Manchester Literary Club.

THE DIALECT OF LANCASHIRE.

The Folk-Speech of Lancashire.

Of the Lancashire dialect there is not even a decent vocabulary, though it is highly important to the philologist, on account of its grammatical structure and its many genuine Saxon terms. The mixture of population consequent upon the spread of the cotton manufacture has greatly deteriorated the purity of the Lancashire speech ; but the Laird of Monkbarns might still find the genuine Saxon guttural in the mouths of the old people.

> R. Garnett, *in Quarterly Review, Vol. LV.* (1836) *p.* 357.

Our words, scattered through districts and used by a population [which is] yet held marvellously together amongst immigrants twenty-fold their number, require collection. Collier's diligent accumulation a century ago is invaluable, but the very glossary which accompanies his book shows that his verbal knowledge was defective. Grimm *(Deutsche Grammatik,* vol. i. p. 222) says it yet remains [in order] to explain Anglo-Saxon to enquire closely into the play (spielarten) of dialects which must be gathered with a reference to place and time, and this can only be done in England. We are satisfied there is no speech so original and important to the end thus proposed as our own neglected South Lancashire patois.

> T. Heywood, F.S.A., *in Chetham Society's Miscellanies, Vol. III.* (1862) *p.* 36.

One might write a dissertation to prove the vigour, the terseness, and the venerable antiquity of this [the Lancashire] variety of speech, which ought to be studied as an independent idiom : and not confounded with corrupt and vulgar English, like the English of the uneducated Londoner. But such a dissertation would be written, however eloquently, in vain. The old provincial languages are passing away from the face of the island, and the time is at hand when the pure dialect of Lancashire will have given place to the English of the schoolmaster and the penny-a-liner. This may be in many ways a great gain. It will bring an important population into closer and easier relation with the other inhabitants of the island. But it will not be an unmixed gain ; and a thousand pregnant turns of expression, a thousand keen-edged phrases that have been sharpened by the wit of many generations, will be lost for ever to our soft-tongued posterity.

> *Wenderholme : a Story of Lancashire and Yorkshire Life.*
> *By* Philip G. Hamerton.

TEMPORARY PREFACE.

[*Issued with the* FIRST PART.]

IN these prefatory remarks it is not intended to do more than indicate, as briefly as possible, the general scope of the Glossary, and to offer such observations as seem absolutely necessary for the due comprehension of the plan pursued. The portion now published will amount, it is estimated, to rather more than a third of the Glossary proper. On its completion, the words themselves will be reprinted—apart from the meanings, notes, and illustrations—accompanied by a representation of the pronunciation according to the Glossic system of Mr. A. J. Ellis. This will be followed by a General Introduction, embodying remarks on the grammatical structure and peculiarities of the dialect, and on the variations of idiom and pronunciation as observable in the several districts of the county. It is proposed also to include, in this section of the work, an essay on the capabilities of the dialect and a bibliographical survey of its literature.

A fairly well-defined difference exists between the dialect of the northern and southern portions of Lancashire. Mr. A. J. Ellis, in the classification of the existing English dialects which he proposes to adopt in Part V. of his *Early English Pronunciation*, and the outlines of which he laid before the Philological Society on the 5th of March, 1874, places Lonsdale, North and South of the Sands, in the Northern English Dialect group, along with Westmorland, Cumberland, and portions of Durham and Yorkshire; whilst the rest of Lancashire is placed in the North-Western English Dialect group, along with Derbyshire, Cheshire, and Shropshire. In view of the division thus indicated, it is urged by some authorities that the dialect of each section should be glossed separately, and it is certain that whatever has been done in the past has been done upon this principle. The present is the first attempt to deal with the dialect of the county in one united collection; and the further we have progressed in the work the less reason have we seen for treating Lancashire on a plan at variance with that adopted in regard to other counties. We have found it impossible, for example, to deter-mine the precise line of demarcation. Some observers fix it as far north as the Lune; others at the Ribble; and others still further south, at a point between Chorley and Bolton. Again, a very large number of words and idioms, and many peculiarities of grammar and pronunciation are common to both sections of the county. Our valued contributor and fellow-labourer, the late Mr. T. T. Wilkinson, F.R.A.S., of Burnley, a close observer of the dialect in his neigh-bourhood for more than forty years, marked almost every one of the Furness words contained in our preliminary draft lists as being also current in East Lancashire. There are differences of pronunciation, of course, but in the main it is obvious that the earlier language was substantially the same in both localities. Similarly, whilst many of the words current in the Fylde, the tract of country between the Wyre and the Ribble, are not now to be found elsewhere in Lanca-shire, the majority of its provincialisms have a close affinity with those in use both in the north and south of the county. In point of fact the differences between the dialect of Lonsdale and that of South and East Lancashire are not greater, in several important particulars, than those observable in different localities within the South-east Lancashire area, where the dialect of Bolton is distin-guishable from that of Rochdale, and the patois of Oldham from that of Ashton-under-Lyne and Stalybridge. Here, as elsewhere, rivers have a dividing effect on the dialect. Mr. James Pearson reports that in the Fylde (not an extensive district) there are three or four different pronunciations, and almost, one might say, as many dialects.

Where a river is fordable or crossed by a bridge, the dialect is the same on both sides of the river; but where the river is unfordable and there are no ready means of communication, the dialect on the two sides is different. Speaking broadly, then, it may be said that whilst minute differences prevail all over the county, the dialect changes by almost imperceptible degrees as it advances northward. The links which bind the northern and southern varieties are traceable without much difficulty when the words are gathered together in one glossary and placed, as it were, side by side. Finally, since the county plan has been adopted as a rule throughout England, there seems to be no sufficient reason why Lancashire should be the only exception.

The Manchester Literary Club, with which the project originated, fortunately possesses some peculiar facilities for its adequate execution. It not only numbers amongst its members the chief writers in the dialect, but also residents in, or representatives from, all parts of the county. The manner in which the shire has been mapped out among the contributors is somewhat as follows :—

Furness, or Lonsdale North . .	Mr. J. P. Morris.
Lonsdale South	Mr. H. T. Crofton.
The Fylde	The late James Pearson.
Mid-Lancashire (Preston and neighbourhood)	Mr. Charles Hardwick, Mr. J. H. Haworth, and Mr. E. Kirk.
East Lancashire (Burnley and Cliviger)	The late T. T. Wilkinson, and Mr. James Standing.
Bury and Walmersley	The late Joseph Chattwood and the Rev. Addison Crofton.
Rochdale	Mr. Edwin Waugh.
Saddleworth	Mr. Morgan Brierley.
Moston	Mr. George Milner and Mr. Joseph Ramsbottom.
Failsworth and Hollinwood . .	Mr. Benjamin Brierley and Mr. James Dronsfield.

The first name in this list suggests the observation that the Editors had at the outset an invaluable body of information concerning the dialect of Furness in Mr. J. P. Morris's Glossary of its Words and Phrases—a collection which leaves almost nothing to be desired, and is a model of what a local glossary should be. Notwithstanding our invasion of a domain which he had made his own, Mr. Morris has worked most cordially with us, and has rendered valuable assistance in many ways. The late Mr. James Pearson, at a very early stage of the work, contributed a large MS. collection of words in in use in the Fylde, the result of years of assiduous observation and research. Other manuscript lists were placed at our service, as follows :—

1. Words in use in Ormskirk.   Compiled by W. Hawkshead Talbot.

2. Words in use in Clifton and Irlam. Compiled by W. Chorlton.

3. Words in use in Ashton-under-Lyne. · Compiled by Dr. Clay.

4. Words in use in Rossendale. Compiled by John Ashworth.

5. Collections made at Walmersley, near Bury, and other places. By the Rev. Addison Crofton, of Reddish.

6. Collections made at Lancaster, Preston, Morecambe, Chipping, Burton, and other places in South Lonsdale and Mid-Lancashie. By H. T. Crofton.

7. A Collection of Lancashire Words. By the Rev. John Davies, author of the *Races of Lancashire.*

8. A List of South Lancashire Words. By John Jackson, of Warrington.

9. A List of Words used in and around Cartmel, in Furness. By W. Hunter, of Height, Cartmel.

Other contributions have been received from Mrs. G. Linnæus Banks, Mr. W. E. A. Axon, and the Rev. Elkanah Armitage, of Waterhead, Oldham. For the MS. lists, 1 to 4, we are indebted to the courtesy of the Manchester Literary and Philosophical Society ; and for the collections of Mr. Jackson and Mr. Hunter (8 and 9) to the Rev. John Davies. The available printed materials will be found enumerated in the list of Authorities.

One of the chief difficulties of a glossarist is the orthography. In our case, the words have been given, whenever practicable, in the spelling adopted by the most trustworthy of the county writers, among whom Mr. Edwin Waugh stands pre-eminent, on account not only of his genius and knowledge, but of his minute observation and scholarly study of the dialect. Where this aid is lacking, a form of spelling has been employed which represents the nearest approach to the pronunciation, so far as that can be conveyed in ordinary English. It is intended hereafter, as already stated, to·reprint the whole of the words accompanied by Glossic symbols. This portion of the work has been kindly undertaken by Mr. Thomas Hallam, who will also, it is expected, contribute an essay upon the general subject of Lancashire dialectal pronunciation.

In the Etymological notes, it has been the anxious desire of the Editors to restrict the information within safe and sound limits, and, above all, to avoid guesses. They have been aided in the prosecution of this endeavour by the Rev. Walter W. Skeat, who has kindly found time from his numerous and pressing labours to revise the proofs, and to enrich the notes with many valuable and interesting suggestions.

The illustrations are arranged in chronological order. The passages from Anglo-Saxon [i.e., First English], Middle English, and modern authors are followed by examples in the Lancashire dialect from the works of county writers ; and when not obtainable from books an example is given, wherever practicable, of the current colloquial usage of the word. The South-East Lancashire examples of colloquial use have been contributed by Mr. George Milner ; East Lancashire by Mr. T. T. Wilkinson ; the Fylde by Mr. James Pearson ; and the Furness examples by Mr. J. P. Morris.

In the General Introduction it will probably be found desirable to explain at some length the plan of procedure in the matter of inclusion and exclusion—to show why words which have a place in some of the extant fragmentary glossaries of the Lancashire dialect, as, for example, Mr. Peacock's Lonsdale collection, are omitted in the present work, and why others are included. It must suffice at present to say that in our compilation, as a rule, the inclusive system has been adopted. All dialectal words known to have currency in the county, and all archaisms the use of which at any period can be verified, have been comprehended in the Glossary, without reference to the fact that some of them may be in use in other parts of England. On the other hand, it has not been thought necessary to encumber the work with archaic declensions, or with the merely provincial spellings of words common in standard English, as both these classes will be dealt with collectively and exhaustively hereafter. Where this rule has been departed from, it has been because the words in question were so peculiar in form that if met with by the ordinary reader in a dialectal book they would not be understood. Other words, again, have been recorded, such as *afeard*, *beck, busk, buss, clip, don*, and the like, which occur occasionally in the poetry of the day, or, more often, in our older standard literature, but which have dropped out of the ordinary speech, and, when given in dictionaries of the language, are marked as "obsolescent" or "obsolete." As these are still employed in the every-day talk of the Lancashire people, it has seemed to us that they had a just claim to a place in a Glossary of the dialect.

It remains for the Editors to tender their warm acknowledgments to all who have kindly assisted them in the preparation of the Glossary. In addition to those already mentioned, they are indebted for valuable suggestions and assistance to Dr. Richard Morris, president of the Philological Society; Mr. F. J. Furnivall, M.A.; and Mr. J. A. Picton, F.S.A., of Liverpool. Their chief thanks are due to the Rev. Walter W. Skeat, M.A., the indefatigable director of the English Dialect Society, whose ripe experience and accurate scholarship have been placed unreservedly at the service of the Editors. The labours of the glossarist, under the most favourable circumstances, are arduous and trying. In the present instance they have been materially lightened by Mr. Skeat's generous and never-failing aid.

MANCHESTER, *December*, 1875.

Authorities:

BEING A LIST OF THE PRINCIPAL BOOKS AND EDITIONS
QUOTED AND CONSULTED.

I.

ANGLO-SAXON AND MIDDLE-ENGLISH.

A.D.
680. CÆDMON. Metrical Paraphrase, Anglo-Saxon and English, by B. Thorpe, F.S.A. 1832.

880 KING ALFRED. Anglo-Saxon Version of the History of the World, by Orosius. Edited by the Rev. Dr. Bosworth. 1859.

995. Heptateuchus, Liber Job, et Evangelium Nicodemi, Anglo-Saxonicè. Ed. by Thwaites. Oxon, 1698. [Quoted as the A.S. version of the Bible : Old Testament.]

995. Anglo-Saxon Gospels. Edited by the Rev. J. Bosworth. 1865.

1210. Ancren Riwle [? Dorsetshire]. Ed. by J. Morton. London, 1853.

1303. ROBERT MANNYNG. Handlyng Synne. Ed. by F. J. Furnivall. Roxburghe Club, 1862.

1320. Early English Metrical Romances [written in Lancashire]. Ed. by John Robson. Camden Society, 1842.

1320. Cursor Mundi [Northumbrian Dialect]. Ed. by Dr. Richard Morris. Early English Text Society. 1874-5.

1330. English Metrical Homilies. Ed. by John Small, M.A. Edinburgh, 1862.

1340. HAMPOLE. The Pricke of Conscience, by Richard Rolle de Hampole. [Northumbrian dialect.] Ed. by Dr. Richard Morris. Philological Society, 1863.

1340. HAMPOLE. English Prose Treatises, Ed. by Rev. G. G. Perry. E.E.T.S., 1866.

1350. The Romance of William of Palerne. Ed by the Rev. W. W. Skeat. E.E.T.S., 1867.

1350. The Alliterative Romance of Joseph of Arimathie, or the Holy Grail. Ed. by Skeat. E.E.T.S., 1871.

1360. The Gest Hystoriale of the Destruction of Troy. Ed. by Panton and Donaldson. E.E.T.S., 1869 and 1874.

1360. Early English Alliterative Poems in the West Midland Dialect [Lancashire]. Ed. by Dr. Richard Morris. E.E.T.S., 1864.

1360   Sir Gawayne and the Green Knight. West Midland Dialect [Lancashire].
       Ed. by Dr. Richard Morris. E.E.T.S., 1864.

1360. Morte Arthure. Ed from the Thornton MS., by the Rev. G. G. Perry.
       E.E.T.S., 1865. Re-edited by E. Brock. E.E.T.S., 1871.

1362. LANGLAND. Alliterative Vision of William concerning Piers the Plow-
       man. Text A, from the Vernon MS. Ed. by the Rev. W. W. Skeat.
       E.E.T.S., 1867.

1377. LANGLAND, William's Vision concerning Piers the Plowman. Text B.
       Ed. Skeat. E.E.T.S,, 1869.

1375. JOHN BARBOUR. The Bruce. Ed. by Jamieson.

1380. JOHN WYCLIF. Version of the Gospels. Ed. by Rev. J. Bosworth. 1865.

1380. GEOFFREY CHAUCER. Aldine Edition. Ed. by Dr. Richard Morris.
       Six volumes. Second Edition. 1870. One or two quotations have
       been made from Tyrwhitt's Edition.

1440. JOHN LYDGATE. Storie of Thebes. Quotations made from Skeat's Speci-
       mens of English Literature. 1871.

1440. Promptorium Parvulorum. Ed. by Albert Way, M.A. Camden Society,
       1865.

1440. Thornton Romances. Camden Society, 1844.

1482. Revelation to the Monk of Evesham. Arber's Reprint.

1513. GAWIN DOUGLAS. Translation of Virgil's Eneid. Quoted from Skeat's
       Sp. Eng. Literature. 1871.

1528. WILLIAM TYNDALE. Version of Gospels. Ed. by Rev J. Bosworth. 1865.

1570. ROGER ASCHAM. The Scholemaster. Arber's Reprint.

1579. STEPHEN GOSSON. The Schoole of Abuse. Arber's Reprint.

1590. EDMUND SPENSER. Globe Edition of Poems. Ed. by Dr. Richard
       Morris. 1869.

1600   WILLIAM SHAKSPERE. The quotations are made from the First Folio
       Edition of 1623 (Booth's Reprint), and the acts, scenes, and lines are
       numbered according to the Globe Edition, edited by W. G. Clark and
       W. Aldis Wright, 1866. The dates affixed to the plays are those of
       the first mention, first printing, or first known production on the stage.

1610. The Bible : Authorised Version.

II.

WRITERS IN THE DIALECT.

ALMOND, JOHN (Blackburn) :
   A Day at Blackpool. 1872.

BAMFORD, SAMUEL [b. 1788, d. 1872] :
   Passages in the Life of a Radical. Two volumes. 1840.
   Walks in South Lancashire and its Borders. 1844.
   Edition of Tim Bobbin. 1850.
   Poems. 1864.

BARBOUR, DR. HENRY :
   Forness Folk : or Sketches of Life and Character in Lonsdale, North of the
   Sands. 1870.

BIGG, J. STANYAN (Ulverston) [b. 1828, d. 1865] :
   Shifting Scenes. 1862.

BRIERLEY, BENJAMIN :
Marlocks of Merriton. 1867.
The Fratchingtons. 1868.
Red Windows Hall. 1869.

BRIGGS, JOHN [*b.* 1787, *d.* 1824] :
Remains. Kirkby Lonsdale, 1825.

BYROM, JOHN [*b.* 1691, *d.* 1763] :
Miscellaneous Poems. Two volumes. First edition, 1773

COLLIER, JOHN [*b.* 1708, *d.* 1786] :
The Works of Tim Bobbin, in Prose and Verse. Rochdale edition, 1819

GIBSON, ALEXANDER C. :
High Furness Dialect Sketches, in his book on the Folk-Speech of Cumberland. 1868.

LAHEE, MISS M. R. :
The Carter's Struggles. Manchester, ab 1865.
Betty o' Yep's Laughable Tale. Manchester, ab. 1865.

LONSDALE MAGAZINE :
Vols. I. and II. Kirkby Lonsdale, 1820-1.
Vol. III. Kendal, 1822.

MORRIS, J. P. :
Sketches in the Furness Dialect. Carlisle, 1867.

RAMSBOTTOM, JOSEPH :
Phases of Distress : Lancashire Rhymes. Manchester, 1864.

RIDINGS, ELIJAH :
The Lancashire Muse. Manchester, 1853.

SCHOLES, JOHN :
Tim Gamwattle's Jaunt fro' Smobridge to Manchester o' seein't Queen.
Manchester, 1857.

STANDING, JAMES :
Echoes from a Lancashire Vale. Manchester, 1870.

WILSONS, THE :
Songs of the Wilsons. Ed. by John Harland, F.S.A. Manchester, no date.

WAUGH, EDWIN :
Sketches of Lancashire Life and Localities. Manchester, 1855.
Poems and Lancashire Songs. 1859.
The Barrel Organ. 1865.
Besom Ben. 1865.
Ben an' th' Bantam. 1866.
Tattlin' Matty. 1867.
The Dead Man's Dinner. 1867.
Th' Owd Blanket. 1867.
Dulesgate. 1867.
Home Life of the Lancashire Factory Folk during the Cotton Famine. 1867.
Sneckbant, or Th' Owd Toll-bar. 1868.
Yeth-bobs an' Scaplins. 1869.
Jannock [Furness dialect]. 1874.
Old Cronies. 1875.
Sancho's Wallet [in the *Sphinx*]. 1870.
The Chimney Corner [in the *Manchester Critic*]. 1874.

III.

WORKS RELATING TO THE DIALECT OR TO LANCASHIRE.

The Lancashire Dialect. Illustrated in Two Lectures. By the Rev. William Gaskell, M.A. 1854.

Essay on the South Lancashire Dialect By Thomas Heywood, F.S.A. Chetham Society's Publications, vol. 57. Manchester, 1862.

Notes on the South Lancashire Dialect. By J. A. Picton, F.S.A. Liverpool : Privately printed.

Glossary of the Dialect of the Hundred of Lonsdale. By R. B. Peacock. Ed. by Rev. J. C. Atkinson. Philological Society's Transactions, 1867.

A Glossary of the Words and Phrases of Furness. By J. P. Morris. 1869.

History of the Chapelry of Goosnargh. By Henry Fishwick, F.S.A. 1871.

Lancashire Legends and Traditions. By John Harland, F.S.A., and T. T. Wilkinson, F.R.A.S. 1873.

Ballads and Songs of Lancashire. Collected and edited by John Harland. Second Edition. Revised and enlarged by T. T. Wilkinson. 1875.

IV.

DICTIONARIES, GLOSSARIES, AND MISCELLANEOUS.

Altenglische Sprachproben. By Edward Mätzner. Erster Band. Berlin, 1869.

Anglo-Saxon and English Dictionary. By the Rev. Joseph Bosworth, D.D. 1868.

Bible Word-Book, The. By J. Eastwood, M.A., and W. Aldis Wright, M.A. 1866.

Dictionary of the Old English Language, compiled from writings of the 12th, 13th, 14th, and 15th Centuries. By Francis Henry Stratmann. Krefeld, 1873.

Dictionary of Obsolete and Provincial English. Compiled by Thomas Wright, M.A. Two volumes. 1869.

Dictionary of the French and English Tongues. By Randle Cotgrave. 1611.

Dictionary of the English Language. By Samuel Johnson. Fifth Edition, folio. 1784.

Dictionary of the English Language. By Charles Richardson, LL.D. Two volumes. 1844.

Dictionary of English Etymology. By Hensleigh Wedgwood. Second Edition. 1871.

English Dialect Society's Publications. 1873-4.

Glossary of the Dialect of Cumberland. By Robert Ferguson. 1873.

Glossary of North Country Words. By John Trotter Brockett, F.S.A. Third Edition. Two volumes. Newcastle-on-Tyne, 1846.

Glossary of Northamptonshire Words and Phrases. By Anne Elizabeth Baker. Two volumes. 1854.

Glossarial Index to the Printed English Literature of the Thirteenth Century. By Herbert Coleridge. 1859.

Glossary illustrating the Works of English Authors, particularly Shakspere and his contemporaries. By Robert Nares, M.A., F.R.S. New Edition, by J. O. Halliwell and T. Wright. Two volumes. 1872.

Historical Outlines of English Accidence. By Dr. Richard Morris. Second Edition. 1872.

Icelandic-English Dictionary. By Richard Cleasby and Gudbrand Vigfusson, M.A. Oxford : Clarendon Press, 1874.

Philology of the English Tongue. By J. Earle, M.A.

Shaksperian Grammar. By E. A. Abbott, D.D. 1873.

Songs and Ballads of Cumberland and the Lake Country. By Sidney Gilpin. Three volumes. 1874.

Sources of Standard English. By T. L. Knighton Oliphant. 1873.

Specimens of Early English, from A.D. 1298 to A D. 1393. By Dr. R. Morris and the Rev. W. W. Skeat, M.A. 1872.

Specimens of English Literature from A D 1394 to A D. 1579. By the Rev. W. W. Skeat. 1871.

ABBREVIATIONS.

A.S.	Anglo-Saxon—used for First English.
Cf.	*Confer*, compare.
Dan.	Danish.
Du.	Dutch.
Fr.	French.
Ger.	German.
Icel.	Icelandic.
Lat.	Latin.
Mœs.-Goth.	Mœso-Gothic.
Mid. E.	Middle English.
O. Fr.	Old French.
Sc.	Scottish.
Suio-Goth.	Suio-Gothic.
Sw.	Swedish.
W.	Welsh.

Glossary of the Lancashire Dialect.

A.

A, *v.* have. In Mid. E. *a* is often used for *have* in the imperative mood, as "*A* mercy, madam, on this man here."—*William of Palerne*, l. 978.

J. STANYAN BIGG. 1862.	Though I'd *a* geen my silver watch Just for ya single word.—*Shifting Scenes*, p. 172.
COLLOQUIAL USE. 1875.	God *a* mercy ! Yon chylt's afire.

A, *prep.* on, in. A.S. *on* is equivalent both to *on* and *in* in Mod. Eng. Icel. *á*, upon or in.

WICLIF. 1380.	Thei wenten *a*foote frö alle citees.—*Mark* vi. 33.
JOHN OF TREVISA. 1387.	Also, of þe forseyde Saxon tonge þat is deled *a* thre [= divided in three].—*Vol.* ii., c. 59, l. 199.
SHAKSPERE. 1597.	The flattering index of a direfull pageant ; One heav'd *a* high, to be hurled downe below. <div align="right">*Richard III.*, iv. 4, 85.</div>
	[Also : *a* Monday, *Hamlet*, ii. 2, 406 ; *a* my word, *Taming of Shrew*, i. 2, 108 ; stand *a* tiptoe, *Henry V*, iv. 3, 42 ; a plague *a* both your houses, *Romeo*, iii. 1, 94 ; and many others.]
RAMSBOTTOM. 1874.	*A*-thattens [= in that way] eawr Harry's for dooin', aw see ; He's sowt him a sweetheart an cares nowt for me. <div align="right">*Unpublished MS.*</div>
COLL. USE. 1875.	" Did he goo to th' buryin' ? " " He did : he went *a*-horseback."

AA (N. Lanc.) *v.* to owe, as "I *aa* him nowt." Aa pronounced like *ah*, long. Icel. *á*, pres. of *eiga*, to own. A.S. *áh*, pres. of *ágan*, to own, to owe. Scot. *awe*.

> I've little to spend, and naething to lend,
> But deevil a shilling I *awe*, man.
> BURNS : *Tarbolton Lasses*.

AAM, *v.* to mock. A person repeating another's words in an ironical manner is said to be " aamin after him." Aa pronounced like *ah*, long.

AAMAS (N. Lanc.), } *sb.* alms, gifts. A.S. *œlmesse.* Icel. *almusa.*
AUMAS (E. Lanc.), } Mod. Scottish *awmus* or *awmous.* Aa pronounced like *ah*, long.

ROBERT OF GLOUCESTER. 1298.	Reufol he was to neody men, of his *almesse* large and fre.—*p.* 330.
NORTHUMBRIAN DIALECT. About 1330.	He mette A beggar that him cumly grette, And said, " lef sir, par charité Wit sum *almous* thou help me." *English Metrical Homilies.*
HAMPOLE. 1340.	First, through byhing of paynes þat greves, With *almus*, þat men to the pure gyves. *Pricke of Conscience,* 3608.
CHAUCER. 1370.	Hir herte is verrey chambre of holynesse, Hir hond, mynistre of fredom and *almesse.* *Man of Lawes Tale,* 69.
BURNS. 1786.	While she held up her greedy gab Just like an *aumous*-dish.—*The Jolly Beggars.*

The following is still remembered in Furness as the usual address of beggars :

" Pity, pity paamas,
Pray give us *aamas* ;
Yan for Peter, two for Paul,
Three for God at meead us all."

COLL. USE (East Lanc.)   He lives o' *aumas.*
1875.

AAN (North and Mid. Lanc.), *adj.* own. A.S. *ágen*, own, from *ágan*, to possess.

HAMPOLE. 1340.	Ilk man þat here lyves, mare or lesse, God made til his *awen* lyknesse.—*P. of C.* 90.
BLIND HARRY. 1461.	In at the dur he went with this gud wiff, A roussat goun of hir *awn* scho him gaif. *Wallace,* 238.
WILLIAM DUNBAR. 1503.	And lat no fowll of ravyne do effray, Nor devoir birdis bot his *awin* pray. *Thistle and Rose,* stanza 18.
GAWIN DOUGLAS. 1513.	Ilke fair cite Stude, payntit, euery fyall, fayn, and stage, Apon the plane grund, by thar *awyn* vmbrage. *Trans. of Virgil's Æneid,* Bk xii., 71.
BURNS. 1786.	Wha's *ain* dear lass, that he likes best, Comes clinkin down beside him. *Holy Fair : Poems,* i. p. 27.

1820.	Yan o' Slaff sons gat wedt, an' hed a son of his *aan.* *Lonsdale Magazine,* vol. ii. 90.
J. P. MORRIS. 1867.	Some said at it wos t' fellas they co'd spekalaters 'at bowte up o' t' stuff, an' then selt it owt at the'r *aan* price.—*Invasion o' U'ston,* 4.

ABACK, *adv.* back, behind, at the back of.   A.S. *on-bæc.*

1350.

> Betere hit were douhtilyche to diȝen on or oune,
> Þen wiþ schendschupe to schone and vs *a-bak* drawe.
> *Joseph of Arimathea,* 495.

WICLIF.
1380.

> Jesus seith to hem I am, and Judas that betraide him stood with hem, and whanne he seide to hem, I am, thei wenten *abak* and felden doun on the erthe.
> *John* xviii.

1440.

> *Abacke,* or backward.   Retro, retrorsum.
> *Prompt. Parv.*

COLL. USE.
1875.

> Just as aw coom up he wur hidin' *aback* o' th' hedge.

ABACK-A-BEHEEND, ⎫ *sb.* a place behind or out of the way;
ABACK-A-BEHINT, ⎭ used in the superlative sense.

COLL. USE.
1875.

> Wheer does he live?—Eh! aw know no'; *aback-a-beheend,* wheer nob'dy comes.

ABBER, *conj.* but.   (See also EBBER.)

COLL. USE.
1875.

> Thae'll not goo, Jim, belike?—*Abber* aw will, shuse what thae says.

ABEAR, *v.* to endure, to tolerate.   A.S. *abéran.*

COLL. USE.
1875.

> I conno' *abear* th' seet on't.

ABIDE, *v.* to suffer, to endure, to tolerate.   A.S. *abidan,* from *bidan,* to wait.   Icel. *biða,* to wait, endure, suffer.   Goth. *beidan.* Swed. *bida.*   Dan. *bie.*

WEST-MID. DIALECT (Lanc.)
1360.

> Þen is better to *abyde* the bur vmbe-stoundes.
> *Allit. Poems,* c. 8.

SHAKSPERE.
1595.

> 1. In the sense of endure :—
>   What fates impose, that men must needs *abide.*
>   It boots not to resist both wind and tide.
>   *Third K. Henry VI.,* iv. 3, 58.

1598.

> 2. In the sense of tolerate :—
>   I cannot *abide* swaggerers.
>   *Second K. Henry IV.,* ii. 4, 118.

COLL. USE.
1875.

> He wur soa ill he cudn't *abide.*

ABOON, *prep.* above, over, more than.   A.S. *abufan;* Icel. *ofan.*

HAMPOLE.
1340.

> Bathe fra *aboven* and fra bynethe.—*P. of C.,* 612.

CHAUCER.
1370.

> And specially *aboven* every thing
> Excited he the poepul in his preching.
> *Sompnoures Tale,* 7.

CHEVY CHASE.
Prob. after 1460.

> Ther begane in Chyviat the hyls *abone* yerly on a monnyn-day.
> *Chevy Chase* (Ashmole MS. 48), 14.

BURNS.
1786.

> An honest man's *aboon* his might.—*Poems,* iii. 53.

JOHN COLLIER. I'd naw gett'n forrud, back ogen, *aboon* a mile or
1750. so, ofore eh saigh [I saw] a parcel o' lads on hobble-
 tyhoys.— *Works*, p. 43.

WAUGH. *Employer:* Wheer hasto bin wortchin at ?
1870. *Carter:* I've druvven for Owd Copper Nob *aboon* nine
 year.— *Sancho's Wallet,* in the *Sphinx,* vol. iii. 90.

ACKER, *v.* to falter, to hesitate, to cough. Welsh *achrethu,* to
tremble or quake : this would apply to the first meaning. Welsh
hochi, to hawk, to throw up phlegm, would apply to the last.
Danish *harke* has the latter meaning.

COLL. USE. 1. He *ackers* and haffles : he's lyin'.
1874.
 2. He *ackers* and spits : he's done [*i e.,* exhausted].

ACKERSPRIT, *sb.* a potato with roots at both ends. The literal
sense is a land-sprout, which will equally apply to a turnip,
mangel-wurzel, or any other root. A.S. *æcer,* a field, land.
Goth. *akrs.* A.S. *sprit,* a sprout. Cf. A.S. *æcersprangas,* saplings ;
from *æcer* and *springan,* to spring.

ADDLE, *v.* to earn. Icel. *ödlask,* to acquire, to gain. The word
was formerly used in the sense of to grow, to increase. Thus
Tusser, in his *Husbandrie* (1573), wrote :

> Where ivy embraces the tree very sore,
> Kill ivy, or else tree will *addle* no more.

> It's I con plough, and I con sow,
> An' I con reap, an' I con mow,
> An' I con to the market go,
> An' sell my daddy's corn and hay,
> An' *addle* my sixpence ivvery day.
>   *Harland's B. and S. of Lanc., p.* 182.
> [The editor says the song, "Dick o' Stanley Green,"
> from which this verse is taken, is a great favourite
> in North Lancashire.]

WAUGH. The old woman said her husband was "a grinder
1867. in a cardroom when they geet wed, an' he *addled*
 about eight shillin' a week."
    Home Life Lanc. Factory Folk, p. 102.

AFEARD, } *p. adj.* afraid, frighted, terrified. A.S. *afæ'ran,* to
AFEART, } terrify, to frighten ; from *fæ'r, sb.* fear, which from
fæ'r, adj. sudden. The word is generally used in Lancashire
without the prefix, as *feard, feart, q.v.*

A.S. VERSION OF BIBLE. The clause "they were afraid," in Gen. xlii. 35,
995. appears in the A.S. version as "hig wurdon ealle
 afærede," i.e., "they all became *afeard.*"

HAMPOLE. For he es *afered* þat he sal be peryst ;
1340. And þat drede til hym es a grete payn.
        P. of C., 2943.

CHAUCER. To be in his goode governaunce,
1380. So wis he was, she was namore *afered,*
     Troylus and Creseide ; iii. 477.

LYDGATE. After 1420.	Nat astonned, nor in his hert *afferde*, But ful proudly leyde hond on his swerde. *Storie of Thebes*, ii. 1069.

SPENSER. 1579.	He from his wide devouring oven sent A flake of fire, that flashing in his beard, Him all amaz'd, and almost made *afeard*. *F. Q.*, Bk. i. canto xi. stanza 26.

SHAKESPERE. 1598.	But tell me, Hal, art thou not horribly *afeared ?* *I. Hen. IV.* ii. 4. 4, 401.

BEN JONSON. 1620	And his lip should kissing teach, Till he cherish'd too much beard, And make Love, or me *afeard*. *Underwoods ; Cel. of Charis*, ix.

[Dr. Johnson (1755) said the word *afeard* " is now obsolete : the last author whom I have found using it is Sedley." He died about 1728]

DICKENS. 1857.	" It's no reason, Arthur," said the old woman bending over him to whisper, " that because I am *afeared* of my life of 'em, you should be." *Little Dorrit*, p. 19, Household Eu.

COLL. USE. 1875.	" Get on wi' thee, mon ; what arto *feard* on ?" " Aw'm noan *afeard* on thee."

AFORE, *prep*. before, at some previous time, earlier than, in front of. A.S. *onforan*; which occurs in the Chronicle, anno 875. The A.S. also exhibits the form *œtforan*, but *a-* commonly corresponds to the A.S. *on-*.

ATHANASIAN CEEED. Trans. about 1549.	None is *afore*, or after other.

SPENSER. 1579.	For of their comming well he wist *afore*. *F. Q.*, iii. 3, 15.

IBID.	They him saluted, standing far *afore*. *F. Q.*, i. 10, 49.

SHAKESPERE. 1608.	If your diligence be not speedy, I shall be there *afore* you. *King Lear*, i. 5, 375.

RAMSBOTTOM. 1864.	O' reawnd agen aw kiss mi brids, *Afore* hoo packs 'em off to bed. *Lancashire Rhymes*, p. 13.

WAUGH. 1870.	Aw've sin sich like as thee *afore*. *Besom Ben*, c. 7, p. 88.

B. BRIERLEY. 1870.	Aw sed *afore*, aw'd bin livin' for th' last fortnight like a feighter. *Bundle o' Fents*, i. p. 30.

WAUGH. 1874.	Now, Sally, gan thi ways *afore* me, an' oppen t' door. *Jannock*, c. iii., p. 18.

AFTERINS, AFTHERINS, *sb*. that which is left ; generally applied to the last milk from a cow.

COLL. USE. 1875.	Jem, let owd Mally have a quart o' *aftherins* for a custhert or two.

AGATE, *adv.* and *part.* started, begun of, in hand, doing, continuing, teasing. Icel. *gata*, road or way. Dan. *gade.*

WAUGH.
1865.

1. On foot or in hand.
  What have they *agate* at th' owd mill ?
  Besom Ben, c. i. 17.

2. Started ; begun of.
  " Well, are yo ready ?"
  "Ay, get *agate*," said Twitchel.
  Ibid, c. iii., 34.

3. Doing.
  Get forrard wi what thae'rt *agate* on just now,
  and dunnot be a foo !   *Ibid*, c. viii 94.

4. On the way.
  Thae'rt olez *agate* o' makin' a bother abeawt
  nought.   *Ibid*, c. ix. 105.

1866.

5. Going on or continuing.
  Thae connot stir while this rain's *agate*, so say
  not a word.   *Owd Blanket*, c. iii. 61.

COLL. USE.
1875.

6. Teasing.
  Mother, aar Jem's *agate* on me again.

AGEN } *prep.* against, in an opposite direction to.   A.S. *agen,*
AGAIN }   *ongean;* Icel. *gegn;* Dan. *igjen;* Swed. *igen;* Ger. *gegen.*

WILLIAM OF PALERNE.
1350.

Riȝtly þenne þemþerour wendes him euene till,
þe child comes him *agayn* & curtesliche him gretes.
William of Palerne, 232.

EDWIN WAUGH.
1857.

An' then, by guy, he's hardly wit enough to keep
fro runnin' *again* woles i'th dayleet.
Lanc. Sketches, p. 28.

JOSEPH RAMSBOTTOM.
1864.

An' o' thattens their little tongues ran ;
Bo sich prattlin' o' went *agen* th' grain.
Lancashire Rhymes, p 20.

AGEN, *prep.* contiguous, near to.   A.S. *ongean,* towards.

COLL. USE.
1875.

Agen th' heawse-eend wur a little cloof o' full o
brids an' fleawrs.

AGG, *v.* to tease, to worry.   May perhaps be referred to the Indo-European *ak*, expressing sharpness ; whence Lat. *acutus;* Icel. *eggja*, to incite, provoke ; E. to *egg* on, *edge*.   In this case the original sense is to prick, goad.

COLL. USE.
1875.

'A done wi' thi' Nan, thae'rt aulus *aggin'* at mi.

AIGREEN, *sb.* the house-leek.   Dr. Johnson spells the word *aygreen.* In Mid. English, *ay-green* would mean ever-green.

AIMT, *p. p.* intended.

WAUGH.
1866.

Hoo'd ha made a rare wife for onybody 'at had
ony sense—hoo would that! Aw'd *aimt* her doin'
weel, and hoo met [might] ha done weel, too.
Owd Blanket, iii. 54.

AISTER-BO,
AISTHER-BO, } (Pron. of Easter ball), *sb.* an Easter dumpling.

COLL. USE.
1875.

Well, mother, it's Aister Sunday t'morn; yo'n
mak us some *Aisther-bo's* aw reckon.

AKRAN, *sb.* an acorn; also called *hatchorn*. Goth. *akran* meants
fruit in general, from *akr*, cultivated land. In the cognate tongues
it became limited to the fruit of the oak. Icel. *akarn;* Dan.
agern; A.S. *æcorn;* Ger. *æckern.*

ALD,
AAD, } (North Lanc.) *adj.* old. A.S. *eald.* The Mid, South, and
East Lanc. form is *owd.*

HAMPOLE.
1340.

He prayses *ald* men and haldes þam wyse.
P. of C., 794.

BURNS.
1780.

'Twas in that place o' Scotland's isle,
That bears the name of *Auld* King Coil.
Twa Dogs: Poems i. p. 1.

J. P. MORRIS.
1867.

As *ald* Dryden said, "It wos ivery thing be torns,
but nowt lang." *T' Lebby Beck Dobby*, 4.

AITHER (North Lanc.), *adj. con.* and *pron.* either. The South and
East Lancashire form is *oather.* There can be little doubt that
aigther, ayther, was the original pronunciation of *either.* A.S.
ægther.

HAMPOLE.
1340.

þat *ayther* hand may chaung sone.
P. of C., 1274.

WEST-MID. DIAL. (Lanc.)
About 1360.

By trw recorde of *ayþer* prophete.
Allit. Poems, A. 830.

Sir T. MALLORY.
1485.

And seyne salle ȝe offyre, *aythyre*, aftyre oþer.
Morte Arthure, 939.

About 1500.

On *ather* part, and is assemblit so.
Lancelot of the Laik, 2629.

AJEE, *adv.* in a flutter.

WAUGH.
1859.

An' when aw meet wi' my bonny lass,
It sets my heart *ajee.*
Lanc. Songs: Sweetheart Gate.

AJEE, *adj.* partly open, awry, oblique.

COLL. USE.
1875.

Tint dur; its *ajee.*

ALE-POSSET, *sb.* warm milk and beer sweetened.

WAUGH.
1849.

There's some nice bacon-collops o'th hob,
An a quart o' *ale-posset* i'th oon.
Songs: Come Whoam to thi Childer.

ALE-SCORE, *sb.* a debt at the alehouse. A *score* was originally a stick or piece of wood with notches cut in it (from A.S. *scyran*, to shear or cut), used in keeping count. When a certain number had been notched, the stick was cut, and called a *tally* (French *taillé*, cut off). The tally varied from 10 to 100 notches ; but, in reck-onings, twenty was the usual number. Hence, the *score* became synonymous with the recorded debt of so many pints of ale drunk. When chalk marks were substituted for the notches on the tally, each mark indicated a notch, and a line drawn diagonally made a tally, two tallies making a score.

SHAKESPERE. 1594.	*Jack Cade :* There shall bee no mony ; all shall eate and drinke on my *score*. *Second King Hen. Sixth*, iv. 2, 78.
1598.	*Score* a pint of bastard in the Halfe Moone. *First King Hen. Fourth*, ii. 4, 29.
COLL. USE. 1875.	Hast paid thi *alescore* at th' Blue Bell yet ?

ALE-SHOT, *sb.* a reckoning at the alehouse. Icel. *skot* = (1) a shot ; (2) a *scot*, or contribution.

SHAKESPERE. 1598.	*Falstaffe :* Though I could scape *scot*-free at London, I fear the *shot* heere ; here's no scoring, but vpon the pate. *First King Hen. Fourth*, v. 3, 30.
1598.	*Speed :* Ile to the ale-house with you presently, where, for one *shot* of five-pence, thou shalt have five thousand welcomes.—*Two Gent. of Ver.*, ii. 5, 8.
1623.	*Posthumus :* If I prove a good repast to the spec-tators, the dish payes the *shot*.—*Cymb.*, v. 4, 157.
COLL. USE. 1875.	He's an *aleshot* at th' back o' th' door yon, th' length o' my arm.

ALLUM, *v.* (Mid. Lanc.) to beat.

COLL. USE. 1875.	Well, Joe, what did th' master say to thi for playin' truant ?—O, he dudn't say varry mich, bod he *allum'd* me reet weel for it.

ALONG, ⎫ *conj.* on account of, owing to, that by which something
ALUNG, ⎭   is caused. A.S. *gelang*, owing to. It is different from the ordinary *along*, which is A.S. *andlang*. Chaucer uses *long on*, on account of. Shakespere has *long of (Cymb.* v. 5. 271*)*.

CHAUCER. 1370.	On me is nought *alonge* thin yvel fare. *Tr. and Cr.*, Bk. ii., 1000.
JOHN GOWER. 1393.	But if it is *along* on me, Of þat ȝe vnauanced be. *Confessio Amantis*, Sp. Ear. Eng. ii. 272, 55.
Sir WALTER SCOTT. 1831.	My poor father !—I knew it would come to this— and all *along* of the accursed gold. *Fortunes of Nigel*, c. xxiv.
COLL. USE. 1875.	It wur o' *alung* o' thee that aw geet into this scrape.

ALP, *sb.* a bullfinch. " *Alpe*, a bryde [bird], *Ficedula*"; Prompt. Parvulorum. See Way's note, which gives *blood-olf* as the Norfolk word for bullfinch; whilst *green-olf* is the green grosbeak. In Icel. *álpt* or *álft* is the common word for a swan. See *alp* in Ray's Gloss. (E. D. S.), p. 77.

> About 1370. In many places wexe nyghtyngales,
> *Alpes*, fynches, and wodewales.
> *Romaunt of the Rose*, 657.

AMACKLY, *adv.* in some form or fashion, partly so, a little in that way. A.S. *macian*, to make ; also, to act, conduct, bear oneself.

AMOON, *prep.* among. A.S. *amang*, from *mengan*, to mix.

> Waugh. Look heaw aw ruvven mi breeches *amoon* th' thorns.
> 1865. *Besom Ben*, p. 57.

AM'DY, *sb.* anybody. One of those contractions which abound in the dialect : ex gr. *beleemy*, believe me ; *ot iddn*, that you had ; *didney*, did you ? etc.

> Ramsbottom. Toime wur, if *amdy* dust ha worn
> 1864. Sich things as neaw are worn by me,
> Ut folks ud sheawt wi jeers an' scorn.
> *Lanc. Rhymes : Gooin' t' Schoo*, 88.

> Ibid. Aw'st twitch *am'dy's* nose ut looks croot.
> 1867. *Poacher Tom : Country Words*, No. 17, p. 264.

AN, *conj.* if. Icel. *en* = than, if.

> John Ford. *Gril :* Fool, fool, fool ! catch me *an* thou canst.
> 1629. *Phi :* Expel him the house ; 'tis a dunce.
> *Lover's Melancholy*, act iii. sc. 1.

> Ben Jonson. Nay *an* thou dalliest, then I am thy foe,
> 1601. And fear shall force what friendship cannot win.
> *Poetaster.*

> Coll. Use. Aw'll warm thee, *an* thae does it.
> 1875.

AN', *conj.* and. A.S. *and ;* High Ger. *und ;* Dutch, *en.*

> Robert of Gloucester. Thys King Knout was tuenty ger King of Engelond,
> 1298. *An* in a thousend ger of grace and thyrtty, ych vnderstonde,
> *An* syxe, he deyde at Ssaftesbury. p. 324.

> Burns. Our Laird gets in his racked rents,
> 1780. His coals, his kain, *an'* a' his stents.
> *Twa Dogs.*

> Ramsbottom. Aw find a wuld o' pleasant things
> 1864. Come creawdin' reawnd sometimes, aw'm sure ;
> *An* some ut God's denied to kings,
> *An's* gan i' plenty unto th' poor.
> *Lancashire Rhymes*, p. 12

ANCIENTRY, *sb.* old things, antiquities. Lat. *ante.* Prov. *antes.*
It. *anzi,* before ; whence *anziano.* Fr. *ancien,* ancient, belonging
to former times.—Wedgwood.

> SHAKESPERE.
> 1600.
>
> Wooing, wedding, and repenting, is as a Scotch
> jigge, a measure, and a cinque-pace : the first suite is
> hot and hasty like a Scotch jigge (and full as fantas-
> ticall), the wedding manerly modest (as a measure,
> full of state and *aunchentry*), and then comes repent-
> ance, and with his bad legs falls into the cinque-pace
> faster and faster, till he sinkes into his graue.
> *Much Ado,* ii. 1, 76.

> FULLER.
> 1660.
>
> Samuel Ward was born at Bishop's Middleham, in
> this county ; his father being a gentleman of more
> *ancientry* than estate.   *Worthies: of Durham.*

> WAUGH.
> 1871.
>
> Eawr Charley—eh, there connot be
> Another pate like his ;
> It's o' cromfull o' *ancientry,*
> An' Roman haw-pennies !
> *Lanc. Songs : Eawr Folk.*

ANCLEJACK, *sb.* a heavy shoe tied round the ancle. *Jack* is employed in a variety of senses for anything rough or homely :
Jack-et, Jack-boots, Jack-plane, Black-Jack, etc. *Jack-boots* come
up the thigh ; *Ancle-jacks* only over the ancle.

> WAUGH.
> 1865.
>
> His feet were sheathed in a pair of clinkered *ancle-
> jacks,* as heavy, and nearly as hard, as iron.
> *Besom Ben,* c. i., p. 6.

ANCLEF, *sb.* ancle. A.S. *ancleow ;* Flemish, *enkel ;* Ger. *enkel.*

> COLL. USE.
> 1875.
>
> Yore Jack's knockt his *anclef* out wi' jumpin'.

ANENST (Fylde and N. Lanc.), *prep.* opposite to. A corrupted
form of Mid. E. *ageines* or *on-yeines* = against ; due to confusion
with *anent,* which is a quite different word, from A.S. *on-emn.*
So also M.E. *amonges* is now *amongst.*

> BEN JONSON.
> 1610.
>
> And right *aninst* him a dog snarling.
> *Alchemist,* act ii.

> COLL. USE.
> 1875.
>
> We come to *anenst* thidder. We stopt *anenst* th'
> yate.

ANGER, *v.* to vex, to irritate. *Angry* (*adj.*) is applied to an in-
flamed sore. Cf. A.S. *ange,* trouble, vexation ; from same root
as Lat. *angor, anxius.*

> S. GOSSON.
> 1579.
>
> Or as curst sores with often touching
> Waxe *angry,* and run the longer.
> *Schoole of Abuse,* p. 21.

> SHAKESPERE.
> 1602.
>
> *Iago :* Do you finde some occasion to *anger* Cassio,
> either by speaking too loud, or tainting his discipline.
> *Othello,* ii. sc. 1.

POPE,
1738.

It *anger'd* Turenne, once upon a day,
To see a footman kick'd, that took his pay :
But when he heard th'affront the fellow gave,
Knew one a man of honour, one a knave,
The prudent general turn'd it to a jest,
And begg'd he'd take the pains to kick the rest.
Epilogue to Satires, ii., Aldine Ed.,
Vol. iii., p. 115.

COLL. USE.
1875.

Yon lad's foot gets no betther ; he's bin walkin'
this mornin', an his stockin' mun 'a *angert* it.

ANGS (North Lanc.) *sb.* the beard of coarse barley.

ANGUISHOUS, *adj.* sorrowful, in pain. Fr. *angoisse ;* Old Fr.
angoisseux. See ANGER.

ROBERT OF GLOUCESTER.
1298.

Kyng Arture was *anguysous* in his companye
That the luther traytor adde of scaped hym so tuye
[twice]. *Chronicle*, p. 222.

About 1370.

But I wille that thou knowe hym now
Gynning and eende, sith that thou
Art so *anguisshous* and mate
Diffigured oute of a-state
Ther may no wreeche have more of woo,
Ne caityfe noon enduren soo.
Rom. of the Rose, 4672.

CHAUCER.
1380.

Fortherover, contricioun schulde be wounder
Sorwful and *anguissheous.*
Persones Tale, iii. 16, p. 284.

JOHN LYDGATE.
1420.

But *anguysshous,* and ful of bysy peyne,
He rode hym forth. *Storie of Thebes*, pt. ii, l. 1217.

COLL. USE.
1875.

He lookt quite *anguishous,* an aw felt sorry for him.

ANOTHER-GATES, *adv.* another kind, a different sort. Low
Ger. *gat* is applied, like *way*, not only to a road, but to manner,
kind, sort.

BUTLER.
1663.

When Hudibras, about to enter
Upon *anothergates* adventure,
To Ralpho call'd aloud to arm
Not dreaming of approaching storm.
Hudibras, pt. i., canto 3, l. 427.

ANOYOUS, } *adj.* provoking, teasing, annoying, unpleasant. From
ANOYFUL, } E. *annoy ;* etym. doubtful.

CHAUCER.
1380.

Alle taryinge is *anoyful.*
The Tale of Melibeus, Ald. Ed. iii., 144, 25.

CHAUCER.
1370.

Right so farith it som tyme of deedly synne, and of
anoyous venial synnes, whan thay multiplien in a
man. *The Persones Tale*, iii. 291, 18.

COLL. USE.
1875.

Yo're varra *anoyous;* give oer.

APPERN, *sb.* an apron. Old Fr. *naperon*, properly the intensitive of *nappe*, a table cloth. In Ælfric's Dialogues (tenth century) we find A.S. *barm-clath* (an apron) explained by Lat. *mappula*. In the Promptorium Parvulorum (1440) we have *barmclothe* or *naprun* explained by Lat. *limus*, which signifies an apron in the modern sense.

B. BRIERLEY. 1867.	"Poo thi *appern* off, Pincher." Pincher took off his apron, which was a white linen one, such as were mostly worn by handloom weavers. *Marlocks of Meriton*, 26.
COLL. USE. 1875.	He's teed to his mam's *appern*-string.

AREAWT, *prep.* out of doors, outside.

JOHN COLLIER. 1750.	I'r no sooner *areawt* boh a threave o' rabblement wur watchin on meh at t' dur. *Works*, 58.
BAMFORD. 1820.	And why comes a gentleman riding alone ? And why doth he wander *areawt* such a night. *Homely Rhymes : The Wild Rider.*
RAMSBOTTOM. 1864.	Theaw God above, alone to-day *Areawt* i'th' broad, green fields aw've come, Aw want a twothri words to say, Aw shouldno like to say awhoam. *Lanc. Rhymes : Preawd Tum's Prayer*, 59.
WAUGH. 1868.	Whatever art doin' *areawt* sich a day as this ? *Owd Bl.*, c. iii., p. 52.

ARK, *sb.* a press to keep clothes in ; a large chest for holding meal or flour. About Oldham and Hollinwood ark is a repository. The country "badger" (q. v.) or provision-dealer will say malt-ark, flour-ark, meal-ark, and so on. A.S. *arc, earc*, a coffer, chest, vessel.

A.S. TRANS. BIBLE. 995.	Oð thone dæg the Noe on *earce* eode. [Until the day that Noah entered into the ark.]—*Luke* xvii. 27.
TYNDALE. 1528.	*Arke*, a cofer or chest, as our shrines, saue it was flatte, and the sample of ours was taken thereof. *Workes*, p. 11.
EARL OF SURREY. 1557.	In the rich *ark* Dan Homer's rhymes he placed Who feigned gests of heathen princes sung. *Sonnets : Praise of Psalms of David*, 4.
SPENSER. 1579.	Then first of all came forth Sir Satyrane, Bearing that precious relicke in an *arke* Of gold. *F. Q.*, Bk. iv., c. 4, 15.
BIBLE. 1610.	An *ark* of bulrushes. *Exodus* ii. 3.
JOHN HIGSON. 1852.	The domestic arrangements [of the farmhouses] included flour and meal coffers, apple *arks*, oatmeal fleak, etc. *Gorton Historical Recorder*, p. 12.
IBID.	She had secreted a small quantity of tea in her meal *ark*. *Ibid*, p. 14.
COLL. USE. 1875.	Go an treyd t' meyl into th' *ark*.

ARLES, *sb.* money paid to bind to bind a bargain ; earnest money, paid to servants on hiring. Sometimes called God's penny. Gael. *arlas*, earnest-money ; Welsh, *arles*, a gift, benefit, advantage.

About 1750.

Arles were low an' makin's were naethin' man,
Lord ! how Donald is flytin' an' frettin' man.
Donald Macgillivray : Hogg's Jacobite Relics.

ARN-LOIN (Cliviger), *sb.* straightened circumstances.

JAMES STANDING.
1870.

W'en missed th' way to fortun: what ! this is th' *arnloin*,
Wheer Jone-o'-Tums says a chap's hard to work,
An a woman's to toil and slave like a Turk.
Echoes from a Lancashire Vale, p 13.

ARR, *v.* to snarl.   Hence *R* was called the dog's letter ; *Rom. and Jul.*, ii. 4., 222.

SIR THOMAS NORTH.
1579.

A dog is, by nature, fell and quarrelsome, given to *arre* and war upon a very small occasion.
Trans. of *Plutarch's Morals*, p. 726.

COLL. USE.
1875.

Co' that dog in, dost no' see how it keeps *arrin'* at yon felly ?

ARR, *sb.* a scar, a mark, a rough seam, a wart.   ARR'D, *v.* marked with scars ; as "pock-arr'd," marked with smallpox. Dan. *ar ;* Icel. *arr, örr ;* Sw. *ärr ;* N. Fris. *aar*, a scar, cicatrix, seam.

COLL. USE.
1875.

He wur *arr'd* o' ower wit' smo-pox.

ARRAN,
ARRANT, } *sb.* an errand.   A.S. *ærend*, a message, tidings.
ARNT,

ANGLO-SAXON BIBLE.
995.

ða hatedon hine his leode, and sendon *ærend*-racan æfter him. [But his citizens hated him, and sent messengers after him.]   *Luke* xix. 14.

1440.

Ernde, negocium, nuncium.—*Prompt. Parv.*

JOHN COLLIER.
1750.

Neaw meh mind misgives meh ot yoar'n gooin a sleeveless *arnt*.   *Works*, p. 42.

RAMSBOTTOM.
1864.

Som'dy sent Will an *arnt* th' tother day,
An' they gan him a cake to bring whoam ;
So he shar'd eawt wi Nanny and Bob,
An' a bit he put bye for eawr Tom.
Lanc. Rhymes, p. 18.

WAUGH.
1867.

Theyn keep 'em scrubbin floors. an' runnin *arrans*, an' swillin, an' scutterin up an' deawn stairs.
Owd Bl., c. iii., 71.

ARRANT, } *adj.* downright, thorough.   Applied to a rogue, vaga-
ARREN,   } bond, or fool.

SIR P. SIDNEY.
1580.

Country folk, who hallooed and hooted after me, as at the *arrantest* coward that ever showed his shoulders to the enemy.

POPE.
1737.

> Know, there are rhymes, which, fresh and fresh apply'd,
> Will cure the *arrant'st* puppy of his pride.
> > *Horace*, b. 1, Epist. 1, Aldine Ed., p. 42.

JOHN COLLIER.
1750.

> For then it wou'd be os plene [plain] as Blackstone-
> Edge ot tearn [they were] mayin [making] o *arron*
> gawby on meh.   • *Works*, p. 58.

COLL. USE.
1875.

> He's an *arran'* thief, and as big a rogue.

ARRONLY, *adv.* exceedingly.

JOHN COLLIER.
1750.

> I're *arronly* moydert [I was completely bewildered].
> > *Works*, p. 58.

ARTO, *v. pron.* art thou?   Mid. E. *artow*, from A.S. *eart þu.*

NORTHUMB. DIALECT.
Before 1300.

> Mi leser [deliverer] *artou*, night and dai,
> Fra mi faes ben wrathful ai.
> > *Metrical English Psalter*, ps. xvii., l. 121.

CHAUCER.
1380.

> "*Artow* than a bayely?"   "Ye," quod he.
> He durste not for verray filth and schame
> Sayn that he was a sompnour, for the name.
> > *Freres Tale*, l. 94.

BAMFORD.
1864.

> I stoode beside Tim Bobbin' grave,
>   'At looks o'er Ratchda' teawn ;
> An' th' owd lad 'woke within his yerth
> An' sed, " Wheer *arto'* beawn ?"
> > *Homely Rhymes*, p. 80.

WAUGH.
1867.

> " Nea then," replied Tim, "what *arto* doin' snoorin
> i'bed at this time o'th day ?"   *Owd Bl.*, p. 14.

ARTONO, } *v. pro.* and *adv.* art thou not? A.S. *eart þú ná?*
ARTN'TO, }

WAUGH.
1867.

> Aw think thae'rt a bit thrutch't i' thi mind this
> morning abeawt summat, *artn'to?* *Owd. Bl.*, p. 10.

ARVAL (N. and Mid. Lanc.) *sb.* a funeral feast. Probably from *arf-ale*, inheritance-ale, or feast made by an heir on coming into property. Cf. Icel. *arfr.;* A.S. *yrfe*, an inheritance.

> That *arval* which Thorward and Thord held in
> honour of their father, was the most famous ever
> known in Ireland.—*Landnamabok*, iii. c. 10.

ARVAL-BREAD, *sb.* cakes used at a funeral.

ASHELT, *adv.* probably, likely; also, easily. Cf. Icel. *heldr*, rather ; which is Mœso-Goth. *haldis*, rather; connected with Goth. *hulths*, favourable ; M.E. *hold*, favourable = M.E. *as hold*, i. e. as favourably, as soon.

JOHN COLLIER.
1750.

> Boh eh thowt eh could *ashelt* sell hur eh this tother
> pleck. [But I thought I could probably sell her in
> this other place.]   *Works*, p. 49.

ASIDE, *prep.* beside.

> COLL. USE.
> 1875.
>
> Eawr Mally stoode *aside* on me while th' rushcart were gooin' by.

ASK, *adj.* hard, dry. Icel. *heskr, hastr,* harsh.

> COLL. USE.
> 1875.
>
> 1. It's an *ask* wind this mornin.
> 2. This ale has an *asky* taste.

ASKE, } *sb.* a water-newt, a lizard ; *pl.* askerds. Gael. *asc,* an
ASKER, }   adder, a snake. A.S. *apexe,* newt, salamander.

> About 1330.
>
> Snakes and nederes thar he fand,
> And gret blac tades gangand,
> And *arskes,* and other wormes felle.
>   *Eng. Met. Homilies : Sp. E. Eng.,* p. 95, l. 177.

> COLL. USE.
> 1875.
>
> He went a-fishin' an' cowt nowt nobbut *askerds.*

ASSAL-TOOTH, (N. and E. Lanc.) *sb.* a molar tooth. Icel. *jaxl,* a molar tooth.

> COLL. USE.
> 1875.
>
> Some co'n em *wang* an otners *assal*-teeth.

ASS, *sb.* ashes from coal. Ess, in South-East Lanc. ; Ass, in North-East Lanc. A.S. *æsce,* ashes.

> COLL. USE.
> 1875.
>
> Now, wench, get that *ass* up and mop th' harston.

ASSCAT, *sb.* a child who plays near or in the ashes ; a term of contempt applied to lazy persons who hang habitually over the fire. A.S. *æsce,* ashes.

ASTITE, *adv.* as soon ; as quick ; by-and-by. Icel. *tiðr,* frequent ; neut. *titt* (used as adv.) soon ; Sw. *tidt,* soon.

> HAMPOLE.
> 1340.
>
> For a best, when it es born, may ga
> *Als-tite* aftir, and rin to and fra.   *P. of C.,* 470.

> WEST.MID. DIAL. (Lanc.).
> 1360.
>
> Bot þer on-com a bote *as-tyt.*
>   *E. Eng. Allit. Poems,* A. l. 644.

> IBID.
>
> And þay token hit *as-tyt* and tented hit lyttel.
>   *Ibid,* B. l. 935

> COLL. USE.
> 1875.
>
> I can go *astite* as him.

ASTO, *vb. pron.* hast thou ? Mid. E. *hastow,* hast thou ?

> COLL. USE.
> 1875.
>
> Why, Jim, thae's never browt o' that lumber wi' thi' *asto ?*

ASWINT, *adj.* crooked, oblique. Dutch, *schuin,* oblique, sloping.

> COLL. USE.
> 1875.
>
> He geet it *aswint,* an cudna set it straight hissel.

ATAFTER, *prep.* after.

CHAUCER.
1340.

At after souper [supper] felle they in treté [treaty].
Frankeleynes Tale, l. 483.

WAUGH.
1868.

He gave another glance at the window, and said,
" Ay; it is a bonny neet, for sure, *at-after* this storm.''
Sneck-bant, p. 14.

ATHATNS (S. Lanc.),
ATHATNESS (Mid Lanc.), } *adv.* in that way.

RAMSBOTTOM.
1864.

An' *o'thattens* their little tongues ran ;
Bo sich prattlin' o' went agen th' grain.
Lanc. Rhymes, p. 20.

ATHIS'NS (S. Lanc.),
ATHISNESS (Mid Lanc.), } *adv.* in this way.

COLLIER.
1750.

Let's stick toth' tone tother's hond then. *Athiss'n*
we went into th' leath. [Let us stick to one another's
hand then. In this way we went into the barn.]
Works, p. 71.

COLL USE.
1875.

Th' owd felly kept waggin' his yed, th' fust *a-this'ns*
an' then a-that'ns.

ATOP, *prep.* on the top.

WAUGH.
1867.

Aw're so mad at him, 'at aw up wi' th' rollin'-pin,
an aw took him straight *a-top* o' th' yed wi't—sich a
cleawt !   *Owd Bl.* c. iii., p. 65.

ATTER, *sb.* poison, filth, corrupt matter issuing from a wound.
A.S. *ater, atter,* poison.

LANGLAND.
1377.

Alle þe oþer þer it lyth [enuenymeþ] þorgh his *attere.*
Piers Plowman, Bk. xii., 256.

1430.

I may drede at my departyng
þat it wole be *attir* and ille.
Hymns to the Virgin and Christ, p. 24-62.

1440.

Attyr, fylthe, sanies. A.Sax. *atter,* venenum.
This sore is full of matter, or atter ; *purulentum.*
Prompt. Parv.

GASKELL.
1854.

Lancashire people often call a bad, irritating temper, an *attern*-temper, poisoned or poisoning temper
Lect. Lanc. Dial. p. 30.

COLL. USE.
1875.

He's fair *attert* wi' dirt.

ATTERCOP, *sb.* a spider. A.S. *atter-coppa,* a venomous insect, a
spider.

WYCLIF.
1380.

The eiren [eggs] of edderes thei to-breeken, and
the webbis of an *attercop* thei wouen.
Isaiah lix. 5.

See a curious tale of the effect of the venom of the *atturcoppe* at Shrewsbury, in the preface to Langtoft's Chron. Hearne, i. p. cc. In Trevisa's version of the Polychronicon, it is said that in Ireland "there ben *attercoppes* (bloode-soukers) and eeftes that doon none harme." *Prompt. Parv.* pp. 16 & 17.

COLL. USE. 1875.

Th' wimmen lace thersels up so, they look like *attercops*.

ATTERCOB, *sb.* a spider's web.

COLL. USE. 1875.

Th' blackberries wur o covered wi *attercobs*.

ATTERING, *adj.* venomous. See ATTER.

ATWEEN, *prep.* between.

SPENSER. 1579.

And then *atweene* her lilly handes twaine
Into his wound the juice thereof did scruze.
F. Q., iii., c. v., st. 33.

ATWIXT, *prep.* between.

Before 1370.

Grete love was *atwixe* hem two.
Bothe were they faire and bright of hewe.
Rom. of Rose, 854.

SPENSER. 1579.

And with outrageous strokes did him restraine,
And with his body bard the way *atwixt* them twaine.
F. Q., i. c. viii., st. 13.

COLL. USE. 1875.

He geet *atwixt* t' wheels.

AUMRY, ⎫ (N. Lanc.), *sb.* a pantry or cupboard. See *awmebry*
AUMBRY, ⎭ in Prompt. Parv. Properly = Low Lat. *almarium*, = Lat. *armarium;* but, as P. P. shows, mixed up with *elemosinarium*.

WILLIAM MORRIS. 1868.

But she across the slippery floors did go
Unto the other wall, wherein was built
A little *aumbrye*. *Jason*, p. 152.

WAUGH. 1874.

We'n tarts, an' cheese, an' a cowd saddle o' mutton
i' t' *aumry* yon, at's never bin cut intill.
Jannock, ii. p. 13.

AVYSE, *sb.* advice, counsel. Fr. *ávis*, from Low Latin, *advisum*, *advisare*, equivalent to an interview face to face, *ad-visum*.

CHAUCER. 1370.

Ye have erred also, for it semeth that yow sufficeth to have been counseiled by these counseilours only, and with litel *avys*. *Tale of Melibeus*, iii., 161, 18.

SPENSER. 1579.

But I with better reason him *aviz'd*.
F. Q., iv. c. viii., st. 58.

COLL. USE. 1875.

I offered him *avyse*, and he wodn't hev it.

AW, *pron.* **I.**

| WAUGH.
1865. | "*Aw* live a bit aboon Whi'toth," replied Ben,
"up Lobden gate on, at a plaze they co'n 'Th'
Ricklin's.'"   *Besom Ben*, p 88 |
| WAUGH.
1867. | He knocked with his empty pot upon the table, and
said, "*Aw* think *aw*'ll have another"
Dulesgate, p. 18. |

AWF, *sb.* an elf, an idiot, a changeling. A.S. *ælf, elf;* Icel. *álfr;*
Dan. *alf;* Flem. *elf, alf.*

| SHAKESPERE.
1602. | We'll dresse
Like vrchins, *ouphes*, and fairies, greene and white.
Merry Wives, iv. 4, 48. |

| JOHN COLLIER.
1750. | What an *awf* wur I to pretend rime weh yo.
Eawther an His Buk : Works, p. xxxvi. |

AWHOAM, *prep.* and *sb.* at home.

| WAUGH.
1859. | So, we'n bide one another, whatever may come ;
For there's no peace i'th world iv there's no peace
awhoam.   *Lanc. Songs : Jamie's Frolic.* |

AWMAKS, *pron.* and *sb.* Pronun. of *all makes.* All sorts or kinds.

| COLL. USE.
1875. | He sells childer's stuff an' *awmaks* o' things. |

AWSE, *v.* to offer, to attempt. See also Oss.

WAUGH. 1859.	A mon 'at plays a fiddle weel, Should never *awse* to dee. *Lanc. Songs : Eawr Folk.*
WAUGH. 1865.	Come, owd dog, *awse* to shap. *Besom Ben*, c. iv. p. 42.
JOHN HIGSON. 1866.	Aw shackert un' waytud till ten, Bu' Meary ne'er *awst* to com eawt. *Harland's Lancashire Lyrics*, p. 187.

AW'ST, *pron.* and *v.* I shall.

		Sing.	*Plu.*
First Person	. . .	Aw'st	We'st
Second Person	. .	Thea'st	Yo'st
Third Person	. . .	He'st	They'st

| WAUGH.
1857. | "Do you ever think of delving the ground up,'
said I. "Delve ! nawe." answered he ; "*aw'st* delve
noan theer."—*Lanc. Sketches : Grave of Grislehurst
Boggart*, 208. |
| COLL. USE.
1875. | *Aw'st* draw mi brass t'morn, an then *thea'st* have a
new cwot. |

AWTS, *sb.* refuse of hay ; left meat ; fragments. Probably Lancashire pronunciation of *orts.* See *orts* in Wedgwood.

| JOHN COLLIER.
1750. | So away we went, an begun o' cromming o' th'
leawphoyles [loop-holes] an' th' slifters i'th' leath
woughs full o' *awts*.   *Works*, p. 44. |

AWVISH, *adj.* queer; naughty. See Awf, *ante.*
AWVISHLY, *adv.* awkwardly.

<table>
<tr><td>COLLIER.
1750.</td><td>When he coom in ogen, he glooart *awvishly* at Mezzil fease [= When he came in again, he stared queerly at Mezzil-face]. *Works,* p. 53.</td></tr>
<tr><td>COLL. USE.
1875.</td><td>Keep out of his road aw tell thi, he's an *awvish,* nowty felly.</td></tr>
</table>

AX, } *v.* to ask. A.S. *âscian, âcsian,* to ask, inquire, demand.
ASH, } The A.S. verb is spelt indifferently *ascian, acsigan, ahsian,* or *axian.*

<table>
<tr><td>E. ENG. MET. ROMANCES.
Ab. 1400.</td><td>Gawan *asshes,* Is hit soe ?—p. 69.</td></tr>
<tr><td>COLLIER.
1750.</td><td>Then, as I thowt he tawkt so awkertly, I'd *ash* him for th' wonst whot uncoths [news] he heard sturrin. — *Works,* 51.</td></tr>
<tr><td>BAMFORD.
1864.</td><td>Curridge, meh lads, ween goo an' see't,
It isno' dark, for th' moon gi's leet;
Iv't be a Ludd, ween at him smash,
Iv boggart, aw'll some questions *ash.*
Poems, p. 164.</td></tr>
<tr><td>RAMSBOTTOM.
1864.</td><td>Then *ax* thisel if thea should fret,
When thea's laid by two hundhret peawnd.
Lanc. Rhymes, p. 41.</td></tr>
<tr><td>WAUGH.
1857.</td><td>Scratching his head. and looking thoughtfully among the houses, he said, " Scowfil ?" [*i e..* pron. of Schole-field.] Aw know no Scowfils, but thoose at th' Tim Bobbin aleheawse; yodd'n better *ash* theer."
Lanc Sk. : Cottage of Tim Bobbin, c. iii., p. 53.</td></tr>
<tr><td>WAUGH.
1865.</td><td>Well, go thee in an' *ax* him then, as thae'rt so cliver !
Besom Ben, p. 58.</td></tr>
</table>

AXED (S. and E. Lanc.), }
ASHT   (ditto) } *v. pt. t.* asked. See Ax.
AISHT   (Furness), }

<table>
<tr><td>A.S. TRANS. GOSPELS.
995.</td><td>And he on wege his leorning-cnihtas *ahsode* [other copies *acsode, axode, axsode*], Hwæt secgaþ men þæt ic sy ?= And he in the way his learning-knights [disciples] *axed,* What say men that I am ?
Mark viii. 27.</td></tr>
<tr><td>WYCLIF.
1380.</td><td>He *axide* his disciplis.—*Mark* viii. 27.</td></tr>
<tr><td>CHAUCER.
1380.</td><td>And to her housbond bad hir for to seye,
If that he *axed* after Nicholas,
Sche schulde seye, sche wiste nat wher he was.
Milleres Tale, l. 226.</td></tr>
<tr><td>THOMAS OCCLEVE.
About 1420.</td><td>Alle that they *axed* haden they redy.
De Regimine Principum, st. 600.</td></tr>
<tr><td>JOHN COLLIER.
1750.</td><td>Then I *asht* him what way eh munt gooa.
Works, p. 47.</td></tr>
<tr><td>IBID.</td><td>Justice *axt* meh whot eh wantut.—*Works,* p. 48.</td></tr>
</table>

WAUGH.
1859

My cheek went as red as a rose ;
There's never a mortal can tell
Heaw happy aw felt ; for, thea knows,
One couldn't ha *axed* him theirsel'.
Lanc. Songs : Dule's i' this Bonnet.

RAMSBOTTOM.
1864.

" Eh, Jim," hoo said, " this lass ull dee,
An' thea's ne'er once e'er *ax'd* to see't."
Lanc. Rhymes, p. 38.

AXEN (S.-E. Lanc.), } *v. pres. t.* ask.   Used in Lancashire in
ASHEN (N.-E. Lanc.), } the plural.

CHAUCER.
1390.

But shortly, lest this tales sothe were,
She dorst at no night *axen* it for feere.
Troylus and C., Bk. iv., 643.

COLL. USE.
1875.

Yo're noan shaumefaced ; yo *axen* [or *ashen*] for
anoof.

AXINS, *sb.* askings, applied to marriage banns.

WAUGH.
1875.

" Eh. Dick, whatever mun I do if my faither finds
this out ?"   " Thou mun do as I towd tho, an' let me
put th' *axins* up.   Mon, th' owd chap 'll come to, if
we getten wed."—*Old Cronies*, iv. p. 43.

COLL. USE.
1875.

Well, thae'rt for bein' wed at th' lung length ; aw
yer thae's getten th' *axins* in.

AYLA (Fylde),   } *adj.* shy, backward, shamefaced.   John Ray,
AYLO (S. E. Lanc.), } in his glossary of North Country words
(1691) has " *Heloe*, or *Helaw*, bashful;" and Ralph Thoresby, in
the list of Yorkshire words (presumably from the neighbourhood
of Leeds), sent to Ray in 1703, gives " *Hala*, bashful, nicely
modest."   (See E. D. S. Reprinted Glossaries, Part III.)   See
also " *Hala*, bashful," in the Rev. W. Thornber's " Glossary of
old words used in the Fylde ;" *History of Blackpool*, p. 108.

WAUGH.
1874.

There's some fresh-poo'd sallet theer, an' some
cowd beef, an' some cheese—so reitch to, an' dunnot
be *ailo*, for I'm nobbut a poor hond at laithin' (in-
viting).—*Chimney Corner : Manch. Critic, July* 24,
1874.

B.

BABS, *sb. pl.* pictures; chiefly pictures in a book. The word is another form of "babes," and it is almost solely used in talk to very little children; as, "There's a *bab* o'er lev" (= there's a baby, or, a picture, over the leaf). Again, in Waugh's "Come whoam to thi Childer an' Me," "I've a book full o' *babs*" means "I've a book full of pictures." Compare the expression *babies in the eyes*, explained by Nares, where *baby* means the small image or picture of oneself, as seen in the eye of another person.

> WAUGH.   Aw've a drum an' a trumpet for Dick;
> 1859.   Aw've a yard o' blue ribbon for Sal;
>   Aw've a book full o' *babs ;* an' a stick
>   An' some 'bacco an' pipes for mysel.
>   *Lanc. Songs : Come Whoam to thi Childer.*

BACKBOTE, *pt. t.* of backbite. See BOTE.

> WAUGH.   They natter't, an' braw'lt, an' *backbote ;* and played
> 1865.   one another o' maks o' ill-contrive't tricks.
>   *Barrel Organ,* p. 15.

BACKEND, *sb.* the latter part of the year. Also applied occasionally to the after part of any period, as a week or a month.

> J. P. MORRIS.   I'se gäèn tà leeàv mè spot [situation] this *back-end*.
> 1859.   *Furness Glossary,* p. 6.
> WAUGH.   "Aw say, Dan," said Ben, addressing the old
> 1869.   fiddler, "thae'll remember that greight wynt-storm
>   'at happen't i'th' last *back-end*."
>   *Yeth-Bobs and Scaplins,* c. iii., p 45.

BACKSET, *sb.* something to fall back upon; a support or supporter.

> COLL. USE.   1. Hoo's noan so badly off; hoo's a bit ov a *back-*
> 1875.   *set* i' th Bank.
>   2. Feight him, Jim; aw'll bi thi *backset.*

BACKSIDE, *sb.* the court-yard or ground at the back of a house.

> COLL. USE.   He used t' sit smookin' of a neet at th' *backside*,
> 1875.   among his bits o' posies.

BADGER, *sb.* the keeper of a small provision shop; also, in North Lanc., a travelling dealer in butter, eggs, etc. "There can be little doubt," says Mr. Wedgwood, "that E. *badger*, whether in the sense of a corn-dealer or of the quadruped, is directly descended from the Fr. *bladier*, a corn-dealer."

> WAUGH.   Eawr Alick keeps a *badger's* shop.
> 1859.   *Lanc. Songs : Eawr Folk.*

RAMSBOTTOM.
1364.

For th' *badgers* soon began to show
  They knew they'd weary toimes to pass ;
They manisht t' let us wortchers know
  They'd nobbut sell for ready brass.
      Lanc. Rhymes : Takin' Stock, p. 46.

BADLY, *adj.* unwell, sickly.

COLL. USE.
1875.

" Heaw's Ailse ?"
" *Badly, badly ;* hoo's noan lung for this world."

BAG, *sb.* a discharge from employment.   Cf. " to get the *sack*."

WAUGH.
1870.

" He geet th' *bag* for that," said Ben.   " Sarve
him reet," replied the fiddler.   "But he never wur
very breet."— *Yeth Bobs*, c. i., p. 26.

IBID.
1875.

Here : I'll ha' this job settle't afore thou comes out
o' that seck [sack]. I've gan thee th' *bag* mony a
time, but thou's taen it thisel' at last.
      Old Cronies, c. iv., p. 48.

BAG, *v.* to discharge from work.

COLL. USE.
1875.

He'll *bag* thi, as sure as thae'r wick, if thae comes
late again.

BAGGIN', *sb.* an afternoon meal, originally carried in a bag.

COLLIER.
1750.

Meh deme's gon fro whoam, an hoo'll naw cum
agen till *baggin'*-time.   *Works*, p. 41.

BAMFORD.
1850.

In the afternoon, oatcake and cheese, or butter, or
oatcake and buttermilk, sufficed for *bagging*.
      Ed. of Tim Bobbin : Intro. p. ix.

WAUGH.
1857.

They [two weavers] had come out of their looms
to spend their " *baggin'*-time" in the open air, and
were humming one of their favourite songs.
      Lanc. Sketches, p. 51.

IBID.
1867.

One day, as aw wur busy i'th kitchen, makin'
some cakes for th' *baggin'*, in comes Owd Plunge.
      Owd Blanket, c. iii., p. 64.

BAIGLE, *sb.* Pron. of *beagle*, the dog with which the hare is hunted.
The word, however, is much used figuratively, as in the common
expression, " Thae'rt a bonny *baigle*," where the phrase is applied
to anybody who is startlingly kenspeckle, or curious, or out of
the ordinary way, in dress or person.

WAUGH.
1865.

" Well, thae'rt a bonny *baigle*, owd mon," said
Enoch, laughing.
" *Baigle !*" replied Twitchel ; "feel at mo ! Aw
met ha' bin in a traycle-tub !"
      Besom Ben, c. v., p. 56.

BAIN (N. Lanc.), *adv.* near, adjacent, convenient.   Icel. *beinn*,
direct ; *beint*, straight.

ANON.
About 1350.

Yff ye wyll oghtte that we kanne doo,
Ye thar bot [need only] commande hus [us] thertoo,
  And haffe your servandes *beyn*.
      Sir Amadas, in *Weber's Metrical
      Romances*, iii. 264 ; l. 512.

1860. *Bane* ta Claapam town-end lived an aud Yorkshire
tike.—*Ball. and Songs of Yorkshire*, p. 160.

A. C. GIBSON.
1868.

On my objecting to quit the smoother and shorter
road for the longer and rougher, he persisted, "It
may bee as yee say, beeath t' better an' t' *bainer*, bit
nowte wad hire me to teeak t' rooad ooer Oxenfell at
this hour o' t' neet."—*Folk-Speech of Cumberland:*
Ex. of Dialect of High Furness, Lancashire, p. 90.

BAK-BREDE, *sb.* a broad thin board, with a handle, used in
riddling out the dough of oatcakes before they are put on the
spittle, and turned down on the *bak-stone*. A.S. *bacan*, to bake,
and *bred*, a board.

BAKIN'-SPITTLE, } *sb.* a peculiar shovel, made of wood, generally
BACK-SPITTLE, } shod with iron, used in baking oatcakes.
Spittle is here a diminutive of *spade ;* see SPADE in Wedgwood.

B. BRIERLEY.
1867.

An owd oak *back-spittle* he slung by his side.
Marlocks of Merriton, p. 58.

WAUGH.
1868.

Aw'm dampish abeawt th' legs wi' wadin' through
th' weet moor; but o' tother's as dry as a *bakin'-spittle.*
Sneck-Bant, c. i., p. 7.

BAKSTER, *sb.* a baker.

WEST MID. DIALECT.
About 1360.

Bochers, bladsmythis, *baxters* amonge.
Gest Hystoriale of Troy, l. 1592.

LANGLAND.
1377.

Brewesteres and *bakesteres*, bocheres and cokes.
Piers Plowman, b. iii. 79.

BAKSTON, *sb.* a plate, stone, or slate for baking upon.

WAUGH.
1869.

This oatcake is baked upon a peculiar kind of stone
slab, called a *back-stone*, and the cry of "Havercake
backstones" is a familiar sound in Rochdale and the
villages round it, at this day.
Lanc. Sketches, p. 129.

BALDER (Burnley and Cliviger), *v.* to break stones on the road.

BALDERER, *sb.* a stonebreaker. See above.

BANDIN', }
BANDT, } *sb.* a cord or string ; also a belt.   From A.S. *bænd*,
BANT, } a band.

WAUGH.
1865.

"Howd fast, good bally-*bant !*" cried Ben, gazing
up and clasping his hands. "Howd fast ! Iv thae
gi's way, aw'm done for !"
Besom Ben, c. ii., p. 23.

COLL. USE.
1875.

1. Hast getten a bit o' *bandin'* abeawt thi ? Mi
shoon han comn unteed.
2. Si tho ! yon horse's bally-*bandt* wants tightenin'.

BANDY-CAD (Mid Lanc.), } *sb.* a game played with a *nurr* and
BANDY-GAD (S. E. Lanc.), } crooked stick ; also called *shinty*.
Much the same as the *hockey* of the South of England.   *Bandy*

is to strike from side to side. See BANDY in Wedgwood. *Cad* is the same as *cat* in the game of tip-cat; it simply means a *cut* bit of wood or fragment of wood; cf. W. *cat*, a piece; *cwtan*, to cut. See CUT in Wedgwood.

R. COTGRAVE.
1611.

"*Bander*, to bend a bow; . . . . also, to *bandie*, at tennis." "Jouer à bander et à racler contre, to *bandy* against, at tennis; and, by metaphor, to pursue with all insolency, rigour, extremity."—*French Dict.*

BANDYHEWIT, *sb.* a sarcastic or contemptuous name for a dog. It means bandy-houghed, crooked or bending in the *houghs.* Brockett has "*heuk-bane*, the hucklebone."

COLLIER.
1750.

I'd o' mind t' cheeot (God forgi' meh) on sell him meh sheep-cur for o *bandyhewit:* tho' I no moor knew, in th' mou in th' moon, whot a *bandyhewit* wur.   *Works,* p. 47.

BANG, *v.* to excel, to surpass.   Icel. *bang,* a hammering; *banga,* to beat.

MISS GILPIN.
1805.

We've *bang'd* the French, aye, out an out,
An duin the thing complete.
        Cumb. Ballads, First Series, p. 168.

COLL. USE.
1875.

Well, that *bangs* o' 'at ever aw seed i' mi life.

BANGBEGGAR, *sb.* a name for a person who kept off noisy intruders during church time.   From *bang,* to beat.

WAUGH.
1865.

Just then owd Pudge, th' *bangbeggar,* coom runnin' into th' pew, an' he fot Dick a souse at back o' th' yed wi' his silver-nobbed pow.—*Barrel Organ,* p. 29.

BANNOCK,
BUNNOCK (Mid. Lanc.), } *sb.* an oatmeal cake.   Gael. *bonnach,* the same.

BURNS.
1780.

Bannocks o' bear meal,
Bannocks o' barley,
Here's to the Hielandman's
Bannocks o' barley.
        Songs: Bannocks o' Barley.

E. KIRK.
1875.

Bunnock is a common term in North Lancashire for a small cake, the principal ingredients of which are oatmeal and treacle.   The cakes vary in size from two to four inches in diameter, and are not, I think, identical with the Scotch *bannock.*—*Local Notes and Queries,* 692, *M. Guardian,* March 22.

BANSIL,
BANSELL,
BENSIL (Goosnargh and Lonsdale), } *v.* to beat.   Cf. Du. *bons,* a bounce, thump; *bonzen,* to thump.   Cf. *bang.*

COLL. USE.
1875.

Aw'll *bansell* thi hide for thi, if thae'rt not off.

BANT, *sb.* vigour, strength.

B. Brierley. 1867.	He're sure to gallop when he should ha' walked, an get to th' end of his *bant* in no time. *Red Windows Hall,* c. xiv., p. 107.
Coll. Use. 1875.	He's good for nowt : there's no *bant* in him : he can noather eyt [eat] nor wark.

BANT, *v.* to manage, to achieve, to conquer. As : " Conto *bant* it ?" (= Canst thou achieve it ?)   " Conto *bant* him ?" (= Canst thou conquer him ?)

Waugh. 1874.	They keepen tryin.' . . . . They keepen comin' to th' edge of a scar, where they can see no fur [further], an' then they han to turn back, an' start again. It's my belief, owd lad, 'at they'n never *bant* it. *Chimney Corner: Manch. Critic,* March 7, 1874.
Ibid. 1875.	" Nay," cried Craddy ; " I've done very weel ! I couldn't *bant* another smite ! " *Owd Cronies,* c. iii. p. 36.

BANYAN-DAY, *sb.* the day when the week's odds-and-ends are eaten up.   At Goosnargh, pronounced Banny-ann-day.

Daily News. 1874.	Jack Mooring, a Trafalgar man, age 93. " On the important question of victualling the ships, Jack has no doubt whatever that the present generation have made advances upon the practice of their grand-fathers. In his time ' there were often six upon four aboard ship, and two *banyan* days in a week,' which, being translated, is, the rations for four men were served out amongst six, in addition to which, on two days out of the week, no rations were served out at all."— *Correspondent's Letter from Haslar Hospital, Portsmouth,* March 17, 1874.

BARFOOT, *adj.* barefoot.   A.S. *bærfôt.*

Before Chaucer. About 1350.	*Barfoot* and ungert Gamelyn in cam. *Cokes Tale,* 215.
About 1400.	In sumer ge habbeð leave *barfot* gan and sittan. *Reliquiæ Antiquæ,* vol. ii , p. 3.

Waugh. 1874.	"Aye, aye, Sam," said Jone, "*barfoot* folk shouldn't walk upo' prickles." " It just depends," replied Sam, " whether they liken it or not." *Chimney Corner: Manch. Critic,* March 14, 1874.
Note. 1875.	In North Lancashire, the phrase "*barfoot* feet " is used ; and the term "*barfoot* clogs " is applied to clogs without irons, which are regarded as a token of the wearer's poverty.

BARIHAM,   ) *sb.* a horse-collar.   A.S. *beorgan,* to pro-
BARKHAM (Cliviger), ʃ   tect, and Eng. *hames.*   It means a protection against the *hames;* also used in the form *hamberwe,* or *hamborough.*   See Hames in Wedgwood, and Barkhaam, in Brockett.

BARKEN'D (Lancaster), *p. part.* caked, encrusted. Icel. *börkr*, E. *bark*, i.e. of a tree, etc.　Cf. *bark*, to form a crust, in *Hamlet*, act i, sc. 5, l. 71.

> COLL. USE.　　　Eh! thae art mucky; it's fair *barken'd* on thi.
> 1875.

BARKL'T, *p. part.* applied to hair upon which dirt has hardened; also to a wound when the blood has hardened upon it.　See BARKEN'D *ante.*

BARLEY, ⎫ *v.* to bespeak, to lay claim to; generally used by
BALLA,　⎭　children.　The phrase *balla me* is exactly the French *baillez moi.*

> COLL. USE.　　　*Balla* me th' apples.
> 1875.

BARM, *sb.* the bosom.　A.S. *bearm*, bosom; Goth. *barms*, a lap, bosom; Icel. *barmr*, border, edge, lap, bosom; Swed. *barm.*

> ANGLO-SAXON GOSPELS.　　　Gód gemet and full, and geheapod and ofer-
> 995.　　　flowende hig syllaþ on eowerne *bearm.*　[= Good
> 　　　measure and full, heaped and overflowing. they shall
> 　　　give into your bosom.]　　　*Luke* vi. 38.
>
> ROBERT MANNYNG.　　　Befyl hyt so vp-on a day
> 1303.　　　Þat pore men sate yn þe way,
> 　　　And spred here hatren [clothes] on here *barme*
> 　　　Aȝens þe sonne þat was warme.
> 　　　　　　*Handlying Synne*, l. 5581.
>
> 1320.　　　For sco rad, þat moder mild
> 　　　And in hir *barm* sco ledd hir child.
> 　　　　　*Cursor Mundi* (Cotton MS.), l. 11601.
>
> WEST MID. DIAL. (LANC.)　　　As lyttel barneȝ on *barme* þat neuer bale wroȝt.
> 1377　　　　　　*Allit. Poems*, C. l. 510.
>
> CHAUCER.　　　And slepyng in hir *barm* upon a day
> 1380.　　　Sche made to clyppe or schere his heres away.
> 　　　　　*The Monkes Tale*, l. 76.
>
> GAWIN DOUGLAS.　　　Zephyrus comfortabill Inspiratioun
> 1513　　　Fortill ressaue law in hyr *barm* adoun.
> 　　　　　*Prologue Eneid*, book xii., l. 75.

BARMSKIN, *sb.* a leather apron.　From *barm*, the lap, and *skin.* The A.S. word was *barm-cláp*, barm-cloth.

> 1440.　　　*Barnyskyn, barme skyn*, melotes, melota.
> 　　　　　　　*Prompt. Parv.*
>
> JOHN COLLIER.　　　"Neaw lads," sed Hal, "mind yer hits: I'll lap
> 1750.　　　meh honds eh meh *barmskin* ot hoo cannah scrat
> 　　　meh."　　　　*Works*, p. 45.

BARN, *sb.* a child.　A.S. *bearn*, M.E. *bern, barn*, from A.S. *beran*, to bear.

> ANGLO-SAXON GOSPELS.　　　Þisse worulde *bearn* synd gleawran þisses leohtes
> 995.　　　*bearnum.*　[= The children of this world are wiser
> 　　　than the children of this light.]　　　*Luke* xvi. 8

1272.

Of qwom that blisfulle *barne* in Bedelem was born.
E. Eng. Met. Rom. A. xviii.

1320.

Þis ilk stern þam come to warn
Apon þat mont in forme o *barn,*
And bar on it liknes of croice.
Cursor Mundi (Cotton MS.), l. 11417.

WILLIAM OF PALERNE.
1350.

And was a big bold *barn* and breme of his age.
Spec. of E. English, l. 18.

WEST MID. DIALECT.
About 1360.

Many wyves, for woo, of þere wit past,
And þere *barnes* on brest bere in þere armes,
Hyd hom in houles.
Gest Hystoriale of Troy, l. 8143.

WEST.MID. DIAL. (Lanc.).
1377.

We leuen on marye þat a grace of grewe
þat ber a *barne* of vyrgyn flour.
Allit. Poems, A. l. 426.

SHAKSPERE.
1611.

Good-lucke (and 't be thy will) what have we heere!
Mercy on's, a *barne ;* a very pretty *barne !* A boy
or a child, I wonder ?
Winter's Tale, act iii., sc. 3, l. 69.

JOHN COLLIER.
1750.

It lawmt [= lamed] th' *barn* ot wur ith' keather.
Works, p. 66.

J. P. MORRIS.
1867.

Peggy Wilson was lettin her lile *barn* sowk when
she heard on't ; an i' her horry she shov'd t' *barn*
int'l an ald brek ubben.—*T' Siege o' Brou'ton,* p. 5.

BARN'S-LAKINS, *n.* children's playthings. Icel. *barna-leikr,* a
child's play ; from Iccl. *barn,* a child ; and *leikr,* a game. Icel.
leika, to play ; Sw. *leka.* Mœso-Goth, *laikan,* to play. But the
word is also A.S. ; cf. A.S. *bearn,* a child ; *læ'can,* to play ; *lác,*
a game.

BARROW HOG, *sb.* a male swine. A.S. *bearh,* Mid. E. *barh.*

About 1300.

He wile of bore wurchen *bareg.*
Owl and Nightingale, l. 408.

PHILEMON HOLLAND.
1600.

I mean no other swine but such as feed and root in
the field : among which the female, especially a guelt
that never farrowed, is more effectual than a (tame)
bore, *barrow-hog,* or a breeding sow.
Plinie, b. xxviii., c. 9.

BASH, *adj.* shy, bashful. From O. Fr. *esbahir.* The word is used
as a verb by the older writers.

WICLIF.
1380.

Thes thingis herynge we dredden, and oure herte
bashede. *Joshua* ii. 11.

SIR T. MALORY.
1469.

I wende no Bretouns walde bee *basschede* for so
lyttille. *Morte Arthure,* l. 2121.

About 1515.

Because they *bashed* them at Berwick, that boldeth
them the more.
Ballads and Songs of Lanc., p. 22
(The Flodden Field).

PHILEMON HOLLAND.
1600.

Are you not ashamed, and *bash* you not to broach
and set abroad, in the view and face of the world,
such mockeries of religion ? *Livius,* p. 320.

BASIER, *sb.* the auricula. F. C. H., in *Notes and Queries* (third series, ii. 305), says : " It seems probable that *basier* was originally *bear's ear*, the usual name for the auricula in the eastern counties ; a name founded no doubt upon the resemblance of the leaf to an ear, which gave occasion to the botanical name of auricula.

> Our flocks they're all folded, and young lambs sweetly do play,
> And the *basiers* are sweet in the morning of May.
> > *Ballads and Songs of Lanc.* (May Song, by a Swinton Man), p. 88.

BASS, *sb.* iron pyrites or shale, found in coal ; coal which will not burn.

COLL. USE.
1875.

That coal's nowt but *bass.*

BASTE, *v.* to beat, to whip or thrash. Swed. *bösta*, to thump. Icel. *beysta*, to beat, to thrash, to belabour.

BUTLER.
1663.

> We whilom left the captiv'd knight
> And pensive squire both bruised in body
> And conjur'd into safe custody,
> Tir'd with dispute and talking Latin
> As well as *basting* and bull-baiting.
> > *Hudibras*, part ii., canto i., l. 32.

COLL. USE.
1875.

Thae'llt get a rare *bastin'*, mi lad, when thae gets whoam.

BAT, *sb.* a child's shoe, made without a welt.

BAT, *sb.* (1) speed or force ; (2) fashion, way, or manner ; (3) a blow. A.S. and Gael. *bat*, a bat ; an imitation of the sound of a blow. Cf. M.E. *batte*, to strike, beat : " *Battede* hem on the bakkes" (Piers Plowman, A. iii. 192).

MARK LONSDALE.
1780.

For at yae *batt* he fell'd me flat.
> *Cumb. Ballads*, 277.

About 1450.

Glad to please you to pay, lest any *bats* [blows] begin.
> *Ballads and Songs of Lanc.*, p. 5. (From MS. vol. Chetham Lib.)

WAUGH.
1868.

1. Speed or force :—
" By th' mon," said he, as he turn't his collar up and cruttle't into th' nook, "it's [rain's] comin' deawn full *bat*." *Sneck-Bant*, c. ii., p. 35.

IBID.
1868.

2. Fashion, way, or manner :—
" How's Billy Kettle gettin' on, Ben ?" " Oh, abeawt th' owd *bat*. As greedy as ever." *Sneck-Bant*, c. ii., p. 34.

B. BRIERLEY.
1867.

3. A blow :—
Aw up wi my fist an gan her a *bat* between th' een. *Red Winaows Hall*, c. iv., p. 25.

BATCH-CAKE, *sb.* a small cake made out of a batch of dough intended for ordinary bread. *Batch* is from Mid. E. *baken*, A.S. *bæcan*, to bake. *Cake* is Icel. *kaka*, E. *cake* or *cate*.

BATE, *v.* to abate, to lessen, to take something from, to deduct, to diminish, to keep back part of a payment. O. Fr. *battre*, to beat or break down.

SHAKESPERE.
1598.

Falstaff: Bardolph, am I not fallen away vilely since this last action ? Do I not *bate* ? Do I not dwindle ? Why, my skin hangs about me like an old lady's loose gown ; I am withered like an old apple-john. *I. King Hen. Fourth*, iii. 3, l. 1.

IBID.
1623.

Ariel to Prospero. Thou didst promise
To *bate* me a full year. *Tempest*, i. 2, l. 249.

[See also : Rather than she will *bate* one breath, *Much Ado*, ii. 3 ; Bid the main flood *bate* his usual height, *Mer. of Venice*, iv. 1, l. 72 ; I will not *bate* thee a scruple, *All's Well*, ii. 3, l. 234; Who *bates* mine honour shall not know my coin, *Timon of Ath.* iii. 3, l. 26 ; Neither will they *bate* one jot of ceremony, *Corio.* ii. 2, l. 144.]

MILTON.
1650.

I argue not
Against Heaven's hand or will, nor *bate* a jot
Of heart or hope ; but still bear up and steer
Right onward. *Sonnet* xxii. *To Cyriac Skinner.*

DRYDEN.
1700.

And, lest some thorn should pierce thy tender foot,
Or thou should'st fall in flying my pursuit !
To sharp uneven ways thy steps decline ;
Abate thy speed, and I will *bate* of mine.
Ovid Met. b. i.

COLL. USE.
1875.

Well, what'n yo *bate* ? Aw'st noan gie that mich, as heaw it is.

BATE, *v.* to start from a certain place ; used in games.

COLL. USE.
1875.

Wheer did he *bate* from ?

BATMAKER, *sb.* a maker of children's shoes.

RICH. BUXTON.
1849.

When about twelve years of age I went to learn the trade of a *batmaker ;* that is, a maker of children's smaller leather shoes.
Botanical Guide to Manch. Plants, p. iv.

BATTER, *sb.* a woman employed in beating raw cotton to clean it. The operation is now generally done by machinery. See BAT, a blow.

COLL. USE.
1875.

" Who wur it ?" " One o' thoose *batters* at th' · fine mill."

BATTIN, *sb.* a bundle of straw.

COLL. USE.
1875.

Heaw much a *battin*, mestur ?

BATTRILL, *sb.* a short staff; a batting staff used by laundresses. Shakspere uses *batlet, As You Like It,* ii. 4, 49. Formed from A.S. *bat,* by addition of the suffixes *-er* and *-el,* like *pickerel* from *pike.*

BAUTERT, *p. part.* applied to hair upon which dirt has hardened. See BARKL'T. The same as the Northampt. *bolter,* to clot, form into lumps, coagulate; *blood-boltered* means clotted with blood. Cf. Du. *bult,* a bunch, boss, knob.

> SHAKSPERE. For the blood-*boltered* Banquo smiles upon me.
> 1610. *Macbeth,* act iv., sc. i., l. 122.

BAUKS, *sb. pl.* as *sb. sing.,* a hayloft. For *balks;* from A.S. *balca,* a beam. The use of the plural is easily explained; the loft would be between the *balks* or rafters. Chaucer has the very phrase, "in the *balkes,*" for "among the rafters" (*C. T.* 3626).

BAUKS, *sb. pl.* obstacles, discouragements, disappointments. For *balks.* *Balk* has the successive senses of beam, partition, obstacle.

> JOHN COLLIER. We geet up whot we cou'd, an I eet it snap, for
> 1750. beleemy Meary I're so keen-bitt'n I mede no *bawks*
> at o heyseed. [= We got up what we could, and I
> ate it quickly, for, believe me, Mary, I was so hungry
> I did not hesitate at all at the hayseed (*i e.,* that
> covered the food).] *Works,* p. 68.
>
> WAUGH. He made no moor *bawks* at th' job, but set tone
> 1857. foot onto th' top-bar, an' up he went into th' smudge-
> hole.
> *Lanc. Sketches: Ramble Bury to Rochdale,* p. 28.

BAWSANT, *adj.* streaked with white on the face, like a badger. O. Fr. *bauçant,* a horse marked with white. Bas Breton, *bal;* W. *bal,* a white mark on the face of animals. Prompt. Parv. "*Bawstone* or *bawsone,* or a gray, *Taxus, melota.*"

BE, *prep.* by. A.S. and Mid. E. *be, bi.*

> HAMPOLE. Thai may defende tham *be* na ways.—*P. of C.,* 5359.
> 1340.
> IBID. Sothely þay sall joye nowe *be* in-ʒettynge of grace,
> and in tym to come *be* syghte of joye.
> *Prose Treatises,* p. 4.
>
> COLL. USE. Nay, thae mun goo wi me; awst noan tak that
> 1875. gate *be* mysell.

BEAR, *sb.* a doormat.

BEARIN', *pres. part.* going towards.

> COLL. USE. He'r *bearin'* towart th' Whoite Moss when aw
> 1875. met him.

BEARIN', *sb.* a weaver's burden; usually applied to the week's work when taken back to the employer.

COLL. USE.
1875.

He'd his week's *bearin'* upo' his shoother.

BEAWN, *part.* Pron. of *boun* or *bown.* (1) Prepared, destined, setting out, going; (2) compelled; (3) about to. Icel. *búinn,* prepared, ready, p. p. of *búa,* to prepare. Mid. E. *bowne.*

1272.

But to serue the pore folke he was fulle *bowne.*
E. Eng. Met. Rom. A. xxvii.

WEST MID. DIAL. (Lanc.)
1360.

"Wy stonde ȝe ydel þise dayeȝ longe."
Þay sayden her hyre [= hire, wages] watȝ nawhere *boun.*   *Allit. Poems,* A. 532.

1440.

ffor-thi they busked theme *bownne* with baners displayede.
Morte Arthure (E. Eng. Text Soc.), l. 1633.

1490.

And euery knyght vpone his horsȝ is *boun.*
Lancelot of the Laik, 1036.

BAMFORD.
1843.

Th' owd lad 'woke within his yerth,
An' sed, "Wheer arto' *beawn?*"—*Poems,* p. 80.

WAUGH.
1865.

"They're just *beawn* to tak it in," replid the land-lord.   *Besom Ben,* c. viii., p. 93.

IBID.
1869.

"Artn'to *beawn* to ha' some bacon?"
Sneck-Bant, c. i., p. 13.

IBID.

" ..rto for flittin? or thae'rt *beawn* to a rushbearin sor wheer?"   *Ibid.,* c. iv., p. 71.

BEAWT, *prep.* pron. of *bout,* without, unless. A.S. *bútan,* without.

ANGLO-SAXON GOSPELS.
995.

And wæs dead *bútan* bearnum. [= And was dead (died) without children.]   *Luke* xx. 29.

WILLIAM OF PALERNE.
1350.

And as bliue, *boute* bod, he braydes to þe quene,
And hent hire so hetterly to haue hire a-strangeled.
William of Palerne, l. 150.

WEST-MID. DIALECT (Lanc.)
1360.

To wham god hade geuen alle þat gayn were,
Alle þe blysse *boute* blame þat bode myȝt haue.
Allit. Poems, b. 259.

About 1816.

He said, "Yore o'erpaid last toime ot yo coom."
Aw said, "If aw wur, 'twur wi wayving *beawt* loom.   *Ballads and Songs of Lanc.,* p. 171.

WAUGH.
1857.

Mary. Well let's ha't; an' mind to tell no lies abeawt th' lad i' thy talk.
Jone. Bith mon, Mary, aw connut do, *beawt* aw say at he's oather a pretty un or a good un.
Lanc. Sketches, p. 28.

BEAWLT'NT, *p. p.* bowled.

COLLIER.
1750.

They order't wheel-barrow with spon-new trindle t' be fotcht 'Twur dun, an' they *beawlt'nt* him away to th' urchon in a crack.
Works: Introduction, p xxxviii.

BECK (North Lanc.), *sb.* a small stream. Icel. *bekkr;* Swed. *bäck,* a stream. Cf. Ger. *bach,* a brook.

> 1440.   *Bek,* watyr, rendylle. Rivulus, torrens.
> > *Prompt. Parv.*

> ——   When moor or moss do saffron yield,
> And *beck* and sike run down with honey.
> > *Ballads and Songs of Lanc.,* p. 31.

>   (I have) watched
> SOUTHEY.   The *beck* roll glittering to the noon-tide sun,
> 1795.   And listened to its ceaseless murmuring.
> > *Joan of Arc,* i. 235.

BECK-BIBBY (Furness), *sb.* the water-ousel. See BECK. For *bibby* cf. Lat. *bibo,* to drink, and Mid. E. *bibble,* to sip, to tipple.

BEEANY-PRICK (Furness), *sb.* a stickleback ; so called from its prickly spines. *Beeany* = bony.

BEEAS, *sb.* beasts, cattle. The plural of *beast,* formed by dropping the *t,* the plural *s* not having been suffixed.

> A. C. GIBSON.   Dunnot ye knā 'at t' farmers mā's t' brackens i' t'
> 1868.   back-end, ut bed thér *beeas's* wi' ?
> > *Folk-Speech of Cumberland:* Example of Dialect
> > of High Furness, Lancashire, p. 69.

BEE-BO, *sb.* sleep ; used only to a child.

> COLL. USE.   1. Hush-a *be-bo,* mi little darlin'.
> 1875.   2. Come, thae mun goo to *be-bo* neaw ; it's lung
> past thi toime.

BEEN, *adj.* nimble, active, lithe. Icel. *beinn,* direct ; Sc. *bain.* Prompt. Parv. "*Beyn,* or plyaunte, *flexibilis.*" Comp. Mid. E. *bayn,* ready. " So *bayn* wer thay bothe two his bone for to wyrk," (E. E. Allit. Poems, C, l. 136).

BEEST,   }   *sb.* the first milk after calving. A.S.
BEESTINS,   }   *bysting,* the same ; from A.S. *beost,* the
BEEAS-MILK (N. Lanc.) }   same. Cf. Ger. *biest-milch.*

> 1440.   *Beestnynge* mylke.   *Prompt. Parv.*

> BEN JONSON.   So may the first of all our fells be thine
> 1625.   And both the *beestning* of our goats and kine.
> > *To Pan,* Hymn 4.

> PHILEMON HOLLAND.   A cow hath no milke ordinarily, before that shee
> 1601.   hath calved. The first milke that shee giveth downe,
> is called *beestins,* which, unless it be delaied with
> some water, will soone turne to be as hard as pumish
> stone.   *Plinie,* b. ii., c. 12.

> ————

> GASKELL.   *Beeost* and *beestins* are yet, as among our Anglo-
> 1854.   Saxon forefathers, used to denote the first milk which
> is given by a cow after calving.
> > *Lect. Lanc. Dialect,* p. 17.

> COLL. USE.   It's as thick as *beestins.*
> 1875.

BEET, *v.* to kindle or amend the fire. A.S. *bétan*, to amend, to better ; also. to kindle a fire. Comp. Sc. *beet*, to kindle. From the root of *better*.

KING ALFRED. 880.	Þa het he *bétan* þær-inne mycel fýr, forþon hit wæs ceald weder. [= Then commanded he to kindle therein a great fire, because it was cold weather.] *Tr. of Orosius*, bk. vi. cap. 32 ; ed. Bosworth.
WEST-MID. DIAL. (Lanc.) 1320.	Wyth blys and bryȝt fyr *bette*. *Sir Gawayne & G. K.*, l. 1368.
About 1350.	The fourth statute, To purchase ever to here, And stiren folke to love, and *beten* fire On Venus awter. *Court of Love*, l. 323.
WEST-MID. DIAL. (Lanc.) 1360.	Quyl I fete sum quat fat þon þe fyr *bete*. [While I fetch some vessel do thou the fire kindle, or mend] *Allit. Poems*, B, l. 627.
CHAUCER. 1380.	And on their auter, wher I ryde or go, I wol do sacrifice, and fyres *beete*. *Knightes Tale*, l. 1394.
TUSSER. 1580.	Yokes, forks, and such other let bailiff spy out, And gather the same as he walketh about ; And after, at leisure, let this be his hire, To *beath* them and trim them at home by the fire. *December Husbandrie*.
BURNS. 1786.	Or noble Elgin *beets* the heav'nward flame. *Cotter's Sat. N.* l. 113.
IBID.	It heets me, it *beets* me, And sets me a' in flame. *Ep. to Davie, a Brother Poet*, l. 111.
JOHN SCHOLES. 1857.	Then aw *beetud* fire, un rattl't fire-potter ogen't back o'th grate. *Jaunt to See th' Queen*, p. 14
COLL. USE. 1875.	1 (To kindle). Tha mun get up an' *beet* t' fire to-morn. 2 (To trim or amend). Come, stir about—*beet* up th' fire, and make things tidy.

BEETINS, *sb. pl.* short lengths of yarn, used by weavers to piece up broken ends in a warp. Possibly for *beetings*, i.e. mendings; from Mid. E. *bete*, to mend.

BEETLE, *sb.* a large wooden hammer, with more handles than one. The phrase " *beetle*-finish" is applied to cloth in the bleaching of which a large hammer is used. A.S. *betel, bytl*, a mallet ; from *bat*. Properly a diminutive, but generally used when the instrument is of large size.

995.	In the A.S. translation of Judges iv. 21, it is said that Jael smote Sisera by driving the tent-peg "mid anum *bytle*," with a mallet.
SHAKESPERE. 1600.	*Chief Justice:* Fare you well. Commend mee to my cosin Westmerland. [*Exit*. *Falstaff:* If I do, fillop me with a three-man-*beetle*. *Second Part K. Henrv IV.*, i. 2, 253.

[Nares (1822) says a three-man-beetle was one so heavy that it required three men to manage it.]

BEAUMONT & F.
1610.

Have I lived thus long to be knock'd o' th' head
With half a washing-*beetle ?—Tamer Tamed*, ii. 5.

BEE'TLIN'-STEÄN (Furness), *sb.* Pron. of *beetling*-stone ; a stone upon which clothes are *beetled* or beaten.

BEET-NEED,) *sb.* a help that may be had at will.
BOOT-NEED (Mid. Lanc.) | A.S. *bot,* a remedy, *boot ;* from A.S. *bet,* better ; *bétan,* to make better, to amend. See BEET.

BEGGAR-BERM, *sb.* barm of the poorest kind, given away to those who beg barm, because it is hardly good enough to sell. The word is commonly applied to anything worthless, especially to worthless talk.

WAUGH.
1874.

"I don't believe i' none sich like things." said the landlord. "It's o' *beggar-berm* an' bull-scutter."
Chimney Corner : Manch. Critic, May 31, 1873.

BEGGAR-INKLE, *sb.* a coarse narrow tape, hawked by beggars. Of *inkle,* Wedgwood says : Fr. *ligneul, lignol,* strong thread ; O.E. *liniolf. Lvnyolf* or *inniolf,* threde to sow with schone or botys; indula, licinium (Prompt. Parv.). The loss of the initial *l,* of which we have here an example, would convert *lingle* into *ingle* or *inkle.*

SHAKESPERE.
1611.

Hee [Autolycus] hath ribbons of all the colours i'th rainebow ; . . . *inckles,* caddysses, cambrickes, lawnes. *Winter's Tale,* iv. 4, 205.

[Also : "What's the price of this' *yncle ?*" *L. L. Lost,* iii. 1, 139. "Her *inkle,* silk, twin with the rubied cherry." *Pericles,* v., Chorus.]

BELEAKINS, *intj.* for "By our ladykin," a diminutive of "By our Lady."

SHAKSPERE.
1600.

By'r lakin, a parlous fear.
Mids. N. Dream, iii. 1, 14.

LANCASHIRE AUTHOR.
1548.

"Thou udgit," quo hoo, "but where dus he dwel ?"
"*Belakin,*" quo hee, "but I connau tel."
"*Warrikin Fair :*" *Gentleman's Mag.,* Sept., 1740.
See also, *Ballads and Songs of Lanc.,* p. 52.

BELDER, *v.* to make a noisy cry, to roar; lit. to bellow. From A.S. *bellan,* Icel. *belja,* to roar.

COLL. USE.
1875.

Make less noise, mon ; it'll do thi no good to *belder* loike that.

BELIKE, *adv.* surely, certainly, probably.

CHAUCER.
1370.

For sche was wilde and yong, and he was old,
And demed himself *belik* a cokewold [*i.e.,* a cuckold.]
Milleres Tale, l. 40.

ARCHB. WHITGIFT. 1570.	I have spoken before, and declared why I do vse it rather than any other ; I have laboured it, noted it, I am acquainted with it, and *belike*, I red it, before you knew whether there was any such booke or no. *Defence*, p. 508.
SIR THOMAS NORTH. 1579.	Moreover he received fourscore milch kine to the pail, and neatherds to keep them, having need of cowes milke *belike*, to heal a disease that fell upon him. *Plutarch*, p. 252.
SHAKSPERE. 1603.	*Ophelia.* What meanes this, my lord ? *Hamlet.* Marry this is Miching Malicho, that meanes mischeefe. *Ophelia.* *Belike* this shew imports the argument of the play. *Hamlet.* We shall know by these fellowes: the players cannot keep counsell, they'l tell all. *Hamlet*, iii. 2. 146. [The word *belike* occurs forty-two times in Shakspere.]
WORDSWORTH. 1805.	Some female vendor's scream, *belike* The very shrillest of all London cries. *Prelude*, p. 146.
IBID.	Things that I know not of *belike* to thee are dear. *Pet Lamb.*
COLL. USE. 1875.	Thae'rt not gooin' yet *belike!*

BELIVE, *adv.* bye-and-bye, quickly. A.S. *be*, by, and *life*, dat. of *lif*, life ; lit. with life.

ROBERT OF GLOUCESTER. 1298.	This noble erl with the Britones ageyn ys fou wente *biliue*, And fagt, and slow faste. P. 162.
ROBERT MANNYNG. 1303.	Þe pore man hente hyt vp *belyue*, And was þerof ful ferly blyþe. *Handlyng Synne*, l. 5619.
CHAUCER. 1380.	He sent hem word by lettres they schulden hye *blyve*, Yf they wolde speke with him whil he was on lyve. *Cokes Tale of Gamelyn*, l. 19. [See also "ride *blyve*," Freres Tale, l. 222]
WYCLIF. 1380.	And so *bliue* doynge down into the erthe the sackis, eche opnyde. *Genesis* xliv. 11. [Authorised Version : Then they *speedily* took down every man his sack to the ground, and opened every man his sack.]
SPENSER. 1579.	*Hobbinol.* God shield, man, hee should so ill have thrive, All for he did his devoyre *belive*. *Sheapherds Calendar*, September, 227.

LANCASHIRE AUTHOR. 1515.	To Skipton in Craven then he come *belive*. *Ballads and Songs of Lanc.*, p. 21. (Flodden Field.)

BELL, *v* to roar, to cry loudly. A.S. *bellan*, to roar.

JOHN COLLIER. 1750.	Then th' battril coom, on whether it lawmt [lamed] th' barn ot wur ith' keather [cradle] I know naw, for I laft it rooaring an *belling*. *Works*, p. 66.

BER, *sb.* force.   Icel. *byrr,* a fair wind.   The peculiar sense of the
Mid. E. *bur,* impetus, force, is not found in Icelandic.

West.Mid. Dial. (Lanc.). 1377.	Such a *burre* myȝt make myn herte blunt. *Allit. Poems,* A. l. 176.
Ibid.	Þen is better to abyde þe *bur* vmbe-stoundes. *Allit. Poems,* C, l. 7.
1440.	Brethly bessomes with *byrre* in berynes sailles. *Morte Arthure,* l. 3662.
Waugh. 1867.	A dog sprang from the kennel. Ben sprang for- ward, right into the fat cook's arms. . . . " Thae's knockt th' breath eawt o' me, welly !" said the cook. " Thae'd no need to come i' sich a *ber !* Th' dog would ha' bitten noan on tho." *Owd Blanket,* c. ii. p. 37.

BERM-BO, *sb.* Pron. of *barm ball.* A light pudding, made of
flour, yeast, and suet.

Waugh. 1867.	The children were all eating a kind of light pud- ding, known in Lancashire by the name of *berm-bo,* or *berm*-dumpling, made of flour, and yeast, mixed with a little suet. *Home Life Lanc. Factory Folk,* c. xix. p. 166.

BERM-YED, *sb.* Pron. of *barm-head.* App. to a man of confused
thought, and also to one of flighty and excitable mind—frothy,
fitful, and wild.   Burns uses it in something of this sense when
he says ·   My *barmy* noddle's working prime.

Waugh. 1865.	Aw'll be bund 'at Enoch's hooked it on in a mis- take. Th' *berm-yed* doesn't know what he's doing th' tone hauve of his time.—*Besom Ben,* c. ii., p. 25.

BERRIN', *sb.* Pron. of *burying,* a funeral.

Waugh. 1855.	I' tho dees through it, aw'll bi' fourpence or fippence toawrd thi' *berrin'.* *Lanc. Sketches* (Bury to Rochdale), p. 29.

BESSY (Furness), *sb.* the yellow-hammer, or yellow bunting.
Emberiza citrinella.

BETHINK, *v.* to call to mind.

Robert of Gloucester. 1298.	Tho the emperour herde this, he by gan hym *by-* *thenche,* And hys wraththe toward the kyng, for drede of the erl quenche. P. 58.
Dan Michel. 1340.	Riȝuolnesse zayþ. " Yef we longe godes drede and be-þenchinge of dyaþe were stille : riȝt hit is þet þe spekinde wel more we by stille." *Sermon on Matthew* xxiv. 43, l 100.
Shakspere. 1602.	*Othello.* If you *bethinke* your selfe of any crime Vnreconcil'd as yet to Heauen, and grace, Solicite for it straight. *Othello,* v. 2, 26.

| Bishop Beveridge. 1700. | *Bethink* yourselves beforehand what mercies you want, for which you should pray unto him. |
| | *Works,* vol. ii. Ser. 145. |

| Coll. Use. 1875. | Aw've seen him afore, that's sartin ; but, for mi loife, aw conno *bethink* me wheer. |

BETHOUGHT, *pt. t.* called to recollection. *Pl.* BETHOUGHTEN.

| Robert of Gloucester. 1298. | And some *bythogte,* and told wat the bytokne was, That the dragon of by Weste bytokned the king Arture. P. 203. |

| Chaucer. 1370. | But atte laste his mayster him *bythoughte* Upon a day, when he his papyr soughte Of a proverbe, that saith this same word, Wel bette is roten appul out of hord Than that it rote al the remenaunt. *Cokes T.* l. 39. |

| Shaksperz. 1603. | *Polonius.* What ist, Ophelia, he hath said to you ? *Ophelia.* So please you, something touching the lord Hamlet. *Pol.* Marry, well *bethought :* Tis told me he hath very oft of late Giuen priuate time to you. *Hamlet,* i. 3, 88. |

| Coll. Use. 1875. | 1. Hast *bethowt* thi yet ? 2. Han yo *bethowten* yoursells ? |

BEZZLE, *v.* to waste, to squander ; generally applied to drinking. Prob. a dimin. of E. *booze,* to drink freely. Cf. our present word *embezzle,* to make away with wrongfully.

| Bishop Hall. 1597. | O mee ! what odds there seemeth 'twixt their chere And the swolne *bezell* at an alehouse fyre, That tonnes in gallons to his bursten paunch Whose shiny droughts his draught can never staunch. *Satires,* Bk. V. Sat. 2. |

| Milton. 1641. | They that spend their youth in loitering, *bezzling,* and harlotting.—*Animad. upon Remons. Def.* |

| John Collier. 1750. | So I seete on restut meh, on drank meh pint o ele ; boh as I'r naw greadly sleckt, I cawd for another, on *bezzilt* tut, too ; for I'r as droy as soot.—*Works,* p. 54. |

| Ibid. | In idd'n made strushion, on *bezzilt* awey moor brass inney hadd'n, yo met'n ha tawkt. [= If you had made destruction and squandered away more money than you had, you might have talked.]—*Works,* p. 55. |

BEZZLER (Furness), *sb.* anything very great.

BIB-AN-TUCKER, *sb.* Primarily, certain parts of dress, but used figuratively to express the whole costume.

| Coll. Use. 1875. | 1. Wheer's he for ? He's getten his best *bib-an-tucker* on. 2. Aw put him his best *bib-an-tucker* on an' went to look for a place for him. |

BIDDEN-WEDDING (N. Lanc.), *sb.* a wedding to which it was formerly the custom in North Lanc. to invite the whole country-side. From Mid. E. *bidde*, to invite. The custom seems to be alluded to in Piers the Plowman, b. ii. 54, where it says that a large number of retainers

> Were *boden* to þe *brydale* on bothe two sydes,
> Of alle maner of men, þe mene and þe riche.

BIDDY, *sb.* a louse.

BIDE, *v.* to dwell, to live with ; to endure.   Pt. t. *bode.*

T. HARDY. 1874.	I've been with her all through her troubles, and was with her at the time of Mr. Troy's death and all. And if she were to marry again I expect I should *bide* with her.—*Far from the Madding Crowd*, c. 49.
WAUGH. 1859.	"Forgi' mo, lad, do : For aw'm nobbut a foo,— An *bide* wi' mo, neaw, till aw dee ! " So we'n *bide* one another, whatever may come. *Lanc. Songs* (Jamie's Frolic).
IBID. 1875.	So he gran' an *bode*, fro day to day ; an' he'd a deeol to *bide*, for Nan went wur an' wur. *Old Cronies*, v. 52.

BIG, *sb.* a teat, where the "familiar" was said to draw blood from the body of a witch. From the same root as *big* and *bulge ;* applied to the breast, it means that which *bulges*. Ray has, "*bigge*, a pappe or teat. *Essex*."

BIGG, *v.* to build. A.S. *byggan*, to build, inhabit ; perhaps not a native word, but taken from Icel. *byggja*, to build ; from the root of *bua*, to prepare.   Cf. A.S. *búan*, to inhabit.

1272.	Of box and of barberè, *byggyt* ful bene. *E. Eng. Met. Rom.* A. st. vi.
IBID.	That is batelt aboute, and *biggutte* fulle bene. *Ibid.* st. lii.
ROBERT MANNYNG. 1303.	And of Gryme, a fisshere, men redes git in ryme, That he *bigged* Grimesby, Grime that ilk tyme.
IBID.	Kirkes and houses brent, nouht than wild he spare. Ther the Inglis had *bigged*, he mad it wast and bare.
HAMPOLE. 1340.	Men ete and drank, shortly to telle, Ilkan with other, and salde and bought, And planted, and *bygged*, and houses wroght. *Pr. of C.* l. 4848.
WEST MID. DIAL. (Lanc.) 1360.	I haf *bigged* Babiloyne, burʒ alþer-rychest, Stabled þer-inne vche a ston in strenkþe of myn armes. *Allit. Poems*, B, l. 1666.
1440.	When erthe appone erthe hase *bigged* vp his bourris. *Religious Pieces*, p. 95, l. 11.
WAUGH. 1869.	Then they *bigged* yon new barn upo' th' knowe. *Lanc. Sketches*, p. 205.

BIGG (Furness), barley. Icel. *bygg*, barley.

J. STAGG.   An' southy crops o' beans an' *bigg*.
About 1804.   *Cumb. Ball.* p. 221.

BIGGIN, *sb.* a building. See **BIGG**. Icel. *bygging*, a habitation ; from *byggja*, to build.

HAMPOLE.   Þe sevend day *byggyns* doun sal falle,
1340.   And grete castels, and tours with-alle.
                                Pr. of C. l. 4782.

WEST MID. DIAL. (LANC.)   I se no *by-gyng* nawhere aboute.
1360.   *Allit. Poems*, A, l. 931.

WAUGH.   Th' orchart's gwon ; an th' gardens an o' are gwon ;
1859.   nobbut a twothre at's laft o'eranent this *biggin*.
                  Waugh : Lanc. Sk. (Grave of Griselhurst
                  Boggart), p. 205.

BILLET, *sb.* a piece of wood pointed at each end, used in farming. Fr. *billot*, a block ; dim. of *bille*, a log , of Celtic origin. Cf. Irish *bille*, a tree-trunk (Brachet).

BIN, pl. of **BE**.

SHAKSPERE.   *Gower.* He, doing so, put forth to seas,
1608.   Where when men *been*, there's seldom ease.
                      Pericles ii. 1. l. 27.

DR. JOHN BYROM.   Folk cry out. " Hard times," but I never regard
1804.   For I ne'er did, nor will, set my heart upo' th' word ;
         So 'tis all one to me, *bin* they easy or hard.
                  Misc. Poems, vol. i. p. 22.

BIRK (N. Lanc.), *sb.* a birch tree. A.S. *birce;* Icel. *björk*.

JOHN BARBOUR.   Than *byrkis* on athyr sid the way,
1375.   That young and thik war growand ner,
         He knyt to-gidder, on sic maner,
         Tha' men moucht nocht weill throu thaim rid [ride].
                 The Bruce, ed. Jamieson, xi. 394 ;
                 Edinb. MS. fol. 54.

1440.   He fande the rede knyght lyggand,
         Slayne of Percyvelle hande,
         Besyde a fyre brynnande
            Off *byrke* and of akke.
        Ther brent of *birke* and of ake
         Gret brandes and blake.
                 Thornton Romances, p. 30.

BIRL (N. Lanc.), *v.* to pour out. Icel. *byrla*, to pour out ; borrowed from A.S. *byrelian*, to give to drink, which from *byrel*, a cupbearer.

1272.   In bolles *birlutte* thay the wyne.
                  Met. Rom. C, st. xlvi. l. 14.

1330.   And seruanz wur at this bridale
         That *birled* win in cupp and schal.
                  Met. Homilies, l. 120.

WEST-MID. DIALECT (Lanc.)
1360.

Weȝe wyn in þis won, wassayl!" he cryes.
Swyfte swaynes ful swyþe swepen þer-tylle,
Kyppe kowpes in honde kingeȝ to serue,
In bryȝt bolleȝ, ful bayn *birlen* þise oþer,
And vche mon for his mayster maehches alone.
Allit. Poems B, 1508.

WYCLIF.
1380.

Take thou the cuppe of wyn of this woodnesse fro
myn hond, and thou schal *birle* thereof to al hethene
men to whom Y schal sende thee.—*Jer.* xxv. 15.

HALL.
1550.

The olde god of wyne called Baccus *birlyng* the wyne
Henry VIII., fo. lxxiii.

SKELTON.
1508.

(They) Dame Elynour entrete
To *byrle* them of the best.　　　*El. R.*, v. 269.

COLL. USE.
1875.

Birl out th' beer.

BISHOP, *sb.* a pinafore ; a kind of smock or overall, worn by
children.

WAUGH.
1874.

Here ; tak him, an' wesh him ; an' put him a clen
bishop on.—*Chimney Corner Manch. Critic,* March
7, 1874.

BISHOPPED, *adj.* Said of milk, which whilst on the fire, has been
burnt against the sides of the pan, and received a peculiar and
not altogether pleasant flavour. Grose, in his *Provincial Glossary,* says : "Formerly, in days of superstition, whenever a
bishop passed through a town or village, all the inhabitants ran
out to receive his blessing. This frequently caused the milk on
the fire to be left till burnt to the vessel, and gave origin to the
above allusion." Tyndale (see below) seems to point to a more
specious origin of the word, in the rancour of the reformers,
which ascribed every ill that might betide them to the Popish
bishops. Grose's story is obviously an invention.

TYNDALE.
1530.

When a thing spedeth not well, we borow speach
and say, the *bishop* hath blessed it, because that
nothing spedeth well that they medle with all. If
the porage be burned to, or the meate ouer rosted,
we say, the *bishop* hath put his foote in the potte, or
the *bishop* hath played the cooke, because the *bishops*
burn who they lust, and whosoever displeaseth them.
Workes, p. 166.

COLL. USE.
1875.

Neaw, Mally, this is too bad ! Th' milk's *bishopped*
again.

BIT, *sb.* a short time ; as, " I'm coming in a bit." A.S. *bitt,* a bit
or bite ; from *bitan,* to bite.

WAUGH.
1867.

" Wheer are yo beawn to tay mo too ?" " Thae'll
see in a *bit,*" replied Roddle.
Besom Ben, c. vii. p. 89.

DR. BARBER.
1870.

Efter a *bit* I landt at top o' Hasty Gill Brow. I
rested a *bit,* for I's gittin rayder puffy ye knā.
Furness Folk, p. 3.

BI'TH, by the.

WAUGH.
1868.

They very near poo'd me *bith* scuft o' th' neck
Sneck-Bant, c. i., p. 8.

BITH-MASS,
BITH-MASKINS, } a form of oath = by the mass.

COLLIER.
1750.

Neaw, *byth maskins* if I be naw fast.
Works, Intro. xxxv.

WAUGH.
1859.

He begged that aw'd wed him i' May ;—
Bith mass, iv he'll let me, aw will.
Lanc. Songs: Th' Dule's i' this Bonnet.

MISS LAHEE.
1865.

Humph, *beth' mass*, there's olez somebody after thee
for brass.—*The Carter's Struggles*, p. 25.

BITH-MON, an oath, frequently used in the form of By-gum ;
which latter, if not a corruption of the word "God," may be connected with Mid. E. *gome*, A.S. *guma*, a man.

WAUGH.
1855.

Thir't a reet un ; *bith' mon*, arto !
Lanc. Sketches (Bury to Rochdale), p. 30.

MISS LAHEE.
1865.

Beth' mons, aw'll tell thi what, Ned, aw dunnot
care heaw soon tha gets a woife.
The Carter's Struggles, p. 25.

COLL. USE.
1875.

"Am aw to goo at this time o' neet ?"   "Ay,
bith mon, mun tha'."

BITIN'-ON, *sb.* a snack or lunch.

JOHN SCHOLES.
1857.

"Are yo beawn to Australia, Betty ?" said aw,
when aw see'd th' basket. "Bless yo, felli," hoo
said ' it's just o *boitin'-on* fur Throddy an' me an'
Nance."   *Jaunt to see th' Queen*, p. 19.

MISS LAHEE.
1865.

Iv tha taks after thi fayther, tha con do wi a *boitin'-
on*.   *Betty o' Yeps*, p. 19.

WAUGH.
1875.

"Please, sir," she said "I was to ask if ye would
have some bread an' cheese for a *bitin'-on* ?"   "For
a what ?"   "For a *bitin'-on* till t' goose is ready."
Jannock, c. ii. p 14.

BITTER-BUMP, *sb.* the bittern, *Botaurus stellaris*. The syllable
bump refers to the *booming* sound made by it.   The Welsh name
is *aderyn y bwmp*, the booming bird.   "The bittern is now rare
in Britain, owing to drainage.   It has a peculiar bellowing cry,
which has obtained for it such English provincial names as
Mire-drum, Bull-of-the-Bog, etc., and many of its appellations
in other languages, as *Bitour, Botur, Botaurus*."   (Chambers's
Encyclopædia, vol. ii.)

CHAUCER.
1386.

And as a *bytoure bumbleth* in the myre
Sche laid hir mouth unto the water doun.
"Bewrey me not, thou water, with thi soun."
Quod sche.   *Wyf of Bathes Tale*, 1 116.

Sir THOMAS BROWNE.
1646.

That a *bittor* maketh that mugient noyse, or as we term it *bumping*, by putting its bill into a reed as most believe, or as Belionius and Aldrovandus conceive, by putting the same in water or mud, and after a while retaining the ayr by suddenly excluding it again, is not so easily made out.
Vulgar Errors. bk. iii. c. 27.

DRYDEN.
1700.

Then to the water's brink she laid her head,
And as a *bittour bumps* within a reed,
"To thee alone, O Lake," she said, "I tell.
(And as thy queen command thee to conceal.)"
Fables: Chaucer's Wife of Bath's T. (See above.)

TENNYSON.
1864.

Moäst loike a *butter bump*, fur I 'eerd um aboot an' aboot. *Northern Farmer : Old Style*, st. 8.

COLLIER.
1750.

Thoose ot connot tell a *bitter bump* fro a gill-hooter.
Works : Intro. xxxiv.

BLACKBERN, *sb*. the blackberry.

BLACK-CLOCK, *sb*. the cockroach or black-beetle; more commonly called *twitch-clock*. See CLOCK.

BLACK-LAD MONDAY, *sb*. The term in Lancashire originated in the custom at Ashton-under-Lyne of carrying through the town on Easter Monday the effigy of "the Black Lad," said to represent a former lord of the manor, who, through a course of cruelty and oppression, had become obnoxious to his tenants and dependants. It seems probable that the real origin was simply the perambulation of the boundaries. See *The Black Knight of Ashton*, by W. E. A. Axon. 1871.

BLACK-OUSEL, *sb*. the blackbird, *Turdus merula*.

BLAIN, *sb*. a little boil. A.S. *blegen;* Mid. E. *bleine*.

BLASH, *sb*. a sudden flame. A variation of *blaze;* A.S. *blo'ese*.

BLASH-BOGGART, *sb*. a fire-goblin, or flash-goblin; that is, a goblin that flashes and diappears. It is more commonly used figuratively, and is applied to persons who are fiery, wild, or strange in appearance, either in dress or person.

WAUGH.
1868.

When it geet toaurd Setturday, he wur some dirty an' tatter't—a gradely *blash-boggart!* Aw use't to think he slept among th' coals or else on a shelf somewheer. *Sneck-Bant*, c. ii. p. 31.

BLEĀ (N. Lanc.), ⎫ *adj.* livid from cold. The old sense "livid"
BLUĀ (E. Lanc.), ⎭ is retained in the phrase to "beat black and blue." Icel. *blár*, blue; Mid. E. *bla, blaa, blo*. The word is found in *Bleā* Tarn (there are three small lakes so called; one

in Langdale, another in Eskdale, and a third near Watendlath),
and *Bleā* Water, near the south end of Hawes Water. There is
also *Bleās*, or Blue Things, the lower part of one of the Ulls-
water mountains.

HAMPOLE, 1340.	He henged on þe rode tre Alle *bla* and blody.—*Pricke of Conscience*, l. 5260
WEST-MID. DIAL. (Lanc.) 1360.	(The Dead Sea is described as)— *Blo*, blubrande, and blak.—*Allit. Poems*, B., l. 1017.
LANGLAND. 1377.	Fyre shal falle, and brenne al to *blo* askes The houses and the homes of hem that desireth Yiftes or yeres yives bicause of here offices *Piers Plowm.*, B. 3, 97.
COLL. USE. (E. Lanc.) 1874.	Thy skin's turned *blua*.

BLEB, or ⎫ *sb.* a bubble; a raised spot or blister on the skin. *Blob*
BLOB, ⎭ is the usage in South Lancashire; *bleb* in North Lancashire. Cf. Mid. E. *blubber*, a bubble ; and as a verb, to bubble.

WEST MID. DIAL. (Lanc.) 1360.	(The Dead Sea is described as)— Blo, *blubrande*, and blak, unblythe to neghe *Allit. Poems*, B., l. 1017
WEST MID. DIAL. (? North). About 1360.	Till the *bloberond* blode blend with the rayn. [= Till the bubbling blood blent with the rain.] *Gest Hystoriale of Troy*, l. 7642.
COLL. USE (E. Lanc.) 1875.	He scalded hissel, an' his skin wur a' i' *blebs*.

BLEFFIN, a block or wedge.

BLEFFIN-YED (i.e. Bleffin-head), *sb.* a blockhead.

BLETHER, *sb.* nonsense, emptiness of meaning ; that which is
noisy and senseless. Also, *v.* to talk nonsense, to chatter.
Icel. *blaðr*, nonsense ; *blaðra*, to talk indistinctly.

BURNS. 1785.	But I shall scribble down some *blether* Just clean aff-loof. *Ep. to J. Lapraik.*
WAUGH. 1867.	He *blether't* abeawt religion as iv he'd bin i' full trainin for heaven o' his days.—*Owd Bl.*, c. iv., p. 89.
B. BRIERLEY. 1867.	Aw wouldno' care if Jammie o' Tum's didno know on't ; but he'll *blethur* an' talk abeawt it o' winter. *Marlocks of Merriton*, p. 26.

BLETHER-YED *sb.* (pron. of Blether-head), a noisy babbler.

COLL. USE. 1875.	Eh ! what a *blether-yed* thae art : when wilto give o'er talkin'.

BLINKERT, *sb.* a person who is blind of one eye ; or that winks
much with his eyes. Cf. Mid. E. *blinken*, to blink. Archdeacon
Nares has " *Blinkard*, one who blinks."

WITHAL. 1608.	A *blinkard* alwayes good doth mis. *Dictionarie*, p. 288.

COLLIER.
1750.

"Humph," said I, "you understand astrology. I perceive." "Eigh," replied *blinkard*, "I've studit it e'er sin I'r fifteen yer owd." *Works*, p. 293.

BLOWPOKE, *sb.*, a fat pursy fellow; generally one who assumes an air of great importance.

BLUFFIN-YED, *sb.* (i.e. Bluffin-head). Mr. Waugh thinks this is a corruption of "muffin-yed," which is more common, and has some affinity in meaning with bowster-yed (*q.v.*), as representing a person of soft and spongy brains—yielding, strengthless, and flabby. See BLEFFIN-YED.

BLUN, *adj.* blind.

BLUND, *p. part.* blinded.

BLUZZ-BOGGART, *sb.* (Darwen), blindman's-buff.

BO, *sb.* Pron. of Ball, as *beef-bo*, a beef pudding; *Ayster-bo*, a pudding made for Easter Sunday; *berm-bo*, a light pudding.

BOBBERSOME, *adj.* impatient, obtrusive; also, frisky, gay, lively.

COLLIER.
1750.

To comparen me to an urchon [hedgehog], ot has noather heead nor tele. Is not it like running me deawn, an a bit too *bobbersome*?
Works : Intro. xxxviii.

BOBBIN', *part.* fishing for eels with a number of worms strung upon a piece of worsted and tied in a bundle.

BODE, *p. part.* remained, stayed, did abide. A.S. *bád*, from *bidan*.

WEST MID. DIAL. (? North),
About 1360.

He bounet to his batell, *bode* he no lengur.
Gest Hystoriale of Troy, l. 6939.

CHAUCER.
1380.

This joly prentys with his mayster *bood*.
Cokes Tale, l. 35.

SPENSER.
1589.

So there all day they *bode*, till light the sky forsooke.
F. Q. bk. vi c. xi., st. 40.

WAUGH.
1875.

He determin't to make th' best on't. so he gran an' *bode* fro' day to day; an' he'd a deeol to bide, for Nan went wur an' wur.—*Old Cronies*, p. 52.

BODLE, *sb.* half a farthing.

BURNS.
1785.

I'll wad a *boddle*.
The Brigs of Ayr ; Auld Frig, l. 5.

COLLIER.
1750.

Ist naw hav one *boadle* t' spere o meh hoyde silver.
Works, p. 55.

WAUGH.
1868.

"God bless this little lad o' mine !" cried Betty. "He's worth five hundred theawsan million peawnd— i' guinea-gowd—every yure ov his yed ! An aw'll not bate a *bodle* noather !"—*Sneck-Bant*, c. iii. p. 58.

BOGGART, } *sb.* a spirit, a ghost. Welsh *bwg, bwgan, bygel,* a
BUGGART, } hobgoblin ; Gaelic *bocan.* Spenser and Shakspere
use the word in its shorter form *bug* or *bugge.*

SPENSER.
1589.

Each trembling leafe and whistling wind they heare,
As ghastly *bug,* does greatly them affeare.
F. Q., bk. ii., c. iii , s. xx.

SHAKSPERE.
1611.

Hermione.   Sir, spare your threats.
The *bugge* which you would fright me with I seeke.
Winter's Tale, act iii , sc. 2, l. 93.

[See also *Hamlet,* v. 2, 22, "With ho, such *bugges*
and goblins ;" *T. of S.,* i. 2, 211, "Tush, tush, feare
boys with bugs ;" and *Cymbeline,* v. 3, 51, "The
mortal *bugs* o' th' field."]

COLLIER.
1750.

On then I'r ill breed [frightened] ogen, for I thowt
I'd seen a *boggart.*   *Works,* p. 52.

WAUGH.
1855.

When one gets a few miles off any of the populous
towns in Lancashire, many an old wood, many a
lonesome clough, many a quiet stream and ancient
building, is the reputed haunt of some local sprite or
boggart. . . In such places the legends and superstitions of the forefathers of Lancashire are cherished
with a tenacity which would hardly be credible to
the inhabitants of great cities in these days.—*Lanc.
Sketches : " Grave of Grislehurst Boggart,"* p. 198.

JOHN SCHOLES.
1857.

When we wur gooin' by *Boggart-*hole Cloof,
Throddy towd us o tale ov o *boggart* ot us't to haunt
theerabeawts. Ghosts un *boggarts* ar not hauve us
mich tawkt abeawt neaw us thae us't to be.
Jaunt to see th' Queen, p. 60.

WAUGH.
1859.

Then he look'd i' my face, an he said,
" Has th' *boggarts* taen houd o' my dad ?"
Poems and Lanc. Songs, p 54.

MISS LAHEE.
1865.

At that toime ther'n no new-fangled things code
foire engins, an'railway styemers skrikin'away through
th' country, enoo to flay a *buggart* eawt o' th'greaund.
Betty o' Yeps, p. 6.

BOGGLE, *v.* to blunder, to hesitate. See BOGGART. Cf. Welsh
bygwl, to threaten ; *bygel,* a scarecrow, from *bwg,* a spectre.

SHAKSPERE.
1598.

Bertram —My lord, I do confesse the ring was hers.
King.—You *boggle* shrewdly, every feather starts you.
Love's Labour Lost, v. 3, l. 231.

ARCHBP. TILLOTSON.
1664.

When a sinner is first tempted to the commission
of a more gross and notorious sin, his conscience is apt
to *boggle* and start at it.   *Sermons,* vol. i., ser. 10.

REV. W. GASKELL.
1854.

We sometimes hear Lancashire people say, he
" *boggled* " at a thing, when they mean that the person of whom they are speaking, started from. or took
fright at it. I might very well have said that I *boggled*
at my lecture to-night.—*Lectures Lanc. Dial,* p. 10.

COLL. USE.
1875.

What dost *boggle* at it so lung for ! Get done, mon,
or gie it up !

BOGIE, *sb.* a small hand-cart, a rude contrivance for moving heavy articles, consisting of a simple plank on low wheels.

BOH (S. E. Lanc.), } *prep.* (var. pron.) But.   Robert of Gloucester,
BUD (E. Lanc.), } Robert Mannyng, and Gawin Douglas have
BOD, } *bote* and *bot.*

COLLIER. 1750.	*Boh* heaw went'n ye on ? Wur th' justice awhoam ? *Works,* p. 45.
JAMES BUTTERWORTH. 1790.	*Boh* aw soon towd um, awre gooin to Owdham, Un aw'd ha'e a battle wi' th' French. *Harland's Ball. & Songs of Lanc. :* " *Jone o' Greenfilt,*" l. 218.
WAUGH. 1867.	They nar. *bod* one bed, yo see. *Home Life, Factory Folk* (Preston), c. ix. p. 81.
JOHN ALMOND. (Blackburn, E.L.) 1872.	" *Bud* yo've hit th' wrong mon," sed th' parson's voice fro' t' other side " Never mind," sed Mary Ann ; " pass it on to th' reight un." *Day at Blackpool,* p. 7.

BOKE, *v.* to point the finger at.

JOHN SCHOLES. 1857.	Betty wur *bokin* hur finger at um, un aw crope behoint hur.—*Jaunt to see th' Queen,* p. 57.
WAUGH. 1874.	I went quietly up to him, an' *boked* my finger at his oppen e'e. *Chimney Corner: Manch. Critic,* Aug. 14.

BOLL, *sb.* a boggart, an object of fear.   Probably a contraction from *boggle*

BONK, *sb.* (var. pron.) a bank.   A.S. *banc.*

WEST-MID DIAL. (Lanc.) 1320	Ouer at þe Holy-Hede. til he hade eft *bonk* In þe wyldrenesse of Wyrale. *Sir Gawayne,* l. 700.
IBID. 1360.	And by þyse *bonkeȝ* þer I con gele. And I se ne by-gyng nawhere aboute. *E. E. Allit. Poems,* A. l. 930.
IBID	And bowed to þe hyȝ *bonk* þer brentest hit wern. *Ibid.,* B. l. 379.
GAWIN DOUGLAS. 1513.	Quhil the reflex of the diurnal bemys The beyn *bonkis* kest ful of variant glemys. *Spec. Eng. Lit.* p. 129, l. 61.

BOOF, *sb.* the bough of a tree ; also, the shaft of a cart.

BOON-PLOO (N. Lanc.) *sb.* a day's ploughing given to each other by neighbouring farmers, or to the lord of the manor, or by a sub-tenant to the holder of the land.   From *boon* and *plough.*

'BOON-SHEARIN' (N Lanc.), *sb.* a quantity of shearing given as in the case of a boon-ploo.

BOORTREE (S. Lanc.), } *sb.* the elder tree.   Tomlinson (in Ray)
BORTREE (N Lanc.), } gives the form *bore-tree,* and derives it from *bore.*   There is no proof of this.

BOOSE, ⎫ *sb.* a cattle-stall. Often used for the upper part of the
BOOST, ⎭   stall where the fodder is placed: as, " Yo'll find it in
th' cow's *boose*." Figuratively, a seat. A.S. *bós, bósig*, a stall,
manger, crib.

<table>
<tr><td>1440.</td><td>*Booc* or *boos*, netystalle (*boce*, K. *bose*, netis stall,
H.P.)   *Prompt. Parv.*</td></tr>
<tr><td>H. Fishwick.
1871.</td><td>One of the every-day proverbs in use here (Goos-
nargh, in the Fylde) is : "A famine begins in the
cow *boost*."
     Hist. Chapelry of Goosnargh, c. xi. p. 200.</td></tr>
<tr><td>Waugh.
1874.</td><td>"Now lads," said Giles, "are yo getten sattle't
into yer *booses* ?"—*Old Cron'es*, p. 33.</td></tr>
</table>

BOOTHER, or ⎫
BOOTHER-STONE, ⎭ *sb.* (var. pron.) a boulder-stone.

<table>
<tr><td>Ramsbottom.
1864.</td><td>O ! it wur hard eawrsels to dhraw
Fro' th' things i' th' heawse we'd awlus known ;
For eawr warm beds t' put up wi' sthraw ;
For every cheer a *boother-stone !*
                Lanc. Rhymes, p. 66.</td></tr>
<tr><td>Waugh.
1867.</td><td>Jenny, bring him a cheer [chair], lass. Thae stons
theer as gawmless as a *boother-stone !*
                Tattlin' Matty, p. 9.</td></tr>
</table>

BOOZE, *v.* to drink hard. Du. *buizen;* Swiss *bausen*, to take deep
draughts, drink deep, to tope.

<table>
<tr><td>Sir Thomas North.
1579.</td><td>[Sylla] falling into such company, by drinking,
bowsing, and making good cheer, he suddenly became
another manner of man.—*Plutarch*, p. 387.</td></tr>
<tr><td>Spenser.
1589.</td><td>Still as he rode he somewhat still did eat,
  And in his hand did beare a *bouzing* can,
Of which he supt so oft, that on his seat
  His drunken corse he scarse upholden can.
             F. Q., bk. i. c. 4, st. 22.</td></tr>
<tr><td>Beaumont & Fletcher.
1613.</td><td>Come, prithee, let's shog off, and *bowse* an hour or
two ; there's ale will make a cat speak at the Harrow.
           Coxcomb, act ii. sc. 1.</td></tr>
<tr><td>Pope.
1728.</td><td>Rous'd at his name, up rose the *bowsy* sire,
And shook from out his pipe the seeds of fire.
               Dunciad, iv. 493.</td></tr>
<tr><td>Coll. Use.
1875.</td><td>He's done nowt but *booze* for a for:nit.</td></tr>
</table>

BORNE, ⎫
BOYRN, ⎭ *v.* to swill, to wash. Cf. A.S. *burne*, a stream.

<table>
<tr><td>Collier.
1750.</td><td>Theaw meh be shure I're primely *boyrnt*, on os
weet as ewer eh could sye. I lookt licker a dreawnt
meawse in [than] o mon.—*Works.* p. 49</td></tr>
<tr><td>John Scholes.
1857.</td><td>Theaw wur thur thinkin' abeawt *boyrnin'* an'
weshin' when we lookt at them fountains.
         Jaunt to see th' Queen, p. 56.</td></tr>
</table>

WAUGH.
1867.

Whatever arto doin areawt [outside] sich a day as this ? What, its enough to *borne* th' buttons off thi clooas. Thae'rt fair sipein' fro yed to fuut.
Owd Blanket, c. iii p. 52.

IBID.
1868.

Eh, heaw it did come deawn ! It's a good while sin aw wur as primely *borne't* as aw've bin this time.
Sneck-Bant, c. i. p. 7.

BORRANS (North Lanc.) *sb.* rough, craggy places, to which foxes run for safety. Gael. *borr, borra*, a knob , *borrach*, a projecting bank.

BORTREE - JOAN (N. Lanc.) *sb.* elderberry wine. The Rev. Addison Crofton writes : " Nurse says it used to be the custom [at Lancaster] to invite friends to take *bortree-joan*, usually served in coffee-cups, and always hot. The housemaid proffered us a¹' some one day here [Burnage], sent by her mother from L caster." 1875. See BOORTREE.

BOSKIN, *sb.* a cattle-stall. From *boose*, with the suffix *kin*. See BOOSE.

BOSS, *sb.* a fat, lazy woman ; a term of reproach. Cf. Fr. *bosse*, a boss ; Du. *bos*, a bunch, bundle.

COLL. USE.
1875.

Hoo's a great idle *boss*. Look at her childer, they'n tell thi what hoo is.

BOSTIN' (Mid. Lanc.), *sb.* the rack or trough in a stable, in which the fodder is placed. See BOOSE and BOSKIN.

BOTE, *p. p.* did bite. Earle *(Philology English Tongue)* gives pres. *bite ;* preterite, *bote*, bit ; part. *bitten, bit ;* and says the form flourished chiefly from the fifteenth to the seventeenth century.

WEST MID. DIAL. (Lanc.)
1330.

And *bote* þe best of his bracheȝ [hounds] þe bakkeȝ in sunder.　　　　*Sir Gawayne*, l. 1563.

LANGLAND.
1362.

Lourede he foule,
His body was bolled. for wraþþe he *bot* his lippes.
Piers Plowman, A-text, v 66.

1400.

He was the burlokke [st] blonke, ther evyr *bote* brede.
Met. Rom., A. xliii., l. 2.

WAUGH.
1855.

"That's just reet," as Pinder said, when his wife *bote* hur tung i' two !　　　*Lanc. Sketches*, 26.

IBID.
1867.

His wife's as nice a lass as ever *bote* off th' edge ov a cake.　　　　*Owd. Bl.*, c. iii., p. 51.

RAMSBOTTOM.
1864.

Mi feyther lookt eawt into th' sthreet,
An' *bote* his lip, bo never spoke.
Lanc. Rhymes, p. 73.

BOTH', *prep.* but the : as, " Aye, *both*' time's past."

BOTS (N. Lanc.) *sb. pl.* intestinal worms in animals. Gael. *botus,* a
bott: *boiteag,* a maggot.

SHAKSPERE. 1593.	Why Petruchio is comming, in a new hat and an old jerkin ; . . . his horse . . . possest with the glanders, and like to mose in the chine ; troubled with the lampasse, infected with the fashions full of windegalls, sped with spavins. raied with the yellows, past cure of the fives, starke spoyl'd with the staggers, begnawne with *bots.* *Taming of Shrew,* act iii. sc. 2, l. 49
IBID. 1598.	*Second Carrier :* Pease an beanes are as danke here as a dog, and this is the next way to give poore jades the *botles.*—*First King Hen. IV.* act ii. sc 1. l. 9
PHILEMON HOLLAND. 1601.	If the same be conveighed downe by a horne into the throat of horses and such like beasts, they will cure the wringing torment of the *botts* that fret and gnaw them in the bellies.—*Plinie,* b. xxviii. c. 11.
OLIVER GOLDSMITH. 1764.	After he [the chapman] had examined the horse round, finding him blind of one eye, he would have nothing to say to him : a fourth knew by his eye that he had the *botts.*—*Vicar of Wakefield,* c. 14.

BOUGHT, | *sb.* the bend, as the *bought* or *boot* of the elbow. A.S.
BOOT, | *búgan, beógan,* to bow, bend, stoop, give way,
Mid. E. *boght, bight ;* Dan. *bugt,* a bend.

WEST-MID. DIAL. (Lanc.) 1330.	Bi þe *hyȝt* al of þe þyȝes.—[= By the fork of the thighs.] *Sir Gawayne,* l. 1349.
SIR P. SIDNEY. 1583.	Now of her knees My tongue doth tell what fancy sees, Whose *bought* incavd doth yield such sight, Like cunning painter shadowed white. *Arcadia,* b ii.
SPENSER. 1589.	And as she lay upon the durtie ground. Her huge long taile her den all overspred, Yet was in knots and many *boughtes* upwound Pointed with mortall sting. *F. Q.,* bk. I., c i., st. 15.
MILTON. 1645.	In notes, with many a winding *bout* Of linked sweetness long drawn out. *L'Allegro,* l. 139.

BOOKTH,
BUGTH, } *sb.* bigness, bulk.   Cf. Icel. *búkr,* bulk.

JOHN COLLIER. 1750.	This wur a nice trick oth' *bookth* on't, wur it naw ? *Works,* p. 68.
JOHN SCHOLES. 1857.	Wi his beein' sich a *bookth,* an' so clumsy ov his legs, he'd o bin toilt to deeoth e wamblin' deawn theer. *Jaunt to see th' Queen,* p. 46.
WAUGH. 1865.	Hasto forgetten me pooin' tho eawt o' that greight tub i' Bull Robin back-yard, when thae'er abeawt th' *bugth* ov er Billy ? Whau thae'd happen be five year owd, or so. *Besom Ben,* p. 43.
B. BRIERLEY. 1869.	"Owd Tabby's getten her hay in?" "Good crop?" "Middlin' i' *bukth,* an' as sweet as a posy." *Red Windows Hall,* c xi., p. 83.

E.

BOOLER (Lancaster), *sb.* a child's hoop. This is not "bowler," but is probably formed from the word *bool* or *bule* (*q.v.*), the hoop being generally made from pieces of wood similar to those used for the handles of osier market-baskets.

BOWSTER, *sb.* a carriage for timber. A.S. *bolster.*

BOWSTER-YED (Lit. Bolster-head), *sb.* applied to a light-headed person, or one of confused brain, with no power of orderly thought ; and, as bolsters are generally stuffed with feathers or some kind of light, fluzzy, yielding stuff, there is a certain figura-.tive fitness in the application.

WAUGH.
1869.

If a poor lad happens to be born wi a hair-shorn lip, or his yure a bit cauve-lickt. he's sure to be punce't for't, oather by one *bowster-yed* or another— though he's no moor to do wi't nor he has wi makin moonleet. *Yeth-Bobs,* c. i., p. 12.

BOWT-RUSHES, *sb. pl.* choice rushes used in the making of rush-carts.

BRABBLE, *v.* to chatter noisily. Cf. Du. *brabbelen,* to confuse, to stammer.

BRABBLEMENT, *sb.* noisy talk.

JOHN SCHOLES.
1857.

In a bit ther wur sich o clatter an' *brabblement* omung us, us made rare spooart fur thoose us wur eawt on't. *Jaunt to see th' Queen,* p. 56.

BRACKEN-CLOCK (Furness), *sb.* a small beetle.

BRAD, } *v.* to spread, to open wide, to extend, to make broad.
BREAD, } A.S. *bræ'dan,* to extend.

WEST.MID. DIAL. (Lanc.).
1320.

He were a bleaunt of blwe, that *bradde* to the erthe. [= He wore a robe of blue that extended to the earth] *Sir Gawayne & G. K.,* l. 1928.

1350.

He made hire to knele a-doun and a bok *bradde,* Radde a gospel þer-on and bad hire up rise.
Joseph of Arimathie, l. 642.

JOHN COLLIER.
1750.

Nor ist oboon two eawrs sin furst time ot eh *brad* meh een on him. *Works,* p. 63.

JOHN SCHOLES.
1857.

A noice clen cloth wur *brad* up o' th' table
Jaunt to see th' Queen, p. 22.

BRADE, *sb.* a board, a shelf. A.S. *bred,* a plank, board ; Swed. *brädd,* a board.

WEST-MID. DIAL. (Lanc.)
1360.

He [Jonah] watȝ flowen for ferde of þe flode lotes Into þe boþem of þe bot [boat] and on a *brede* lyggede.
E. E. Allit. Poems, C, l. 183.

1440.

Brede, or lyttel borde. *Mensula, tabula, asserulus.*
Prompt. Parv.

BRADE, *sb.* bread, but usually applied to oaten cake.

WAUGH.
1857.

"Win yo have hard *brade ?* Which side dun yo come fro ?" "I come from Manchester," said I. "Fro Manchester, eh ! Whau, then, yoddn rather ha' loaf-*brade*, aw'll uphowd yo." "Nay, nay," said I, "I'm country-bred ; and I would rather have a bit of oat-cake." That's reet ; aw'll find yo some gradely good stuff ! An it's a deeol howsomer nor loaf, too, mind yo."—*Lanc. Sketches* (Bury to Rochdale), p. 24.

BRADE-FLEIGH, } *sb.* a wooden frame, crossed by cords, and
BRADE-FLAKE, } hung below the ceiling, used to lay oatcakes upon to dry and harden.

BAMFORD.
1840.

The large *bread-flake* in the kitchen was speedily unthatched. *Life of Radical*, vol. i., p. 234.

WAUGH.
1857.

When I asked a villager whether Gamershaw Boggart was ever seen now, he said, "Naw ; we never see'n no boggarts neaw ; nobbut when th' *brade-fleigh's* empty !"—*Lanc. Sketches* (Birthplace of Tim Bobbin), c. ii., p. 79.

IBID.
1866.

Upon a *brade-fleigh* or bread-rack, which was suspended from the ceiling, like a great square harp, a few oat-cakes were spread, with their ends curled up about the strings.—*Ben an' th' Bantam*, c. i., p. 11.

BRAGGAT, } *sb.* new alé spiced with sugar ; a sweet drink, made
BRAGGET, } of the wort of ale, honey, and spice ; mulled ale, prepared and drunk in many places on Mid-Lent Sunday, which is hence called Braggat Sunday. W. *bragawd ;* Sc. *bragwort.*

CHAUCER.
1386.

Hir mouth was sweete as *bragat* is or meth.
Milleres Tale, l. 75.

1440.

Bragett, drynke. *Mellibrodium bragetum.*
Prompt. Parv.

HOLLINSHED.
1586.

Before she putteth her first woort into the furnace, or mingleth it with the hops, she taketh out a vessel full of eight or nine gallons, which she shutteth up close, and suffereth no aire to come into it till it become yellow, and this she reserveth by itself unto further use, calling it *brackwoort.*
Descrip. of England, c. vi.

BEN JONSON
1610.

Captaine, if ever at the bozing ken,
You have in draught of Darby drilled your men ;
And we have serv'd there armed all in ale
With the browne bowle, and charg'd in *bragget* stale.
Masques : Gypsies Metamorphosed.

REV. W. GASKELL.
1854.

Consulting my school recollections again, there used to be, and there may be yet, and I hope there is for the sake of school-boys, a Sunday in the year known as *Bragget*-Sunday, because on that day they were indulged in a kind of sweet drink which bore this name, and was composed, I believe, of ale, sugar, and nutmeg This evidently corresponds to the *bragawd* of the Welsh, which denotes a liquor made of the wort of ale—*brag* signifying malt in that language, as in Cornish and Gaelic—mixed with mead and spiced. We find it mentioned both by Aneurin and Taliesin, two British poets flourishing in the sixth century, and in the laws of Hoel Dha, in the tenth century.—*Lect. Lanc. Dialect*, p. 8.

BRAID, *v.* to resemble; to be like.   Icel. *bregða við*, to resemble.

COLL. USE. 1875.	He *braids* o' th' lot; he's nooan a good un.

BRAK, broke.   A.S. *bræc.*

ROBERT MANNYNG. 1303.	Out of hys mouth me thoghte *brak* A flamme of fyre bryght and clere. *Handlyng Synne*, l. 5922.
Before 1380.	He smot the wyket with his foot, and *brak* awey the pyn. *Cokes Tale of Gamelyn*, l. 298.

BRANDRETH, *sb.* a gridiron.   A.S. *brandreda;* Icel. *brand-reið,* a grate.

BRANGLE, *sb.* a quarrel or squabble.

BRAN-NEW, *adj.* quite new.   See *brand-new* in Jamieson.

COLL. USE. 1875.	Come that's *bran-new*, thae's never towd that afore.

BRANT, *adj.* steep, as applied to a hill.   Thus, *Brant* Fell, near Windermere; *Brant*wood, Coniston, a wood on a steep hill side. Sw. *brant*, steep; Icel. *brattr*, steep. Cf. W. *bryn*, a hill.

WEST-MID. DIAL. (Lanc.) 1320.	[He] seȝe no syngne of resette, by-sydeȝ nowhere, Bot hyȝe bonkkeȝ and *brent*. *Sir Gawayne & G. K.*, l. 2164.
IBID. 1360.	Þe byggyng thay leveȝ And bowed to þe hyȝ bonk þer *brentest* hit wern. *E. E. Allit. Poems*, B., l. 378.
ROGER ASCHAM. 1544.	A man maye, I graunt, sit on a *brante* hyll syde. *Toxophilus*, A., p. 58 (Arber's reprint).
JOHN BRIGGS. 1822.	Ye'll find it a lang way an' varra *brant*. *Remains*, p 106.

BRASH, *adj.* rash.   Gael. *bras*, rash.   Cf. W. *brys*, haste.

BRASH, *sb.* an eruption.   Cf. Gael. *briseadh*, a breach, a bursting; W. *brech*, an eruption.

BRASS, *sb.* money.

JOHN COLLIER. 1750.	I thowt I'll know heaw meh shot stons ofore I'll wear [spend] moor o meh *brass* o meh brekfust. *Works*, p. 55.
RAMSBOTTOM. 1864.	Beawt wark, thae knows weel, there's no *brass*. *Lanc. Rhymes*, p. 15.
WAUGH. 1867.	"Dost want any *brass?*" said she. "Well, ay," replied Ben. "Thae may gi mo sixpence" *Owd Bl.*, c. i, p. 23.

BRAST, *v.* to burst.   A.S. *berstan*, p. t. *bærst.*

WEST MID. DIAL. (Lanc.) 1360.
Þe bur ber to hit baft þat *braste* alle her gere.
E. E. Allit. Poems, C., l. 148.

WYCLIF. 1380.
This Judas hadde a field of the hire of wickednesse, and he was hanged, and to-*brast* in the myddil and alle hise entrailis weren shed abrood.   *Acts,* c. i.

CHAUCER. 1386.
And bothe his yën *brast* out of his face.
Man of Lawes Tale, l. 573.

GAWIN DOUGLAS. 1513.
The fyry sparkis *brastyng* from his eyn.
Prologue Eneid, b. xii. 39.

1551.
When he was hanged *brast* asonder in the myddes and all hys bowels gushed out.—*Bible : Acts,* c. i.

SPENSER. 1590.
No gate so strong, no locke so firm and fast, But with that piercing noise flew open quite or *brast.*
F. Q., Book I., c. viii , l. 4.

MISS LAHEE. 1865.
Aw had mi fayther an' ir lads laughin' fit to *brast* their soides.   *Betty o' Yep's Tale,* p. 10.

WAUGH. 1869.
Eawr Billy cried, poor lad. . . . Every time that aw slipt, or gav a bit ov a clunter again a stone, he *brast* eawt again, as iv his heart wur breighkin.
Yeth-Bobs, c. ii., p. 33.

BRAST-OFF, *v.* to start, to begin.

WAUGH. 1875.
Silence, lads ; Jem's gettin' his top-lip ready. *Brast-off,* Jem.   *Old Cronies,* c. vii., p. 85.

BRAT, *sb.* a coarse apron.   A.S. *bratt,* a cloak, probably borrowed from the Celtic ; cf. Gael. *brat,* a mantle ; W. *brat,* a rag.

CHAUCER. 1386.
And a *bratt* to walke in by daylight.
Ed. Tyrwhitt, l. 16349.

J. P. MORRIS. 1867.
Them 'at hedn't any pots held owt the'r *brats,* 'an gut a scowp-ful put in.—*Invasion o' U'ston,* p. 6.

WAUGH. 1867.
Aw'd rayther see it nor a *brat*-full o' guinea gowd !
Owd Bl., c. i., p. 19.

BEALEY. 1870.
Hoo awlus like't to gather flowers, An bring 'em whoam to me ; Hoo'd bring her *brat* full mony a time, An sort 'em on her knee.
Poems : Eawr Bessy, p. 157.

BRAWSEN, or **BROSSEN,** *p. p.* and *adj.* burst ; also, overfed.   A.S. *borsten ;* Mid. E. *bresten, brusten, brosten.*   Cf. Dan. *bröst,* hurt, damage.

CHAUCER. 1386.
For with the fal he *brosten* had his arm.
Milleres Tale, l. 641.

IBID.
For I am hole, al *brosten* ben my bondes.
Troylus and Creiseide, l. 976.

JOHN COLLIER. 1750.
If I'd naw bin eh that wofo pickle Ist a *bross'n* weh leawghing.   *Works,* p. 70.

REV. W. GASKELL.
1854.

I have heard of a person who, when charged at table with not eating. said, "Aw've eyten till o'm welly *brossen*," to which the response was, "*Brossen*, for sure ! We wishen we'd owt for t' *brossen* yo wi !"
Lect. Lanc. Dialect, p. 25.

WAUGH.
1857.

There's plenty o' chaps i' Rachdaw teawn at's so *brawsen* wi wit, whol noather me, nor thee, nor no mon elze, con may ony sense on 'em.
Lanc. Sketches (Bury to Rochdale), p. 33.

IBID.
1874.

There's nowt at a' coorse, nor *brawsen* [overfed or bloated] aboot him. He's a well-leukin', clear-skinned, healthy man.   *Jannock*, c. v., p. 36.

IBID.
1874.

"Come, Gavlock, owd brid, wakken up ; thour't noan sto'in, arto ?"   "By th' mon, it's gettin' time, I think. Thou doesn't want to see me *brawsen*, doesto ? I measur't a hond-bradth off between my singlet an' th' table afore we started, an' they're welly met."
Old Cronies, p. 34.

BRAZIL, *sb.* anything very hard.   "It is not a little singular," says Way, in his notes to *Promptorium Parvulorum*, "to find so many notices as occur of Brazil-wood, considerably anterior to the discovery of Brazil by the Portuguese captain, Peter Alvaris Capralis, which occurred 3rd May, 1500. He named it the land of the Holy Cross, 'since of store of that wood called *Brasill*.' Purchas's Pilgrimes, vol. 1. In the Canterbury Tales, the host, commending the Nonnes Preeste for his health and vigour, says :

Him needeth not his colour for to dien
With *Brasil*, ne with grain of Portingale."

WAUGH.
1867.

"Aw could like to gi' tho summat that would tak tho off whoam " said the doctor.   "Aw'm as hard as *brazill*," said Tip ; "kill mo !"
Owd Bl , c. iv., p. 85.

IBID.
1874.

"How didto goo on wi Owd Sniggle *?*"   "Oh, he's as hard as *brazzil* ! But I banted him i' th' end."
Chimney Corner : Manch. Critic, May 2, 1874.

BREAD-AND-CHEESE, *sb.* the leaves of the hawthorn.   Also, in N. Lanc. the leaves and flowers of the *Oxalis acetosella*. A phrase used by children.

BREAST-HEE, *sb.* the mouth of a tunnel leading to a coal-pit which has been made in the side of a hill, the shaft being horizontal instead of vertical.

BAMFORD.
1850.

At the time when Tim Bobbin was spending his days at Milnrow . . . the collier brought his coal to daylight at the mouth of a tunnel, or what was called a *breast-hee*. generally opening out, not unlike a large black sough, on some hill-side.
Ed. of Tim Bobbin : Intro. iii.

WAUGH.
1857.

A long-limbed collier lad began to hum, in a jolting metre, with as much freedom of mind as it he was at the mouth of a lonely *breast-hee* on his native moorside. a long country ditty.
Lanc. Sketches : Cottage of Tim Bobbin, p. 44.

IBID.
1874.

He took me up one street an' down another, till we coom to th' end of a ginnel 'at looked as dark as a *breast-hee* col-pit. — *Chimney Corner : Manchester Critic*, March 21, 1874.

BREED, *adj.* frightened.   Icel. *bregða*, to startle, to be amazed.

JOHN COLLIER.
1750.

I'r so feerfully *breed* at meh hure stood on eend.
Tim Bobbin : Works, p. 51.

COLL. USE.
1875.

He was fair *breed.*

BREOD, *sb.* a cake—not bread.

COLL. USE.
1875.

Wilto have *breod* or loaf ?

BRETHER, *sb. pl.* brothers.   In the oldest English the plural of *brother* was *brothru (brothra)*.   In the thirteenth century this became, 1, *brothr-e;* 2, *brothr-e-n (brotheren)*; 3, *brethr-e;* 4, *brethr-e-n;* 5, *brotheres (brothers)*.   In the Northern dialects in the fourteenth century we find *brethre* becoming *brether.* " These be my mother, *brether*, and sisters." Bp. Pilkington (died 1575). The *e* in *brethren* seems to have arisen from the dative singular *(brether)*.   Dr. Morris's *English Accidence*, p. 96.

WEST MID. DIAL. (LANC.)
1320.

Þis kyng lay at Camylot upon kryst-masse
With mony luflych lorde. ledeȝ of þe best,
Rekenly [nobly or princely] of þe rounde table alle
  Þo rich breþer.—*Sir Gawayne & G. K*, l. 37.

HAMPOLE.
1340.

That ilka tyme when yhe did oght
Until ane of þe lest þat yhe myght se
Of my *brether*, yhe did til me.—*Pricke of C.*, l. 6176.

DUNBAR.
About 1500.

My *brethir* oft hes maid the supplicationis.
Spec. Eng. Lit., p 117, st. 6.

BRERE, *sb.* a briar.   A.S. *brêr;* Mid. E. *brere.*   Names of places in Lancashire, *Brere*cliffe, *Brere*croft.

WILLIAM OF PALERNE.
1350.

Blake-beries that on *breres* growen.
W. of Palerne, l. 1809

WEST-MID. DIAL. (Lanc.)
1360.

His browes bresed [rough] as *breres* aboute his brode
  cheekes.   *E. E. Allit. Poems*, B, l. 1694.

WYCLIF.
1380.

That is brynginge forth thornes and *breris*.
Hebrews, c. 6

GAWIN DOUGLAS.
1513.

Welcum the byrdis beild upon the *brer.*
Prologue of the xii. buk of Eneados, l. 257.

SPENSER.
1579.

The gentle shepheard satte beside a springe,
All in the shadowe of a bushye *brere.*
Shepheardes Calender, December, l. 1.

WILLIAM BROWNE.
1614.

I wonder he hath soft'red been
  Upon our common heere,
His hogges doe rent our younger treen,
  And spoyle the smelling *breere.*
Shepheard's Pipe, Ec. 2.

DRYDEN.
1680.

A thicket close beside the grove there stood.
With *breers* and brambles choked, and dwarfish wood.
Theodore & Honoria, l. 103

BREWIS, *sb.*, oatcake or bread toasted, and soaked in broth or stew. Welsh *brywes;* A.S. *brîw, brîwas,* the small pieces of meat in broth ; pottage.

BECON.
1550.

We were weary of the comfortable manna, and a pleasure to return unto Egypt, where we might sit among greasy fleshpots, eating beef and *brewis* knuckle-deep. *A Comfortable Epistle,* c. iii.

Rev. W. GASKELL.
1854.

In Lancashire, bread soaked in broth, or in the fat that drips from meat when being roasted, is known as *brewis.* A writer in the reign of Edward VI. refers to "*browess* made with bread and fat meat." *Lect. Lanc. Dialect,* p. 13.

JOHN SCHOLES.
1857.

Ut last theyrn as scarce to be fund as drops o' fat on Owdham *breawis.*—*Jaunt to see th' Queen,* p. 13.

BREWITS (S. E. Lanc.)) *sb.* the rim or brim of a hat, A.S. *brerd;*
BRUART (E. Lanc.)) Mid. E. *brurd,* top, brim.

A. S. GOSPELS.
1000.

And hig gefyldon þá oð þone *brerd* [= and they filled them up to the brim].—*John* ii. 7.

WAUGH.
1868.

Theer stoode Sneck-bant i'th dur-hole, as quiet as a dreawnt meawse, wi th' rain drippin' off his hat *brewits.* *Sneck-Bant,* c. ii., p. 38.

BREWSTER, *sb.* a brewer.

LANGLAND.
1377.

Brewesteres and baksteres, bocheres and cokes. *Piers Plowman,* B text, Passus iii., l. 79.

BRICKLE,) *adj.* fragile, brittle. A.S. *brecan,* to break. Mid. E.
BRITCHEL,) *bruchel, brukel, brikle.*

SIR THOMAS MORE,
About 1500.

Suche as didde their endevour to break his bondes, and to shake his yoke from them, those he shall spyte of their teeth, rule with an yron rod and as a *brickell* earthen pot in pieces al to frush them. *Workes,* p. 1398.

SPENSER.
1591.

But th' Altare, on which this Image staid, Was (O great pitie !) built of *brickle* clay, That shortly the foundation decaid, With showres of heaven and tempests worne away. *Ruines of Time,* l. 498.

Rev. W. GASKELL.
1854.

Brickle is a true Lancashire adjective, formed just as properly from the A.S. *brecan* as brittle is from *brytan ;* only as the Mæso-Gothic is *brickan,* it may boast most likely of a higher antiquity than "brittle." By the same process as that which changed *circ* into church, and *cicen* into chicken, *brickle* is sometimes converted into *britchle.*—*Lect. Lanc. Dialect,* p 21.

JOHN SCHOLES.
1857.

Thoose ur yoar Manchistur cheers [chairs], ar thi?—us *britchel* us egg-shells, ur o cake o' brayd uts bin on th' fleak fur o thri wik. They arnah fit to peeorch o hen on. *Jaunt to see th' Queen,* p 47.

WAUGH.
1874.

Thou costs moore tor breighkage than thi wage comes to! Thou'rt like as if thou'd a malice again aught 'at's *britchel.—Chimney Corner: Manchester Critic*, Feb. 28, 1874.

BRID, *sb.* a bird.   A.S. *brid*.

1300.

Lenten ys come wiþ loue to toune,
Wiþ blosmen and wiþ *briddes* roune,
þat ul þis blisse bryngeþ.
Proverbs of Hendyng: Sp. E. Eng., p. 48.

WEST MID. DIAL. (Lanc.)
1320.

Bryddes busken to bylde and bremlych syngen
For solace of þe softe somer þat sues þer·after.
Sir Gawayne & G. K., l. 509.

IBID.
1360.

Fro þe burne to þe best, fro *bryddeȝ* to fyscheȝ.
E. Eng. Allit. P., B, l. 288.

WICLIF.
1380.

It shal make grete braunchis, so that *briddis* of hevene mowe dwelle undir the shadewe ther-of.
———   *Mark* iv. 32.

WAUGH.
1859.

He're very fond o' singin-*brids*
That's heaw he geet his name.
Lanc. Songs: Chirrup.

RAMSBOTTOM.
1864.

O' reawnd agen aw kiss mi *brids*
Afore hoo packs 'em off to bed.
Lanc. Rhymes, p. 13.

WAUGH.
1868.

"Middlin o' *brids* upo' th' moor this time, aw think," said Ben. "Ay," replied Randal, "but they're terrible wild upo' th' wing."   *Sneck Bant*, ii. 24.

BEALEY.
1870.

An' seemed to sing an' nestle theer,
Just like a little *brid*.   *Poems*, p. 156.

BRIDE-WAIN, *sb.* a bidden wedding, *q.v.*

BRIG (North and Mid. Lanc.) *sb.* a bridge. The most southerly point of the county where "brig" is used instead of "bridge" is believed to be Bamber Brig, a few miles south of Preston. It occurs, however, in Collier's *Tim Bobbin*. A.S. *bricg;* Icel. *bryggja*.

WEST MID. DIAL. (Lanc.)
1320.

And he ful chauncely hatȝ chosen to þe chef gate,
þat broȝt bremly þe burne to þe *bryge* ende, in haste;
þe *bryge* watȝ breme vp-brayde.
Sir Gawayne & G. K., l. 778.

IBID.
1360.

At vch *brugge* a berfray on basteles wyse.
E. E. Allit. P, B, l. 1187.

LANGLAND.
1377.

þe *brugge* is of hidde-wel, þe bette may þow spede.
Piers P., B-text, Pass. v., l. 601.

LAURENCE MINOT.
1352.

Franche men put þam to pine
At Cressy, when þai brak þe *brig*.
Sp. E. E., p. 136, l. 77.

CHAUCER.
1386.

At Trompyngtoun, nat fer fro Cantebrigge,
Ther goth a brook, and over that a *brigge*.
Reeves Tale, l. 1.

JOHN COLLIER.
1750.

I saigh two rotten pynots ot tis seme *brig* os eh coom.   *Works*, p. 50.

COLL. USE (E. Lanc.)
1875.

Pig wouldn't o'er t' *brig*.

BRIGGS, *sb.* irons to set over the fire. Welsh *brigwn*, andirons.

BRINDLE, to be irritated, to show resentment, to bridle up.

COLL. USE.
1875.

He *brindled* up as soon as aw spoke to him.

BROCK, *sb.*, a badger, from the white-streaked face of the animal. Names of places in Lancashire, *Brock*holes, *Brocks*bottom. Gael. *broice*, a mole, a freckle; *brucach*, spotted; *breac*, speckled; Welsh *brech*, *brych*, brindled, freckled; Icel. *brokkr*, a badger; Dan. *brok*, a badger; A.S. *broc*.

LANGLAND.
1377.

And go hunte hardiliche to hares and to foxes,
To bores and to *brockes* þat breketh adown myne
hegges. *Piers Plowman*, B-text, vi. 30

WYCLIF.
1380.

They wenten aboute in *brok* skynnes.—*Heb.* xi. 37.

SHAKSPERE.
1602.

Sir Toby: Marrie, hang thee, *brocke!*
Twelfth Night, ii., v., 114.

BEN JONSON.
1633.

Or with pretence of chasing thence the *brock*,
Send in a curre to worry the whole flock.
Sad Shephera, act i., sc. 4.

REV. J. RELPH.
1740.

" Nea mair i' th' nights thro' woods he leads,
To treace the wand'ring *brock*."
Cumberland Ballads, p. 8.

BRODDLE, *v.* to assume, to swagger. BRODDLIN', *adj.* assuming, swaggering. Cf. Gael. *brodail*, proud, arrogant.

JOHN COLLIER.
1750.

So I gen um her; on still this *broddlin* fussock
lookt feaw as Tunor [a dog's name] when I'd done.
Works, p. 55.

BAMFORD.
1850.

See heaw he *broddles*.
Edition of Tim Bobbin, p. 145.

BROG (N. Lanc.), *sb.* a branch, a bough, a broken branch. Cf. Welsh *brigyn*, a top branch, a twig; *brigau*, the tops of trees.

DR. BARBER.
1870.

Be t' time we'd gitten by t' last *brog* an' off t' sand,
it rooar't an' blew fit to thraa a body over.
Forness Folk, p. 37.

J. P. MORRIS.
1867.

Ye men-fo'k er sic buzzards, if ye sã a *brog* on
t' sand ye wod think it wos t' French
Siege o' Brouton, p. 6.

NOTE.
1875.

After obtaining a safe ford, the guides, on the
Ulverston and Lancaster sands, mark out the track by
inserting branches of trees. This is called " *broggin'*
t' channel."

BROG,
BROGGLE, } *v.* to fish for eels by making the water muddy.

BROKKEN-YURE'T, *adj.* broken-haired; only half-bred. Appl. to anything spurious, especially, in a sarcastic way, to anything pretentious or hypocritical in human character—anything that is not what it seems to be. As regards dogs, it is applied to mongrels: thus, a " brokken-yure't spaniel" is a dog that is not all a spaniel.

B. BRIERLEY.
1860.

Aw ha' no' had so mich o' that *brokken-yurt* sort o' livin as aw're us't have.   *Bunk Ho'*, p. 17.

WAUGH.
1867.

It was a short, bloated man, with a pale, puffed face . . He was dressed in faded black and he carried a large blue umbrella. "Who is it? asked Gablock. "He favvours a *bro.ken-yure't* doctor, or summat."   *Owd Bl.*, c. iv., p. 88.

BRONG, } *v.* brought. Dr. Richard Morris (' *ist. Outlines English*
BRUNG, }   *Accidence*, p. 172), among the verbs peculiarly formed, includes, " Pres. bring, Past, brought, P. part. brought ; O. E. *bringe, brohte, broht.* In the oldest English we also find *bring, brang, brungen*, from which we see that the root is *brang = brag*."

CÆDMON.
680.

He tha bysene from gode *brungen* hæfde ; *i.e*, he had brought those commands from God.
        Cædmon, ed. Thorpe, p. 41.

COLL. USE.
1875.

1. I *brung* it an' he sent it back.

2. Has'nt thae *brung* mi baggin ? Off wi' thi back, sharp.

BROO, *sb.* a brother.

BROODY, *adj.* wanting to sit, applied to fowls.

BROWN-TOMMY, *sb.* a kind of brown bread, made of inferior flour.

COLL. USE.
1875.

" A two-pund loaf, mester." " Which win yo' have—white or brown ?" " Oh *brown-tommy*—its good enough for t' childer."

BRUART, *sb.* a shooting forth or sprouting of corn, fruits, or vegetables ; also, *v.* to sprout. The A.S. *brord*, a shooting blade of corn, occurs in the Northumbrian version of Luke viii. 6.

COLL. USE.
1875.

1. Yo'n a fine *bruart* o' strawberry.

2. Yo'r taties are *bruartin'* finely.

BRUN, *v.* to burn. A.S. *byrnan, brennan.*

ANON.
1350.

For thei had lutherli here lond *brend* and destrued.
        Will. of Palerne, l. 2646.

WAUGH.
1866.

Th' chylt cries i'th keyther ;
Th' cake *bruns* i'th oon :
Th' cow moos i'th milkin-gap,
Bi'th leet o' th' moon.   *Besom Ben*, p. 13.

IBID.
1867.

Yo'n sin that owd yollo rag ov a blanket o' mine, wi' th' hole *brunt* in it, ha'not yo ?
        Owd Bl., c. iii. p. 61.

BRUNFIRE, *sb.* a bonfire.

BRUZZ'D, *p.p.* broken, dulled, bruised, blunted. A.S. *brysan*, to bruise.

SPENSER.
1579.

And, being downe, is trodde in the durt
Of cattell, and *brouzed*, and sorely hurt.
        Shepheardes Calender : Februarie 235.

COLLIER.
1750.

I'd no hurt boh th' tone theawm stunnisht, on th'
skin *bruzz'd* off th' whirlbooan o' mi knee.

Works, p. 45.

COLL. USE.
1875.

"Aw've *bruzzed* mi clog-nose wi puncin' that owd
can."

BUCK, *sb.* a piece of wood, shorter than the ordinary billet, for use
on hard ground.

BUCKED-UP, smartly dressed.

COLL. USE.
1875.

"Hello, Jim,'what art' *bucked-up* for?"   "Gooin'
to Manchester, owd lad."

BUCKFAN, *sb.* a throw in wrestling. A term common in the
Burnley Valley and Todmorden district. At and about Rochdale, the word is applied to riding a culprit, or unpopular person,
on a stang, or pole, as a punishment.

BUCKLE-TO, *v.* to begin in earnest. Probably related to A.S.
bugan, to bow, rather than to Fr. *boucle*.

SPENSER.
1590.

Eftsoones again his axe he raught on hie,
Ere he were throughly *buckled to* his geare.

F. Q. bk. v., c. xi. st. x.

WAUGH.
1874.

I sit down, sometimes, just to gether mi wits
together a bit; an' then I have to *buckle-to* again.
There's nought else for't, yo known.

Chimney Corner: Manchester Critic, April 11.

BULE, *sb.* the handle of a pot, pan, or other utensil. At Lancaster,
the flat wooden handle of an osier market-basket. The word is
obviously a contraction of *bow*, in the sense of something *bent*,
with the suffix *-el*, from A.S. *búgan*, to bend. In exactly the
same way we have Icel. *bygill*, a stirrup, from *bogi*, a bow; and
G. *bügel*, a bent piece of wood or metal, from *bug*, a bend. The
Dan. *böile*, a bent piece, comes very near to the Lancashire form.

BULIN', *v.* linking arm in arm.

BULLART, *sb.* the warden of a bull; lit. a *bull-ward*.

WAUGH.
1874.

A greight brawsen *bullart*, wi' a neck like th' bole
of an oak tree.

Chimney Corner: Critic, Feb. 28, 1874.

BULL-HEADS, }
BULL-JONES, } *sb.* tadpoles.

WAUGH.
1857.

Rolling into the wet ditch at the bottom, to the
dismay of sundry limber-tailed *bull-jones* and other
necromantic fry that inhabit such stagnant moistures.

Lanc. Sketches · Heywood and Neighbourhood, p. 189.

IBID.
1865.

It'd be summat like th' raisin-puddin' 'at owd Mall made, wi' *bull-jones* in it. "Hello, mother!" says little Jerry, "what dun yo' co' this?" "Whau, it's a raisin," said Mally; "get it into tho'." "Well," said Jerry, howdin' it upo' th' end ov his fork, "aw never see'd a raisin wi' a tail on afore!"

Besom Ben, c. i. p. 7.

BULLOCK, *v.* to plague, tease, or bully; to interrupt or baulk by a feint.

COLL. USE.
1875.

That'll noan do; fair play! yo' munnot *bullock* him like that.

BULLOE, *sb.* the sloe or wild plum. Welsh *bwlas*, winter sloes.

BULL-SCUTTER, *sb.* anything worthless and nasty.

WAUGH.
1873.

"I don't believe i' none such-like things," said the landlord. "It's o' beggar-berm an' *bull-scutter!*"

Chimney Corner: Critic, May 31, 1873.

BULLYRAG, *v.* to abuse; to abuse with intention to intimidate.

COLL. USE.
1875.

It's no use *bullyragging* me; thae'll get nowt by it.

BUM, or BUMBAILIE, *sb.* a bailiff who distrains for rent; figuratively, a loud and overbearing person. To *bum*, to dun (Halliwell), and *bailie*, a contraction of *bailiff*.

SHAKSPERE.
1602.

Go Sir Andrew: scout mee for him at the corner of the orchard like a *bum-baylie*.

Twelfth Night, iii 4, l. 193.

CONGREVE.
1700.

Wit: The rogue has no manners at all; that I must own;—no more breeding than a *bum-baylie*, that I grant you.—*Way of the World*, act i.

B. BRIERLEY.
1869.

"I'm in a solicitor's office." "Is that bein' a *bum-baily?*" "Bum-bailiff! I should think not. Do I look like anything of the sort?"

Red Windows Hall, c. viii., p. 58.

COLL. USE.
1875.

1. Bi sharp, bi sharp, lads; here's t' *bum-bailies* come to owd Ned's.
2. Howd thi tongue; thae'rt worse nor a *bumbaily* i'th' heawse.

BUMMEL-BEE, *sb.* the humble-bee. W. *bwmp*, a hollow sound.

BUN, *v.* bound, in the sense of going; also, tied, apprenticed to.

COLL. USE.
1875.

1. "Wheer't 'a *bun?*" "Whoam, to bi sure."
2. "What han they done wi that lad o' theirs?" "*Bun* him to a blacksmith."

BUNHEDGE, *sb.* a hedge made of twisted sticks.

BUNHORNS, *sb. pl.* briars to wind yarn on.

BUNT, *v.* to pack up. Dan. *bundt*, a bunch, a bundle.

BUNT, *v.* to take work home.

BURLY-MAN, *sb.* an officer appointed at a court leet to examine and determine respecting disputed fences.

BURN, *sb.* a burden ; by contraction to *bur'n.*

WAUGH.   Gathering on their way edible herbs, such as
1855.   "green-sauce" or "a *burn* o' nettles," to put in
                 their broth.
                       Lanc. Sketches : Cottage of Tim Bobbin, p. 50.

IBID.   Eh Dimple, thae may well prick thoose ears o'
1868.   thine !   Thae never had as bonny a *burn* o' stuff upo'
                 thi back sin thae began wearin' a tail.
                       Sneck-Bant, c. iii. p. 60.

BURY-HOLE, *sb.* a grave : a word generally used by children.

WAUGH.   The child croodled thoughtfully to himself a minute
1868.   or two, whilst his mother went on dressing him ; and
                 then, suddenly turning up his face, he said, "Eawr
                 little Ben's i'th *bury-hole,* isn't he, mam ?"
                       Sneck-Bant, c. iii. p. 53.

BURYIN', *sb.* a funeral.

MISS LAHEE.   When her husband deed Tim wor axt to th' *berryin'.*
1865.   *Betty o' Yep's Tale,* p. 6.

COLL USE.   Ay, aw'm better now ; but there'd like to bin a
1875.   *buryin'* at eawr heawse, aw con tell thi.

BUSK, *v.* to dress smartly.   Icel. *búa,* to make ready, to dress, equip.   *Busk* is a remnant of the old reflex, *búask,* i.e. *búa sik,* to prepare oneself ; see Dasent, *Burnt Njal,* pref. xvi. note. (Cleasby and Vigfusson.)

—   She had nae sooner *buskit* hirsel,
                    And putten on hir goun,
                 But Edom o' Gordon and his men
                    Were round about the toun.
                       Percy's Reliques : Edom o' Gordon.

WILLIAM MORRIS. Now the next morn, when risen was the sun,
1868.   Men 'gan to *busk* them for the quest begun.
                       Jason, p. 46.

COLL. USE.   "Come *busk up,* an' let's be off."
1875.

BUSS, *sb.* a kiss.   Cf. Fr. *baiser,* to kiss ; but the connection is not certain ; cf. Gael. *bus,* a lip.   In the fifteenth century, according to Richardson, *basse* was the form used.

1561.   For lyppes thynne, not fatte, but ever lene,
                 They serve of naught, they be not worth a bene ;
                 For if the *basse* ben full, there is delite.
                       Court of Love, 795.

SPENSER.   But every satyre first did give a *busse*
1590.   To Hellenore ; so *busses* did abound.
                       F. Q. bk. iii., c. & st. xlvi.

WAUGH.
1859.

God bless it ! Daddy's noan far off ;
Let mammy have a *buss.—Lanc. Songs : Neet-fo'.*

B. BRIERLEY.
1869.

If t' meeans ay, give me a *buss* ; if t' meeans nawe,
give me a smack i' th' face.
Red Windows Hall, c. xiv. p. 112.

BUSS, *v.* to kiss. See BUSS, *ante.*

About 1420.

Lende me your praty mouth, madame,
I wis dere hert to *basse* it swete
A twyse or thryse or that I die.
Ritson : Harleian MS., *temp.* Hen. V.

SIR THOMAS MORE.
About 1500.

Thys good minde, good Lord, will I keepe styll,
and never let it fall out of my hart al the while that
I lye *bassing* with Besse.   *Workes,* p. 557.

SHAKSPERE.
1609.

Ulysses : For yonder wals that pertly front your
towne,   [the clouds,
Yond towers, whose wanton tops do *busse*
Must kisse their owne feet.
Troylus and Cressida, iv. 5, l. 219.

TENNYSON.
1842.

Buss me, thou rough sketch of man,
Far too naked to be shamed !   *Vision of Sin.*

BUTCH, *v.* to kill animals for food. as a *butcher* does.

COLL. USE.
1875.

He use't to be a farmer, but he *butches* neaw.

BUTTLE, *v.* to pour out drink.   Probably *buttle* originally meant a
pitcher, and is a dimin. of A.S. *byt,* a flagon or bottle.

WAUGH.
1865.

"Come," said Enoch, taking up the pitcher, "we'n
buttle once reawnd again."—*Besom Ben,* c. vi. p. 78.

B. BRIERLEY.
1867.

The broad village green *buttled* round its cheap
delights, in pitchers of home-brewed, innocent of any
notion of inebriety.—*Marlocks of Merriton,* p. 5.

WAUGH.
1875.

" *Buttle* out, free ! " cried Giles to the servants, "an
look after these plates ! "—*Old Cronies,* c. iii. p. 34.

BUTTY, *sb.* a confederate.

BUTTY, *sb.* a slice of bread and butter.

COLL. USE.
1875.

Here, little lad, con ta ate a *butty ?*

BUTTY-CAKE,
BUTTER-CAKE, } *sb.* a buttered cake.

JOHN SCHOLES.
1857.

Awm us fond o' fun us a chilt is ov a traycle *butter-
cake.*   *Jaunt to see th' Queen,* p. 6.

WAUGH.
1866.

Aw remember thi mother ga' mo a traycle *butter-
cake* an' a hawp'ny when aw geet tho whoam.
Besom Ben, p. 43.

BUZZERT, *sb.* a moth or butterfly , the cockchafer.   Mr. Wedgwood says : " The name *buzzard* is given to a beetle from the
buzzing sound of its flight, and it is to be thus understood in
the expression *blind buzzard.*   We also say, as blind as a beetle,
as heedless as a cockchafer, from the blind way in which they

fly against one." On the other hand, it is certain that *bosarde* in .the Rom. of Rose, 4033, meant a hawk; O. Fr. *busard.* Mr. Wedgwood's suggestion lacks proof.

COLL. USE.
1875.

He's olez after *buzzerts* and things.

BYNG, *v.* to bewitch.

HARLAND.
1867.

A year of ill-luck comes. . . . The milk is *bynged* or will not churn, though a hot poker has been used to spoil the witchery.—*Lancashire Folklore :* East Lanc. Superstitions, p. 165.

BYRE, *sb.* a cowhouse. A.S. *búr ;* Icel. *búr.*

WAUGH.
1874.

He ["Wonderful Walker"] fed an' looked after his own cattle ; he cleaned his own *byre.*
Jannock, c. viii. p 83

BYZEN, *adj.* blind. A.S. *bisen,* blind.

1250.

Lamech ledde long lif til than
That he wurth *bisne,* and haued a man
That ledde him ofte wudes ner.
Story of Genesis and Exodus, l. 471.

UDALL.
1560.

Thys manne was not purblynde, or a lyttle appayred and decayed in syght, but as *bysome* as was possible to be. *Marke,* c. 8.

SHAKSPERE.
1603.

First Player : But who, O who, had seen the mobled queen, [the flame Run bare-foot up and downe, threatning With *bisson* rheume.
Hamlet, ii. 2, 524.

IBID.
1623.

Coriolanus : How shall this *bisson* multitude digest The senate's courtesie ?
Coriolanus, iii. 1, 131.

COLLIER.
1750.

All Englandshire'll think at yoar glenting at toose fratching, *byzen,* craddingly tykes.—*Works,* p. xxxix.

BYZEN (N. Lanc.), *sb.* an example ; also, a sign or spectacle in the sense of warning, an example to be avoided. A.S. *bysen,* an example ; *bysenian,* to give an example ; *bysenung,* a resemblance. Cf. Icel. *by'sn,* a strange and portentous thing.

NORTHUMB. DIALECT.
1330.

And of child Jesus *bisen* take.
Met. Homilies, p. 110

HAMPOLE,
1340.

Yhit þe bodys of þe world þair kynde,
Shewes us for *bisens* to haf in mynde,
How we suld serve God in our kynde here.
Pricke of Conscience, l. 1026.

WAUGH.
1874.

What it'll be a sham [shame] an' a *bizen* if we connot find him a menseful bit of a dinner.
Jannock, c. ii. p 13.

C.

CAAKERS (N. Lanc.),   *sb. pl.* iron rims on the under side of
CAWKERS (Mid. Lanc.),   wooden-soled shoes. Prob. it means
CAWKINS (East Lanc.),   *treaders;* cf. Lat. *calcare,* to tread;
Gael. *calc,* to ram, drive. The Mid. E. *cauke,* = to tread, occurs
in *Piers Plowman,* xi., l. 350; and B-text, xii., l. 229. See *Calkins*
in Nares and Halliwell. Nares gives " *Calkyns* or *Calkins,* appa-
rently from *calx,* a heel; the hinder parts of a horse-shoe, which
are sometimes turned up." He adds two illustrations, one from
Holinshed's Hist. of Scot., sign. U. 3 b.; the other from the *Two
Noble Kinsmen,* v. 4. See also *Cawker* in Brockett's N. C. Gloss.

CAAKERED, *part.* bound with iron. See CAAKERS.

CADGE, *v.* to beg; to skulk about a neighbourhood. CADGER, *sb.*
one who skulks about for a living.

> COLL. USE.   Well, wi' wortchin' a bit an' *cadgin'* a bit, he maks
> 1875.   out t' best road he con.

CADGE, *v.* to tie or bind a thing.

CADGE, *v.* to stuff the belly. Cf. *cadge*-belly = a full fat belly.
(Halliwell.)

> COLLIER.   While I'r busy *cadging* mey wcm, hoo towd me
> 1750.   hoo lipp'nt hur feather wur turn't strackling.
>   *Works,* 68.

CAFF (N. Lanc.), *sb.* chaff, refuse. A.S. *ceaf;* Du. *kaf.*

> HAMPOLE.   For als fyre þat *caffe* son may bryn
> 1340.   Gold may melt þat es lang þar-in.
>   *P. of C.,* l. 3148.

> SIR DAVID LYNDESAY.   Cum down dastart and gang sell draff,
> 1535.   I understand nocht qnhat thow said;
>   Thy words war nouther corne nor *caff;*
>   I wald thy toung agane war laide.
>   *Satyre of the Thrie Estaits.*

> 1440.   [In the sense of refuse.]
>   *Caffe* of creatours alle, thow curssede wriche!
>   *Morte Arthure,* l. 1064.

CAFFEL (N. Lanc.) *v.* to entangle. Icel. *kefla,* to gag; *kefli,* a gag.
Mid. E. *kevel,* a gag.

CALD (N. Lanc.), *sb.* and *adj.* cold. A.S. *ceald, cáld;* Icel. *kaldr.*

> HAMPOLE.   For now es *cald,* now es hete,
> 1340.   Now es dry, and now es wete.
>   *Pricke of Conscience,* l 1438.

F

HAMPOLE.
1340.

And I fand Ihesus wery in þe way, turment with hungre, thirste, and *calde.*　　*Prose Tracts,* p. 5.

WEST-MID. DIAL. (Lanc.)
1360.

Þy corse in clot mot *calder* keue.
　　　　　　E. Eng. Allit. Poems, A, l. 320.

A. C. GIBSON.
(Dialect of High Furness).
1873.

It was a *cald,* sleety, slattery sooart of a day.
　　　　　　Folk-Speech of Cumberland, p. 68.

CALE, *sb.* a turn in rotation.　Cf. Icel. *kall,* a call, a calling on, a claim.

WAUGH.
1857.

There's a deal on 'em 'ud go deawn afore me. Aw'd may somebody howd back whol their *cale* coom!—*Lanc. Sketches:* "Bury to Rochdale," p. 32.

JOHN SCHOLES.
1857.

Th' Prince o' Wales comes next: he'll ha' th' creawn when his *cale* comes.
　　　　　　Jaunt to see th' Queen, p. 41.

CALE, *v.* to supersede unjustly; to take a place, turn, or opportunity from a person by force or fraud.

COLL. USE.
1875.

It's noan reet; aw've bin waitin' moor nor an hour, an' he's gone in and *caled* mi.

CALF-LICK,　⎱ *sb.* a word used to describe the hair on the forehead when it lies obstinately backwards.
CAUVE-LICK,　⎰

COLL. USE.
1875.

Yo' may comm his yure as yo' like, but it'll noan lie down; he's a *cauve-lick,* like his fayther.

CALLET (N. Lanc.) *sb.* a drab, a dirty woman; a contemptuous term for a woman.　Cf. Gael. *caile,* a quean; *cailleach,* an old woman.

BEN JONSON.
1605.

Mos: What is the injurie, lady?
Lady:　　　　　　Why, the *callet*
You told me of, here I have tane disguis'd.
　　　　　　Volpone, iv. 3.

SHAKSPERE.
1611.

A *callat*
Of boundlesse tongue, who late hath beat her husband And now bayts me.　　*Winter's T.,* iii. 3, 90

[See also "base borne *callot* as she is," *Second Hen. VI.,* i. 3, 86; "to make this shamelesse *callet* know her selfe," *Third Hen. VI,* ii. 2, 145; "a beggar in his drinke could not have laid such termes upon his *callet,*" *Othello,* iv. 2, 120.]

CALLIERD (Fylde), *sb.* a hard blue stone.　Cf. *Calyon,* rounde stone.　Rudus.　Hic rudus esto lapis, durus, pariterque rotundus.　*(Prompt. Parv.)*　Mr. Way, the editor, in a note, says: "In the accounts of the churchwardens of Walden, Essex, in 1466-7, among the costs of making the porch, is a charge 'for the foundacyons, and *calyon,* and sonde.'　Hist. of Audley End, p. 225.　Among the disbursements at Little Saxham hall, in 1505, is one to the chief mason, for the foundation within the

inner part of the moat, ' to be wrought with *calyons* and breke.'
Rokewode's Hundred of Thingoe, 141." Cf. Fr. *caillon*, a flint;
Welsh *callestr*, flint; W. *cellt*, a flint-stone. Although this is
marked as a Fylde word, there is a country place near Rochdale
called " Th' Callierds."

CAM, *sb.* contradiction, crooked argument.   Welsh *cam*, sb. an injury, wrong.

SHAKSPERE.
1623.

Sicinius [referring to the crooked reasoning of
Menenius Agrippa] :   This is cleane *kamme*.
Brutus· Meerely awry.
Corio., act iii., sc. 1, l. 304.

COLL. USE.
1875.

1. When he meets wi *cam* there's no good to be done.
2. It's clean *cam*, an' nowt else.

CAM, *v.* to wear awry : generally applied to a shoe.   Welsh *cam*,
crooked.

REV. W. GASKELL.
1854.

When I was a lad, an old cobbler, who mended
my shoes, used constantly to charge me with what he
called a sad trick of "*camming*" them, which meant
wearing them out of shape, either at the heel or at
the side.   *Lect. Lanc. Dialect*, 7.

COLL. USE.
1875.

He *cams* his shoon at th' heel.

CAM, *v.* to cross or contradict; to oppose vexatiously; to quarrel.
Welsh *cam*, sb. an injury; *camu*, to bend.

COLL. USE.
1875.

I'll *cam* him, an' get up his temper.

CAMMED (South Lanc.),   } *adj.* and *adv.* crooked; also, bad-
CAIMT (North and E. Lanc.), }   tempered, ill-natured.   W. *cam*,
crooked; *camu*, to bend.   A *cammed* nose in Mid. E. = a flat
nose.   Cf. "*campe* hores" = crooked rough hairs, *Early Eng.
Allit. Poems*, B, l. 1695.   Chaucer, in the *Reeves Tale* (l. 14), has
"round was his face, and *camois* was his nose," *i.e.* crooked or
curved was his nose; again, *Reeves Tale*, l. 54,

This wenche thikke and wel i-growen was,
With *camoys* nose, and eyghen gray as glas.

Cf. also, Morecambe Bay = the crooked sea bay; Cam, the
crooked river; Camden, the crooked wooded vale.

COLLIER.
1750.

Good lorjus deys ! it's not to tell heaw *camm'd*
things con happ'n !   *Works*, 61.

REV. W. GASKELL.
1854.

Cammed is an epithet which is often applied to a
temper that is not quite so even and straight as it
should be, as "Eh ! hoo's in a terrible *cammed*
humour to-day !"   *Lect. Lanc. Dialect*, p. 7.

WAUGH.
1875.

I doubt this bit o' supper hasn't agreed wi' tho
very weel, for thou'rt gettin' *camm'd* as a crushed
whisket.   *Old Cronies*, c. vi., p. 60.

CAMPERKNOWS, *sb.* ale pottage, in which are put milk, sugar, and spices.

CAMPLE (N. and S. E. Lanc.), } *v.* to retort, to contend. W. and
CEMPLE (E. Lanc.), } A.S. *camp,* Sw. *kamp,* a conflict.
W. *campio,* to strive at games ; Mid. E. *kempe,* to strive, to fight.
" There es no kynge undire Criste may *kempe* with hym one."
(Morte Arthure, 2633.) A.S. *cempa,* Mid. E. *kempe,* a soldier,
champion. Ger. *kampeln,* to debate, dispute.

WAUGH. 1867.	"Ger off witho, Ben, do!" replied Betty. "Thae'll ston here o' day *camplin* an' talkin thi stuff ! " *Owd Blanket,* c. i., p. 25.
IBID. 1875.	Then Nan lost no time, but coom back to hersel'; An' hoo *cample't* an' snapt, as no mortal can tell ; An' poor Tum o' Pobs soon found out that his wife, Though an angel at first, wur a divul for life. *Old Cronies,* c. v., p. 51.

CAMPLE, *sb.* a chat, a conversation.

WAUGH. 1867.	"Well," said she, "drop in some day th' next week, iv yor this gate on. Yo know aw've no neighbours to have a bit ov a *cample* to." *Tattlin Matty,* c. ii., p. 23.

CAMRIL, } *sb.* the lower part of a horse's leg. Cf. W.
CAMMEREL (Fylde), } *cambren,* a crooked stick. Mid. E. *gambrel,* a bent stick ; from *cam,* crooked.

COLL. USE. 1875.	Hit it o'er th' *camril* an it'll goo.

CANDLE-BARK (Fylde), } *sb.* a candle-box. See *Bark* in
CANNEL-BARK (N. Lanc.), } Brockett's Glossary.

CANK, *v.* to talk, to chatter. Cf. Icel. *kank,* gibes ; *kankast, v.* to jeer, gibe.

JOHN SCHOLES. 1857.	Peg Yep and me wur suyne awhoam, un mony o' pleasant *cank* win had o'er eawr jaunt, bith' fire-side sin. *Jaunt to see th' Queen,* p. 61.
B. BRIERLEY. 1869.	Well, aw'll just have a bit of a *cank* wi' thee, as theau maks so mich trouble. *Red Windows Hall,* c. xiv., p. 108.

CANKERT, *part.* ill-natured. Lat. *cancer.*

JOHN SKELTON. 1522.	He rages and he raues, And cals them *cankerd* knaves. *Poems:* "Why come ye nat to Courte?" l. 331.

WAUGH. 1866.	" Aw think hoo's a bit *cankert* is th' owd besom," said the landlord. "*Cankert?* Eh, aw think hoo is. Yo should hear her when she's in a tantrum " " Then her ailment hasn't touched her tung. like?" continued the landlord. "Tung! no ! Aw believe she'll talk in her coffin." *Ben an th' Bantam,* c. v., p. 78.

CANKIN'-PLECK, *sb.* a place to chat in.   **Cf.** A.S. *plæc,* a space.

COLLIER.
1750.

Boh here's a fine droy *canking-pleck* under this thurn.
Works, p. 41.

WAUGH.
1874.

Come, owd lad, let's wind a bit! There's a nice
conkin'-pleck bi th' side o' th' well, here. What
saysto!
Chimney Corner: Manchester Critic, May 2.

CANNEL-BONE (N. Lanc.), *sb.* the collar bone.

1272.

The squrd [sword] squappes in toe,
His *canel-bone* allsoe,
And clevet his schild clene.   *Met. Rom.,* p. 19

CANT, } *adj.* cheerful, lively, comfortable, chatty; very old but
CANTY, } in good health. **Mid.** E. *cant,* bold, vigorous.

LAURENCE MINOT.
1352.

þe King of Beme was *cant* and kene,
Bot þare he left both play and pride.
Sp. E. Eng., p. 137, l. 107.

1440.

A *kaunte* herte.   *Morte Arthure,* l. 2195.

BURNS.
1786.

Contented wi' little, and *cantie* wi' mair.
Poet. Works, Aldine Ed. ii., p. 253.

MISS LAHEE.
1865.

" Hoo's a gradely *cant* owd lass, an' can tell some
rum skits," says my mother.
Betty o' Yep's Tale, p. 3.

WAUGH.
1868.

The farmer's wife came to the door. She was
about sixty-five years of age; but she was a fine,
healthy, cheerful woman still . . . round, and
sound, and as fresh-coloured as a well-grown apple.
" Hoo is yon, sitho," said the old farmer, " hoo is
yon—as *cant* as a kitlin'."
Sneck-Bant, c. iv., p. 76.

CANTLE, *sb.* a canfull.

CANTLE, *sb.* a piece of anything.   **Mid.** E. *cantle,* O. F. *chantel,*
Dan. *kant,* an edge, border; It. *canto,* a side, corner. **Cf.** W. *cant,*
a rim or edge of a circle.

CHAUCER.
1386.

For nature hath nat take his bygynnyng
Of no partye ne *cantel* of a thing,
But of a thing that parfyt is and stable.
Knightes Tale, l. 2149.

FAIRFAX.
1600.

There armours forged were of metal frail,
On ev'ry side a massy *cantel* flies.   *Tasso,* vi., 48.

SHAKSPERE.
1598.

Hotspur . See, how this River comes me cranking in,
And cuts me from the best of all my land,
A huge halfe Moone, a monstrous *cantle* out.
First K. Hen. IV., iii. 1, 98.

IBID.
1623.

Scarus : The greater *cantle* of the world is lost
With very ignorance ; we have kist away
Kingdomes and provinces.
Ant. & Cleo., iii. 10, 4.

BEAUMONT & FLETCHER.
1600-1625.

Do you remember
The *cantel* of immortal cheese ye carried with ye ?
Queen of Corinth, ii.

CAP, } *v.* to out-do, to surpass, to astonish, to crown.   Cf. Welsh
COP, }   *cop,* top ; A.S. *copp, cop,* head, top.

| SHAKSPERE. 1600. | *Orleance :* Ill will never sayd well. *Constable of France :* I will *cap* that proverbe with, There is flatterie in friendship. *K. Hen. V.*, iii. 7, 123. |

| WAUGH. 1859. | Eawr Johnny gi's his mind to books ; Eawr Abram studies plants,— He *caps* the dule for moss an' ferns, An' grooin' polyants.   *Lanc. Songs,* p. 47. |

| IBID. 1865. | "Well," said Twitchel, "it *caps* o', iv th' maister's taen it into his yed to goo into th' jackass line !" *Besom Ben,* c. ii., p. 26. |

| MISS LAHEE. 1865. | Well, that *caps* o' at ever aw yerd. *Carter's Struggles,* p. 60. |

| DR. H. BARBER. 1870. | It's a queerly mannisht job, an *caps* many a yan. *Furness Folk,* 22. |

CAP-RIVER, *sb.* a termagant.   Lit. a cap-tearer.

| WAUGH. 1873. | He's a terrible hen-peckt chap, too, for their Sally's a gradely *cap-river* when hoo starts. *Chimney Corner : Manchester Critic,* May 17. |

CAPPEL, *sb.* a patch on a shoe.   Lit. a small cap.

| COLL. USE. 1875. | Nay, that shoe's noan done yet ; thae mun get a *cappel* put on it. |

CAPPER, *sb.* something which another cannot do ; something
which cannot be excelled.   See CAP.

| WAUGH. 1868. | "Well," said Betty, as she stirred the fire, after Ben had disappeared, "that's a *capper* of a tale, as heaw !"   *Sneck-Bant,* c. i., p. 9. |

| COLL. USE. 1875. | That's a *capper* for him, an' no mistake. |

CARKIN' *v.* to talk in an anxious or harassing manner ; pertina-
cious grumbling.   Welsh *carc,* care.

CARLIN'S, *sb.* boiled peas.   Brockett says, " In the North carlings
are served at table on the second Sunday before Easter, called
Carling Sunday, formerly denominated Care Sunday, as Care
Friday and Care Week were Good Friday and Holy Week ; supposed to be so called from being a season of great religious care
and anxiety."

CARR, *sb.* a marshy place ; a flat, low-lying land.   Dan. *kær,* a
marshy place.   Cf. Sc. *carse.*   See *N. and Q.* 4th s., vols. xi. and
xii. for discussion on *carr,* as connected with names of places in
the Northern counties and Lincolnshire.   There is a place called
Gatley *Carrs* a few miles south of Manchester.

CARRWATER, *sb.* red peaty water.

CARRY, *adj.* red, peaty.

CARRY-PLECK, *sb.* a place boggy with carrwater. Cf. A.S. *plæc*, a space.

CART-SWOE (Fylde), *sb.* the rut made by a cartwheel. Cf. A.S. *swæth*, a track.

CAT (E. Lanc.),
CATTY (N. Lanc.), } *sb.* a game played with a small piece of wood.

CATTER, *v.* to lay up money, to thrive. Cf. Sc. *cater*, money; Eng. *cater*, to provide; O. Fr. *acater;* Fr. *acheter*.

CAUSEY, *sb.* a sidewalk.

CAWVE (S. Lanc.),
CAWF (E. Lanc.), } *sb.* a calf.

COLLIER.
1750.

On me *kawve* (the dule bore eawt it een for meh) took th' tit for it mother, on woud need seawk her.
Works, p. 41.

B. BRIERLEY
1868.

Theau fastened on me like a clemmed leech, or as a hungry *cawve* does its moather.
Fratchingtons, c. iii., p. 35.

CECKLE (*c* hard), *v.* to retort impertinently; to laugh derisively. Lit. to cackle.

CECKLY (Mid. E. and S. Lanc.),
COCKLY (North Lanc.), } *adj.* unsteady, uneven.

CEFFLE (*c* hard), *v.* to cough slightly and sharply. A dimin. of *cough*.

CHAFF, *v.* to chew.

CHAFFS (N. Lanc.), } *sb. pl.* jaw bones. A.S. *ceaflas*, jaws; Icel.
CHUFFS (S. Lanc.), } *kjaptr*, the mouth, jaws; Dan. *kjæft*, jaw; Sanskr. *jambha*, the jaws. Mid. Eng. *chaft*, jaw; *chaft-ban*, jaw-bone.

CHANG (N. and E. Lanc.), *sb.* noisy talk.

CHAP, *sb.* a man; also a sweetheart. Mid. E. *chapman*.

DR. JOHN BYROM
1750.

For you are to consider, these critical *chaps*
Do not like to be snubb'd; you may venture, perhaps,
An amendment where they can see somewhat amiss;
But may raise their ill blood, if you circulate this.
Misc. Poems, vol. i., p. 214.

N. LANC. DIALECT.
1822.

Thear was ya *chap* weaven some red stript stuff, like Betty Dixon window cortans; and another *chap* was meakan a thing like a girt lang sile.
Lonsdale Magazine, iii., p. 339.

JOHN SCHOLES.
1857.

There wur women un' fellis, un lasses un their *chaps*.
Jaunt, p. 15.

WAUGH.
1874.

I geet croppen into th' kitchen, amung a rook o' *chaps* fro th' moor-ends.
Chimney Corner : Manchester Critic, Aug. 14

CHAPPIN', *sb.* courting ; applied to a woman.

> B. BRIERLEY.   "Matty," said he, " heaw is it theau's ne'er begun
> 1867.   o' *chappin* yet ? "   "What's that yo sen, Sam ? "
>   said Matty, without turning to her interrogator, as it
>   the question did not interest her.   "Heaw is it
>   theau's ne'er begun o' cooartin' ? "   "Nob'dy's ne'er
>   axt me ; that's heaw it is," was the ready and unex-
>   pected reply.   *Marlocks of Merriton,* p. 15.

CHAR, ⎱ *v.* to work at occasional jobs ; applied to house work.
CHARE, ⎰ A *chare* (not used in Lancashire as a *sb.*) is a turn of
work. A.S. *cyre,* a turn ; *cérran,* Du. *keeren,* to turn ; Gael. *car,*
turn, twist. Swiss, *es ist mi cheer,* it is my turn ; *cher um cher,* in
turns, turn about. See Wedgwood.

> TWELFTH CENTURY.   Wiken and *cherres* [= services and turns].
>   *O. E. Hom.,* First Series, p. 137.
>
> WEST-MID. DIALECT. Thou schal cheve to the grene chapel, thy *charres*
> 1320.   to make.   *Sir G. & G. Knight,* l. 1674.
>
> SHAKSPERE.   *Cleopatra :*   Commanded
> 1608.   By such poore passion as the maid that milkes
>   And does the meanest *chares.*
>   *Ant. & Cleop.,* iv. 15, l. 73.
>
> COLL. USE.   Hoo weshes for th' folk at th' Rectory, and *chars*
> 1875   for a day now and then.

CHAR, *v.* to stop or turn back. A.S. *cerran,* Mid. E. *cherren,* to
turn. To turn (cf. E. *churn)* is the primary meaning. Cf. *ajar,*
older form a-*char,* on-*char.*

> TWELFTH CENTURY.   Hwan ic a3en *cherre* [return].
>   *O. Eng. Hom.,* First Series, p. 79.
> WEST MID. DIAL. (Lanc.) Bi that I *charre* hider [= by that I return hither].
> 1320.   *Sir Gawayne & G. K.,* l. 1678.

CHAT (Mid. and E. Lanc.), *sb.* a small potato.

CHATS
CHATWOOD, ⎱ *sb.* small twigs for lighting fires.

CHATS, *sb.* the catkins of the maple and other trees. Cf. þe *chattes*
of hasele. *Voiage of Maundevile,* ed. Halliwell, p. 168. F. *chat,*
a cat. *Catkin* is the dimin. of *cat.*

CHATTER-BASKET, *sb.* an incessant talker ; gen. appl. to a child.

> COLL. USE.   Come, little *chatter-basket,* it's toime for bed.
> 1875.

CHASE (E. Lanc.), ⎱ *sb.* hurry.
CHASS (N. Lanc.), ⎰

> COLL. USE.   Wot are yo in sich a *chase* for ?
> 1875.

CHAW, ⎱ *v.* to chew. A.S. *ceówan,* Mid. E. *cheowen,* to chew. The
CHOW, ⎰ form *chaw,* says Nares, occurs in the version of the Bible

of 1611 (Ezek. xxix. 4, xxxviii. 4), but the spelling was altered without remark early in the eighteenth century. Dryden used both forms, *chaw* and *chew*.

1440.　　　*Chowynge* (or chewynge), masticacio.
　　　　　　　　　　　　　　　　　Prompt. Parv.

SPENSER.　　And next to him malicious Envie rode
1586.　　　Upon a ravenous wolfe, and still did *chaw*
　　　　　　Between his cankred teeth a venmous tode,
　　　　　　That all the poison ran about his chaw ;
　　　　　　And inwardly he *chawed* his own maw
　　　　　　At neighbours welth, that made him ever sad.
　　　　　　　　　　　　　F. Q. b. i., c. iv. st. 30.

IBID　　　This with sharpe teeth the bramble leaves doth lop,
　　　　　　And *chaw* the tender prickles in her cud.
　　　　　　　　　　　　　Virgil's Gnat, st. 11.

DRYDEN　　This pious cheat, that never sucked the blood
1700.　　　Nor *chawed* the flesh of lambs, but when he could.
　　　　　　　　　　　　　The Cock and the Fox, l. 484.

COLL. USE.　　What's to do ? Thae looks as if thae'd fair *chaw*
1875.　　　me up.

CHEAN (S. Lanc.), *sb.* a woollen warp.

CHEEP, *v.* to chirp ; to make a slight sound ; to tell only a little. Cf. Sc. *chieper*, a cricket.

WAUGH.　　Aw couldn't find i' heart or mind
1859.　　　To *cheep* o' weddin' for a while.
　　　　　　　　　　　Lanc. Songs　Bonny Nan, p. 64.

IBID　　　He'll sit by th' fire, hour after hour, an never
1867　　　*cheep*. But, eh, yo should yer him when he's had a
　　　　　　gill or two.—*Tattlin' Matty*, c. i., p. 10.

CHEWTER-YED (E. Lanc.),　⎫
CHOWTER-YED (Mid. Lanc.),⎬ *sb.* a blockhead.
　　　　　　　　　　　　　　⎭

CHIEVE, *v.* to prosper, to thrive, to succeed. Mid. E. *cheve*, from Fr. *chevir*, to compass, manage.

LANGLAND.　　And somme chosen chaffare ; they *cheven* the bettere,
1377.　　　As it semeth to owre sight that such men thryveth.
　　　　　　　　　　　　Piers Plowman : Prologue, l. 31.

CHAUCER.　　He took out of his oughne sleeve
1380.　　　A teyne of silver (evil mot he *cheeve !*)
　　　　　　　　　　Chanounes Yemannes Tale, l. 213.

CHIG (E. and N. Lanc.), *v.* to chew. Cf. W. *cegio*, to mouth ; Gael. *cagainn*, to chew.

COLL. USE.　　1. I've gin him sommat to *chig*.
1875.　　　2. Let him *chig* that.

CHIG (Fylde), *v.* to remove the stalks from gooseberries.

CHILDER,
CHILTHER, } *sb. pl.* children. A.S. *cild*, pl. *cildra*, sometimes *cildru.*

ORRMIN.
1200.

"Orrmin (whose book, the metrical paraphrase of the Gospels, is the most Danish poem ever written in England, that has come down to us) uses *chilldre* for the plural of *child*. Our corrupt plural *children* came from the south, as did also *brethren* and *kine*.
Oliphant's Standard English, pp. 93 and 102.

NORTHUMB. DIALECT.
1250.

Of mouth of *childer* and soukand
Made þow lof in ilka land
For þi faes. *Northumbrian Psalter*, Ps. viii., l. 5.
(Surtees Society.)

WEST MID. DIAL. (Lanc.)
1320.

Nay, frayst I no fyʒt, i fayth I þe telle,
Hit arn aboute on þis bench bot berdleʒ *chylder*.
Sir Gawayne & G. K., 279.

HAMPOLE.
1340.

Thay ere lyke unto the *childir* that rynnes aftere buttyrflyes. *Prose Treatises*, p. 39.

WYCLIF.
1380.

Forsothe the *childer*, wymmen, and the ʒeldingus wenten in, and tolden to hir. *Esther* iv. 4.

WAUGH.
1858.

God bless tho, my lass; aw'll go whoam,
An aw'll kiss thee an th' *childer* o' reawnd.
* * * * *
But aw've no gradely comfort, my lass,
Except wi' yon *childer* and thee.
Lanc. Songs: "Come whoam to thi childer an me," p. 7.

CHILDERS'-DAY (Fylde), *sb.* Innocents' Day.

CHILT,
CHOILT, } *sb.* pron. of Child.

WAUGH.
1855.

Besides, he's somebory's *chylt*, an' somebory likes him too, aw'll uphowd him.—*Lanc. Sketches*, p. 27.

JOHN SCHOLES
1857.

Then hoo clipt *chilt* in hur arms.—*Jaunt*, p. 59.

CHIMBLEY,
CHIMDY, } *sb.* a chimney.

WAUGH.
1859.

Tum Rindle lope fro' the *chimbley* nook
As th' winter sun wur sinkin.
Lanc. Songs: "Tum Rindle," p 69.

B. BRIERLEY.
1868.

A church wi a *chimdy* o'th top ud be moore i' thy road, aw think. *Fratchingtons*, c. iv., p. 48.

CHINCOUGH, *sb.* the whooping cough. Cf. Sw. *kik-hosta*, G *keich-husten*, Du. *kieck-hoest*, *kink-hoest*, the whooping cough, from the sharp *chinking* sound by which it is accompanied. To *chink* with laughter, to lose one's breath with laughter and make a crowing sound on recovering breath. *Wedgwood.*

COLL. USE.
1875.

Yo' mun tak him onto th' Whoite-Moss every day if yo' want'n t' cure him o' that *chin-cough*.

CHINK, *v.* to lose one's breath with coughing or laughter.

COLL. USE.
1875.

He fair *chinked* again.

CHIP (N. Lanc.), *v.* to trip a person up. Icel. *kippa*, W. *cipio*, to pull or snatch. Cf. Du. *kippen*, to seize.

CHITTER (E. and N. Lanc.), *v.* to talk quickly. A dimin. of *chatter.* Mid. E. *chiter*, to chirp as birds to.

<table>
<tr><td>WYCLIF.
1380.</td><td>These hethen men, the londe of which thou schalt welde, heren hem that worchen by *chiteryng* of briddys.   *Deut.* xviii. 14.</td></tr>
<tr><td>CHAUCER.
1386.</td><td>They may wel *chiteren*, as doon those jayes.
     *   *   *   *
But to her purpos schal thay never atteyne.
    Chanoune Yemannes Tale, l. 386.</td></tr>
<tr><td>1440.</td><td>*Chyteryn* as byrdys, supra in chaterynge.
    Prompt. Parv.</td></tr>
</table>

CHITTY (E. and N. Lanc.), *sb.* a cat ; also, the wren, commonly called Chitty-wer-wren.

CHITTY (S. Lanc.), *sb.* the lesser red-poll linnet. In Manchester and the suburbs it is also called the greybob.

CHITTY-FACE, *sb.* a child with soft sleek cheeks.

CHOCK, *sb.* a wedge for fastening the cart to the shafts.

<table>
<tr><td>COLL. USE.
1875.</td><td>Put thoose *chocks* in an' let's be gooin'.</td></tr>
</table>

CHOCK-FULL, *adv.* full to choking, *i.e.* to the cheeks. Mid. E. *cheke-ful*, choke-full, from A.S. *ceoce*, Mid. E. *cheke*, cheek.

<table>
<tr><td>1440.</td><td>Charotteȝ *chokkefulle* chargyde with golde.
    Morte Arthure, 1552.</td></tr>
<tr><td>COLL. USE.
1875.</td><td>He's *chock-full* o' nowtiness.</td></tr>
</table>

CHOLES, *sb. pl.* the jaws. A.S. *ceole*, the jaw, throat.

<table>
<tr><td>MIDLAND DIALECT.
1394.</td><td>Blowen bretfull of breþ, and as a bagge honged
On boþen his chekes, and his chyn wiþ a *chol* lollede
    Peres the Ploughman's Crede, 223.</td></tr>
<tr><td>1440.</td><td>Chavylbone or *chawl*-bone, mandibula.
    Prompt. Parv.</td></tr>
<tr><td></td><td>[See also, *Chaul, Alisaunder of Macedoine*, ed. Skeat, 1119; *Choule, Poems of John Audelev* [Shropshire, 1426], 77; *Chaules, Mapes Latin Poems*, ed. Wright, 338; *Chawleȝ, E. Eng. Allit. Poems*, c. 268 (West Mid. Dial., 1360).]</td></tr>
<tr><td>WAUGH.
1857.</td><td>Are yo noan flayed o' throwing yor *choles* off th' hinges ?—*Lanc. Sketches:* Bury to Rochdale, p. 30.</td></tr>
<tr><td>IBID.
1857.</td><td>Ay, it's a grand meawth ; and a rook o' th' prattiest teeth ut ever wur pegged into a pair o' *choles!*
Lanc. Sketches: Birthplace of Tim Bobbin, p. 80.</td></tr>
</table>

CHOM, CHOMP, *v.* to chew. E. *champ.*

> COLL. USE.
> 1875.
>
> He looks as if he wur awlus *chommin'* summut in his meawth.

CHOUP (N. Lanc.), *sb.* the bright red fruit of the dog-rose *(Rosa canina).*

> J. P. MORRIS.
> 1872.
>
> Her cheeks were rosy as a *choup,*
> Her een wi' luvv was breet.   *Maggie Bell.*

CHOVE, *v.* to wear by friction.

> COLL. USE.
> 1875.
>
> It's getten *choved* at th' edges.

CHOTTY, *sb.* a blockhead.

CHUCK, *sb.* a hen. Cf. E. *chick;* A.S. *cycen.*

> COLL. USE.
> 1875.
>
> Thoose *chucks* are i'th garden again.

CHUCK, *sb.* a term of affection for a child or a woman.

> SHAKSPERE.
> 1610.
>
> Be innocent of the knowledge, dearest *chuck.*
>   *Macbeth,* iii. 2, 45.

> COLL. USE.
> 1875.
>
> Come, my little *chuck,* let mammy put it to bed.

CHUCK, *v.* to throw.

> COLL. USE.
> 1875.
>
> Get into th' water, aw tell thi. If thae doesn't,
> a-v'll *chuck* thi in !

CHUFFIN-YED, *sb.* a blockhead.

> 1490.
>
> *Choffe* or *chuffe,* rusticus.—*Prompt. Parv.*

> NASH.
> 1592.
>
> That these men by their mechanicall trades should come to be sparage gentlemen and *chuff-headed* burghomasters.   *Pierce Penilesse.*

> SHAKSPERE.
> 1598.
>
> *Falstaff :* Are ye undone ? No, ye fat *chuffes ;* I would your store were heere.
>   *First K. Hen. IV.,* ii. 2, 93.

CHUNNER, *v.* to grumble in a low tone, to murmur.

> JOHN SCHOLES.
> 1857.
>
> Bob wur *chunnerin'* summut to hissel abeawt th' principul o' perpettyul motion.   *Jaunt,* p. 31.

CHURN (N. Lanc.), *sb.* the daffodil.

CHURN-GETTIN' (S. Lanc.), *sb.* a night feast after harvest.

> WAUGH.
> 1866.
>
> A company of haymakers, on their way home from a "*churn-gettin*"—as the hay-harvest supper is called—came up the road.
>   *Ben an th' Bantam,* c. vi., p. 118.

CHURN-MILK (S. Lanc.), *sb.* milk after the butter has been taken from it; buttermilk.

<table>
<tr><td>WAUGH.
1867.</td><td>There wur a chap stonnin' at a shop-dur, at th' side ov a mug-full o' churn-milk.
Owd Blanket, c. iii., p. 76.</td></tr>
<tr><td>COLL. USE.
1875.</td><td>"What has to had for thi dinner?" "Nowt but a 'tatoe and a sope o' churn-milk."</td></tr>
</table>

CHURN-SUPPER, *sb.*, an evening feast to celebrate the close of the hay harvest. See CHURN-GETTIN'.

<table>
<tr><td>WAUGH.
1868.</td><td>We're o' up to th' neck, gettin ready for th' churn-supper.
Sneck-Bant, c. iv., p. 81.</td></tr>
<tr><td>IBID.
1869.</td><td>The fiddler had been specially invited to enliven the rustic gathering which thronged the old house at Th' Nine Oaks Farm at the annual churn-supper, as the feast of the hay harvest is called in South Lancashire. The churn-supper at Nine Oaks was famous all over the Forest of Rossendale, no less on account of the number of the guests and the bounty of the cheer, than on account of the presence of a minstrel so well known and so universally welcome as Dan o' Tootlers was in those days.— Yeth-Bobs, c. i., p. 15.</td></tr>
</table>

CHURN-YED, *sb.* (pron. of Churn-head), a person of confused wits.

<table>
<tr><td>WAUGH.
1866.</td><td>Nea then, Twitch, has thae no moor sense nor botherin' wi' sich a churn-yed as that?
Ben an th' Bantam, c. v., p 97.</td></tr>
</table>

CHYLT-LITTLE, *sb.* childhood.

<table>
<tr><td>WAUGH.
1869.</td><td>In a bit, we wur as thick as iv we'd every one bin mates together fro' chylt-little.
Yeth-Bobs, c. ii , p. 34.</td></tr>
</table>

CIPHER, *sb.* an insignificant person; also, a name given to an assistant operative in a cotton mill.

CLAAK, *v.* to catch hold of, to clutch. Mid. E. *clechen, cleken.*

<table>
<tr><td></td><td>Sir Clegis clynges in and clekes another.
Morte Arthure, l. 1865.</td></tr>
</table>

CLACK, *v.* to chatter. Icel. *klaka*, to twitter, to chatter.

<table>
<tr><td>1225.</td><td>Þu clackest oft and longe.
Owl and Nightingale, l. 81.</td></tr>
<tr><td>COLL. USE.
1875.</td><td>Thae'rt clack clack, o' day lung.</td></tr>
</table>

CLACK, *sb.* continual chatter; a sharp sound, frequently repeated.

<table>
<tr><td>MISS LAHEE.
1865.</td><td>Wi' that mi mother ses to me, "Do howd thi clack, Betty." Betty o' Yep's Tale, p. 8.</td></tr>
</table>

CLAG (N. and E. Lanc.), *v.* to adhere. A.S. *clæg*, sticky earth, clay; Dan. *klæg, kleg*, loamy, sticky.

<table>
<tr><td>COLL. USE.
1875.</td><td>This bread's noan hauf baked; it clags i' mi meawth.</td></tr>
</table>

CLAM (N. Lanc.), *v.* to dry up, to clog up. A.S. *clám*, a bandage; also clay.

> WEST MID. DIAL. (Lanc.)
> 1360.
>
> And þenne *cleme* hit with clay comly withinne
> And al þe endentur dryuen daube withouten.
> *E. Eng. Allit. Poems* B, 1. 312.

CLAM-RATTAN (N. Lanc.), *adj.* app. to a farm where the soil is poor and unproductive. See CLEM.

CLAM-STAVE-AN'-DAUB, *sb.* a combination of clay or mud and sticks, used in the making of walls. A.S. *clam*, clay, and *stœf*, a staff or stick.

> REV. W. GASKELL
> 1854.
>
> *Clam-stave-an'-daub* still, in some parts of the county, denotes the rude walls (such as are found in the East, and referred to in the Scriptures as those which "thieves break through") made simply of mud and sticks. *Lect. Lanc. Dialect*, p. 18.

CLANTER (N. and S. Lanc.),⎫ *v.* to make a noise in walk-
CLUNTER (E., S., and Mid. Lanc.),⎭ ing.

> WAUGH.
> 1869.
>
> Every time that aw slipt, or gav a bit ov a *clunter* again a stone, he brast eawt again.
> *Yeth-Bobs*, ii. 33.

CLAP, *v.* to put a thing in a place; to pat. G. *klappen*, to do anything with a clap. To *clap* in E. is used in the sense of doing anything suddenly. (Wedg.) Icel. *klappa*, to pat, stroke gently.

> SHAKSPERE.
> 1593.
>
> The silly boy, believing she is dead,
> *Claps* her pale cheek, till *clapping* makes it red.
> *Venus and Adonis*, 467.

> IBID.
> 1597.
>
> *Mercutio:* Thou art like one of these fellowes, that when he enters the confines of a Taverne, *claps* me his Sword upon the Table, and sayes, God send me no need of thee. *Rom. and J.* iii., i. 6.

> WAUGH.
> 1869.
>
> It wur one o' th' leet horse, a fine yung chap as ever aw *clapt* een on. *Yeth-Bobs*, c. i., p. 22.

> COLL. USE.
> 1875.
>
> 1. He *claps* his hat deawn as if he belunged to th' place.
> 2. He's chokin'—*clap* his back.

CLAP-BREAD, *sb.* a thin cake of oatmeal unleavened. Also called haver-bread.

CLAP-CAKE, *sb.* The same as CLAP-BREAD.

CLARTY, *adj.* sticky; also filthy. Cf. Mid. E. *bi-clarten*, to defile. Cf. also, Du. *klad*, a stain, spot of dirt; *kladaig*, dirty, nasty, slovenly; E. *clot, clotty, clotted*, etc.

> NORTHUMB. DIALECT.
> 1330.
>
> Þat spatel þat swa bi*clarted* þi leor. [= That spittle that so defiled or besmeared thy face]
> *O. Eng. Hom.*, First Series, p. 279.

CLASHY (N. Lanc.), *adj.* wet and uncomfortable, as applied to weather.

> DR. BARBER.
> 1870.
> "Slashy weather, maister," I sed. "Ey, varra *clashy*," t' chap sed. *Forness Folk*, 39

CLAT (E. and Mid. Lanc.)} *sb.* tiresome talk. Cf. Du. *klatteren*, to
CLATE (S. Lanc.) } rattle.

CLATCH, }
CLUTCH, } *sb.* a brood of chickens. Icel. *klekja*, to hatch.

> WAUGH.
> 1868.
> It would ha' stode (wearied) a *clatch* of ducks.
> *Sneck-Bant*, c. i., p. 7.

CLAW (Fylde), }
CLEAW (S. and E. Lanc.), } *sb.* a floodgate in a watercourse.
CLOOSE (N. Lanc.), } From Lat. *claudere*.
CLOW (E. and Mid. Lanc.), }

> 1220.
> Water et ter mulne *cluse* [= water at the mill-dam.]
> *Ancren Riwle*, ed. Morton, p. 72.

> 1440.
> *Clowys*, water schedynge (*clowse*, watyrkepyng ; *clowse*, water shettinge). *Sinogloatorium.*
> *Prompt. Parv.*

CLAWK (E. and Mid. Lanc.), *v.* to scratch. From Mid. E. *claw*, to scratch, or tickle. As in Second King Hen. IV. (act ii., sc. 4, l. 281), the Prince says of Falstaff, "Looke, if the wither'd elder hath not his poll *claw'd* like a parrot."

CLEAN, *adv.* entirely.

> BIBLE.
> 1610.
> Is his mercy *clean* gone for ever ?
> *Psalm* lxxvii. 8.

> WILLIAM MORRIS.
> 1868.
> Then loud they shouted, *clean* forgetting fear.
> *Jason*, p. 113.

> COLL. USE.
> 1875.
> Aw his brass is *clean* gone.

CLEAVIN' (Cartmel), *sb.* the last furrow in ploughing.

CLECK, } *sb.* a small catch, designed to fall into the notch of a
CLICK, } wheel ; also a door-latch. Cf. G. *klinke*, *klinge*, a latch. Fr. (patois of the Hainault), *cliche*, a latch. See Wedgwood, Click ; Clicket. Cf. W. *clicied*, a clicket, latch, catch ; Suio-Goth. *klinka*, a door-bolt ; Du. *klink*, a latch.

> LANGLAND.
> 1377.
> For he hath þe keye and þe *cliket*.
> *Piers Plowman*, B-text, v. 1. 613.

> CHAUCER.
> 1386.
> This freissche May, that I spak of so yore,
> In warm wex hath emprynted the *cliket*,
> That January bar of the smale wiket,
> With which into hys gardyn ofte he wente,
> And Damyan, that knew al hir entente,
> The *cliket* counterfeted prively ;
> Ther nys no more to saye, but hastily
> Som wonder by this *cliket* schal betyde,
> Which ye schal heeren. if ye wol abyde.
> *Marchaundes Tale*, 1 872.

CLECK, } *v.* to catch at hastily. Cf. A.S. *ge-læccan*, to catch,
CLICK, } seize.

About 1400.	Thenne Sir Gaẇan bi the coler, *clechis* the knyȝte.
	E. Eng. Met. Romances, p. 23.
1440.	He *clekys* owthe Collbrande fulle clenlyche burneschte.
	Morte Arthure, l. 2123.

Miss Lahee.	Hoo *cleekt* howd o' mi hond, an' away we seet to
1865.	ir heause. *Betty o' Yep's Tale*, p. 3.
Dr. Barber.	She *clickt* t' glass off teeable an' wod gie him nowte.
1870.	*Forness Folk*, p. 33.

CLEG, *sb.* the gadfly.   Icel. *kleggi*, the horse-fly.

| Coll. Use (E. L.) | Hoo sticks like a *cleg*, an' will hev it. |
| 1875. | |

CLEM (S. Lanc.),   } *v.* to starve from want of food.
CLAM (E., Mid., and N. Lanc.), } Du. *klemmen*, to pinch; O. L.
Ger. (bi-)*klemman ;* O. H. Ger. (bi-)*chlemmen*, to clam ; Du.
kleumen, to be benumbed with cold.

West Mid. Dial. (Lanc.)	Ne best bite on no brom, ne no bent nauþer,
1360.	Passe to pasture, ne pike non erbes,
	Ne non ox to no hay, ne no horse to water ;
	Al schal crye for-*clemmed*.
	E. Eng. Allit. P., C, l. 392.

Ben Jonson.	Hard is the choice
1599.	When valiant men must eat their arms or *clem*.
	Every Man out of his Humour, iii , 6.

Massinger.	My intrails
1620.	Were *clamm'd* with keeping a perpetual fast.
	Roman Actor, ii., 2.

Lees & Coupe.	Booath *clemmin*, un starvin, un never a fardin,
1790.	It ud welly drive ony man mad.
	Harland's Lanc. Ballads : " Jone o'
	Grinfilt," p. 217.

Gibson.	We s' niver, I's insuer us,
(Dialect of High Furness.)	Be neeàkt or *clemm'd* or càld.
1866.	*Folk-Speech Cumb.*, p. 86.

Waugh.	There's a brother o' mine lives wi' us ; he'd a been
1867.	*clemmed* into th' grave but for th' relief.—*Factory Folk*
	during the Cotton Famine, c x., p. 92.

| B. Brierley. | Theau fastened on me like a *clemmed* leech. |
| 1868. | *Fratchingtons*, c iii , p. 35. |

CLEWKIN, *sb.* twine, string.   A.S. *cliwe*, a clew, hank ; Mid. E.
cleowe.

B. Brierley.	Aw've nowt nobbut a shillin', an' some copper, an'
1867.	a knife, an' a bit o' *clewkin*.
	Marlocks of Merriton, c. ii., p. 28.

CLEWKIN'-GRIN, *sb.* a game-snare, made of twine. *Clewkin*
(which see), and A.S. *grin*, a snare.   A *grin* is the true Mid. E.
form ; corrupted to *gin*, from confusion with *engine*.

| Collier. | He throttlt eawr poor Teawzer in o *clewkin-grin*. |
| 1750. | *Works*, p. 44. |

CLICK, *sb.* a blow. "We have the notion of a short quick movement in E. dial. *click, clink,* a smart blow." (Wedgwood). Cf. Du. *klink,* a blow.

COLL. USE.
1875.

Be quiet, or thae'll get a *click* i'th ear-hole.

CLIM, *v.* to climb. See CLOM.

COLL. USE.
1875.

He *clim* up th' broo an' wur off like a redshank.

CLINKER, *sb.* a strong nail for shoes. Cf. Du. *klinken,* to rivet.

BAMFORD.
1850.

[In Tim Bobbin's time, 1750, the men wore] very strong shoes, nailed with *clinkers,* and fastened by straps and buckles.
Intro. to Ed. of Tim Bobbin, p. viii.

WAUGH.
1865.

His feet were sheathed in a pair of *clinkered* anclejacks, as heavy, and nearly as hard, as iron.
Besom Ben, c. i., l. 6.

IBID.
1869.

"Aw'm beawn to a churn-supper at Th' Nine Oaks," said the fiddler. "Th' dule theaw art!" replied Ben "Eh, thae will tickle yon owd *clinkert* shoon o' theirs up aboon a bit!"
Yeth-Bobs, c. i., l. 16.

CLINKER, *sb.* a hard metallic cinder. Du. *klinker,* a brick.

COLL. USE.
1875.

His grate bars are o' full o' *clinkers.*

CLIP, *v.* to embrace; to cling round the neck. A.S. *clyppan,* to embrace, clasp, make much of, admire. Mid. E. *clippen;* Icel. *klypa,* to clasp.

About 1196.

The whiche reverently he *clyppyd* to hym, and with coffis and terys watryd the fete of the crosse
Revelation to Monk of Evesham.
Arber's Reprint, p. 25.

ANON.
1350.

Þe cherl ful cherli þat child tok in his armes,
And kest hit and *clipped.*
William of Palerne, Sp. E. Eng. p. 140, l. 62.

CHAUCER.
1386.

For whiche ful oft ech of hem seyde, "O swete! *Clippe* Ich yow thus, or elles I it meete."
Troylus and Crysede, Bk. ii., l. 1294.

SHAKSPERE.
1608.

O, let me *clip* ye
In arms as sound as when I woo'd.
Corio. I., vi., l. 29

SHELLEY.
1821.

As a dying meteor stains a wreath
Of moonlight vapour, which the cold night *clips,*
It flushed through his pale limbs, and passed to its eclipse.   *Adonais,* st. xii.

WAUGH.
1871.

He's gone! he's gone!
Aw'm lonely under th' sky!
He'll never *clip* my neck again
An' tell me not to cry.
Lanc. Songs : Willy's Grave.

G

CLIPPINS, *sb. pl.* something cut off; used in Lancashire as applied to wool. Icel. *klippa*, to cut, clip, shear; *klipping*, a shearing; *klippingr*, a shorn sheepskin. Dan. *klippe*, to cut.

> BAMFORD.
> 1864.
>
> Whilst Sir John Cop' mun sit at top,
> Upon a seck o' *clippins*.
> *Homely Rhymes*, p. 136.

CLIT-CLAT, *sb.* a noise made by a talkative person. Cf. Du. *klikklak*, the clashing of swords.

> COLL. USE.
> 1875.
>
> Aw con yur (hear) his *clit-clat* gooin' on yet, as if he'd only just started.

CLOAK'N (S. Lanc.),
COAKIN (E. Lanc.), } *sb.* the sharp part or cramp of a horse-shoe. E. *calkin*.

> SHAKSPERE & FLETCHER.
> About 1612.
>
> On this horse is Arcite,
> Trotting the stones of Athens, which the *calkins*
> Did rather tell [*i.e.* count] than trample.
> *Two Noble Kinsmen*, ed. Skeat, act v, sc. 4, l. 54.
>
> W. W. SKEAT.
> 1875.
>
> *Calkins*, the parts of a horseshoe which are turned up and pointed to prevent the horse from slipping. Also spelt *cawkins* and *calkers*. It is the diminutive of A.S. *calc*, a shoe, a word probably borrowed from the Lat. *calceus*. Florio explains the Italian rampone as "a *calkin* in a horse's hoof to prevent him from slipping."
> *Note on above passage in new edition.*
>
> COLL. USE.
> 1875.
>
> Th' mare up wi hur *coakin*, an knockt it deawn.

CLOCK, *sb.* a beetle : generally used with a descriptive prefix, as bracken-clock, black-clock, twitch-clock, and so forth. The entry "*chuleich*, scarabæus" occurs in an Old High Germ. gloss. See Garnett's *Essays*, p. 68. No such word as *clock* is to be found in A.S. dictionaries.

> COLL. USE.
> 1875.
>
> Lanc. Proverb : If yo kill a *clock*, it'll rain to-morn.

CLOCKS, *sb. pl.* ornaments woven into a stocking.

> BAMFORD.
> 1850.
>
> He's stockin's wi' *clocks*.
> *Ed. of Tim Bobbin*, p. 149.
>
> COLL. USE.
> 1875.
>
> Young Girl *loq.* : Eh ! but I like *clock*-stockin's.

CLOD, *sb.* the ground. Cf. Dan. *klat*, a bit of ground.

> WAUGH.
> 1857.
>
> We asked him whether the spot we were upon was Grislehurst ; and he replied, "Yo're upo' th' very *clod*."—*Lanc. Sk.* : Grave of Gris. Boggart, p. 204.
>
> IBID.
> 1865.
>
> " Th' dog would ha' toucht noan o' thee, iv thae'd bin upo' thi own *clod*," said Sally. "Who arto ?"
> *Besom Ben*, c. v. p. 54.

CLOD, *v.* to throw missiles. Originally *clod* = clot, a lump ; then to throw a lump of something.

> WAUGH.
> 1867.
>
> "Mistress, dun yo know at yo'n laft a mug eawt ?"
> "Eh, ay," hoo says, "aw have." "Well," he said ;

COLL. USE.
1875.

"hadn't yo better tak it in ? There's a rook o' chaps bin *cloddin'* at it."—*Tattlin' Matty*, ii., l. 19.

"Jem, does ta know yon felly ?" "Now [no]."
"Then *clodd* a stone at him."

CLOG, *sb.* a shoe with a wooden bottom. Cf. G. *klotz*, a block, log ; *klotz-schuh*, a wooden shoe ; Wedgwood.

LANC. BROADSIDE.
About 1830.

To Lunnon aw'll walk, wi meh *clogs* on meh feet.
Bal. and Songs of Lanc. p. 174 :
Jone o' Grinfilt.

RAMSBOTTOM.
1864.

Doff thi *clogs* and warm thi feet.
Lanc. Rhymes, p. 41.

CLOM,
CLOMB,
CLŌME, } *v.* climbed.
CLUM,

CHAUCER.
1384.

But up I *clombe* with alle payne.
House of Fame, bk. iii., l. 28.

MILTON.
1667.

So *clomb* this first grand thief into God's fold.
Paradise Lost, iv., l. 192.

WILLIAM MORRIS.
1868.

So when she had *clomb* up the slippery bank
And let him go, well nigh adown she sank.
Jason, p. 17.

REV. W. GASKELL.
1854.

The Lancashire dialect has been peculiarly reten-tive of the Anglo-Saxon preterite, generally preferring the strong conjugation to the weak. A Lancashire man does not say " he climbed a hill," but he " *clom* " it.—*Lect. Lanc. Dialect*, p 24.

COLL. USE.
1875.

He *clomb* o'er th' wall, an' set off loike leetnin'.

CLOMP, } *v.* to make a noise in walking. Cf. Du. *klomp*, a log, a
CLUMP, } clog, a wooden shoe.

REV. W. GASKELL.
1854.

Dost think at aw's ha nowt for t'do, bo go *clumpin'* up an deawn a-seechin' yore Tummus ?
Lect Lanc. Dialect, p. 29.

JOHN SCHOLES.
1857.

Deawn stairs aw *clompt* i' mi clogs, o' purpose to ma' Peggy yer [hear] ut aw wur gettin' mi ready.
Jaunt, p. 14.

CLOOAS (S. Lanc.),
CLEEAZ (N. Lanc.), } *sb. pl.* Pron. of clothes.

COLLIER.
1750.

As I'r donning meh thwooanish [wet] *clooas*.
Works, p. 55.

LANC. BROADSIDE.
About 1816.

Eawr Marget declares, if hoo'd *clooas* to put on,
Hoo'd go up to Lunnun to see the great mon.
Ball. and Songs of Lanc.: Jone o' Grinfilt
Junior, p. 172.

WAUGH.
1859.

So aw iron't o' my *clooas* reet weel,
An aw hanged 'em o'th maiden to dry.
Songs : Come whoam to thi' Childer.

DR. BARBER.
1870.

He donn't some sailor's *cleeaz* an watch't at back of a dyke till full seea.
Forness Folk, p. 50.

CLOOF, *sb.* a clough, a wooded ravine.   Icel. *klofi*, a cleft or rift in a hill closed at the upper end.   Mid. E. *clough.*

1440.   The cragge with *cloughes* fulle hye.
                                                Morte Arthure, 941.

WAUGH.   "A jackass!" cried Jem.   "Wheer han yo let o'
1865.   this?"   "We fund it powlerin abeawt i' th' *cloof,*
                yon," replied Enoch.   *Besom Ben,* v., p. 59.

CLOT-YED (South Lanc.),   ⎱ *sb.* a lout, a stupid fel-
CLOT-HEEAD (Mid., E., and N. Lanc.),   ⎰ low.   Cf. Du. *kloet,*
a pole ; also, a booby.   Dan. *klods,* a log ; also, a lout.

COLL USE.   Let it abee, tha greyt *clot-yed.*
1875.

CLOUDBERRY, *sb. Rubus chamæmorus,* which grows on Pendle— a semi-arctic plant, which Prof. Forbes considered to belong to the glacial era.   See Murray's *Handbook for Lancashire,* p. 220.

PHILEMON HOLLAND.   But when Ribell commeth into Lancashire . . .
1601.   Pendelhill advanceth itselfe up to the skie with a
                      loftie head, and in the very top thereof bringeth forth
                      a peculiar plant which, as though it came out of the
                      clowdes, they tearme *clowdes-bery.—Trans. of Cam-
                      den's Britain* (ed. of 1637), p. 749.

CLOUT, *v.* to strike or beat.   Du. *klotsen,* to strike.

COLL. USE.   Aw'll *clout* thi yed for thi if thae'rt not off.
1875.

CLOUT, *sb.* a cuff or blow with the hand.

1440.   That he na gafe hym swylke a *clowte.*
                                        Thornton Romances, p. 113.

SHAKSPERE.   *Scarus :* O my brave Emperor, this is fought indeed,
1608.   Had we done so at first, we had droven them home
                      With *clowts* about their heads.
                                        Ant. and Cleo., iv., sc. 7, 4.

COLL. USE.   Give him a *clout,* mon, an' ha' done wi' it.
1875.

CLOUT, *sb.* a piece of cloth used for domestic purposes, as dish-clout ; a patch of leather or iron.   A.S. *clût,* a little cloth ; Mid. E. *clout, clutian, clutien,* to patch.   Icel. *klutr,* a kerchief. Dan. *klud.*   Welsh *clwt.*

1280.   A kevel [= gag] of *clutes.*   *Havelok,* 547.
LANGLAND.   They wesshen hym and wyped hym and wonden hym
1377.   in *cloutes.*   *Piers Plowman,* B-text, ii., l. 220.
1440.   *Clowte* of cloth (cloute or ragge), scrutum, panni-
                culus, pannucia.   *Clowte* of a schoo [= shoe], pic-
                tasium.   *Prompt. Parv.*

                                        A *clout* about that head
SHAKSPERE.   Where late the Diadem stood, and for a Robe
1603   About her lanke and all ore-teamed Loines,
                A blanket.   *Hamlet,* ii. 2, l. 529.

SHAKSPERE.
1612.

I thought he slept, and put
My *clowted* Brogues from off my feete, whose rudenesse
Answered my steps too lowd.
Cymbeline, iv. 2, l. 213.

MILTON.
1634.

The dull swain
Treads on it daily with his *clouted* shoon.
Comus, l. 634.

WAUGH.
1869.

A tattered *clout* may lap
A very noble prize ;
A king may be, by hap,
A beggar i' disguise.
Lanc. Songs : God bless thi Silver Yure !

WAUGH.
1875.

I doubt there's moore *clout* than dinner about this
tale o' thine. *Old Cronies*, c. vii., p. 67.

CLOUT-NAIL, *sb.* a large nail, used for fixing iron clouts on the wooden axle-trees of carts.

CLOZZUM, *v.* to embrace, to hold fast, to clutch.

CLOZZUMS, *sb. pl.* talons, embraces, clutches.

CLUDDER,) *v.* to crowd or heap together. Welsh *cludair*, a pile,
CLUTTER,) a heap ; *cludeirio*, to heap together ; A.S. *clúd*, a little hill.

REV. W. GASKELL.
1854.

In Lancashire, when things are heaped higgledy-piggledy, it is common to say "they're aw in a *clutter*," or, " they're aw *cluttered* together."
Lect. Lanc. Dialect, p. 11.

J. P. MORRIS
1867.

O' t' poor wimmin i' t' town *cludder'd* round about
'em wi' basens, pots, an cans of o' kinds.
Invasion o' U'ston, p. 5.

COLL. USE.
1875.

Th' fields are aw *cluttert* wi' daisies.

CLUNCH, *sb.* a clodhopper or boor. Cf. Dan. *klunt*, Du. *klont*, a log.

COTGRAVE.
1611.

Casois, a country clown, boore, *clunch*, hinde.
French Dictionary.

CLUNTER-YED, *sb.* a stupid fellow. See above.

COAK (E. and Mid. Lanc.),)
COWK (S. Lanc.),) *v.* to strain, to vomit.

COLLIER.
1750.

I con heardly tell the, I'm so whaugish [= faint,
sickly], for I'm ready t' *cowk'n* with th' thowts ont.
Works, p. 45.

COB, *v.* to excel, to surpass. A.S. *cop*, a cap, top ; W. *cop*, a top.

REV. W. GASKELL.
1854.

A common expression in Lancashire is, " that *cobs*
aw," which is equivalent to " that beats everything,"
—the same idea. *Lect. Lanc. Dialect*, p. 8.

COB, *v.* to catch, to take hold of.

COLL. USE.
1875.

Cob howd of it mon, and dunna shoo it into th'
water.

COB, *v.* to strike, to throw. In Mid. Lanc. to thrash, applied to the master's punishment of boys at school. Welsh *cob*, a knock, thump ; *cobio*, to knock, thump.

REV. W. GASKELL.
1854.

> When boys are throwing stones, you may often hear them say "give o'er *cobbin*."
>
> *Lect. Lanc. Dialect*, p. 8.

JOHN SCHOLES.
1857.

> Aw'll *cob* him into th' steyme wayter th' furst toime ut aw catch him gooin' o courtin' up yon lone.
>
> *Jaunt*, p. 18.

COB, *sb.* something round, as a *cob* of coal, a *cob* of bread. Welsh *cobyn*, a bunch, cluster.

REV. W. GASKELL.
1854.

> Lancashire men call a round lump of coal a "*cob* of coal," and distinguish the larger pieces from the small as "*cob*-coal." *Lect. Lanc. Dialect*, p. 8.

WAUGH.
1859.

> Aw've just mended th' fire wi a *cob*.
>
> *Lanc. Songs*. "Come Whoam."

COBBLE-STONE, *sb.* a rounded stone.

—

> My Gammer sure intends to be uppon her bones,
> With staves or with clubs, or else with *coble-stones*.
> *Gammer Gurton's Needle*, ii , sc. 5.

COCKERS, *sb. pl.* stockings ; hose without feet. A.S. *cocer*, a sheath ; Du. *koker*, a sheath, case, quiver.

WEST-MID. DIAL.
1360.

> With rent *cokre3*, at the kne.
>
> *E. Eng. Allit. Poems*, B, l. 40.

LANGLAND.
1377.

> And cast on me my clothes yclouted and hole,
> My *cokeres* and my coffes for colde of my nailles.
> *Piers Plowman*, B-text, vi , l. 61.

1440.

> *Cocur*, boote. Ocrea, coturnus.—*Prompt. Parv.*

BROCKETT.
1829.

> There is a small place not far from Bolton, called Duff-*Cocker*, where, my friend Mr. Turner informs me, it used to be the fashion for the country people who came from church or market to pull off their stockings, and walk barefoot home.
> *Gloss. North Country Words*, p. 101.

COCKLE, *v.* to wrinkle. Properly, like *coggle*, *joggle*, to shake or jerk up and down, then applied to a surface thrown into hollows and projections by partial shaking, by unequal contraction. A *cockling* sea is one jerked up into short waves by contrary currents. (Wedgwood.)

COLL. USE.
1875.

> It's poor stuff—it'll *cockle* th' first time thae gets it rained on.

COD, *sb.* a husk, a pod of peas or beans. A.S. *codd*, a scrip, small bag ; Sw. *kudde*, a sack, bag, pod ; Icel. *koddi*, a pillow ; Welsh *côd*, *cwd*, a bag or pouch.

CODDLE, *v.* to make much of, to pet, to over-nurse ; also, to parboil.

COKE (N. and E. Lanc.) *sb.* the pith of anything ; the core of a fruit. Du. *kolk,* a pit, hollow, whirlpool ; cf. Gael. *caoch,* empty, hollow.

HAMPOLE.
1340.

Alle erthe by skille may likend be
Til a rounde appel of a tre,
That even in myddes has a *colke.*
Pricke of Conscience, l. 6443.

YORKSHIRE DIAL.
1450.

Tille an appylle she is lyke,
    *   *   *   *   *
It is full roten inwardly,
At the *colke* within.   *Townley Mysteries,* 281.

COLLOCK, *sb.* a large pail. Cf. Icel. *kolla,* a pot or bowl without feet.

COLLOP, *sb.* a slice, a rasher of bacon. Mr. Wedgwood says : " From *clop* or *colp,* representing the sound of a lump of something soft thrown on a flat surface. Du. *klop,* It. *colpo,* a blow." Cf. Sw. *klappa,* Du. *kloppen,* .to beat. But the word occurs in Old Swedish. Ihre says—" *Kollops,* edulii genus, confectum ex carnis fragmentis, tudite lignea probe contusis et maceratis."

LANGLAND.
1377.

I have no salt bacoun
Ne no kokeney, bi cryst, *coloppes* for to maken.
Piers Plowman, B-text, vi., l. 286.

SHAKSPERE.
1592.

Fye, Joan, that thou wilt be so obstacle :
God knowes, thou art a *collop* of my flesh.
First Hen. VI. v., 4, l. 17.

BIBLE.
1610.

Because he covereth his face with his fatness, and maketh *collops* of fat on his flanks.—*Job.* xv. 27.

WAUGH.
1859.

There's some nice bacon *collops* o'th hob,
An' a quart o' ale-posset i' th' oon.
Lanc. Songs : " Come Whoam."

HARLAND.
1867.

Originally, *collops* were simply slices of bread, but these were long ago discarded for slices or rashers of bacon.—*Lanc. Folk-Lore,* p. 217.

COLLOP-MONDAY, *sb.* the Monday before Lent.

HARLAND.
1867.

In Lancashire and other Northern counties. three days in Shrovetide week had their peculiar dishes ; viz.. *Collop Monday,* Pancake Tuesday, and Fritters Wednesday.—*Lanc. Folk-Lore,* p. 217.

COLLYWEST, *adj.* in the other way, or opposite direction ; entirely wrong ; contrary. This is said, in Hartshorne's Salopia Antiqua, to have a proverbial reference to Colley Weston, in Northamptonshire.

COLL. USE.
1875.

Never mind him ; he ne'er agrees wi' onybody ; he's awluz *collywest.*

COM,
COOM, } *v.* came. A.S. *com,* pt. t. of *cuman : Ic com,* I came.

LANGLAND.
1362.

Beestes that now ben mouwen banne the tyme
That evere that cursede caym *com* upon eorthe.
Piers Plowman, A-text, x., l. 165.

REV. W. GASKELL
1854.

A Lancashire man does not say he " came," but he " coome."   *Lect. Lanc. Dialect,* p. 24.

COME-AT, *v.* to come near.

> COLL. USE.　　　　Howd back! Let me *come-at* him.
> 1875.

COME-BY, *v.* to obtain; also, obtained, won.

> COLL. USE.　　　　Aw his brass hez bin honestly *come-by*.
> 1875.

COMFORTABLE, *sb.* a woollen wrapper for the throat.

COMM, *v.* to comb.　A.S. *cemban,* Mid. E. *kemben,* to comb.

> COLL. USE.　　　　Wesh thi face an' *comm* thi yure.
> 1875.

COMN, *v. pl. and pp.* come, as "they are comn.'

> WAUGH.　　　　Aw've just time to gi' tho another bit ov a ditty
> 1868.　　　　afore we *comn* to yon heawse.　What's it to be?
> 　　　　　　　　　　　　　　*Sneck-Bant,* c. iv., p. 70.

CON (N. Lanc.), *sb.* a squirrel.　Cf. E. *coney,* a rabbit.

> NORTH LANC. DIALECT.　Our young friend dissipated our fears by telling us
> 1821.　　　　that *con* was only the provincial name for a squirrel.
> 　　　　　　　　　　　　　*Lonsdale Magazine,* ii., 124.

CONDLE, *v.* to get angry.

CONNY (N. Lanc.), *adj.* large; app. to quantity or size.

> J. P. MORRIS.　　There's a *conny* lock on 'em thrang i' t' hay-field
> 1869.　　　　owerbye.　　　　　*Furness Gloss.,* p. 21.
>
> DR. BARBER.　　Jim had suppt a *conny* lot, but he was nin soft.
> 1870.　　　　　　　　　　　　　*Forness Folk,* p 4.

CONNY (North and East Lanc.), *adj.* handsome, good-looking, agreeable, snug, clever, knowing.　Cf. Icel. *konr,* royal; A.S. *cyne,* royal, gentle.　Some of the meanings are to be referred to the root *ken,* to know.　Cf. Sc. *canny.*

> COLL. USE (N. Lanc.)　Ay, he's a gay *conny* fella, an' th' lasses like him
> 1875.　　　　weel.

COOTER, *sb.* Pron. of coulter, a ploughshare.

COOTH,
COWTH, } *sb.* a cold.　A.S. *coth, cotha,* disease, sickness.

> 1150.　　　　*Cothe* other qualm.
> 　　　　　　　　　　　*Old Eng. Hom.,* Second Series, 1. 177.
>
> 1440.　　　　*Cothe,* syncope.　　　　　*Prompt. Parv.*

COP, *sb.* the top or head of anything.　A.S. *copp,* W. *cop,* the head, top, apex.　O. Fris. *kop,* the head.

> DORSET DIALECT.　From the tures *coppe.*　　　*Ancren Riwle,* 1. 228.
> 1220.
> WYCLIF.　　　The *coppis* of the hillis.　　　*Genesis,* c. 8.
> 1380.
> CHAUCER.　　Upon the *cop* right of his nose he hade
> 1386.　　　　A werte.　　　*Prologue to Cant. Tales,* 1. 554.
>
> IBID.　　　　Thoo gan I up the hille to goone
> 　　　　　　　And fonde upon the *cop* a woone.
> 　　　　　　　　　　　　　*House of Fame,* iii., 75.
>
> BEN JONSON.　　Marry she's not in fashion yet; she wears a hood,
> 1610.　　　　but 't stands *a-cop.*　　　*Alchemist,* ii., 6.

COP, *sb.* a small oval-shaped bundle of spun cotton thread, prepared in that form for the manufacturer of cloth. W. *cob*, a tuft.

COPPY, *sb.* a small field.

> DR. BARBER. 1870.
>
> He hed a bull-*coppy* i' t' front o' t' house, reet afoar t' winda, but bars went across to keep t' bull frae brekkin it. *Forness Folk*, p. 44.

COPPY-STOOL (N. and E. Lanc.), *sb.* a small stool for children.

COPSTER, *sb.* a spinner. See COP. Cf. W. *cob*, a tuft; also, a spider.

CORBY, *sb.* a carrion crow; the raven. Mid. E. *corbyal;* Lat. *corvus;* Icel. *korpr;* Swed. *korp;* O. Fr. *corbel.*

> WEST MID. DIAL. (Lanc.) 1360.
>
> That wat3 the raven so ronk that rebel wat3 ever ;
> He was colored as the cole, *corbyal* untrue.
> *E. Eng. Allit. Poems*, B. 1. 455.

> GAWIN DOUGLAS. 1513.
>
> Quhil *corby* gaspyt for the fervent heit.
> *Prol. Æneid*, Bk. xii., l. 174.

CORN-BOGGART, *sb.* a scarecrow, set up to frighten birds from the wheat.

> WAUGH. 1874.
>
> It'd make a rare *corn-boggart !* There's no gradely brids i' this world 'at durst come within hauve a mile o' thoose brids 'at's i' that pictur !
> *Chimney Corner : Manchr. Critic*, Feb. 27.

COST'N, *ind. pl.* of the verb Cost.

COSTRIL, *sb.* a small barrel. Mid. E. *costrelle*, a small barrel.

> CHAUCER. 1386.
>
> And therwithal a *costrel* taketh he tho
> And seyde, " Hereof a draught, or two,
> Yife hym to drynke whan he gooth to reste."
> *Legende of Goode Women;* Ypermystre, 105.

COTTER, *sb.* a blow.

> COLL. USE. 1875.
>
> Aw gan him such a *cotter* as he'll noan forget.

COTTER, *v.* to drive with blows.

> MISS LAHEE. 1865.
>
> Beawt moor ado aw *cotter'd* th' cat out.
> *Carter's Struggles*, p. 24.

COTTER, *v.* to fasten, to secure.

> COLL. USE. 1875.
>
> *Cotter* them shutters, an' let's get to bed !

COTTER (S. Lanc.),
COTTRILL (E. and Mid. Lanc.), } *sb.* an iron pin to fasten a bolt.

COTTERS, *sb. pl.* entanglements.

> COLL. USE. 1875.
>
> I can't get th' *cotters* out o' mi hair.

COUP (N. Lanc.), *sb.* a cart, *i.e.* a cart that can be *couped* or tilted

COW, *v.* to rake or scrape together. See *Coul*, to scrape; *Coulrake*, a scraper, in Halliwell's Dict.

MID. LANCASHIRE.
1734.

It was also ordered that "all persons refusing to clean or *cow* the streets opposite their respective houses should be fined 6d. after notice from the serjeant with his bell" (Minute Book of Kirkham Bailiffs.)
Fishwick's Hist. Kirkham, c. i., p. 24.

COW-GRIP, *sb.* a trench in a shippon, to carry off the water.

COW-QUAKES (Fylde), *sb. pl.* cold winds in May.

COW-RAKE, *sb.* a rake without prongs, for scraping up mud. See Cow.

MISS LAHEE.
1865.

Beawt moor ado aw cotter'd th' cat out wi' th' cowrake, for aw wor feeort on it oather bitin' or scratchin' mi.   *Carter's Struggles,* p. 24.

COW-SKARN (N. Lanc.),
COW-SHARN (E. and Mid. Lanc.),
COW-CLAP (S. Lanc.),
COW-SWAT (N. Lanc.),
} *sb.* cow dung.   Skarn = Icel. *skarn*, A.S. *scearn*, Mid. E. *sharn*, dung.

CRAA (N. Lanc.), *sb.* a crow.

CRAAM (N. Lanc.) *sb.* a curved three-pronged fork, used in getting cockles. Called *crome* in Norfolk, a form which occurs in the Paston Letters. Cf. Du. *krom*, crooked.

JOHN BRIGGS.
1822.

They struck a small instrument with three crooked prongs, called a *craam*, into the sand, close beside these holes, where they were sure to find a cockle.
Remains, p. 32.

CRACK, *sb.* a chat.   Cf. Welsh *crecian*, to chatter.

WAUGH.
1859.

Aw can do wi a *crack* o'er a glass.
Lanc. Songs: Come Whoam to thi Childer.

IBID.
(Furness Dialect.)
1874.

I hope I'm not tirin' ye wi' these aad-warld *cracks* o' mine.   *Jannock,* c. vii., p. 62.

CRACK, *v.* to boast. A.S. *cracian* is to *crack;* but *crake* is to *croak*, to *crow*. Cf. Icel. *kráka*, a crow. Mid. E. *crake*, to break, boast.

CHAUCER.
1380.

He *crakkede* boost [boast] and swor it was not so.
Reeves Tale, l. 81.

SHAKSPERE.
1598.

And Ethiopes of their sweet complexion *crack.*
Love's Labour Lost, iv. 3, l. 268.

COLL. USE.
1875.

He's awluz *crackin'* about his feyther, as if nob'dy else could do nowt bur him.

CRACKED, *adj.* silly, foolish, witless.

WAUGH.
1868.

"Some folk reckon't he're *crack't*," continued Ben. "Well," replied Randal, ' he happen wur, a bit. Mon, he coom ov a crack't mak'; an' he're like to keep th' owd system."—*Sneck-Bant,* c. ii., p. 28.

CRADDA (N. Lanc.), *sb.* a lean person or animal.

COLL. USE.
1875.

Wy thou's grown a fair *cradda*.

CRADDY (S. Lanc.),
CRATTY (E. Lanc.),
CRATTAN (Leyland),
CRODDY (Oldham),
} *sb.* a feat, a surpassing act, a challenge.

REV. W. GASKELL.
1854.

A common amusement with boys is to set one another what they call "craddies," trials of strength
and daring; and I have sometimes fancied that this
word (as no other better derivation has been given of
it) might be derived from the Welsh *crad*, which signifies heat, vigour, strength, as in this game these
qualities are required.—*Lect. Lanc. Dialect*, p. 10.

WAUGH.
1865.

They had made up their minds, as Enoch said, to
" set th' owd lad a bit ov a *cruddy*."
Besom Ben, c. vi., p. 62.

B. BRIERLEY.
1869.

Geoffrey set a "*craddie*," as he called it. He
jumped the brook and dared you to follow.
Red Windows Hall, c. xii., p. 96.

CRAMM'D, *part.* snappish, ill-tempered.

MISS LAHEE.
1865.

" Hello, theer, what the hangments don yo want
here at this toime o'th' neet ? Donnot yo see at we're
o' i' bed ?" " Well, well, donnot be so *cram'd*,
mon." *Carter's Struggles*, p. 56.

CRANCH, *v.* to grind anything with the teeth ; to eat green fruit.

CRANKY, *adj.* difficult to deal with ; awkward tempered.

WAUGH.
1855.

He're a fine, straight-forrud man, wi' no maffle
abeawt him, for o' his quare, *cranky* ways.
Lanc. Sketches : Cottage of Tim Bobbin, p. 55.

CRAP, *v.* to put strips of leather on the sole of a clog or wooden shoe.

COLL. USE.
1875.

He's a handy chap—he can *crap* his own clogs.

CRAP, *sb.* money.

COLLIER.
1750.

" I'm poor, God wot." " Heaw so ?" " My
crap's aw done." *Works*, p. 33.

CRAPPLE, *v.* to scramble.

WAUGH.
1874.

As soon as he could *crapple* up to his feet again, he
went at this gatepost, hommer an' tungs, wi' his fists.
Chimney Corner : Manch. Critic, March 28.

CRATCHINLY, *adv.* and *adj.* feebly, weakly.

COLLIER.
1750.

There's an owd *cratchenly* gentleman, ot wooans
[lives] ot yon heawse. *Works*, p. 56.

B. BRIERLEY.
1869.

"These owd timber-lifters," he said, taking stock
of his legs, "are gettin' as *cratchinly* as an owd wis-
ket. They keepn foin' eaut wi' one anotłter upo' th'
road." *Red Windows Hall*, c. xi., p. 82.

CRATCHINS, *sb.* the refuse or parched membrane left after lard, tallow, or any fatty substance is melted or rendered.

CREAWSE, *adj.* amorous, lascivious. Mid. E. *crus*, which occurs in Havelok, l. 1966 ; perhaps from Swed. *krusa*, (1) to curl, (2) to compliment excessively ; see Atkinson. Sc. *crouse.*

CREE, *v.* to soften wheat, barley, or rice by simmering.

CREEAN (N. Lanc.) *v.* to bawl, to shout.

CREEL, *sb.* a frame to wind yarn upon.

CREEM, *v.* to give or take privately , also, in the latter sense, to steal.

> COLLIER.
> 1750.
>
> I cawd for·summot t'eat. Hoo browt me some hog-mutton on special turmits. I *creemt* Nip neaw on then o lunshun [*i.e.*, I stole Nip (the dog) now and then a luncheon]. *Works,* p. 53.

CREETCHY, *adj.* sickly, ailing, feeble, shaky.

> COLL. USE.
> 1875.
>
> His barns are *creetchy*-like an' poorly.

CREWEL-BO, *sb.* a ball covered with parti-coloured worsted.

CRICK, *sb.* a local pain, particularly applied to a pain in the neck. Mid. E. *crik*, spasms. Cf. W. *crych*, a wrinkle. Allied to *crook.*

> ——
>
> Thou might stomble and take the *crik.*
> *Rel. Antiq.*, ii. 29.

> 1440.
>
> *Crykke*, sekeness, crampe, spasmus, tetanus.
> *Prompt. Parv.*

> COLL. USE.
> 1875.
>
> Aw've got a *crick* i' mi neck wi' sittin' wi th' dur oppen.

CRICKET, *sb.* a stool or low seat.

> WM. CARTWRIGHT.
> 1641.
>
> I'l stand upon a *cricket*, and there make Fluent orations to 'em.
> *Comedies ·* "Lady Errant."

> COLLIER
> 1750.
>
> I poo'd o *cricket*, an keaw'rt meh deawn i'th' nook.
> *Works,* p. 52.

> BAMFORD.
> 1850.
>
> Poo that *cricket* to th' foyer.
> *Ed. Tim Bobbin* p. 151.

CRILL, *sb.* a shiver.

> WAUGH.
> 1865.
>
> He began to be aware that there was a deeper silence around him than before, and it sent a cold *crill* all over him. *Besom Ben*, c. iv., p. 37.

> IBID.
> 1867.
>
> Aw felt a bit of a cowd *crill*, for summut towd mo there wur misfortin afoot.
> *Dead Man's Dinner*, c. ii., p. 18.

CRINKLE (S. Lanc.), *v.* to bend under a weight. A.S. *crincan*, to cringe, submit. Cf. Icel. *kring*, round ; *kringla*, a circle , Du. *krinkelen*, to wind about.

CROMPY (S. Lanc.), } *adj.* full of action, restless.
CRAMPY (E. Lanc.), }

CRONK, *sb.* the note of a raven. Also, croaking, prating. Icel. *krunk*, the raven's cry ; *krunka*, to croak.

> COLL. USE (E. L)
> 1875.
> Let's ha less o' thi *cronk* ; thaa'rt wur nor a crow.

CRONK, *v.* to croak, to prate. See CRONK *ante.*

CRONKY, *adj.* rough, uneven. See CRANKY.

CROODLE, *v.* to hum or murmur quietly to oneself.

> WAUGH.
> 1868.
> The child *croodled* thoughtfully to himself for a minute or two, whilst his mother went on dressing him ; and then, suddenly turning up his face, he said, "Eawr little Ben's i'th' bury-hole, isn't he, mam ?"
> *Sneck-Bant,* c. iii., p. 53.

CROOIN' (E. Lanc.), *v.* creeping close together.

CROOKELT, } *adj.* crooked. Du. *kreukelen,* to crumple ; Platt
CROOT, } Deutsch, *krukeln.*

> REV. W. GASKELL.
> 1854.
> There are some words common to the Dutch and the Lancashire that are not found in the Anglo-Saxon, or appear in a different form. Thus, in Dutch, *kreukelen* is to crumple ; and in Lancashire we hear of a *crookelt* pin ; and when a person has displaced or twisted things, "he's gone an' *crookelt* 'em."
> *Lect. Lanc. Dialect,* p. 27.

> B. BRIERLEY.
> 1868.
> Aw'll stop here an' wind for thee till aw'm as *croot* as owd Ailse o' Beaukers. *Fratchingtons,* p. 52.

CROP, *v.* to spring.

> RAMSBOTTOM.
> 1864.
> Bo jeighs [joys] *crop* up i' th' midst o' cares.
> *Lanc. Rhymes,* p. 12.

CROPE, *v.* p. t. of the verb to creep = crept. A.S. *Ic creáp,* I crept ; Mid. E. *crop, creop.*

> LANGLAND.
> 1377.
> *Crope* into a kabau for colde of thi nailles.
> *Piers Plowman,* B-text, iii., l. 190.

> CHAUCER.
> 1380.
> He wende have *crope* by his felaw Jon,
> And by the myller in he creep anon.
> *Reeves Tale,* l. 339.

> COLLIER.
> 1750.
> Aw *crope* fur into th' chimney. *Works,* p. 52.

> JOHN SCHOLES.
> 1857.
> Aw slipt off mi shoon, un *crope* sawfli eawt.
> *Jaunt,* p. 14.

> WAUGH.
> 1859.
> One neet aw *crope* whoam when my weighvin were o'er. *Lanc. Songs:* "Jamie's Frolic," l. 1.

> B. BRIERLEY.
> 1867.
> "Where's Jammie o' Tums ?" demanded Bowley.
> "He *crope* eawt abeaut an heaur sin," replied Sogger.
> *Marlocks of Merriton,* p. 30.

CROPPEN, *p. p* crept. A.S. *p. p. cropen.*

REV. W. GASKELL.
1854.

The Lancashire dialect often retains the Anglo-Saxon " en " of the past participle, in cases where it is omitted in the present English. For instance, instead of " crept," we have " *croppen.*"
Lect. Lanc. Dialect, p. 25.

JOHN SCHOLES.
1857.

Wi'n *croppn* close together, wi'rn so feeurt, un durst goo na furr.　　*Jaunt,* p. 60.

WAUGH.
1868.

Just when th' storm wur ut th' height, aw geet *croppen* into a grand owd chimbley-nook.
Sneck-Bant, c. i., p. 8.

CROSS-PATCH, *sb.* a peevish person. " *Patch,* a fool; perhaps from wearing a *patched* or parti-coloured coat. Thus Shakspere in *Mer. Ven.* ii. 5, 'The *patch* is kind enough, but a huge feeder.' The term *cross-patch* meant originally 'ill-natured fool.' " (Nares.)

COLL. USE.
1875.

Eh, what a *cross-patch* hoo is ! It's a wonder thae can live wi' her.

CROUSE (N. and E. Lanc.), *adj.* brisk, pert.　See **CREAWSE.**
O. E. *crus, crous,* brisk, nimble, angry.

N.E. MID. DIALECT.
About 1280.

And drive hem ut thei he weren *crus.*
Havelok, l. 1966.

BURNS.
1786.

Now they're *crouse* and canty baith,
Ha ha, the wooing o't.　　*Duncan Gray.*

CROVUKT (N. Lanc.), crushed up, crowded.　Welsh *crybwch,* shrunk.

J. P. MORRIS.
1869.

We wer o' *crovukt* in a heeàp.
Furness Glossary, p. 23.

CROW-BOGGART, *sb.* a scare-crow.

CROWD, *sb.* a fiddle.　Welsh *crwth,* a fiddle.

SPENSER.
1594.

Harke ! how the minstrils gin to shrill aloud
Their merry musick that resounds from far,
The pipe, the tabor, and the trembling *croud,*
That well agree withouten breach or jar.
Epithalamion, l. 129.

CROW-GATE, *sb.* the direct road, as the crow flies.

WAUGH.
1855.

If he wishes to know the country and its inhabitants, he must get off that, " an' tak th' *crow-gate.*"
Lanc. Sketches, p 43.

CROWNER,
CRUNNER, } *sb.* a coroner.

SHAKSPERE.
1602.

Oliver : Go thou and seek the *crowner,* and let him sit o' my coz.　　*Twelfth Night,* i. 5, l. 3.

IBID
1803.

Second Clown : Therefore make her grave straight ; the *crowner* hath sate on her, and finds it Christian buriall.　　*Hamlet,* v. i , l. 3

COLL. USE.
1875.

Eh dear o' me ! Th' *crunner* 'll ha' to sit o'er him.

CROW-SWING, *sb.*, a bar in a chimney to hang pans upon.

CRUD, ⎱ *v.* to curdle. Welsh *crwd*, a round lump ; Mid. E.
CRUDDLE,⎰ *crudden*, to curd, coagulate.

WYCLIF.
1380.
Whether not as mylc thou hast mylkid me, and as
chese thou hast *crudded* me?   *Job*, x. 10.

1440.   *Cruddin*, coagulare.   *Prompt Parv.*

SPENSER.
1579.
Comes the breme Winter with chamfred browes,
Full of wrinckles and frostie furrowes,
Drerily shooting his stormy darte,
Which *cruddles* the blood and pricks the harte
        Shepheardes Calender, Februarie, l. 43

COLL. USE.
1875.
Th' milk's *cruddl't* again ; it's that thunder.

CRUDS, *sb. pl.* curds. Welsh *crwd*, a round lump , Mid. E. *crudde*,
curd.

LANGLAND.
1377.
A fewe *cruddes* and creem.
        Piers Plowman, B-text, vi. 284.

1440.   *Crudde*, coagulum.   *Prompt. Parv.*

S. GOSSON.
1579.
Making black of white, chalke of cheese, the full
moone of a messe of *cruddes*
        Schoole of Abuse (Arber's Ed), p. 18.

COLL. USE.
1875.
Street cry : " *Cruds* an' whey, *cruds* an' whey ! "

CRUDDLE,⎱ *v.* to bend ; to sink down from weakness.   Allied to
CRUTTLE,⎰ *crouch*.

COLLIER.
1750.
I'r ready t' *cruttle* deawn, for theau moot o knockt
meh o'er with a pey.   *Works*, p. 56.

JOHN SCHOLES.
1857.
He cudnah help hissel, boh he quoyutly *cruttl'd*
deawn between th' two cheers [chairs].
        Jaunt, p. 47

IBID.
Aw laight [laughed] till mi soides wur us *crutil't* us
o pair o'. blacksmith's ballys.   *Jaunt*, p. 38.

WAUGH.
1868.
He *cruttle't* into th' nook, like a freetn't hedgehog.
        Sneck-Bant, c. ii., p. 35

CRUMMOCK. *sb.* a crooked stick.   Cf. Du. *krom*, crooked.

T. T. WILKINSON.
1873.
Lanc. Proverb : He'll go through th' wood, an' ta'
th' *crummock* at last.—*Lanc. Legends, &c.*, p. 201.

CRUMPER, *sb.* a big, strong, thorough fellow ; also, something
done in a forcible and complete way.

WAUGH.
1855.
Jone : " Ned's some gradely good points in him,
too." *Sam.:* " There isn't a quarer o' this country-
side, as hea't be ; an' there's some *crumpers* amoon
th' lot."   *Lanc. Sketches*, p. 27.

IBID.
1874.
" Well, if ever ! " said Betty ; " that sheds [excels]
o' ! " " It's a *crumper* for sure," said Flop, " an' it
reminds me o' Ben o' th' Biggins an' th' gate-post."
        Chimney Corner : Manch. Critic, March 28.

CRUTCH, *v.* to crowd.

CUCKOO-MEAT, *sb.* a large clover.

CUCKOO-SPIT, *sb.* the froth found on grass or plants, enclosing an insect *(Cicada spumaria)*.

> WAUGH.
> 1855.
>
> It was one of those old-fashioned hedges which country lads delight in * * where they could fight and tumble about gloriously * * then roll slap into the wet ditch at the bottom, among *"cuckoo-spit"* and *"*frog-rud,*"* and all sorts of green pool slush. *Lanc. Sketches*, p. 189.

CUCKSTOOL, *sb.* the stool upon which shrews were formerly ducked. It was in use in Manchester as late as 1775, and was a wooden chair placed upon a long pole, which was balanced on a pivot, and suspended over a pond called Pool-house and Pool-fold ; afterwards it was placed over the Daub-holes (Infirmary pond), and was employed for the punishment of scolds and prostitutes. See Manchester *Historical Recorder*, in which there is a facsimile of an old engraving of the cuckstool. According to Blount, this apparatus was in use in the Saxon era, when it was named the *scealfing-stól*.

> RANDOLPH.
> 1643.
>
> *Plus.* And here's a cobler's wife brought for a scold.
> *Nim.* Tell her of *cooking-stooles.*
> *Muses Looking-Glasse.*

> HARLAND & WILKINSON.
> 1873.
>
> That the *cuck-stool* was in request at Liverpool as late as the year 1695 may be inferred from an item in the parochial expenditure of that year, which runs thus :—" Paid Edward Accres for mending the *cuck-stool*, fifteen shillings." According to Mr. Richard Brookes *(Liverpool from 1775 to 1800)*, it was in use in 1779. At Ormskirk, the ducking-stool was removed in 1780. It was in use to a late period at Great Carlton, in the Fylde, and in the ancient borough of Kirkham.
> *Lancashire Legends and Traditions*, p. 167—171.

CUCKSTOOL-DUB, *sb.* the pool in which the cuckstool was used.

CUD'N, pl. of the verb could.

CULVER, *sb.* the dove or pigeon. A.S. *culfre.*

> SPENSER.
> 1595.
>
> Lyke as the *culver* on the bared bough
> Sits mourning for the absence of her mate.
> *Sonnet* 88.

> IBID.
> 1590.
>
> All comfortlesse, upon the bared bow,
> Like wofull *culvers*, doo sit wayling now.
> *Teares of the Muses*, l. 245.

CUMMINS, *sb. pl.* sprouts of barley in malting.

CURTNER, *sb.* a curtain.

CUSH, } *sb.* a child's name for a cow. Icel. *kussa*, a cow ; *kus*,
CUSHY, } a word used to call cows.

CUSHY-COW-LADY, *sb.* the lady-bird or lady-fly ; *coccinella.*

CUT, *sb.* a canal.

WAUGH.
1867.

After the superintendent had gone away, some of the men said much and more, and "if ever he towd ony moor lies abeawt 'em, they'd fling him into th' *cut.*" *Home Life Factory Folk,* iii. 30.

CUT, *sb.* a weaver's term for a piece of calico when taken from the loom.

BAMFORD.
1844.

" How much may you have for weaving a yard of calico?" "A yard, mon ! they'n so mitch a *cut.*" " And how many yards are there in a *cut?*" "Why, theer's thirty yards i' th' Smithy-nook cal' [calico]; an they gettin' fro a shilling to eighteenpence a *cut.*"
Walks in South Lancashire p. 270.

IBID.

Toilonett is a neat light cloth, made of black cotton warp, and shot with white woollen yarn in hand The pieces, or *cuts,* are thirty yards in length. A weaver will be four days in dressing his warp, and about eight in weaving a *cut.*—*Ibid.* pp. 29, 30.

CUTS, *sb. pl.* lots, or chances ; pieces of paper, sticks, or straw, cut into different lengths, and then used in drawing lots.

CHAUCER.
1380.

Now draweth *cut,* er that we forther twynne ;
Which that hath the schortest schal bygynne.
" Sire knight," quoth he, " maister and my lord,
Now draweth *cut,* for that is myn accord."
  *   *   *   *   *
Anon to drawen every wight bigan,
And schortly for to tellen as it was,
Were it by aventure, or sort, or cas,
The soth is this, the *cut* fil to the knight,
Of which ful glad and blithe was every wight.
Prologue Cant. Tales, 1. 835.

SHAKSPERE.
1598.

Dromio S.   You are my elder.
Dromio E. That's a question, how shall we trie it?
Dromio S. Wee'l draw *cuts* for the signior ; till then ; lead thou first.
Com. of Errors, v. i. 420

IZAAK WALTON.
1653.

Piscator : Come on, my masters, who begins ? I think it best to draw *cuts,* and avoid contention.
Peter : It is a match. Look, the shortest *cut* falls to Coridon.
Coridon : Well, then, I will begin, for I hate contention.   *Complete Angler,* c. v.

COLL. USE.
1875.

Let's draw *cuts* for it ; that'll be fair enough.

CUTTER, *v.* to make much of. Allied to *coddle, cuddle.*

COLLIER.
1750.

I dunnaw meeon heaw folk harbort'n't or *cuttertn't* o'er thee.   *Works,* p. xxxvi.

CUTT'RIN, *sb.* muttering, whispering. O. Sw. *kuttra,* to chatter ; Sw. *kuttra,* to coo.

H

D.

DAB, *sb.* a blow with something moist or dirty.

> COLL. USE. If he comes courtin' here again of a Friday neet
> 1875.   aw'll give him a *dab* wi' th' dish-clout.

DAB, *adj.* clever, expert. Probably as doing a thing at a *dab,* or skilfully and quickly.

DAB, *sb.* a clever person, an expert.

> WAUGH.   I've often heard 'em say that he was quite a *dab*
> 1874.   at a bit o' tailorin' or shoemakin'.
>   *Jannock,* c. 8, p. 82.

DACKER, *adj.* unsettled; generally applied to the weather.

DAD, *sb.* father. W. *tad;* Lapponic *dadda* (in children's language), father. Almost, says Wedgwood, as universally spread as *Baba* or *Papa.*

> SHAKSPERE.   *Bastard:* Zounds, I was never so bethumpt with
> 1598.   words,
>   Since first I cal'd my brother's father *dad.*
>   *King John,* ii. 1, 466.

> RAMSBOTTOM. If ther wur bo some wark for his *dad,*
> 1864.   An' his mam ud keep th' things Will could do ;
>   For his velveteen breeches hoo'd sowd,
>   An' his jacket, his cap, an' shoon, too.
>   *Lanc. Rhymes,* p. 19.

> WAUGH.   "Here, *dad,*" cried he, holding out the remains of
> 1866.   his bread and cheese to a tall mower who sat below ;
>   "here, *dad,* aw connot height no moor." . . .
>   Then stretching out his arms, he said, "*Dad,* heighve
>   mo deawn. Aw want to goo and play mo wi' yon
>   tother."   *Ben and th' Bantam,* c. iii., p. 54.

> IBID.   Tom Pobs wur a good-nature't sort ov a lad ;
> 1875.   He wove for his livin', an' live't with his *dad.*
>   *Old Cronies,* c. v., p. 50.

DAD,
DADE,   *v.* to lead. Richardson says *dade* is a word
DAWD (E. Lanc.),   peculiar to Michael Drayton (a native of
                      Warwickshire) ; and Dr. Johnson says it
means—to hold up by a leading-string. To *dade,* continues Richardson, seems to = to move, or cause to move, cautiously, slowly. Allied to *dandle.*

> DRAYTON.   Which, nourished and bred up at her most plenteous
> 1622.   pap,
>   No sooner taught to *dade,* but from their mother trip,
>   And in their speedy course strive others to outstrip.
>   *Polyolbion,* s. i.

DRAYTON.
1622.

The little children when they learned to go,
By painful mothers *daded* to and fro.
Earl of Surrey to Lady Geraldine.

WAUGH.
1859.

" Aw'm gettin' done up," to their Betty he said ;
"Dost think thae could doff mo an *dad* mo to bed ? "
Lanc. Songs : Owd Enoch, p. 72.

DADDLE (E. and Mid. Lanc.), *v.* to assist a child to walk.

DADDLE, *v.* to reel or waver on the road. Cf. F. *dandiner.*
"*Dandiner,* to go gaping illfavouredly, looking unsteadily ;"
Cotgrave.

DADIN'S,
DADLIN'S (E. Lanc.)
DAWDLIN'S (E. Lanc.),
DADIN'-STRENGS (S. E. Lanc.),
} *sb. pl.* leading strings.

JOHN SCHOLES.
1857.

Aw've livt e' Smobridge evvur sin' awre e' *dadin-strengs.*

DAFF, *v.* to daunt. Allied to DEAVE, q.v.

DAFFOCK, *sb.* a slattern. Mid. E. *daffe* + ock. See DAFFEY.

COLL. USE (E. Lanc.)
1875.

Whod a *daffock* hoo is !

DAFFY (N. and E. Lanc.), *sb.* a foolish person. Mid. E. *daffe,* a
dolt. Cf. Old Sw. *döf,* stupid ; Mœso-Goth. *daubs,* dull, hard of
heart ; Icel. *dofi,* torpor ; *dofna,* to be dead or numb, appl. to a
limb.

LANGLAND.
1362.

" þou dotest *daffe,*" quaþ heo, "dulle are þi wittes."
Piers Plowman, A-text, i., l. 129.

IBID.
1377.

" þow doted *daffe,*" quod she. " dulle arne þi wittes."
Ibid, B-text, i., l. 138.

CHAUCER.
1380.

And when this jape is told another day,
I sal be held a *daf,* a cokenay.—*Reeves Tale,* l. 287.

1440.

Daffe, a dastard, or he that spekyth not yn tyme.
Prompt. Parv.

J. P. MORRIS.
1869.

Ye men-folk er sic buzzards, if ye sā a brog on t'
sand ye wod think it wos t' French. I've neā patience
wi' sic *daffys.* *Siege o' Brouton,* p. 6.

DAFFY-DOWN-DILLY, *sb.* the daffodil.

SPENSER.
1579.

Strowe me the ground with *Daffadowndillies,*
And Cowslips. and Kingcups, and loved Lillies.
Shepheardes Calender : April, l. 140.

OLD SONG.
Com. in Lanc.

Roses and lilies and *daffy-down-dillies.*

DAFT, *adj.* soft, foolish, silly. See DAFFEY. *Daffe* + ed, *i.e.* verb
formed from sb., and then p. p. of verb used.

SIR D. LYNDESAY.
1552.

Thou art the *daftest* fuill that ever I saw.
Three Estaits.

BURNS.
1786.

Or maybe, in a frolic *daft*,
To Hague or Calais taks a waft.—*Twa Dogs*, I. 155.

J. P. MORRIS.
1867.

On he went croonin t'll his-sel scraps of a *daft* ald
sang he'd offen heeàrd sung at t' Spavin'd Horse.
Lebby Beek Dobby, p. 6.

COLL. USE.
1875.

Come sharpen up mon, thae looks as if thae'rt *daft*.

DAG, *v.* to shear sheep.   Mid. E. *daggen*, to cut into jagged edges.
The expression "leet *dagge* his clothes" in Piers the Plowman,
B. xx. 142, means— "he caused his clothes to be curiously cut;"
in allusion to the fashion of the period.

DAG, *sb.* a leathern latchet.

DAG, *sb.* dew on the grass. Icel. *dögg*, dew ; see also Icel. *deigr*,
damp, wet, lit. "doughy." Cf. Icel. *deig*, dough ; Mœso-Goth.
daigs, dough, from a verb of which the earliest trace is the
Mœso-Goth. *deigan*, to form by hand, as a potter forms clay.

DAG, *v.* to trail in the dew, wet, or mire.   See DAG *ante.*   Icel.
döggva, to bedew.

B. BRIERLEY.
1869.

The dame proceeded to pin up her dress, to prevent
its being "*dagged*," as she expressed herself, in the
dew.   *Red Windows Hall*, p. 25.

DAGGY (E. Lanc.), *adj.* dirty, wet, drizzly.   See DAG *ante.*

COLL. USE.
1875.

It's varra *daggy* to-day.

DAGLOCKS, *sb. pl.* the wool cut off a sheep.   See DAG, *verb.*

DALE (Chipping ; and Burrow, near Kirkby-Lonsdale), *sb.* an un-
separated portion of a field, belonging to a second owner, and
which is often unmarked, or only shown by stakes in the hedge
and stones at the corners of the *dale.*   A.S. *dæl*, a portion.

COLL. USE.
1875.

1. (Burrow.) We've two *dales* in Hardgroves
Bodom.
2. (Chipping.) A *dale* of about a quarter of an
acre on Black Moss belongs to this farm.

DANK, *v.* to depress ; lit. to damp.

BAMFORD.
1864.

Put th' Kurn-bill i' the divel's hons
'At it no moor may *dank* us.
Homely Rhymes, p. 135.

DANK,
DONK,
} *adj.* damp, depressing.   Akin to *damp.*

COLLIER.
1750.

I doft meh *donk* shoon on hoyse, on me doage
clooas.   *Works*, p. 54.

DANNET (N. Lanc.),
DO-NOWT (S. and E. Lanc.),
} *sb.* a term of reproach ; lit. dow-
nought ; from the verb *dow*, to
be worth.   Cf. in E. D. S. Reprinted Glossaries, 1873, *dannat*

(North of England), *sb.* a bad person; *donnot* (E. Yorkshire), *adj.* good-for-nothing, bad; *dannot* (West Riding), *sb.* a good-for-nothing, a wretch. The verbs *dow* and *do* are confused even in modern ordinary English. " That will *do* " is a corruption of " that will *dow*."

J. P. MORRIS.
1857.

T'ăld woman shouted, " Cu' thy ways on, th'ou *dannet*." *Siege o' Brou'ton*, p. 5.

COLL. USE (S. and E. L.)
1875.

He's a *do-nowt* an' maks his mother keep him.

DARK, *adj.* blind.

COLL. USE.
1875.

Help him o'er th' road, poor lad, he's *dark*.

DARKENIN', *sb.* twilight. A.S. *dearcung*, twilight.

A. C. GIBSON
(Dial. of High Furness).
1868.

He niver durst bide by his-sel' efter t' *darkenin'*. *Cumb. Folk-Speech*, p. 95.

DARRACK (N. Lanc.), *sb.* a day's work. A.S. *dægweorc*, the same.

DASHIN, *sb.* a tub used for kneading oatmeal dough.

COLLIER.
1750.

He nipt up th' *deashon*, ot stoode oth' harstone, on whirl'd it at meh. *Works*, p. 66.

DATALLER (S. Lanc.),   ⎫ *sb.* a day labourer. Marshall's
DAYTAL-LABOURER (Furness), ⎬   East Yorkshire Glossary
(E. D. S. Reprint, 1873, p. 25) has " *Daitle* (that is, day-tale) *adj.* by the day; as, daitle-man, a day-labourer; daitle-work, work done by the day." Brockett (Gloss. N. Country Words) has, " *Daytaleman*, a day-labourer, chiefly in husbandry—one who works by day-tale, *i.e.* a man whose labour is *told* or reckoned by the day, not by the week or year." Cf. Icel. *dagatal*, a tale of days.

DATELESS, *adj.* stupefied, foolish, disordered in mind. For *deedless*. So Icel. *dáðlauss*, lit. deedless, means lubberly, impotent. See *Deedless* in Atkinson's Cleveland Glossary.

MISS LAHEE.
1865.

Theer sit Jinny starin' at th' owd lass loike one *dateless*. *Betty o' Yep's Tale*, p. 15.

WAUGH.
1867.

They carried her into Sally Grimshaw's, an' laid her upo' th' couch cheer, as *dateless* as a stone. *Dead Man's Dinner*, p. 19.

IBID.
1869.

Th' White Heawse had to goo into other honds, for th' poor owd crayter wur getten quite *dateless*, an hoo wur takken to live wi some relations. *Yeth Bobs*, c. ii., p. 40.

DATHIT (Furness), *interj.* a mild curse on making a mishap.

DAUB, ⎫ *sb.* clay or marl; also, the clay mixed with chopped straw.
DOBE, ⎬ formerly used for filling in between the timbers of

wooden-framed houses, sometimes called "wattle and daub."
See CLAM-STAVE-AN'-DAUB *ante*.

WEST MID. DIAL. (Lanc.) 1360.	Þenne cleme hit with clay comly withinne, And alle þe endentur drynen *daube* withouten. 　　　　　*E. Eng. Allit. P.*, B., l. 312.
1440.	*Dawber* or cleyman : *dawbyn*, lino, muro. 　　　　　　　*Prompt. Parv.*

COLL. USE. 1875.	Fetch yon lad in, he's messin' hissel wi that *dobe*.

DAUB-HOIL, *sb. i.e.* daub-hole ; a clay or marl pit. See DAUB *ante*.

DAWK (Fylde), 　　　　⎱ *v.* to stoop, to plunge.　Lit. to *duck*.
DEAWK (S. and E. Lanc.), ⎰ Cf. Du. *duiken*, to stoop, dive,
plunge.

COLL. USE. 1875.	I *deawk'd* deawn an' he misst his aim.

DAWKIN', *sb.* a dull, stupid person.　See DAFFY.

DAWKINLY, *adv.* stupidly, foolishly.

COLLIER. 1750.	After looking *dawkinly*-wise a bit.—*Works*, p. 52.

DAZED (Furness), *adj.* starved, cold, stupid, frightened.　Icel.
dasask, to become weary and exhausted from cold or bodily exertion ; *dasaðr*, exhausted, weary ; O. Du. *daesen*, to lose one's wits.

HAMPOLE. 1340.	Brynned ay here in þe calde of malice, And ay was *dased* in charité. 　　　　*Pricke of Conscience*, l. 6646.
WEST MID. DIAL. (Lanc.) 1360.	I stoode as stylle as *dased* quayle [as a dazed quail]. 　　　　*E. Eng. Allit. Poems*, A, l. 1084
CHAUCER. 1384.	Thou sittest at another booke, Tyl fully *dasewyd* ys thy looke. 　　　　　*House of Fame*, ii., 149.
GAVIN DOUGLAS. 1513.	All þe maisters were so mased Þat dom þai stode als þai ware *dased*. 　　　　　　Vol. ii., 567

DEAD-TONGUE (Furness), *sb.* the water hemlock.

DEAVE, *v.* to deafen ; to stupefy with noise.　*Adj.* DEAVIN, deafen-
ing.　Icel. *deyfa*, to stupefy ; O. Sw. *doȝwa*, to deafen, dull, assuage,
stupefy , Dan. *döve*, to deafen, deaden, blunt.

WEST MID. DIAL. (Lanc.) 1320.	Þe dunte [=blow] þat schulde hym *deve*. 　　　　*Sir Gawayne & G. K.*, l. 1286.
BURNS. 1786.	If mair they *aeave* us with their din. 　　　　　*The Ordination*, l. 122.
JOHN SCHOLES. 1857.	Just then th' queen's carridge un o' thoose ut win sin i' th' mornin' rattlt by, un bang went th' *deavin'* din [of cannon] ogen.—*Jaunt to See th' Queen*, p. 55.
COLL. USE. 1875.	Howd thi din, thae fair *deaves* me.

DEAWLDY, *adj.* doleful, depressed, dolorous, despondent. Cf. Icel. *dáligr*, wretched. E. D. S. Reprinted Glossaries, B. 7. (West Riding) has "*dowly, dawly*, adj. lonely, sorrowful;" and Brockett (North Country Words) gives "*Dowley*, lonely, dismal, melancholy, sorrowful, doleful."

WAUGH.
1859.

> Then, Mally, fill it up again ;
> An dunnot look so *deawldy ;*
> There's nought can lick a marlock. when
> One's brains are gettin meawldy !
> *Lanc. Songs :* Tum Rindle.

DEAWN, *adj.* depressed.

COLL. USE.
1875.

> There's summat wrung wi th' owd lad to-day—he looks so *deawn.*

DEAWN-BROO, *adv.* down hill , metaph. for failing or declining.

WAUGH.
1865.

> Owd Roddle was now only the shrunken relic of a very strong man. He had long since begun to grow "*deawn-broo*, like a keaw-tail."
> *Besom Ben*, c. vi., p. 79.

DEAWN-FO. *sb. i.e.* down-fall. A fall of rain or snow.

WAUGH
1855.

> A sawp o' *deawnfo* 'ud do a seet o' good just neaw ; an we'st ha some afore lung, or aw'm chetted.
> *Lanc. Sketches :* Grave of Grislehurst Boggart, p. 209.

DEAWN-LYING, *sb.* an accouchement.

COLL. USE.
1875.

> Hoo's just at th' *deawn-lying ;* poor body ! we'd better see ut hoo's looked after a bit.

DEAWNT, *v.* finished ; taken off or taken down. *Deawnin'*, finishing, *part.* Lancashire weavers call the web, or piece of cloth they are working upon, whether woollen or cotton, a "cut;" and when the entire piece or web is woven, and taken off the loom, the weaver says he has "*deawnt his cut;*" that is, he has taken his finished web down from the loom. So, figuratively, a man who dies, has finished the web of his life.

WAUGH.
1855.

> Aw thought it wur time to sell th' dog, when aw had to ax owd Thunge to lend mo a bite ov his moufin whol aw *deawnt* my piece.
> *Lanc. Sketches :* Birthplace of Tim Bobbin, p. 81.

BAMFORD.
1864.

> And never would she let me wait
> When *downing* on a Friday,
> Her wheel went at a merry rate,
> Her person always tidy.   *Poems*, p. 39.

WAUGH.
1867.

> "Yer, tho', Jone, another cally-weigher [calico-weaver] gone !" "Ay," replied Jone, "th' owd lad's *deawnt* his cut. He'll want no more tickets."
> *Home Life Factory Folk*, c. xiv , p. 127.

DECK, *sb.* a pack, applied to playing cards. Mr. Payne Collier (Ed. Shakspere) says "the word continued in use [as applied to a pack of cards] as late as 1788, being found in the Sessions Paper of that year. Possibly it is derived from the A.S. *decan,* to cover, because one card in a pack covers the other."

SHAKSPERE.
1595.

Gloucester : Alas, that Warwick had no more forecast,
But whiles he thought to steale the single ten,
The king was slily finger'd from the *deck*.
Third K. Hen. VI., v. 1, 42.

DEED, *sb.* doings.

WAUGH.
1867.

We'n had very hard *deed*, maister. Aw consider we'n had as hard *deed* as anybody livin, takkin o together.—*Home Life Factory Folk*, c. xvi. p. 145.

DEET, *v.* to daub, to sully. Also, *adj.* dirty. Probably *deet* is a mere corruption of *dirt*, formerly spelt *drit*. Cf. A.S. *gedritan*, to dirty. The loss of the *r* is well seen in *speak*, a corruption of *spreak*, from A.S. *sprecan*.

MISS LAHEE.
1865.

Betty wor not long afore hoo coome back wi' th' owd paper in her hond, looking as *deet* an' yellow as one of them foreign felleys at aw've sin i' Manchester.
Betty o' Yep's Tale, p. 29.

COLLIER.
1750.

An ill-grim'd an *deet* th' lad wur for shure.
Works, p. 59.

WAUGH.
1867.

He comes noan here! Aw'll not ha' th' heawse *deeted* wi' sich like rubbidge!
Owd Blanket, c. i., p. 11.

IBID.
1867.

"Come in," said the landlady, "an sit tho deawn while eawr lasses getten yon kitchen readied (made right) a bit." "Aw's *deet* this reawm o' yors," said Ben, looking round the parlour. "*Deet*, be hanged!" replied she. "A saup o' clen wayter 'll *deet* nought."
Ibid, c. iii., p 53.

DEET (S. Lanc.), *v.* to dress with size or paste ; a term used by weavers.

COLL. USE.
1875.

When he's *deeted* his yarn he'll come eawt.

DEG, *v.* to sprinkle water upon anything. Icel. *döggva*, to bedew ; cf. Icel. *deigja*, wetness, damp ; Sw. *dagg*, dew. This is probably the same word as that which in Shakspere takes the form of *deck*.

SHAKSPERE.
1623.

Thou didst smile,
Infused with a fortitude from heaven,
When I have *deck'd* the sea with drops full salt,
Under my burthen groaned ?
Tempest, act i., sc. ii., l. 153

REV. W. GASKELL.
1854.

The word which a Lancashire man employs for sprinkling with water is "to *deg*," and when he *degs* his garden he uses a *deggin*-can.
Lect. Lanc. Dialect, p. 28.

MISS LAHEE.
1865.

Si'tho' what a *deggin'* hoo's gin me, an' aw've o' these moiles to gu i' mi weet clothes.
Carter's Struggles, c. vii., p. 53.

DELF-RACK, *sb.* shelf for crockery.   *Delf*= pottery from Delft, and *rack*, an open frame work.

DENE   ) *sb.* a little valley.   A.S. *denu*, a
DEYN or DEIGN (E. Lanc.),)   valley.

A. SAX. GOSPELS.   Ælc *denu* bíþ gefylled ; [every valley shall be filled].
995.   *St. Luke*, iii., 5.

WEST MID. DIAL. (Lanc.)   þou says þou trawez me in þis *dene*,
1360.   Bycause þou may with yзen me se.
                                           E. Eng. Allit. P., A, l. 295.

WAUGH.   In the forest of Rossendale, between Derply Moor
1855.   and the wild hill called Swinshaw, there is a lone
                valley called *Dean*. The inhabitants of this valley
                are so notable for their love of music that they are
                known all through the vales of Rossendale as "Th'
                Deign Layrocks," or "The Lárks of *Dean*."
                Lanc. Sketches : Wandering Minstrels, p. 276.

DESS (Fylde). *sb.* a pile, appl. to straw.   Icel. *des*, a rick, whence *hey-des*, a hay-rick.   It exists in local names, as Desjur-myri in the east, Des-ey in the west of Iceland.

DEVILMENT, *sb.* mischief.

WAUGH.   Yo'n some make o' *divulment* agate i'th chimbley,
1855.   aw declare.   *Lanc. Sketches*, p. 29.

DICKONS, *sb.*, the deuce or devil.

SHAKSPERE.   *Mistress Page :* I cannot tell what the *dickens* his
1602.   name is.   *Merry Wives*, iii. 2, .19.

COLLIER.   "The *Dickons* it is ! " sed I.—*Works*, p. 70.
1750.

DIDDLE-DADDLIN',   dawdling about.

COLL. USE.   Hoo goes abeawt *diddle-daddlin* an' never gets
1875.   nowt done.

DILFA (Mid. Lanc.),) *adj.* doleful, sickly.   In Essex dialect *dil-*
DEALFA (E. Lanc.),) *vered* means exhausted.

DILL, *v.* to lull or soothe a child ; also, to dandle.   Icel. *dilla*, to trill, lull ; *dillindo*, lullaby.

COLL. USE.   Näa ; thee *dill* that chylt an' get it asleep.
1875.

DING, *v.* to knock, to strike, to thrust ; p. t. *dang* and *dung* ; pl. *dungen* : as " He *dang* [or *dung*] him down ;" " They *dungen* him to the floor."   Icel. *dengja*, to hammer , Sw. *dänga :* A.S. *dencgan*, to knock.

HAMPOLE.   Right swa þe devels salle ay *dyng*
1340.   On þe synfulle, withouten styntyng.
                                      P. of Conscience, 7015.

BEN JONSON.
1610.

Surly : Down with the door.
Kustril : 'Slight ! *ding* it open.
Lovewit : Hold, gentlemen, what means this violence.
           Alchemist, v. 5.

DRAYTON.
1627.

This while our noble king
His broad sword brandishing
Down the French host did *ding.*
    Battle of Agincourt : Works, p. 1380.

WAUGH.
1869.

Hoo use't to *ding* me up wi' a bit sometimes when
we wur cwortin.   *Yeth Bobs,* c. i., p. 9.

DING-DONG,
DING-DRIVE (Furness), } *adv.* full speed, without intermission.

COLL. USE.
1875.

He goes at it *ding-dong.*

DINNEL, *v.* to tingle : *din* + el.

COLL. USE.
1875.

My ears *dinnel* as if bells wur ringing in 'em.

DINTLE, *v.* to indent.   A.S. *dynt,* a dint, blow, dent ; Icel. *dynta,*
sb. a dint ; and *v.* to dint.

DITHER (general),
DOTHER (E. Lanc.), } *v.* to shake, to tremble. In some parts
DEDUR (N. Lanc.), } of England, *didder.* A certain kind of
and quaking-grass. grass is called *didder*-grass, totter-grass,
zittern, to tremble ; The cognate form in High German is
a word in common use.

LANCASHIRE DIAL.
About 1400.

He began to *dotur* and dote
Os he hade keghet scathe.
    E. Eng. Met. Rom., C, xvi., l. 11.

IBID.

Gif Menealfe was the more myȝtie
Ȝette dyntus gerut him to *dedur.*
    Ibid, C, xxv., l. 7.

COLLIER.
1750.

I *dithert* ot meh teeth hackt i' meh heeod ogen.
    Works, p. 50.

ELIJAH RIDINGS.
1848.

My honds shak'd loìke an aspen leof,
Aw *dithert* i' my shoon.
    Lanc. Muse : Ale v. Physic, p. 8.

RAMSBOTTOM.
1864.

Hearken th' bonny layrock sing,—
A dark spot *ditherin'* i' th' blue sky.
    Lanc. Rhymes, p. 100.

WAUGH.
1868.

Eh, it ma'es me *dother* neaw, when aw think of a
pickin-peg.   *Sneck-Bant,* c. ii., p. 29.

DIVERSOME, *adj.* fanciful ; hard to please.

WAUGH.
1865.

Musicianers cap'n the world for bein' *diversome,* an'
jealous, an' hard to plez.   *Barrel Organ,* p. 14.

COLL. USE.
1875.

Thae'rt too *diversome* to live ; tha eyts nowt.

DIVULSKIN, ⎱ *sb.* a humorous term of reproach, generally applied
DULESKIN, ⎰ to a mischievous person. Mid. E. *deueles cynnes*,
lit. of the devil's kind or kin.

WAUGH.
1874.
"He's etten all t' goose." "Who hes?" "Yon
divulskin i' t' parlour." *Jannock*, c. iv., p. 29.

DO, ⎱ *sb.* an action or occurrence ; anything of a lively or
DOOMENT, ⎰ stirring nature ; a business, an entertainment.

MISS LAHEE.
1865.
When he started a readin' o'er Jinny's *dooment*, aw
ne'er yerd sich laughin'.— *Betty o' Yep's Tale*, p. 15.

WAUGH.
1867.
"Who are they?" said the landlord ; "conto
make 'em eawt?" "Nawe," answered the carter ;
"but they favvour'n Todmorden chaps. Aw'll be
bund they're upo th' same *dooment*." "Aw dar say
they are," replied the landlord. "They're comed
up a-viewin', aw guess." *Dulesgate*, p. 19

IBID.
1875.
"What the hectum's yon lad doin'." Hoo said,
"I see him ! He's comin' down th' brow, yon, full
pelt, wi' a gun on his shoulder." "O' reet," said
Sam, rubbin' his honds ; "o' reet, keep still. This
is a grand *do*." *Old Cronies*, vii., 89.

DŌ, *v.* to thrive, to be healthy. Cf. Sc. *dow ;* A.S. *dugan*, to profit,
avail, be good for ; cognate with Ger. *taugen*, to be good for.

COLL. USE.
1875.
Old folks will say of a sickly man, "He noather
dees nor *dōes*." Again, "He *dōes* [*i.e.*, thrives] well
in his business."

DOAGE, ⎱ *adj* damp. A.S. *deawig*, dewy, wet. Cf. DEG
DOYCH (E. Lanc.), ⎰ *ante.*

COLLIER.
1750.
I doft meh donk shoon on hoyse. on me *doage*
clooas. *Works*, p. 54.

COLL. USE (E. L)
1875.
Where he weyves is *doych* an' he's getten t' rheumatiz.

DOBBER, *sb.* a lump ; also, a large marble.

WAUGH.
1868.
"Put thi hond o' th' top o' mi yed," said Ben.
"Doesto feel nought?" "Some lumps," said Randal.
"Lumps!" replied Ben ; "Ay, an pummers too.
Ceawnt 'em. Aw think they'n come to seven—
gradely *dobbers*." *Sneck-Bant*, c. ii., p. 30.

DOBBIN, *sb.* a familiar term for a horse.

DOBBIN, *sb.* a small, thick glass tumbler, which holds a fourth or
fifth of a pint. Cf. W. *dobyn*, a half-pint measure.

MICHAEL WILSON.
1830.
Come, Robin, sit deawn, an aw'll tell thee a tale,
Boh first, prithee, fill me a *dobbin* of ale.
Songs of the Wilsons, p. 26.

DOBBY, *sb.* a ghost ; lit. a stupid. See *Dobbie* in Jamieson's Scottish Dict.

J. P. MORRIS.
1867.
Ghosts! Eigh, me lad, we've hed plenty on 'em
i' Forness, but we'd anudder neeàm for em ; we ol'as
co'd 'em *dobbies* or freetnins. Here about U'ston
we'd t' Plunton Ho' *dobby*, Swartmoor Ho' *dobby*,
Ald Ho' *dobby*, Lebby Beck *dobby*, 't Swing Gate
dobby, an' we had t' King's Arms *dobby*, tu.
T' Lebby Beck Dobby, p. 3.

DOFF, *v.* to take off or put off, to undress ; literally, do off.

1440.	And thou my concelle doo, thow *doffe* of thy clothes.
	Morte Arthure, l 1023
SHAKSPERE. 1598.	*Faulconbridge :* Thou weare a lyon's hide ! *Doff* it for shame.
	And hang a calf's-skin on those recreant limbs.
	K. John, iii. 1. 128.

RAMSBOTTOM. 1864.	*Doff* thi clogs and warm thi feet.
	Lanc. Rhymes, p. 40.
WAUGH. 1868.	Come thi ways in, an *doff* tho. An get summat warm into tho—for thae'll do wi't.—*Sneck-Bant*, i., p. 8.
DR. BARBER. 1870.	He hed *doft* his clogs an stockin's, an was paddlin amang watter an soft sand. *Forness Folk*, p. 39.

DOG-CHEAP, *adj.* excessively cheap.

| COLL. USE. 1875. | " Buy it, Mally, it's *dog-cheap*." |

DOG-DAISY, *sb.* the common field daisy, *Bellis perennis ;* sometimes applied to the ox-eye daisy, *Chrysanthemum leucanthemum.*

DOG-ROSE, *sb.* the common wild rose, *Rosa canina.*

DOIT, *sb.* a trifle ; a small share.   Cf. Icel. *dôt*, trumpery, trifles. The Dutch *duit* (pron. *doit*) was a small coin, the eighth part of a stiver, or about half a farthing.

SHAKSPERE. 1611.	*Trinculo :* When they will not give a *doit* to relieve a lame. beggar, they will lay out ten to see a dead Indian. *Tempest*, ii. 2, 32.
IBID. 1623.	*Timon :* How dost like this jewel, Apemantus ?
	Apem. : Not so well as plain dealing, which will not cost a man a *doit.*
	Timon of Athens, i. 1, 214.

| COLL. USE. 1875. | " He's not worth a *doit* " ;   " He hasn't a *doit* in his pocket." |

DOITED, *adj.* silly, foolish.   E. *dote, dotard.*   Cf. Du. *dutten*, to take a nap, from *dut*, a nap ; Icel. *dotta*, to nod from sleep ; *dottr*, a nodder.

| COLL. USE. 1875. | He's *doited ;* ne'er mind him. |

DOLLOP, *sb.* a shapeless lump, a large piece.   Cf. W. *talp*, a mass, a lump.

| COLL. USE. 1875. | Heaw mich ?   Tuppence !   What a *dollop* thae's getten ! |

DOLLY, *sb.* a wooden instrument used in washing clothes.

DON, *v.* to put on, to dress ; lit. to do on ; p. t. did on.   In this form the phrase appears in Morris's *Jason* (p. 15):

Then Jason rose and *did on* him a fair
Blue woollen tunic.

This again is very near to the Lancashire expression, " He *did*
himself up," for " He dressed himself."

1280.	That Grim bad Leve bringen lict, For to *don* on his clothes. *Havelok*, l. 576.
SHAKSPERE. 1600.	What ! should I *don* this robe, and trouble you ? Be chosen with proclamations to-day ; To-morrow yeeld up rule. *Titus Andronicus*, i. 1, 189.

BAMFORD. 1850.	On Sundays and holidays, a pair of lighter shoes, raised at the heels, would be *donned*. *Ed. of Tim Bobbin*, p. vii.
WAUGH. 1867.	Get tho *donned*, an come deawn ! Aw mun be gooin. *Owd Blanket*, c. i. p. 14.
B. BRIERLEY. 1869.	Aw tell eawr Matty sometimes, ut if hoo stonds so lung starin' i'th looking-glass when hoo's *donnin'* her- sell, hoo'll find hoo's getten int' an old maid afore hoo knows gradely where hoo is. *Red Windows Hall*, c. iv p. 26.

DONTLES, *sb. pl.* clothes to be donned. See Don *ante.*

DOSOME, *adj.* healthy. See Dō *ante.*

JOHN SCHOLES. 1857.	Hoo did look sum plump un' *dohsom*. *Jaunt to See th' Queen*, p. 43.
T. T. WILKINSON. 1873.	A quart o' this ale o'th' top ov a beef-steak 'ud mak' a chap's ribs feel *dōsome*. *Legends and Trad. of Lanc.*, 195.

DOSSUCK, } *sb.* a slovenly woman. Perhaps related to Icel. *dasi,*
DOSSY, } a lazy fellow; *dasaðr*, exhausted.

WAUGH. 1875.	Thou'll make a bonny *dossy* of a wife for sombry, when thou comes to be laft to thisel'. *Old Cronies*, ii. 20.
COLL. USE. 1875.	Hoo's a regular *dossuck*, and lies i' bed till noon.

DO-UP, *v.* to fasten. See also *dup* in Shakspere : " And *dupped*
the chamber door." *Hamlet*, iv. 5, 53.

COLL. USE. 1875.	*Do-up* mi dress ; aw connot catch th' hooks.

DOW, *sb.* alms, relief ; lit. a dole, a pittance.

RAMSBOTTOM. 1864.	To get this *dow* aw still con goo. *Lanc. Rhymes*, p. 53.

DOWD, *adj.* flat, dead. Icel. *dauðr*, dead ; *dodi*, deadness, insen-
sibility.

COLL. USE. 1875.	It's as *dowd* as dyke wayter.

DOWLY (N. Lanc.), *adj.* dull, lonely. See DEAWLDY *ante.*

DOYT, *sb.* a finger. Lat. *digitus*, a finger ; Fr. *doigt.*

COLL. USE. 1875.	Keep thi *doyts* off me.

DOYTCH-BACK, *sb.* (*i.e.* ditch back), a fence, a rampart above a ditch.

COLLIER.
1750.

Whether eh lost it ith' bruck, or weh scrawmin o'er th' *doytch-backs,* I no moor know than th' mon ith' moon.   *Works,* 55.

DOXY, *sb.* a term for a sweetheart. The author of Tim Bobbin (see below) applies the word to his wife. Also, an untidy, dirty woman. Probably from the rogue's cant or gipsy language, Nares observes that Autolycus, who sings the song in *Win. Tale,* has a spice of the cant language in his dialect. On the other hand, Dr. Mahn connects the word with Swed. *docka,* a doll, a baby. Cf. Dan. *dukke,* a doll; and perhaps E. *duck,* in the sense of sweetheart.

SHAKSPERE.
1611.

When daffodils begin to peere
With heigh the *doxy* over the dale
Why then comes in the sweet o' the yeere.
                                         Win. Tale, iv. 3, 2.

JOHN GAY.
1728.

Thus I stand like the Turk with his *doxies* around,
From all sides their glances his passion confound.
                                         Beggars' Opera : Finale.

JOHN COLLIER.
1768.

My compliments to all friends ; and tell my *doxy* that her son John is tired with living free as a hawk.
                                         Works (Letters), p. 359.

COLL. USE.
1875.

Thae'rt a bonny *doxy*—get thi weshed !

DRAD, *v.* (past tense and pp. of Dread), feared. A.S. *drædan;* p. t. *drêd ;* pp. *dræden.* Mid. E. *dradde, drad.*

CHAUCER.
1380.

He *dradde* hire so,
And his unworthynesse he ay acused.
                                         Troylus and C., Bk. ii., l. 1080.

HOLINSHED.
1586.

Saw hys people governed with such justice and good order, that he was both *dradde* and greatly beloved.   *Vol. I.,* d. 2.

SPENSER.
1590.

So from immortall race he does proceede,
That mortall hands may not withstand his might,
Drad for his derring doe and bloody deed.
                                         Faerie Queene, Bk. II., c. iv., st. 42.

COLL. USE.
1875.

"He dings her so that hoo's *drad* on him killin' hur."

DRAGGLE-TAIL, *sb.* a dirty person ; one whose skirts have been drawn through the mire.

OLD SONG.
Date uncertain.

'Twas Moll and Bet, and Doll and Kate, and Dorothy
                     Draggletail,
And John and Dick, and Joe and Jack, and Humphrey with his flail.

COLL. USE.
1875.

" Eh, what a *draggle-tail*—howd up thi' petticoats !

DRAFF, *sb.* malt grains after brewing.   Icel. *draf,* husks, dregs ;
A.S. and Du. *drabbe,* dregs, lees.

LANGLAND. 1362.	Þei [hogges] don bot dravele þeron ; *draf* weore hem levere Þen al þe presciouse Peerles þat in Paradys waxen. *Piers Plowman,* A-text, xi , 11.
CHAUCER. 1380.	Why schuld I sowen *draf* out of my fest, Whan I may sowe whete, if that me lest ? *Persones Tale,* Prol., l. 35.
1440.	*Draffe,* or drosse, or matter stamped ; pilumen. *Prompt. Parv.*
SHAKSPERE. 1598.	*Falstaff :* I had a hundred and fiftie tatter'd pro- digals, lately come from swine-keeping, from eating *draffe* and huskes.—*First K. Hen. IV.,* iv. 2, 38.
COLL. USE. 1875.	We mun get some *draff* for these cows.

DRAPE, *sb.* a cow which has ceased to give milk.   See DRIPPINS.

DREE,   ) *adj.* tedious, protracted, monotonous, wearisome.
DREESOME,)   Icel. *drjugr,* lasting ; Swed. *dryg,* long ; Dan.
dröi, large, ample. A.S. *dreógan,* to endure, to suffer ; p. t. *dreah.*
Icel. *drygja,* to lengthen ; Mid. E. *dreghe* (Hamp. *Pricke of C.,*
l. 2235 ; *E. Eng. Allit. Poems,* B, 1224).

COLLIER. 1750.	"Whooas lad arto ?" "Whau," sed he, "I'm Jone's o' Lall's o' Simmys, o' Marriom's, o' Dick's, o' Nethon's, o' Lall's o' Simmy's ith' Hooms." Odd, thinks I t' mehsel, theaws a *dree*-er name than me *Works,* p. 51.
BAMFORD. 1840.	The rain having set in *dree.*—*Life of Radical,* xx., 135.
REV. W. GASKELL. 1854.	Lancashire people talk of "*dree* rain," which often puzzles those who fancy *dree* is a corruption of "dry." And they say it rains "*dreely,*" meaning that it is continuous and enduring.—*Lect. Lanc. Dialect,* p. 22.
WAUGH. 1859.	Aw've brought thi top cwot, doesto know, For th' rain's comin' deawn very *dree.* *Lanc. Songs :* "Come Whoam to thi Childer."
DR. BARBER. 1870.	I fudged away up Gamswell . . . till I began to think it wos langsome and *dreesome* beath. *Forness Folk,* p. 3.

DRINKINS (Lancaster) *sb. pl.* lunch, labourer's dinner.

DRIPPINS, *sb.* the last yield of milk.

DROIT (S. Lanc.), *sb.* a draught of ale ; a team of horses.   A.S.
dragan, to draw.

MISS LAHEE. 1865.	Bessy, lass, bring Jone here a *droite* o' ale, an' a boite o' brade an' cheese.—*Carter's Struggles,* c. i. p. 5.
WAUGH. 1867.	But, come, winnot yo have a *droight* o' ale ? Jenny, fill him a tot. *Tattlin Matty,* c. i. p. 14.
B. BRIERLEY. 1867.	Sogger seized him by the arm, and begged he would partake of "a *droit* o' charmed drink." *Marlocks of Merriton,* c. ii. p. 35

DUB, *sb.* a pool, a marshy place, a muddy hole.   Probably of Celtic origin ; cf. Irish *dôb*, a gutter ; W. *dwfr*, water.

DUBERSOME, *adj.* doubtful, dubious.

DUBBIN, *sb.* an oily paste used for softening shoes.

DUBBLER, *sb.* a large dish.   O. Fr. *doblier*, a plate (Burguy).

| WEST MID. DIAL. (Lanc.) 1360. | A dysche oþer a *dobler* þat dryȝten oneȝ served. [= A dish or a dobler that the Lord once served.] *E. Eng. Allit. Poems*, B, l. 1146. |
| 1440. | *Dobeler*, vesselle.   Lat. parapses. *Prompt. Parv.* |

DUD, *sb.* a teat.   Cf. Mœso Goth. *daddjan*, to suckle.

| COLL. USE. 1875. | Hoo's a rare elder ; an' what *duds* ! |

DUDS, *sb. pl.* clothes.   Icel. *dúða*, to swathe in clothes, *dúði*, swaddling clothes.

| COLL. USE. 1875. | Be sharp and get thi *duds* off, an' away to bed. |

DULE, *sb.* the devil.   Contracted from A.S. *deofol*.

| WAUGH. 1859. | But aw're mazy, an' nattle, an' fasten't to tell What the *dule* it could be that're ailin mysel. *Lanc. Songs :* "Jamie's Frolic." |
| RAMSBOTTOM. 1864. | Aw'r bad enoof i' wark, for sure, Bo stoppin' plays the *aule* wi me. *Lanc. Rhymes*, p. 33. |

DUMMEL-HEEAD (N. Lanc.), *sb.* a blockhead.   A.S. *dumb*, mute, foolish ; cf. Du. *dom*, dull, stupid ; Ger. *dum*, stupid.   Cf. Ger. *dummel-kopf*.

| DR. BARBER. 1870. | "It's a fair sham," she said, "a girt *dummel-heead* it hes à feass for owte."   *Forness-Folk*, p. 32. |

DUMPS, *sb.* a low-spirited condition.   Cf. Du. *dompig*, damp, misty ; *dompen*, to extinguish.

SHAKSPERE. 1607.	*Baptista :* Why, how now, daughter Katherine, in your *dumps* ? *Tam. of Shrew*, ii. 1, 286.
COLLIER. 1761.	I from this cot, this Christmas eve, Write with a troubled mind, believe, And wife in doleful *dumps*. *Works*, 467.
COLL. USE. 1875.	Say nowt to him, he's in th' *dumps* to-day.

DUNDER-HEAD, *sb.* a blockhead.

DUNG-PIKE, *sb.* a dung-fork.

DUMMOCK, *sb.* a small heap of soil or dirt.   Prob. a dimin. of *dam*.   Cf. Du. *dam*, a bank ; Icel. *dammr*.

DUNNOCK, *sb.* the hedge-sparrow. From *dun*, as a colour ; so also *ruddock*, a red-breast, from *red*. The Icel. *dunna*, a wild duck, seems to have been similarly named.

BAMFORD, 1840.	It wur nother gorse-cock, ouzle, nor *dunnock*. *Life of Radical*, xx. 133.
IBID. 1844.	She was of middle stature ; and whilst he was as dark as a *dunnock*, she was of an excessively fair complexion.—*Walks in South Lancashire*, p. 39.

DUR, *sb.* pron. of Door.   A.S. *duru*, a door.

WRITTEN IN LANCASHIRE, About 1400.	Nerre the chapelle *dur* he 30de, Auturs for to lere. *E. Eng. Met. Rom.* B vii. 2.
WAUGH. 1865.	When we'n getten fairly off, thae mun lock th' *durs*, an' pike eawt at th' back after us. *Besom Ben*, c. iii. p. 34.

DUR-CHEEK, *sb.* doorpost.

WAUGH. 1874.	When I geet to th' house, I fund a yello-lookin' mak of a chap rear't up again th' *dur-cheek*. *Chimney Corner : Manc. Critic*, Mar. 21.

DUR-HOLE, *sb.* the doorway.

WAUGH, 1865.	Owd Mally stoode i'th' *dur-hole*, watchin 'em. *Besom Ben*, c. iv. p. 45.
IBID. 1869.	They threatn't mich an' moor that if he didn't howd his din they'd throw him eawt at th' *dur-hole*. *Yeth-Bobs*, c. ii. p. 35.

DUR-STONE, *sb.* the threshold.

COLL. USE. 1875.	He wur stondin' on th' *durstone*, an' would no goo inside.

E.

EÄ (N. and E. Lanc.), *sb.* a river or the channel of a river ; applied also to water generally. A.S. *eá*, water. Mœso-Goth. *ahwa.* Icel. *â.* The word *eá* occurs four times in the A.S. version of Genesis ii. 11—14, where the authorised version has *river.*

EALIN', *sb.* a shed set against another building ; a lean-to. Lit. a *heeling*, from the verb to *heel* or lean over. *Heel* is a corruption from Mid. E. *helden*, A.S. *hyldan*, to incline. See HELDEN in Stratmann, and HEEL in Wedgwood. For the loss of the initial *h*, see ELDER.

EASINS, *sb.* the eaves of a house ; also applied to sloping land. Thus Habergham - Eaves = Habergham slopes (properly slope, as *eaves* is singular). For *evesings*, from A.S. *efesung*, a shearing round, from the verb *efesian*, to shave round ; which from A.S. *efese*, ꞙ brim, edge, margin. Mid. E. *evesunge, evesinge.*

LANGLAND. 1377.	"Ysekeles in *eueses*," i.e., icicles upon the eaveses, P. Plowman, B. xvii 227, where four MSS. read *euesynges ;* also the C-text (xx. 193) has "Isykles in *euesynges*."
1440.	Evese or *evesinge* of a house.—*Prompt. Parv.*
COTGRAVE. 1611.	Severonde, the eaue, eauing. or *easing* of house. *French Dictionary.*

JOHN SCHOLES. 1857	See yo, Tim, hoo sed to me, iv ther is nah o felley peeorcht on th' *yeazin's*, wi o choilt in his arms. *Jaunt to See th' Queen*, p. 31.
COLL. USE. 1875.	Hearken heaw th' rain's dhrippin' off th' *easins* (or *yezzins*).

EASIN-SPARROW, *sb.* the common house-sparrow. From EASIN, *q. v.*

COLL. USE. 1875.	It's nowt but an *easin'-sparrow.*

EAVER (sometimes Ether), *sb.* ꞙ quarter of the heavens, as "the wind is in a rainy *eaver.*"

EAWL-LEET (pron. of Owl-light), *sb.* twilight.

WAUGH. 1867.	"Heaw quiet everything is," said Betty. drawing her chair nearer to Ben's. "Very," replied he, "aw olez think there's summat fine abeawt th' *eawl-leet.*" *Sneck-Bant*, c. i., p. 15.

EAWRSELS,
ERSELS, } *p.* pron. of Ourselves. See also Ursels.

RAMSBOTTOM.
1864.

O ! it was hard *eawrsels* to draw
Fro th' things i' th' heawse we'd awlus known.
Lanc. Rhymes, p. 66.

WAUGH.
1863.

Ben laid his hand upon his shoulder and said,
"Dan, owd lad; we'n o' th' world to *ersels* yet.
There isn't a wick soul i' seet."—*Yeth-B.* c. i., p. 28.

EAWT, *adv.* pron. of Out. A.S. *út* ; Icel. *út.*

WAUGH.
1867.

He ails nought, not he. Go poo him *eawt.*
Owd Blanket, c. i., p. 8.

EAWT-COMER,
EAWT-CUMLIN, } *sb.* one from another district ; a stranger.
From A.S. *cuman,* to come ; cf. O. H. G.
chomeling, a new comer, stranger.

JOHN OF TREVISA.
1387.

Þe longage of Normandy ys *comlyng* of anoþer lond.
Descrip. Britain, l. 193. *(Sp. E. Eng.,*
Pt. ii., p. 242.)

HAMPOLE.
1340.

For I am a *commelyng* toward þe,
And pilgrim, als alle my faders was.
Pricke of Conscience, l. 1385.

WYCLIF.
1380.

A *comelynge* which is a pilgrim at ʒou.
Levit. xviii., 26.

IBID.

Most dere I biseche you as *comelingis* and pilgryms.
I. Peter, ii., 11.

1440.

Comelynge, new cum man or woman ; *Adventicius,*
inquilinus. *Prompt. Parv.*

WILLIAM HARRISON.
1587.

The lawes of Malmutius . . . . indured in
execution among the Britons, so long as our *homelings*
had the dominion of this Ile. Afterwards, when the
comeling Saxons had once obteined the superioritie of
the kingdom, the maiestie of those lawes fell for a
time into . . . decaie —*Description of England :*
Ed. by Furnivall for New Shakspere Soc., Bk. II.,
c. ix., p. 189. ———

JOHN SCHOLES.
1857.

One o theese same hauve-clemm'd *eawtcumblin's*
sed ut Englond awt to bi guvern'd by commun sense.
Jaunt, p. 55.

EAWT-O-FLUNTERS, *adv.* Phr. Out of order. It is obvious that
flunters can hardly mean *order* here ; the phrase is probably a corruption of eawt-*to*-flunters, *i.e.* out to splinters. See FLENDERS,
shreds, splinters, in Brockett. To "fly to *flinders*" means to fly
to pieces. The Dutch *flenters* means tatters. So Nares gives
the Mid. E. *fling* with the sense of a trifle ; lit. a fragment. The
root is the verb to *fling*, which is best illustrated by the Old Swed.
flenga, to beat, and Lat. *fligere :* cf. Lat. *affligere.*

WAUGH.
1865.

When he geet th' organ into his cart, they towd
him to be particular careful an' keep it th' reet side
up ; and he wur to mind an' not shake it mich, for it
wur a thing that wur yezzy thrut *eawt o' flunters.*
Barrel Organ, p. 18.

IBID.
1867.

" Yo'n catched us *eawt-o-flunters,*" said the poor
woman when we entered ; but what con a body do ?
Home Life Lanc. Factory Folk, c. xix., 166.

EDDER (S. Lanc.),
EDTHER (N. Lanc.),
ETHERD (E. Lanc.), } *sb.* an adder. Mid. O. E. *addre, eddre*, probably = *naddre, neddre.* A.S. *næddre, nædre ;* etym. disputed.

1220.

"Þe *nddere*," seið Salomon, "stingeð ul stilliche."
Ancren Riwle, p. 82, 11.

WYCLIF.
1380.

Yee sarpentis, fruytis of *eddris*, hou shulen yee flee fro the dom of helle ?   *Matt.* xxiii , 33.

CHAUCER.
1380

Here may ye see, that dedly synne hath first suggestioun of the feend, as scheweth here by the *neddir.*
The Persones Tale, Ald. ed., vol. iii.,
p. 287, l. 22.

1440.

Eddyr, or neddyr, wyrme ; Serpens.
Prompt. Parv.

COLL. USE.
1875.

He's bin bitten by an *edder* [*edther* or *etherd*].

EDDISH or EDDITCH, *sb.* the first grass after mowing. A.S. *edisc*, aftermath, where prefix *ed* = again. Mid. E. *edisch.*

SIR ANTHONY FITZHERBERT.
1523.

If all shulde lye common, than wolde the *edyche* of the corne feldes, and the undermath of all the medowes be eten in x. or xii. dayes.
The Boke of Surveying.

BP. KENNETT.

Eddish, roughings or after-math in meadows, but more properly the stubble or gratten in corn-fields. This word is in some southern parts corrupted into *ersh*, and in Surrey into *esh*, as a wheat esh, a barley esh.—*Glossarial Collections,* Lansdowne MSS., 1033.

COLL. USE.
1875.

This rain 'ull fotch th' *eddish* up.

EDGE-O'-DARK, *sb.* twilight.

WAUGH.
1868.

It 'll tak thee a greight while to gether fifty shillin' i' tow-brass [toll money], at th' rate we're gooin at— a keaw i' th' forenoon, a wheelbarrow i' th' afternoon, an' happen a jackass at th' *edge-o'-dark.*
Sneck-Bant, c. ii., p. 39.

IBID.

We's be back again abeawt th' *edge-o'-dark*, when th' crow flies home.   *Ibid,* c. iv., p. 72.

EDGRO or ETGRO, *sb.* the aftermath. A.S. *ed*, again + *grow*. Cf. A.S. *edgrówung,* a re-growing.

1440.

Edgrow, gresse. *Bigermen, regermen.*
Prompt. Parv.

COLL. USE (E.L.)
1875.

So mitch for t' gress and soa mitch for t' *etgro.*

EDDERBOWT,
EDTHERBOWT, } *sb.* the dragon-fly. See EDDER, EDTHER + *bolt.*

COLL. USE.
1875.

It'll sting like an *edder-bout.*

EDDERCROP,
EDTHERCROP, } *sb.* a spider. Formed like A.S. *átter-coppa*, a spider, with a variation in the second part.

It is therefore from A.S. *átter*, poison, and *crop*, a top, or bunch, alluding to the supposed poison bag.

JOHN SCHOLES. 1857.	Aw met weel foind o *eddercrop* creepin' o' mi cwoats, hoo sed. *Jaunt*, p. 15.
COLL. USE. 1875.	Th' edges are full o' *edthercrop* neesus (nests).

EE-BREE, *sb.* the eyebrow. A.S. *eáge*, eye, and *bræw*, brow.

COLL. USE. 1875.	He's a fause un, aw con tell bi his *ee-brees*.

EE, *sb.* the eye; EEN, pl. A.S. *eáge*, pl. *eágan*.

CHAUCER. 1386.	Hire nose streight ; hire *eyen* grey, as glas. *Prologue C. T.*, 152.
DUNBAR. 1503.	All present wer in twynkling of ane *E*, Baith beist, and bird, and flowr, befoir the quene. *Thistle and Rose*, 13.
IBID.	Me thocht Aurora, with hir cristall *ene*, In at the window lukit by the day. *Ibid*, 2.
GAWIN DOUGLAS. 1513.	The fyry sparkis brastyng from hys *eyn* To purge the ayr, and gylt the tendyr greyn. *Prologue XII. Book of the Æneid*, l. 39.
SPENSER. 1590.	His belly was upblowne with luxury, And eke with fatnesse swollen were his *eyne*. *Fairy Queen*: I., iv., 21.
IBID.	My star is falne, my comfort done, Out is the apple of my *eine*. *An Elegie: Astrophel*, l. 69.
REV W. GASKELL 1854.	In Anglo-Saxon, one declension of substantives formed the plural in "an," the only relic of which in modern English is in the word "oxen." In Lancashire we have two words as least beside "oxen," in which this form is preserved. They occur in this passage from the "Okeawnt uth Greyt Eggshibishun" :—"They'rne sum uth grandest carpits us ever aw clapt my *een* on ; aw wondur heaw they cud foind e' ther hearts fur to set ther *shoon* on um." *Lect. Lanc. Dialect*, p. 23.
WAUGH. 1859.	Thi cheeks are grooin thinner, An th' leet has laft thi *ee*. *Lanc. Songs*: What ails thee, my Son Robin.
IBID. 1859.	He cried till his *een* were quite red. He likes thee 'some weel, does yon lad! *Ib.*: Come whoam to thi childer.
B. BRIERLEY. 1870.	He oppent a pair o' *een* as wide as a sheead. *Bundle o' Fents*, I., p. 32.

EEM, *v.* to spare time; to find an opportunity; to be able to compass an object; to get into the way of doing a thing. A.S. *efnan*, to be able to perform; Icel. *efna*, to perform, chiefly to fulfil a vow or the terms agreed upon; Dan. *evne*, to have ability; Swed. *ämna*, to form, shape. In like manner, the A.S. *efen*, even, becomes *eme* in provincial English.   Shakspere uses *even* as a verb.

CÆDMON.
About 680.

Efndon únrihtdóm [i e., they performed unrighteous-ness.]   *Ed. Thorpe*, p. 227, l. 7.

DR. BYROM.
1745.

We warken hard as't iz for meeat and clooas,
An connot *eem* to be so feert, God knooas.
                                        Misc. Poems, vol. i., p. 157.

COLLIER.
1750.

E law, whot o cank han we had ! I mennaw [may or must not] *eem* to stey onny lunger.
                                        Works, p 71.

COLL. USE.
1875.

1. Aw've tried mony a time but aw could never *eem* to do it.

2. If aw wur thee aw'd *eem* to do that or elze aw'd see what it sticks on.

EEND-WAY,
EEND-WAYS,
ENDAS (Mid. and E. Lanc.),
} *adv.* outright; at once ; to the ending or finish.   Cf. Spenser's use of *endlong* :—

That who from East to West will *endlong* seeke,
Cannot two fairer Cities find this day.
                                        Fairy Queen, III. ix , 51.

Also Dryden :—

Then, spurring, at full speed, ran *endlong* on.
                                        Palamon and Arcite, iii., l. 691.

COLLIER.
1750.

So I took *eendwey*, for it wur welly neet.
                                        Works, p. 59.

IBID.

Get *eendwey* ; its prime rime efeath.
                                        Works, p 39.

B. BRIERLEY.
1869.

Aw've done seventy odd year beaut bein' drawn like a dobby-hoss ; an' aw meean to do *eend-way*.
                                        Red Windows Hall, c. xiii., p. 104.

WAUGH.
1875.

"Rom a bit o' talk in," said Rondle o' Rogers, "an' get *eend-way*."   *Old Cronies*, c. v., p. 51.

EEN-NEAW (pron. of Even now), *adv.* directly, bye-and-bye, in a short time, a short time ago.

SHAKSPERE.
1595.

Nurse : What's this?   What's this ?
Juliet :   A rhyme I learned *even now*
              Of one I danced withal.
                                        Rom. and Jul., i. 5

BIBLE.
1611.

Moreover the Lord shall raise him up a king over Israel, who shall cut off the house of Jeroboam that day : but what ? *even now.*—1 *Kings*, xiv., 14.

COLLIER.
1750.

I'st tell the moor o that *eend-neaw*.
                                        Works, p. 60.

B. BRIERLEY.
1870.

E'enneaw wi seed Jonathan Grimshaw comin' deawn bi th' side o' th' dingle.
                                        Bundle o' Fents, i., 26.

EET,
ET,
} *v.* ate, did eat.   Pr. t., ate ; imp. t., eet or et ; per. t., eetn or etten ; pr. par., atin. Thus: "Canto *ate* this bread?" "Aw *eet* [or *et*] what thae gan mi."   "He's *etten* o' th' lot."

" Be quiet, aw'm *atin* mi baggin." A.S. *etan*, pt. t. *ǽt*, pl. *ǽton.*
Icel. *eta ;* pret. *át*, pl. *átu ;* pres. *et.*

1320.　　　Þar þai offerd. praid, and snank,
　　　　　Thre dais noþer *ete* ne dranc.
　　　　　　　Cursor Mundi. (Sp. E. Eng., pt. ii. p. 70, l 40.)

HAMPOLE.　　Alswa in þe days of Loth befelle,
1340.　　　Men *ete* and drank, shortly to telle,
　　　　　Ilkan with other.　　　　　*Pricke of C.* l. 4847

WYCLIF.　　Therfore whanne thei hadden *etyn*, Ihesu seith
1380.　　　　　　　　　　　　*John* xxi. 15.

CHAUCER.　　Ful sooty was hir bour, and eek hir halle,
1386.　　　In which she *eet* ful many a sclender meel.
　　　　　　　　　Norme Prest his Tale, l. 12.

EGADLINS, *int.* a diminutive oath.　*Egad*, for *begad*, with dimin. suffix.

JOHN SCHOLES.　　*Egodlins,* Betty, sez aw, aw think wın no need to
1857.　　　goo ony furr.　　　　*Jaunt*, p. 19.

COLL. USE.　　*Egadlins !* wi mun bı sharp eawt o' this pleck or
1875.　　　they'n catch us.
　　　　　　　●

EGODSNAM, *int.* a form of oath ; contraction of "in God's name."

COLLIER.　　Heau's tat *e Godsnum ?*—*Works.* p. xxxvi.
1750.

EGG, *v.* to urge on, to incite.　A.S. *eggian*, to incite.　Icel. *eggja*, to egg on, incite, goad ; from A.S. *ecg*, Icel. *egg*, an edge, point.

1220.　　　Bacbitunge, and fikelunge, and *eggunge* to don eni
　　　　　vuel.　　　　　　*Ancren Riwle*, p. 82.

1350.　　　And next was peynted coveitise
　　　　　That *eggeth* folk in many gise.
　　　　　　　　Romaunt of Rose, 181.

LANGLAND.　　Fader of Falsness, he foundede it him-seluen ;
1362.　　　Adam and Eue he *eggede* to don ille.
　　　　　　　　Piers Plowman : A. Passus I. l. 62.

WEST MID. DIAL (Lanc.)　Bot þur3 þe *eggyng* of Eue he ete of an apple
1360.　　　　　　*Allit. Poems :* "Cleanness," l. 241.

CHAUCER.　　January hath caught so gret a wille,
1386.　　　Thorough *eggyng* of his wyf, him for to pleye
　　　　　In his gardeyn.　　*Marchaundes Tale*, l 890.

1440.　　　*Eggyn*, or entycyn, to doon' welle or yvele ; *Incıto,
provoco.*　　　　　　*Prompt. Parv.*

　　　　　　　――――――――

COLL. USE.　　He *eggs* him on to o' sorts o' mischief.
1875.

EGG-CLOCK, *sb.* a cockchafer.　See CLOCK.

COLL. USE.　　Lancashire Proverb . Kill a *egg-clock* an' it 'll rain
1875.　　　to-morn.

EGGS-AN'-COLLOPS, *sb.* toad-flax, *Linaria vulgaris.*

EH, *pron.* I.　Cf. Icel. *ek, eg*, I.

WAUGH.　　" Aw'm donnin this lad as fast as *eh* con," replied
1868.　　　Betty.　　　　*Sneck-Bant*, c. iii., p 50

EH, *interj.* oh or ah.

WAUGH.
1867.

Eh, Ailse—that blanket, that owd blanket! *Eh,* iv that blanket could talk, Ailse, it could oather make folk laugh or cry!—*Owd Blanket,* c. iii., p. 61.

B. BRIERLEY.
1870.

"*Eh,* whatever is ther' t' do," hoo shrikt eawt.
Bundle o' Fents, i., p. 31.

EIGH, *adv.* aye, yes.

COLLIER.
1750.

Mary : Is Seroh o' Rutchots so honsome ?
Tim : Eigh, hoos meeterly.   *Works,* p. 54.

J. P. MORRIS.
1867.

Tom ex'd t' priest if it was trew 'at ther' wos sich things. "*Eigh,*" said t' āld fella, an' his lile black eyes fair twinkled wi' fun, "*Eigh,* ther's many a million on 'em."   *Lebby Beck Dobby,* p. 5.

EISCH-KEYS (N. and Mid. Lanc.), *sb.* the pods containing the seed of the ash. A.S. *æsc,* ash-tree ; whether the ending is really Å.S. *cæg,* a key, is not proven.

.1440.

Esch key, frute ; Clava in fructinus.—*Prompt. Parv.*

COLL. USE (N. Lanc.
1875.

Child *loq. :* Let's ga an' gedder some *eisch-keys* an' lake at conquerors. [In this amusement the wings of the seed are interlocked ; each child then pulls, and the one whose "keys" break is conquered.]

ELDER, ⎫ *adv.* rather, more easily. Icel. *heldr,* more, rather.
ELTHER, ⎭   Dan. *heller.* Vigfusson says "Only Scandinavian, not being found in Teutonic dialects." Yet it is found in Mœso-Gothic in the form *haldis.* The literal meaning of *haldis* is more favourable, and A.S. *hold,* friendly, is from the same root. Thus *elder* really means "with more pleasure." Cf. A.S. *hyld,* inclination, favour.

WEST MID. DIAL. (Lanc.)
1320.

Gawan goꝫ to þe gome, with giserne in honde,
And he baldly hym bydeꝫ, he bayst neuer þe *helder.*
Sir Gawayne and Grene Kt., l. 375.

WAUGH.
1857.

Aw'd go as fur as oather grace grew or waytur ran, afore aw'd live amoon sich doins. One could *elther* manage we't at th' for-end o' their days.
Lanc. Sketches : Bury to Rochdale, p. 26.

IBID.
1874.

I declare I'd *elder* see 'em wortchin for th' next to nought nor see 'em doin nought. It keeps 'em out o' lumber, an that's summat.
Chimney Corner : Manchester Critic, Feb. 21.

ELDER, *sb.* the cow's udder.

COLL. USE.
1875.

When thaer't milkin', Nancy, thae mun' bi gentle wi hur, hur *elder's* a bit sore.

ELDERS, *sb.* ancestors, parents, betters. A.S. *eldran, yldran,* elders, parents.

LANGLAND.
1362.

God sende to seie, by Samuel mouþe,
þat Agag and Amalec and al his peple aftur,
Schulden dye for a dede þat don hedde his *eldren*
Aꝫeynes Israel and Aaron and Moyses his broþer.
Piers Plowman, A-text ; Passus iii. 246.

WYCLIF.
1380.

And I profitide in the Iewerie aboue manye of myne euene *elderis* in my kynrede, and was more aboundantli a folowere of my fadris tradicions.
Galat. c. i.
[The Authorized Version, in place of "manye of myne, euene *elderis* in my kynrede" has "many my equals in mine own nation."]

CHAUCER.
1386.

For he was boren of a gentil hous
And had his *eldres* noble and vertuous.
Wyf of Bathes Tale, 298.

SIR WALTER RALEIGH.
1610.

Hereof it came, that the word [*elder*] was always used both for the magistrate, and for those of age and gravity ; the same bearing one signification in almost all languages. *Hist. World,* b. i. c 9. s. 1.

SHAKSPERE.
1623.

Cæsar: Forget not in your speed, Antonio,
To touch Calphurnia ; for our *elders* say,
The barren touched in this holy chace,
Shake off their sterrile curse. *Jul. Cæs.,* i. 2, 6.

ELDIN' (N. Lanc.), } *sb.* fuel or fire. The word is
EILDIN' (N., Mid., and S. Lanc.), } ·appl. to any kind of fuel, and to the brushwood of which fences are made. Icel. *elding,* firing, fuel ; Scot. *eilding,* from Icel. *eldr,* fire ; A.S. *æled,* fire ; A.S. *ælan,* to kindle.

1440.

Eyldynge, or fowayle ; Focale.—*Prompt. Parv.*

WAUGH.
1857.

He fetched a great handful of heather from the inner room, and, cramming into the fire-place, put a light to it. Up blazed the inflammable *eilding,* with a crackling sound.—*Lanc. Sketches:* Rochdale to Blackstone Edge, p. 156.

IBID.
1866.

These coals were burnt very sparingly, with dried roots, brushwood, and other bits of dried "*eildin'.*"
Ben an' th' Bantam, c. i., p. 14.

DR. BARBER.
1870.

She'd just thraan down a girt leadd o' fire *eldin',* she'd fetcht off t' fell. *Forness Folk,* p. 15.

ELLY-MOUTH (N. Lanc.), *sb.* a bound or goal in the game of football. Probably a corruption of Mid. E. *hell-mouth,* a common expression due to the fact that the entrance to *hell* was commonly represented by a widely opened *mouth.* See the numerous illustrations in Nares' Glossary, *s. v.* Barlibreak. Herrick wrote an epigram, with the title "Barlibreak, or Last in Hell." *Hell* was the middle compartment of the three which were marked out in playing this game.

ELSIN (S. Lanc.), } *sb.* a sort of shoemaker's awl. The Dutch
ELSON (E. Lanc.). } word for an *awl* (A.S. *æl, awel*) is *els,* from which *elsin* is formed by the addition of the diminutive suffix *in.* Tauchnitz's Dutch Dict. has the entry : "*Els,* f. an awl, elsin."

1440.

Elsyn ; Sibula.—*Prompt. Parv.*

1571.

In the inventory of the goods of a merchant as Newcastle. A.D. 1571, occur "vj doss' *elsen* heftet 12d. j clowte and ⅓ a c *elson* blades."
Wills and Inv.: Surtees Soc. i. 361.

ELT (E. Lanc.) *v.* to stir oaten dough some time after kneading. Icel. *elta*, (1) to chase; (2) to knead, to work. Mid. E. *elten*, to knead.

> COLL. USE.   Hoos *eltin* t' doff an canno' come.
> 1875.

END-IRON (S. Lanç.),   } *sb.* a moveable plate
END-ARNS (E. Lanc. and Goosnargh dist.), }   to contract the fireplace. *End* may be a corruption here, as the common word is *andiron.*

> COLL. USE (E. Lanc.)   Put them *endarns* in an id'l nod brun so monny
> 1875.   coyls.

ENTY (N. Lanc.), *sb.* the last furrow in a rigg. A.S. *ende ;* Icel. *endi*, the end, conclusion.

ER, *pron.* our. A.S. *úre*, lit. of us, gen. pl. of *we.*

> WAUGH.   We'n live't together, an' we'n had th' best ov *er*
> 1867.   days together.   *Owd Blanket,* c. iii., p. 63.

ESHLE-TREE (N. and E. Lanc.), *sb.* an axle-tree. A.S. *eax*, an axle-tree, with the dimin. suffix *el.*

> 1440.   *Axyltre* or *exyltre.* Axis.—*Prompt. Parv.*

ESLINS (N. and E. Lanc.), *sb.* a salmon-fly.

ESS (S. and S. E. Lanc. and Goosnargh dist.), *sb.* ashes. A.S. *asce, ásce ;* Icel. *aska ;* Mid. E. *asche, esche, esse.*

> DAN MICHEL.   Huet am ich bote *esssse* [i e. what am I but ashes.]
> 1340.   *Ayenbite of Inwyt,* p. 137.
>
> [This, however, only illustrates the *vowel;* the consonant is quite different, since the Kentish *ss* means *sh;* and the doubling of *sh* is indicated by the four *esses ;* hence *esssse* = esh-she, a disyllable. Dr. Stratmann seems not to have noticed this, and spells the word wrongly.]
>
> COLL. USE..   Come, lass, sweep th' *ess* up, an' let's bi lookin'
> 1875.   tidy.

ESS-HOLE (S. and S. E. Lanc.), *sb.* the hole under the fire which receives the ashes. See Ess.

> COLLIER.   Deawn he coom o th' harstone, on his heeod i th
> 1750.   *esshole.*   *Works,* p. 52.
>
> B. BRIERLEY.   Theau'rt farrantly yet, if theau'd nobbut keep eaut
> 1868.   o'th' *esshole,* an' smarten thissel' up.
>   *Fratchingtons,* p. 11.

ETTLE (N. and E. Lanc.), *v.* to intend, to purpose. Icel. *ætla*, (1) to think, mean. suppose; (2) to intend of oneself, purpose. Mid. E. *ahtlien, atlien, etlen.*

> WEST MID. DIAL. (Lanc.)   Forþi an aunter in erde I *attle* to schawe.
> 1360.   *Sir Gawayne and Grene Knt.,* l. 27.
>
> WEST MID. DIAL. (Lanc.)   Me bos tellè to þat tolk þe tene of my wylle
> 1360.   And alle myn *attlyng* [purpose] to Abraham vn-haspe
>   bylyne.   *Allit. Poems,* B, l. 687.

WILLIAM (Surname unknown.) þe emperour entred in a wey euene to *attele*,
1360.   To haue bruttenet þat bor at þe abaie seþþen.
Will. and Werwolf, 205.

COLL. USE.   East Lancashire Saying : He's ready to *ettle* but
1875.   never to do.

ETTLE (N. and E. Lanc.), *adj.* stingy.   A.S.·*etol*, greedy, occurring
in the compound *ofer-etol*.

COLL. USE (E. Lanc.)   Hoo's varra *ettle* to-day, an' gi's next to nowt.
1875.

EVVEN-DOWN, *adv.* (N. and E. Lanc), *i.e.* even-down; thorough,
downright.

COLL. USE (E.Lanc.).   I gav him a *evven-down* blow.
1875.

EVVEN-FORRIT (N. Lanc.), ⎱ *adv.*, *i.e.* even fore-right or even-
EVVEN-FURRUD (E. Lanc.),⎰   forward; directly forward.

COLL. USE.   He went *evven-forrud* an' nowt could stop him.
1875.

EVVEN-ON, *adv.* (N. and E. Lanc.), *i.e.* even-on ; close to the
mark.

COLL. USE. (E. Lanc.)   That wur *evven-on* t' hoyle.
1875.

EX,   ⎫
EXT,   ⎬ *v.* pron. of Ax and Asked *(q. v.)* in Furness and E. Lanc.
ESHT,   ⎭

J. P. MORRIS.   A chap i' U'ston . . wos gā'n tā *ex* neābody
1867.   knā's how mitch a pund for it.
Invasion o' U'ston, p. 4.

DR. BARBER.   A slonkin sooart of a chap *ext* for a leet job o'
1870.   some maks at t' pits.   *Forness Folk*, p. 21.

EYSEL, *sb.* a kind of vinegar made from the juice of the wild crab.
O. Fr. *aisil*, vinegar (Roquefort) ; which is said to be from the
Greek ὀξαλὶς, which from ὀξὺς, sharp.

ANON.   That lad her life onely by bread
1370.   Kneden with *eisell* strong and egre.
Romaunt of the Rose, l. 217.

WICLIF.   And thou shalt greithe [make ready] *eysel* veselis
1380.   and phiols.   *Exodus*, xxv. 29.

1440.   *Esylle.* Acetum.   *Prompt. Parv.*

SHAKSPERE.   Whilst, like a willing patient, I will drink
1609.   Potions of *eysell*, 'gainst my strong infection.
Sonnet, c. xi.

REV. W. GASKELL.   I have not heard the word for some thirty years. . .
1854.   I have heard Lancashire people formerly make use of
the expression "as sour as *eysel*."
Lect. Lanc. Dialect, p. 12.

F.

FADDER (Mid. and N. Lanc.), *sb.* father. A.S. *fæder ;* Du. *vader ;* Dan. and Swed. *fader.* Professor Skeat *(Etymological Dictionary)* says " the spelling *fader* is almost universal in Middle English ; *father* occurs in the Bible of 1551. The change from M.E. *fader, moder,* to *father, mother,* is remarkable, and perhaps due to the influence of *th* in *brother* (A.S. *broðor*), or to Icel. *faðir.*" *Father* occurs in Tyndale's New Testament of 1526.

A. C. GIBSON.
(High Furness Dialect.)
1868.

He was niver seen ageean wi neàbody. He partit wi' Betty at her *fadder* duer i' Tilberthet, an' that was t' last on him !   *Folk-Speech of Cumberland,* p. 94.

WAUGH.
(Furness Dialect.)
1874.

Ye see, my *fadder* an' mudder lies buried there—an' my gran-*fadder,* an' my great gran-*fadder,* an' I know not hoo mony mair o' my awn kin.
Jannock, c. vi., p. 55.

FADDLE, *sb.* nonsense, evasive trifling. (Bamford's Glossary.) Usually used with the addition of the word *fiddle.*

COLL. USE.
1880.

Come, no *fiddle faddle ;* out with it at once, mon.

FADGE, *sb.* a burden, part of a horse's load. (Bamford's Glossary.)

FADGE, *v.* to toil.

DR. BARBER.
(Furness Dialect.)
1870.

I set off by t' Gillbanks, an' *fadged* away up Gamswell.   *Forness Folk,* p. 3.

FAFFMENT (N. Lanc.), *sb.* nonsense.

FAIN, *adj.* and *v.* glad, delighted, eager, fond, willing, compelled or obliged. A.S. *fægen,* glad. The word in the forms *fayn, fayne,* and *feyn,* is to be found in the *Alliterative Poems,* West Midland (Lancashire) dialect, 1360 ; Piers Plowman, Chaucer, and is indeed common in Mid. Eng. See also Shakspere's *2 Hen. VI.,* act ii., sc. 1.; Bacon's Essay " Of Empire ;" Burns' *Tam o' Shanter ;* Sir W. Scott's *Black Dwarf,* chap. ii.; Morris's *Jason,* p. 91 ; Forster's *Life of Dickens,* vol. i., p. 182.

MISS LAHEE.
1865.

Aw'm rare an' *fain* at yo could cheat yon owd stingy beggar out of ought.   *Carter's Struggles,* p. 28.

WAUGH.
1867.

."Wed folk, be hanged !" answered Ben. " Aw'm *fain* 'at we are wed, lass; an' that's moor nor some can say."   *Owd Blanket,* c. i., p. 25.

FAIR, *adv.* really, actually, completely.

COLL. USE.
1880.

Aw wur *fair* shuddering wi' cowd.
He wur *fair* gloppent (completely astonished).
He wur *fair* done up.

FAIRIN', *sb.* a gift from the fair.

FAIRISH-ON, *adj.* elderly; also partially intoxicated.

FAND (W. Lanc.), *v.* found. *Cursor Mundi*, A.D. 1320, Cotton and Gottingen MSS., l. 10,993; *Alliterative Poems*, A.D. 1360, A. 870; and in other Northumbrian and West Midland texts.

J. P. MORRIS. (Furness Dialect.) 1867.	Ivery roum an' celler wos rumiged ower an' ower, but they *fand* nowte. *Invasion o' U'ston*, p. 5.
WAUGH. (Furness Dialect.) 1874.	He *fand* that his breeches were getten sadly aat o' gear. *Jannock*, c. vii., p. 61.

FARMOST, *adj.* farthest. Also pronounced *furmost*. Dryden has " Within the *farmost* entrance of the grot." (*Sigismonda*, l. 264.)

COLL. USE. 1880.	He lives at th' *furmost* house i'th' lone.

FARRANT, *adj.* becoming, decent, nice, applied to action or dress. See *Sir Gawayne and the Green Knight* (A.D. 1320), l. 101, for "*farand* fest" = goodly feast; *E. E. Alliterative Poems*, West Mid. (Lanc.) dialect, A.D. 1360, Bk. A., l. 864, for " talle *farande*" = pleasing tale.

FARRANTLY, *adv.* decently. See *E. E. Alliterative Poems*, Bk. C., l. 435, for *farandely* = pleasantly.

FARRANTLY, *adj.* reputable, decent.

COLLIER. 1750.	Yo'ar a ninyhommer t' heed 'ur, for there's none sich *farrantly* talk abeawt 'ur.—*Works: Tim Bobbin*, p. 72.
JOHN SCHOLES. 1857.	Hoo's as hard a wortchin', howsom, *farrently*, daysunt o body us is to bi fund e Smobridge. *Jaunt to see th' Queen*, p. 14.
WAUGH. 1859.	Aw'd tak him just while he're inclined, An' a *farrantly* bargain he'd be. *Lanc. Songs: The Dule's i' this Bonnet*.
B. BRIERLEY. 1868.	Theau'rt *farrantly* yet, if theau'd nobbut keep eaut o' th' esshole, an' smarten thisel up. *Fratchingtons*, p. 11.

FASH, *v.* to trouble, annoy, vex. O.F. *fascher*, "to anger, displease, offend." (Cotgreave.) See Burns' *Epistle to James Smith*.

COLL. USE. 1880.	Tha' doesn't need to *fash* thisell abeawt it. It 'll come reet i'th' end.

FASH, *sb.* the leaves of a turnip or carrot. (Bamford's Glossary.)

FASH (Ormskirk), *v.* to pare, to cut off.

FAST-GATED, *adj.* reckless, thoughtless. Lit. : quick-paced.

WAUGH. 1875.	He didn't like th' notion of his hard-getten brass bein' squander't bi a *fast-gated* spendthrift. *Old Cronies*, c. iv., p. 40.

FATTERT, *v.* embarrassed.

BAMFORD. 1850.	He's quite *fattert* wi' it.—*Glossary*.

FAUSE or FAWSE, } *adj.* wise, cunning, sly.

COLLIER. 1750.	Odd ! but that wur o meety *fawse* owd felly. *Works: Tim Bobbin*, p. 57.
WAUGH. 1876.	He're as *fause* as a boggart, as th' neighbours weel knew, Though—when he'd a mind—he could look like a foo. *Poems and Songs : The Grindlestone.*
IBID. 1876.	Mi faither wur about as *fause* a chap as ever I let on. *Chimney Corner*, c. vii.

FAVVOUR (favour), *v.* to resemble, to have the same outward appearance or form.   This verb is formed from the noun *favour* in its old sense.

WAUGH. 1855.	*Jone.* Yo reckelect'n a 'torney co'in' here once't. What dun yo think o' him ? *Sam.* He *favvurs* a foo, Jone ; or aw'm a foo mysel'.
JOHN SCHOLES. 1857.	Whot ! thoose show dolls ? sed Tum. Thi *favvurn* us iv thid bin tryin' to jump thru th' hoop un ud stuck'n fast i' th' middle on't.—*Jaunt to see th' Queen*, p. 23.
WAUGH. 1867.	"Who are they ?" said the landlord ; "conto make 'em eawt ?" "Nawe," answered the carter ; "but they *favvour'n* Todmorden chaps." *Dulesgate*, p. 19.

FAWN-FRECKLED, *adj.* freckled, having small spots on the face. A Lancashire folk-rhyme runs thus—

> Fawn-freckles han made a vow,
> They'll noan come on a face that's feaw.

This is because freckles are usually found on a fair skin.

FAYBERRY, *sb.* = fairy's berry ; a gooseberry.

| WAUGH. 1868. | "Well," said Randal, "heaw arto for gooseberries ?" "Eh," said Ben, "aw ha'not a *fayberry*-tree i' th' garden." *Sneck-Bant*, c. ii., p. 26. |
| IBID. 1875. | There's a hare under th' *fayberry* tree, at th' bottom o' yo'r garden. Yo' mun be sharp. *Old Cronies*, c. vii., p. 89. |

FEAR, *v.* to frighten, to terrify.   Frequent in Shakspere.   See *Venus and Adonis*, l. 1,094 ; *Ant. and Cleo.*, ii., sc. 6 ; *Tam. Shrew*, i., 2, l. 211.   See FEART.

FEART or FEAR'D, } *v.* afraid, frightened, terrified.   See FEAR, AFEARD.

JOHN SCHOLES. 1857.	*Feeurt*, sez tah ! Aw've sin naut e Manchistur ut con *feeur* me. *Jaunt to see th' Queen*, p. 27.
MISS LAHEE. 1865.	Aw'm *feert* on it deein', cose it's bin ailin' this day or two, an' ud eyt nought.—*Carter's Struggles*, p. 33.
WAUGH. 1866.	Yo'n nought to be *feeor't* on. He's fuddle't to-neet but a quieter chap never broke brade. *Ben an' th' Bantam*, c. vi., p. 114.

FEATHER-YED, *sb.* a light and brainless person.   Tennyson's *Queen Mary*, v. 1., "A fool and featherhead."

FEAW, *adj.* ugly, unhandsome.

> WAUGH.
> 1855.
>
> There never wur a *feaw* face i' this world but there wur a *feaw* fancy to match it, somewheer.
>
> *Lanc. Sketches: Bury to Rochdale.*

FEEÄG (Furness), *sb.* a flatterer. A.S. *fægnian,* to flatter.

FEERIN' }
FEORIN' } *sb. pl.* evil spirits, fearful things.

> WAUGH.
> 1855.
>
> In the lonely detached dwellings which are scattered among the hills and cloughs of the " Edge " [Blackstone Edge] they cling to the speech, and ways, and superstitions of their rude forefathers. A tribe of hardy, industrious, old-fashioned, simple-hearted folk, whose principal fear is poverty and boggarts. They still gather round the fire, in corners where factories have not reached them, on dark nights in winter, to feed their imagination with scraps of old legend, and tales of boggarts, fairies, and *feeorin'* that haunt their native hills and dales.—
>
> *Lanc. Sketches: Rochdale to Blackstone Edge,* p. 124.

> JOHN HIGSON.
> 1852.
>
> As for fact'ry lads, they caren nowt noather for boggarts nur *feorin'.*—*Gorton Historical Recorder,* p. 17.

> JOHN SCHOLES.
> 1857.
>
> Wheer aw wur browt up at, it fair swarmt wi *feeorin'.*
>
> *Jaunt to see th' Queen,* p. 60.

> WAUGH.
> 1859.
>
> Neaw, mother, dunnot fret yo ;
> Aw am not like mysel' ;
> But, 'tis not lung o' th' *feeorin'*
> That han to do wi' th' deil.
>
> *Lanc. Songs: What ails thee, my son Robin?*

FEERSUNS-EEN, *sb.* Shrovetide. Such is Collier's spelling. The more recent form is Fasten-een. See Burns' *Epistle to Lapraik :*—

> On *Fasten-een* we had a rockin,
> To ca' the crack, and weave our stockin.

> COLLIER.
> 1750.
>
> For I should be lose ot *Feersuns-een,* on it matter't naw mitch. *Works: Tim Bobbin,* p. 68.

FEGGUR, *adj.* fairer. (Bamford's Glossary.) A.S. *feger, fegr,* fair.

FELD, *past tense* of *v.* to feel.

FELLY, *sb.* a fellow, a man, a sweetheart.

> WAUGH.
> 1868.
>
> Little Billy put his arm round his mother's neck, and said, "Aw's be a *felly,* soon, shan't aw, mam?" "Ay, in a bit, my love," replied Betty, with a long-drawn sigh ; "in a bit, iv God spares thi life." "Little lads o' groon into *fellys,* don't they mam?" "Ay, if they liven, my love," answered Betty, in a quiet tone.
>
> *Sneck-Bant,* c. iii., p. 53.

> COLL. USE.
> 1880.
>
> Sithee, that first is a *felly;* t'other are o' women.

> IBID.
>
> Mam, eawr Mary's getten a *felly* neaw : aw met 'em i'th lone to-neet.

FELLON (N. Lanc.), *sb.* a sore, a disease in cows.

FELLON-WOOD (N. Lanc.), *sb.* the plant Bitter-sweet *(Solanum Dulcamara).*

FEND, *v.* to provide for, to seek, to strive.   A.S. *fandian, fandigan,* to try, tempt, prove, seek, search out.   *Fend* is used by Burns. See *Poor Mailie.*

COLLIER.
1750.

Nip [a dog] I leet *fend* for hur seln.—*Works: Tim Bobbin,* p. 49.

GASKELL.
1854.

Another common expression is "*fendin'* and provin'." The former word is not, as might be supposed, a corruption of defending, but is from the Anglo-Saxon *fandian,* to try, to seek, to search out. And when a man is "*fendin'* for a livin' for hissel'," or "*fendin'* for his family," he is seeking a means of subsistence for himself or them.   *Lect. Lanc. Dialect,* p. 17.

WAUGH.
1859.

God bless him that *fends* for his livin',
An' houds up his yed through it o'!
Lanc. Songs: God bless these poor folk!

WAUGH.
1867.

The Board gave orders for the man and his wife and three of the children·to be admitted to the workhouse, leaving the other two lads to "*fend* for theirsels," and find new nests wherever they could.
Factory Folk during Cotton Famine, p. 51.

FENDY   (N. Lanc.),
FENSOME   (ditto), } *adj.* adroit ; also neat, becoming.

DR. BARBER.
1870.

She's a gay *fendy* lile body, an' a terble favourite amang o' maks o' foke.   *Forness Folk,* p. 32.

FERRUPS, *int.* an exclamation, as "Wot th' *ferrups* arto doin'?"

MISS LAHEE.
1865.

Whoy, what the *ferrups* don yo myen, felley?
Betty o' Yep's Tale, p. 20.

FEST (N. Lanc.), *v.* (1) to put out to board ; (2) to put out cattle to grass at a rate per head ; (3) to let off any work.

FET, *v.* fetched.   See FOT.

FETTLE, *sb.* condition.

MISS LAHEE.
1865.

Yo'r long traunce 'll ha' made yo' i' rare *fettle* for yo'r breykfast.   *Betty o' Yep's Tale,* p. 6.

WAUGH.
1875.

"Bravo, Jem," said Giles.   "By th' mass, thou'rt i' grand *fettle.*   Thou mends as thou gets owder."
Old Cronies, c. vii., p. 86.

FETTLE, *v.* to mend, improve, set right, dress.   Shakspere uses the word in *Rom. and J.,* act iii., sc. 5, line 154.

COLLIER.
1750.

I think t' be an ostler, for I con *fettle* tits.
Works: Tim Bobbin, p. 71.

WAUGH.
1859.

One neet aw crope whoam when my weighvin' were o'er,
To brush mo, an' wesh mo, an' *fettle* my yure.
Lanc. Songs: Jamie's Frolic.

B. BRIERLEY.
1868.

Peggy. Aw'll fot thi cooat.   Should aw co at little Planker's to get it *fettled?*   Or should aw try to do it misel?
Tim. Theau con just ha' thi own road.   Ift' thinks theau con *fettle* it, theau may try.—*Fratchingtons,* p. 41.

DR. BARBER.
1870.

T' bonny lile lan'lady com in a minute, wi' her yār [hair] o' *fettled* up.   *Forness Folk,* p. 32.

FEWTRILS, *sb.* little things. In Burns' *Address to a Louse* this is given "fatt'rels," and in the glossary is described as "ribbon-ends" :—

> Now haud ye there, ye're out o' sight,
> Below the *fatt'rels*, snug an' tight.

JOHN SCHOLES.
1857.

Peg had hur hoppet ov hur arm wi her odd *fewtrils* in't. *Jaunt to see th' Queen*, p. 28.

FEY, *v.* to remove the earth over stone or slate.

FIR-BOB, *sb.* a fir-cone.

FIRE-POTE,
FIRE-POTTER, } *sb.* a poker.

JOHN SCHOLES.
1857.

Th' monkey wur makkin o *foyar-pótter* ov it neebur's paw. *Jaunt to see th' Queen*, p. 56.

WAUGH.
1867.

We went towards this place with the poker. . . Out came John from the kitchen. "Here, John, owd brid," said one of the carters, "weigh this *fire-potter* for us, wilto?" *Dulesgate*, p. 25.

WAUGH.
1867.

Iv aw wur her mother, see yo, aw'd tak that pouse at top o' th' yed wi' th' *fire-pote* iv ever he darken't my dur-hole upo' sich an arran' as that.
Tattlin' Matty, c. ii., p. 19.

FIRTLE (N. Lanc.), *v.* to intermeddle in small matters; also, to fidget.

FITTED, *v.* suited, served.

COLL. USE.
1880.

"Thae'rt a lung time a getten *fitted*."
"Aye, this mon's so slow : aw nobbut want a bit o' calico."

FLAIGHT, *sb.* a light turf.

FLAKE,
FLEAK,
FLEIGH, } *sb.* a shelf, or a number of cords stretched between two pieces of wood upon which to hang oatcake. See BRADE-FLAKE, BRADE-FLEIGH.

JOHN HIGSON.
1852.

[About the middle of last century] the domestic arrangements included boilers, flour and meal coffers, apple arks, and oat-cake *fleak*, oaten cake and bread forming a considerable portion of their ordinary diet.
Gorton Historical Recorder, p. 12.

B. BRIERLEY.
1868.

Pointing to a *flake* or *fleigh* well thatched with crisp-looking and nicely browned oat-cakes, which curled over the strings that held them like a bishop's hat-brim inverted. *Irkdale*, p. 45.

FLANG, *v.* flung.

WAUGH.
1868.

Grippin' th' poker tight in his reet hond, he shot th' bowt wi' his left, an' *flang* th' dur wide oppen.
Sneck-Bant, c. ii., p. 38.

FLANNIN, *sb.* flannel. The more correct form. W. *gwlanen*, flannel.

BURNS.
1786.

I wad na been surprised to spy
You on an auld wife's *flainen* toy.—*To a Louse*.

FLASH-PIT, *sb.* a pit nearly grown up with reeds and grass.

FLASKER, *v.* to struggle, to flounder.

COLLIER. 1750.	Deawn coom I i'th weter, on *flaskert* int' eh geete howd on a sawgh. [= Down I came into the water, and floundered till I got hold of a willow]. *Works : Tim Bobbin*, p. 49.
B. BRIERLEY. 1868.	A lot o' cowts (colts) ut han kicked an' *flaskert* thersels eaut o' wynt (wind). *Irkdale*, p. 23.

FLASKET, *sb.* a shallow basket. Welsh *fflasged*, a shallow basket.

FLAY, ⎰ *v.* to frighten. See FLAY. *Fley* is A.S. *flégan* (not in
FLEY, ⎱ the dictionaries), another form of *fly'gan*, to put to
flight, in Leo's *Glossar* (not in Bosworth). It is the causal of
A.S. *fléon*, to flee, fly. See FLEZEN in Strutmann, and *Allit.
Poems*, ed. Morris, B. 960 [W. W. S.].

COLLIER. 1750.	True, Tummus, no marvil ot o wur so *flay'd ;* it wur so fearfoo dark ! *Works : Tim Bobbin*, p. 51.
IBID.	These wur'n th' boggarts ot *flayd'n* thee ! *Works : Tim Bobbin, Intro.* p. xxxvii.
DR. BARBER. 1870.	I was *flayte* o' missin' t' train, so meadd t' best o' me way to San' side. *Forness Folk*, p. 16.
WAUGH. 1866.	"What, thae'rt noan fleyed ov a cat, arto?" asked the landlord. "Aw'm *fleyed* o' that cat," replied Ben. *Ben an' th' Bantam*, c. ii., p. 46.
WAUGH. 1875.	"Craddy," said Giles, "draw nar to th' table. Thou looks as if thou were beawn to fire a gun. Thou's no 'casion to be *fleyed*." *Old Cronies*, c. iii., p. 33.

FLAY-CROW (N. Lanc.), *sb.* a scarecrow, a ridiculous object.
Pronounced : Flay-craa.

FLAYSOME, ⎱
FLEYSOME, ⎰ *adj.* fearful.

WAUGH. 1875.	"What, th' boggart?" "Ay ; an' th' warst boggart there is upo' this country-side for *flaysome* deed, an' powlerin' about i' th' neet time !" *Old Cronies*, c. ii., p. 24.

FLEAZY, *adj.* dusty, linty, fibrous.

FLECK, *sb.* a flea.

COLL. USE. 1880.	Aw sent him off wi' a *fleck* in his ear-hole aw con tell yo : he'll noan come a courtin' here again.

FLEED, *v.* flayed, skinned.

FLEET (N. Lanc.), *v.* to skim. See FLET.

FLEETINS, *sb. pl.* the curd of milk from which cream is made.
A.S. *flet*, cream.

GASKELL. 1852.	We have also *fleetins*, from the A.S. *fliete* (cream, that which floats) signifying the curds from which cheese is made. *Lect. Lanc. Dialect*, p. 19.

FLEET-TIME (Ormskirk), *sb.* break of day, twilight.

FLEIGH. See FLAKE.

FLET, *p.p.* skimmed. See FLEET and FLEETINS.

FLET-MILK, *sb.* skimmed milk.

> JOHN SCHOLES.   The'ad bettur may o roice puddin', fur win o deyle o
> 1857.   *flet-milk* laft.   *Jaunt to see th' Queen,* p. 19.

FLINDERS, *sb. pl.* small pieces, fragments. See Burns' *On a Scotch Bard :—*

> 'Twill mak her poor, auld heart, I fear,
>   In *flinders* flee.

FLIPE (N. Lanc.), *sb.* the brim of a hat.

> DR. BARBER.   He hed a terble grand white hat on top of his heead,
> 1870.   wi' girt breadd *flypes* tul it like a collegian ameastt.
>   *Forness Folk,* p. 57.

FLIT, *v.* to move from a house, with the household goods. Mid. Eng. *flitten ;* Dan. *flytte.* See "flitting" in Tennyson's "Walking to the Mail."

> PSALMS OF DAVID.   Thou tellest my *flittings.—Ps.* lvi. 8, *Pr. Bk. Ver.*
> 1625.   Edmund Platt pledges himself "to *flitt* remove and
>   depart out of and from all that capitall messuage or
>   dwelling-house called the Platt."
>   *Booker's Birch,* p. 23.
> MISS LAHEE.   He towd me to tell you ut th' notice stons good, un
> 1855.   yo mun *flit.*   *Neddy Fitton's Visit,* p. 17.

FLITTIN', *sb.* the removal from a house.

FLIZ,
FLIZZIN', } *sb.* a splinter.

FLOOS (Furness), *sb.* a sluice.

FLOOSE or
FLOSS, } *sb.* loose threads, fibres ; a loose texture.

> COLLIER.   Sitch a *floose* o hay follot me ot it driv me shiar deawn.
> 1750.   *Works : Tim Bobbin,* p. 68.

FLOP, *v.* to throw or put down anything suddenly, in such a manner as to make a noise.

> COLL. USE.   Whoile they wur o' sittin' round th' foire as quiet as
> 1880.   mice, a greyt lump o' soot *flopped* deawn th' chimney.

FLOP, *sb.* a noise, a hollow sound.

FLOSH (Furness), *sb.* water, or a watery place. Cf. *flush.*

FLOTE, *v.* (past tense of *Flyte*) to scold or upbraid sharply.

> COLLIER.   Mezzil fease [Mezzil-face] startit to his feet, *flote* none,
> 1750.   boh gran like a foomurt-dog.—*Works : Tim Bobbin,* p. 52.
> WAUGH.   An' er Betty *flote* me, as if aw'd bin th' instigation o'
> 1865.   th' whole consarn.   *Besom Ben,* c. iv., p. 45.

FLUET (Furness), *sb.* a blow with the back of the hand.

FLUNTER, ⎫ *sb.* order; correct arrangement, as in machinery.
FLUNTERS, ⎭ See Eawt-o'-flunters.

FLUSK, *sb.* a whirring sound.

> COLLIER.   I heard th' eawl come into th' hoyle, on presently
> 1750.   summot come with a greyt *flusk* thro' th' riddle.
> *Works: Tim Bobbin*, p. 45.

FLUTTERMENT, *sb.* fluttering excitement.

> WAUGH.   Dan, owd lad, let's have a doance! These toes o'
> 1869.   mine are ram-jam full o' *flutterment!* Strike up 'The
> Flowers of Edinburgh;' aw'll fuut it! Just thee hearken
> my feet, neaw.   *Yeth-Bobs*, c. i., p. 28.

FLUZZ (N. Lanc.), *v.* to blunt.

FLUZZED (N. Lanc.), *adj.* blunt and jagged, or turned up at the
edges; bruised.

FLYRE, *v.* to smile improperly, impertinently, or scornfully. Probably pron. of the old word *fleer.*

FLYTE, *v.* to scold. A.S. *Flítan, flite, he flit;* pt. *flát, we fliton;*
pp. *fliten, gefliten.* To strive, contend, dispute, quarrel, rebel.
Flít, geflit, strife, wrangling.

> BURNS.   And gin she take the thing amiss,
> 1790.   E'en let her *flyte* her fill, Jo.
> "O steer her up."
>
> GASKELL.   When a Lancashire man scolds, he *flytes;* from *flytan,*
> 1852.   to quarrel.   *Lect. Lanc. Dialect*, p. 17.
>
> WAUGH.   Yor noan beawn to *flyte* mo, owd crayter, are yo?
> 1855.   *Lanc. Sketches: Bury to Rochdale*, p. 25.
>
> MISS LAHEE.   Dunnot yo see Mally dar but say so, freetened Bob
> 1865.   met [might] *flite* her for stoppin' Jinny off her feed.
> *Betty o' Yep's Tale*, p. 27.

FOG, *sb.* the later growth of grass; the aftermath.

FOISTY, *adj.* having a musty or bad smell or taste.

> COLLIER.   We'n had enough o this *foisty* matter.
> 1750.   *Works: Tim Bobbin, Intro.*, p. xxxvi.

FOLD,
FOWD, or ⎬ *sb.* a cluster of houses.
FOWT,

> WAUGH.   Wardle *Fold*, near Wardle Hall, was fifty years since
> 1855.   only a small sequestered cluster of rough stone houses.
> *Lanc. Sketches*, p. 124.
>
> WAUGH.   Thou 'rt a town's talk, mon! Th' childer putten their
> 1876.   tungs out at tho, as thou gwos through th' *fowd*.
> *Chimney Corner*, N. S., chap. ix.

FOO-GAUD, *sb.* a plaything.

FOO'-HARD, *adj.* foolhardy.

WAUGH.
1868.

He ails nought 'at aw know on, nobbut he talks to mich off at th' side, neaw an' then ; an' he's *foo-hard*.
Sneck-Bant, c. ii., p. 25.

FOOMERT or FOOMART,

sb. a martin, polecat, or fitchew. Mid. Eng. *folmart*. Prof. Skeat *(Etym. Dictionary)* says, "A hybrid compound ; Mid. E. *ful*= A.S. *fúl,* foul, stinking ; and old French *marte, martre,* a marten. Thus it means 'foul marten.' "

COLLIER.
1750.

He gran like a *foomut*-dog.
Works : Tim Bobbin, p. 52.

WAUGH.
1855.

The moors north of Heywood afford great sport in the grouse season. Some of the local gentry keep harriers ; and now and then a *foomart*-hunt takes place, with the long-eared dogs.—*Lanc. Sketches : Heywood and its Neighbourhood,* p. 182.

WAUGH.
1865.

They turn't up at th' edge-o'-dark, as hungry as two *foomart*-dogs. *Besom Ben,* c. iv., p. 45.

FOOR (N. Lanc.), *sb.* a furrow.

FOOR-BREST (N. Lanc.), *adv.* right in front.

FOO-SCUTTER, *sb.* silly boasting talk. Foo = fool. F. *fou.*

WAUGH.
1866.

"An' aw've a uncle 'at owns two mills i' Darbyshire— my uncle Joe. Thoose two mills are mine when he dees. Crack that nut." "Iv thy uncle Joe owns ony mills i' Darbyshire," said Twitch, "they're coffee mills. Thae desarves jollopin' for talkin' sich-like *foo-scutter* as that."
Ben an' th' Bantam, c. v., p. 96.

FOO-SIDE, *sb.* foolish side, the part most open to be gulled or deceived. Foo = fool. F. *fou.*

WAUGH.
1876.

There is'nt a wick soul i' th' world at hasn't a *foo-side*.

FOR-ALL, *con.* although, notwithstanding.

COLL. USE.
1880.

Well, yo know, he would goo *for-all* it wur so rough and dark ; an' th' eend on't wur he slipt into th' cut, just at th' bridge corner an' wur drownt.

FORCE (N. Lanc.), *sb.* a cascade or waterfall. A fall of water in a narrow gorge. Icel. *fors ;* Dan. *fos.*

FORE-ELDERS, *sb. pl.* forefathers.

WAUGH.
1855.

The entire population [about Heywood], though engaged in manufacture, evinces a hearty love of the fields and field sports, and a strong tincture of the rough simplicity, and idiomatic quaintness, of their forefathers, or *fore-elders*, as they often call them.—*Lanc. Sketches,* p. 183.

J. P. MORRIS.
(Furness Dialect.)
1867.

Some on 'em hes left barns behint 'em 'at m'appen wodn't like tà see the'r *for-elders'* neeàms mix't up wi' sic a bit o' Forness Linch-ta.—*Invasion o' U'ston,* p. 7.

WAUGH.
(Furness Dialect.)
1874.

He's a farmer, an' his fadder afore him was a farmer, an' all his *fore-elders* were farmers.—*Jannoch,* c. v., p. 36.

FORE-END, *sb.* early spring; the beginning of a thing or time; used as the opposite of *far-end.*

> WAUGH.
> 1855.
>
> One could either manage we't at th' *for-end* o' their days. But what, we hannot so lung to do on neaw.
> *Lanc. Sketches,* p. 26.

FORMER, *v.* to order or bespeak. Probably *former* used as a verb. Cf. to *further* a thing.

> JOHN SCHOLES.
> 1857.
>
> As fur mi shoon, awd gettin' o spon-new payre to put on, ut ud bin *formert* o thri wik gon.
> *Jaunt to see th' Queen,* p. 13.

> B. BRIERLEY.
> 1859.
>
> "Aw'm come a-*formerin* a weddin'."
> "*Formering* a wedding! Oh, I see," replied the clerk; "you mean putting up the banns."
> *Lanc. Tales and Sketches,* p. 219.

FORRUD, *adv.* forward.

> BURNS.
> 1786.
>
> Yes! there is ane; a Scottish callan—
> There's ane; come *forrit,* honest Allan!
> *On Pastoral Poetry.*

> WAUGH.
> 1859.
>
> Get *forrud* wi' thy deein'.
> *Lanc. Songs: Owd Pinder.*

FOR-SET (Furness), *v.* to waylay.

FOR-SURE, *adv.* certainly, undoubtedly.

> COLL. USE.
> 1880.
>
> "Wilta come?" "Aw will, *for-sure.*"

FOR-THINK, *v.* to regret, to reconsider.

> WAUGH.
> 1869.
>
> When it geet th' edge-o'-dark, an' nought but th' wild cloof abeawt us, it made me rayther *for-think* ever settin' eawt. *Yeth-Bobs,* c. ii., p. 32.

FOR-TO, *adv.* in order to.

> BIBLE, AUTHOR. VER.
>
> And it came to pass, that there went out some of the people on the seventh day *for to* gather, and they found none. *Ex.* xvii. 27.

FOR-WHY, *adv.* wherefore. A.S. *for-hwi.*

> COLL. USE.
> 1880.
>
> "*For-why?* Because he wur a foo', an knew no better."

FOT or FET, *v.* fetched. A.S. *fetian,* perfect tense; *fette,* to fetch, to bring to.

> CHAUCER.
> 1380.
>
> And thereupon the wyn was *fet* anoon;
> We dronken, and to reste went echoon.
> *Cant. Tales: Prologue,* l. 19.

> SPENSER.
> 1590.
>
> He was unhable them to *fett.*
> *F. Queene,* Bk. ii., canto 9, v. 58.

SHAKSPERE.
1599.

On, on, you noblest English,
Whose blood is *fet* from fathers of war-proof !
King Hen. V., iii., 1, l. 18.

BAMFORD.
1843.

Whilst Bet-at-Joe's nipt up her toes,
And *fot* owd John wi th' fiddle.
Poems : Stakehill Ball, p. 144.

GASKELL.
1852.

The Lancashire dialect has been peculiarly retentive
of the Anglo-Saxon preterite, generally preferring the
strong conjugation to the weak. A Lancashire man
does not say he "fetched," but he "*fet*" or "*fot.*"
Lect. Lanc. Dialect, p. 24.

WAUGH.
1866.

Send yo'r Alick to him, an' tell him to crack o' *fottin*
law iv he doesn't turn up some brass.
Ben an' th' Bantam, c. iv., p. 77.

FOUGHTEN, *part.* of *v.* to fight. Shakspere, *Henry V.*, act iv.,
sc. 6 ; W. Morris, *Jason*, p. 146.

B. BRIERLEY.
1869.

I'd a quiet victory, but like mony a battle of a bigger
sort, it wur unfairly *fowten*, an' had to be bowt (bought)
at last. *Ab-o-th'-Yate in London*, p. 76.

COLL. USE.
1880.

" Hasto *foughten ?* "
" Nawe."
" Then get *foughten* ; an' come whoam wi' thee."

FRAM (N. Lanc.), *adj.* brittle, tender.

FRAMPIT (Ormskirk), } *sb.* an iron ring which slides on the boose-
FRAMPUT (S.E. Lanc.), } stake to fasten cows in their stall.

FRAP (N. Lanc.), *sb.* a blow. F. *frapper.*

FRAP, *sb.* a fit of temper or passion.

COLLIER.
1750.

Come, come, dunnaw fly up in a *frap.*
Works : Tim Bobbin, Intro., p. xxxvii.

WAUGH.
1867.

Dunnot tee fly up i' sich a *frap*, mon,—what, aw
nobbut want a bit ov a wort (word) wi him.
Owd Blanket, c. i., p. 10.

FRATCH, *adj. and v.* quarrelsome ; to quarrel, to dispute.

COLLIER.
1750.

Theydn some o'th' warst *fratchingst* cumpany ot e'er
e saigh. *Works : Tim Bobbin*, p. 52.

A. C. GIBSON.
(High Furness Dialect.)
1868.

As I cūd hear, they wor *fratchin* cruelly o' t' way as
t'ey com. *Folk-speech of Cumberland*, p. 92.

WAUGH.
1875.

" Come, come, lads ; let's ha' no *fratchin'!* Jone
thou'rt gettin' terribly rivven o' at once."
Old Cronies, c. vii., p. 90.

FRAWZIN' (Ormskirk), *sb.* a gossiping person.

FREETNIN' (N. Lanc.), *sb.* a ghost, spirit, or anything uncanny.

J. P. MORRIS.
(Furness Dialect.)
1867.

" Ghosts ! Eigh, we've hed plenty on 'em i' Forness,
but we'd anudder neeàm for 'em ; we ol'as co'd 'em
dobbies èr *freetnins.*" *Lebby Beck Dobby*, p. 3.

FREMD, *sb.* a stranger or guest.

FREMD, *adj.* strange, not related. Thus, a person living with a family to whom he is not related is termed "a *fremd* body." If it were asked, "Is he akin to you?" the answer would be, "Nawe, he's fremd," *i.e.* "he's one of us, but not a relation." A.S. *fremed*, foreign; Mœso-Goth, *framatheis;* G. *fremde*, strange. Burns uses *fremit* for strange. A "fremit man" is a stranger.

CHAUCER. 1380.	Now alle is wel, for al the world is blynde In this matere, bothe *fremed* and tame. *Troylus and Crysede*, Bk. iii., l. 479.
IBID.	A faucon peregryn than seemed she Of *fremde* londe. *Squieres Tale*, pt. ii., l. 82.
SPENSER. 1579.	So now his frend is chaunged for a *frenne*. *Shepheards Calender*, April, stanza 7.

GASKELL. 1852.	*Fremed* or *fremd* in Anglo-Saxon meant foreign, strange ; or, as a substantive, a stranger or guest. We meet with it in Chaucer as *fremde*. In Spenser we have it altered into *frenne*. Sir Walter Scott uses the expression, "like a cow in a *fremd* loaning." Precisely the same meaning is given to the word by Lancashire people. When an individual has been adopted into a family, they say "he is a *fremd*." *Lect. Lanc. Dialect*, p. 20.

FRIST, *sb.* trust.

FRITH (N. Lanc.), *sb.* a wood ; also unused pasture land. W. *ffrith*.

FROG-RUD, *sb.* the spawn of the frog, which may often be seen floating on stagnant pools or ditches.

WAUGH. 1855.	[Lads] soiling their "good clooas," as country mothers used to call them, by tumbling among the dry soil of the hedge-side, and then rolling slap into the wet ditch at the bottom, among cuckoo-spit, and *'frog-rud*, and all sorts of green pool-slush. *Lanc. Sketches*, p. 189.

FROSK (N. Lanc.), *sb.* a frog. A.S. *frox* ; Icel. *froskr*. See FROG in Skeat's *Etym. Dict.*

FRUM, *adj.* brittle.

E. KIRK. 1876.	*Frum* means fragile, or short, in the sense of short-cake, a common word in South Lancashire. A story is told of a country girl giving some pears to the late Lady Houghton, then of Astley Hall, Chorley, and saying, "The're varra gud, an' if yoal nobbut put em under the bowstert abaat a faurtnit they'll be as *frum* as muck" (soil).—*Manchester Guardian Local Notes and Queries*, No. 1,107.

FRUMMETY or FURMETY, } *sb.* new wheat boiled in milk ; from Lat. *frumentum*. See FRUMENTY in Skeat's *Etym. Dict.*

FRUMP, *sb.* a mock or jeer.

FRUPP (N. Lanc.), *adj.* loose, spongy, easily broken.

FUB (Ormskirk), *sb.* long withered grass on old pastures or meadows.

FUD (N. Lanc.), *sb.* the hair of a hare or rabbit.

FUDGE (Ormskirk), *sb.* a fat person.

FULL-MICKLE (N. Lanc.), *adj.* too much ; literally, full much.

FUN, *v. pt. t.* of *verb* find ; for fund, *i.e.* found.

FUR or ⎫
FAR, ⎭ *adj.* and *adv.* further ; also distant.

WAUGH. 1865.	Aw mun clear these brokken pots eawt, afore we gwon ony *fur!* *Besom Ben,* c. ix., p. 102.
IBID. 1866.	Let's see ; my aunt Matty lies i' yon *fur* nook. *Sexton's Story,* p. 24.
COLL. USE. 1880.	Stond *fur ; i.e.* move further back.

FUR-END, *sb.* the furthest end ; the last of any thing.

COLL. USE. 1880.	Well, we'n getten to th' *fur-end* now ; an' the Lord only knows what we mun do for eawr next meal.

FUSSOCK (S.E. Lanc.), ⎫
FUZ, ⎬ *sb.* an idle fat woman.
FUZZOCK, ⎭

COLLIER. 1750.	This broddling *fussock* lookt *feaw* os Tunor [a dog] when I'd done. *Works: Tim Bobbin,* p. 55.
JOHN SCHOLES. 1857.	Yoih ! boh that owd *fussock* ov o woife ov hiz tuk it off mi ogen. *Jaunt to see th' Queen,* p. 20.
WAUGH. 1868.	"Nay," cried Billy ; "thae'rt noan beawn to run off thi bargain becose o' this *fuzzock* makin' her din, arto ?" *Sneck-Bant,* c. ii., p. 40.

FUUTIN, *sb.* = footing ; condition, understanding.

WAUGH. 1876.	Aye, marry : thou may sattle wi' the dule his-sel' upo' that *fuutin'.* *Manchester Critic,* March 3.

FUUTIN, *sb.* = footing ; a fine or contribution paid by an apprentice or other person on the occasion of his entering upon a new trade or situation ; also the entertainment provided by such payment.

COLL. USE. 1880.	"Has he paid his *footin'?*" "Nawe." "Then he starts no work here, aw con tell yo'."

G.

GĀ (N. Lanc.), *v.* to go.   A.S. *gá*, go.

> A. C. GIBSON.   But wrote-for punds *gā's* farder far
> (High Furness Dialect.)   Nor hundreds gién or fund ;
> 1873.   An' sum' may be to t' fooer for t' barnes
>   When we *gā* under t' grund.
>   *Folk-Speech of Cumberland,* p. 87.

GABLOCK, } *sb.* an iron crowbar, a weapon.
GAVLOCK,

> COLLIER.   Truth on honesty gooin' hont eh hont howd'n one
> 1750.   onother's backs primely, on ston os stiff os o *gablock.*
>   *Works,* p. 62.

GAD-ABOUT, *sb.* an idle, rambling person.

GADWAUD (Cartmel), *sb.* a long stick.

GAFFER, *sb.* a master.

> COLL. USE.   Neaw then, shift sharp—here's th' *gaffer* comin'.
> 1880.

GAIN, *adj.* direct, near, convenient, handy.   Icel. *gegn*, short, also serviceable.

> COLL. USE.   Come back, mon ; this is th' *gainest* road.
> 1880.

GAIT (N. Lanc.), *sb.* pasturage for cattle during summer in a common field.

GAITINS (N. Lanc.), *sb. pl.* single sheaves of corn set up on end to dry.

GALE (N. Lanc.), *sb.* the wild myrtle or bog-myrtle, *Myrica gale.*

GALKER, *sb.* a tub to hold wort.

> JOHN SCHOLES.   Some o' thir own brewin' wur browt eawt, ut aw
> 1857.   believe coom fro under th' *galker,* fur it wur onkommon
>   fresh o' berm.   *Jaunt to see th' Queen,* p. 22.

GALLIVANT, *v.* to go about in a loose or aimless manner.

> COLL. USE.   He's *gallivantin'* up and down wi' play-actors instead
> 1880.   o' mindin' his wark.

GALLOWSES, } *sb. pl.* braces, straps to hold up the trowsers.
GALLACES,

> WAUGH.   Goo an' get that jackass in, aw tell tho ! An' then come
> 1865.   an' unbutton my *gallowses.—Besom Ben,* c. 11, p. 28.
>
> IBID.   His breeches wur nobbut fastened wi' one *gallace ;*
> 1868.   tother hanged down beheend, like a razzor-strap in a
>   barber's shop.   *Sneck-Bant,* c. ii., p. 38.
>
> IBID.   I can leet o' nought but two *gallows*-buttons an' a
> 1875.   'bacca papper.   *Old Cronies,* c. ii., p. 25.

GALLOWS, *adj.* cunning, designing, full of duplicity.

> COLL. USE.
> 1880.
> Tha mun look after yore Jem. He's a *gallows* young dog.

GAM (game), *sb.* sport, rollicking, fun.

> WAUGH.
> 1879.
> Thoose began o' snow-bo'in' one another, wi' breek an' stones. . . . It's rare *gam* too—as lung as a body doesn't get hit theirsel'.
> *Chimney Corner*, p. 41.

GAMASHES (N. Lanc.), *sb. pl.* short gaiters or leggings.

GAM-LEG, *sb.* a crooked or feeble leg. *Gammy*, meaning crooked or feeble, is also frequently used as an adjective. Cf. Welsh *cam*, crooked.

> GASKELL.
> 1854.
> I remember that a poor schoolfellow of mine who had a bent leg, which obliged him to use a crutch, was commonly said to have a *gam leg*. I fancied that this was because he was made "game" of, but the reason evidently was because it was bent.
> *Lect. Lanc. Dialect*, p. 8.

GAMMERSTANG (N. Lanc.), *sb.* an awkward, tall, slender person, male or female.

GAN, *v.* gave, given.

> WAUGH.
> 1859.
> My mother's *gan* me th' four-post bed,
> Wi' curtains to't an' o'.
> *Lanc. Songs: Come, Mary, link thi arm.*

GAN,
GANG, } (N. Lanc.), *v.* to go. A.S. *gangan*, Icel. *ganga*, to go.

> DR. BARBER.
> 1870.
> He com i' contact wi' t' middle o' t' beck whār t' stream was *ganging* at a cruel speed. *Forness Folk*, p. 6.

> IBID.
> T' miners *gang* to wark at o' hours o' t' neet.
> *Ibid.*, p. 26.

> WAUGH.
> 1874.
> "Adam," said she, "if I wur thee, I'd *gan* down to t' meadow, an' see what's goin' on."
> *Jannock*, c. ii., p. 16.

GANG (Cartmel), *sb.* a lobby in a farm-house.

GANG-BOOSE, *sb.* a narrow passage from the cow-house to the barn. See BOOSE. A.S. *gang*, a way, path, passage.

GANK, *sb.* a deep, narrow footway.

GANTY, *sb.* a wooden frame on which barrels are placed.

GAR (Cartmel), *v.* to compel.

GARDEN-TWOD, *sb.* a large toad.

> WAUGH.
> 1879.
> Hutch't of a lump, like a *garden-twod*.
> *Chimney Corner*, p. 151.

GARTH (N. Lanc.), *sb.* a small field or enclosure adjoining a house, church, or other building; usually an affix, a's school-garth, church-garth, chapel-garth. W. *gardd*, an enclosure.

TENNYSON. Past into the little *garth* beyond.—*Enoch Arden*.
1864.

WAUGH. When ye get to Seathwaite, ye must gan by all means
1874. into t' *chapel-garth*; an' there ye'll find his gravestone.
Jannock, c. viii., p. 78.

GARTH, *sb.* a hoop; a child's bowling hoop.

WAUGH. Aw seed nobory abeawt, nobbut a bit of a lad mar-
1866. lockin' wi' a *garth*.—*Ben an' th' Bantam*, c. iv., p. 81.

GARTHIN', *v.* repairing a tub by re-hooping it.

WAUGH. I'll have a penk at her piggin', if I have to pay for th'
1879. *garthin'* on 't. *Chimney Corner*, p. 154.

GATE, *sb.* a road, a way; also, a manner or fashion; speed, rate of movement. Icel. *gata*, A.S. *geat*, a way.

WAUGH. One never knows a mon by nobbut meetin' him i'
1865. smooth wayter a time or two. Yo mun see 'em tried o'
gates [= all ways] afore yo known 'em !
Besom Ben, c. vii., p. 84.

IBID. Then Mally trode upo' th' cat, an' away it shot on to
1868. th' top o' th' drawers, eawt o' th' *gate* o' th' row.
Sneck-Bant, c. ii., p. 36.

IBID. Well, thae'll be sure to co' when tho comes this *gate*
on again, an' let's have another look at tho !
Ibid., c. ii., p. 49.

GATE, *v.* to begin; to put a loom in order for working.

WAUGH. Afore tho *gates* a-talkin', goo an' don these dry things.
1868. *Sneck-Bant*, c. i., p. 9.

COLL. USE. Aw con *gate* a loom wi' ony chap i' Owdham (Oldham).
1880.

GATHERIN', *sb.* a suppuration.

COLL. USE. "Oh my ! this *gatherin'* does lutch !" "Well, lass,
1880. we mun poultice it, an' then it 'll soon come to a head."

GAUD-GATHER (Ormskirk), *sb.* a tax-collector.

GAUK-HANDED (N. Lanc.), *adj.* left-handed.

GAUP, *v.* to stare.

GASKELL. In Lancashire, to stare is to *gaup*. When, for instance,
1854. one person runs against another while looking a different
way, it is not unusual to hear, "Na, stupid, what art ta
gaupin' at ?" *Lect. Lanc. Dialect*, p. 27.

GAURDIN (Cartmel), *sb.* wood for hedging.

GAWBY, *sb.* a lout, a silly fellow, a clown.

GAWM, *v.* to understand, to comprehend.

COLLIER. Hoave a duzz'n on um would geaw t' see if they
1750. coud'n mey shift t' *gawm* it, boh it capt um aw.
Works: Intro., p. 37.

GASKELL.
1854.

There is one word that is not found in the Anglo-Saxon language ; nor, as far as I know, in any of the kindred tongues, except that which is the oldest and most venerable of them all. And, if so, this is one of great interest. It is the word *gaum*, to understand. As, for instance, a Lancashire man says, "I conno *gaum* what tha means ;" and from it is formed the adjective *gaumless*. In the version of the Gospels by Ulphilas, "they saw" or "they perceived" is, in one instance, Mark xvi. 4, "*gaum*idedun." It seems to me there can be little doubt that we have in this the original of the Lancashire word. It is the past tense, and the root would evidently be *gaum.—Lect. Lanc. Dialect*, p. 14.

GAWMBLIN, *sb.* a silly fellow ; a half fool.

BAMFORD.
1840.

"As for that *gawmblin* o' mine," she continued, "he met ha' had his coo-dove lung sin, iv he'd nobbut ha' follod th' advice o' Limpin Billy at Ratliffe."
Life of Radical, c. xx., p. 134.

GAWMIN', *v.* understanding ; also considering, cogitating ; at a loss, but trying to understand.

GAWMLESS, *adj.* dull or slow of comprehension ; vacant-minded ; foolish, silly, senseless ; insensible ; idiotic.

COLLIER.
1750.

I steart like o wilcat, on wur welly *gawmless*.
Works : p. 55.

WAUGH.
1865.

"Theer," said Joe, stopping to take breath, "aw think they'n yer that, if they aren't both deof an' *gawmless*."   *Sexton's Story*, p. 20.

B. BRIERLEY.
1868.

Aw'm nobbut a poot yet, an' happen a bit *gawmless*.
Irkdale, c. ii., p. 102.

COLL. USE.
1880.

1. He up wi' his foot an' knockt him *gawmless*.
2. He wur olez a *gawmless* foo'.

GAWMLIN. *adj.* silly, senseless, stupid.

COLLIER.
1750.

Boh mind neaw, theaw *gamblin'* tyke.
Works : Intro., p. 37.

IBID.
1750.

This wur mad *gawmlin'* wark.   *Works*, p. 53.

GAWSTER, } *v.* to boast, to swagger.
GOSTER,

WAUGH.
1875.

An' that set him agate o' bletherin' an' *gosterin'* up an' down like mad.   *Old Cronies*, c. viii., p. 98.

IBID.
1880.

He began o' *gosterin'* an' talkin' about th' horses— he'd ha' this done, an' he'd ha' that done, or else he'd play th' upstroke wi' somebry. *Chimney Corner*, p. 89.

GAWSTERIN', *sb.* boasting.

GAY (N. Lanc.), *adj.* considerable.

A. C. GIBSON.
(High Furness Dialect.)
1873.

Jack Slipe follow't by his-sel' a *gay* bit behint 'em.
Folk-Speech of Cumberland, &c., p. 94.

GAYLY (N. Lanc.), *adv.* very moderately.

DR. BARBER.   T' rooad now wos o' down bank, sooa I manisht *gayly*
1870.   weel.   *Forness Folk.*

GAYLY (Fylde), *adv.* heartily.

GEÀL (N. Lanc.), *v.* to smart or itch with cold.

J. P. MORRIS.   Mi fingers fair *geàl* wi' cald.   *Furness Glossary*, p. 39.
1869.

GEAWL, *sb.* a rheumy discharge from the eyes.

GEAWLT, *part.* festered with a rheumy discharge.

WAUGH.   It're very frosty, an' his een looked white an' wild ;
1865.   an' as *geawl't* as a whelp.
    Lanc. Sketches : Rochdale to Blackstone Edge, p. 130.

GEBBY (N. Lanc.), *sb.* a hooked stick.

GEET, *v. p. t.* got ; *plural,* geet'n or gett'n.

WAUGH.   When it *geet* past midneet, I couldn't prop my een
1879.   oppen no lunger.   *Chimney Corner*, p. 245.

IBID.   We'n o'ertay yo afore yo *getten* to th' Owler Nook.
    Chimney Corner, p. 3.

COLL. USE.   1. What has to *geet* i' thi hond ?
1881.   2. What han they *geet'n* i' that cart ?

GERSE, *sb.* grass.

JOHN SCHOLES.   "David," hoo sed to one o' th' lads, "thee moind
1857.   o' th' stirk breakin' thru yon gap intuth' hay-*gerse.*"
    Jaunt to see th' Queen, p. 19.

DR. BARBER.   Ther' wos jenny-spinners, *girse*-hoppers, an' midges,
1870.   an' bees bumman about i' thowsands.
    Forness Folk, p. 7.

GERSINS', *sb.* moorland pastures.

GETS, *sb.* wages.

COLL. USE.   Tha'll noan marry him, wench, surely.   Why his *gets*
1881.   wouldn't keep hissel, mon, let alone booeth on you.

GEX, *v.* to guess.

COLLIER.   I *gex* I'm him ot to meeons.   *Works*, p. 57.
1750.

IBID.   I heard um say ut *gexing's* o kint lying.—*Works*, p. 73.

GIB (Fylde), *sb.* a hooked stick.

GIFT, *sb.* a small white spot on the finger nail, said to foretell the
    coming of a gift ; sometimes called, also, "a sweetheart."

GILDERT (N. Lanc.), *sb.* a snare of horse-hair.

GILLERS, *sb. pl.* bands of twisted hair.

GILLHOOTER, *sb.* an owl.

COLLIER.   Thoose ot connaw tell a bitterbump fro a *gillhooter.*
1750.   *Works : Intro.*, p. 34.

GILLIVER, *sb.* the gilly-flower.

GIMMER (N. Lanc.), *sb.* a two-year old sheep.

GINGER-TOPPIN', *sb.* applied to the head of a person whose hair is red.

GINN, } (Fylde), *sb.* a road or passage down to the sea. A.S. *ginn,*
GYNN, } an opening, an abyss.

GINNEL, *sb.* a narrow entry; a covered passage between houses. See GINN.

> MISS LAHEE.　　　Underneath this reawm wor a *ginnel* coed th' dark
> 1865.　　　　　entry . . . an' dark it wor, sure enough.
> 　　　　　　　　　　　　　　*Betty o' Yep's Tale,* p. 21.

GIRDLE (N. Lanc.),　} *sb.* an iron plate used for baking, and
GRIDDLE (S. E. Lanc.), } laid upon or suspended over the fire.
Welsh, *greidyl,* a bakestone.

GIRN, *vb.* to grin.

GIRT (N. Lanc.), *adj.* great.

> DR. BARBER.　　　T' aad man meadd a *girt* blast wi' t' horn.
> 1870.　　　　　　　　　　　　　　　*Forness Folk,* p. 6.

GISE (*g* soft; N. Lanc.), *v.* to put cattle out to grass at a sum agreed upon per head.

GIST (*g* soft; N. Lanc.), *v.* to pasture out cattle upon hire.

GISTIN' (N. Lanc.), *sb.* the pasturage of cattle at a price.

GIVE-O'ER, *v.* to cease doing a thing; to discontinue.

> COLL. USE.　　　If tha doesn't *give-o'er* this sort o' wark, tha 'll come
> 1881.　　　　　to a bad end, aw con tell thi.

GIV'EROUS, } *adj.* greedy; also avaricious. A.S. *gifer,* greedy,
GIVERSOME, } voracious, desirous.

> DR. BARBER.　　　He'd hed nowt to itt [eat] o' t' day, an' wos varra
> 1870.　　　　　*gyversom.*　　　　　*Forness Folk,* p. 13.

GIZ, *v.* pronun. of "gives."

> COLL. USE.　　　He *giz* nowt for th' money mon. Wi mun tak eawr
> 1881.　　　　　brass somewheer else.

GLEAD, *sb.* a hawk.

GLENDUR, } *v.* to look intensely or abstractedly; to stare.
GLENTHUR, }

> WAUGH.　　　Wheer the heart will be,
> 1859.　　　　　Th' wits are sure to wander;
> 　　　　　What one likes to see
> 　　　　　At it they mun *glendur.*
> 　　　　　　　　　*Lanc. Songs: These Maund'rin' Een.*

> IBID.　　　Then he grunted, an' mumble't, an' *glendur't* around.
> 1870.　　　　　　　　　　*Lanc. Songs: The Grindlestone.*

GLENT, *sb.* a glance, a quick view.

COLLIER.
1750.

I gan o *glent* into th' shipp'n, on seed o mon stonnin'.
Works, p. 56.

WAUGH.
1875.

" Ay," said Judd, givin' a sly *glent* round th' kitchen ;
" I've stopt to lung." *Old Cronies*, c. iv., p. 44.

GLEY, *sb.* a squint.

JOHN SCHOLES.
1857.

Iv yoan tay notis yoan see ut aw've o sooart ov o *gley*
wi mi een. *Jaunt to see th' Queen*, p. 6.

GLIFF (N. Lanc.), *sb.* a glimpse, a transient sight.

J. P. MORRIS.
(Furness Dialect.)
1867.

I've niver seen yan, an' if ther wos sic a lot we'd o'
hev gitten a *gliff* at yan some time er anudder.
Lebby Beck Dobby, p. 7.

GLIME (N. Lanc.), *v.* to glance aside, to look askance.

GLISK, *v.* to glitter, shine, sparkle, glisten.

GLIZZEN, *v.* to sparkle.

BAMFORD.
1840.

It wur as fair a gowden yallo as ever *glizzent*, wi' white
wings o' th' untherside.—*Life of Radical*, c. xx., p. 133.

GLIZZEN, *sb.* lightning.

BAMFORD.
1840.

Away it went i' th' *glizzen* an' th' thunner-din, o'er th'
moor. *Life of Radical*, c. xx., p. 133.

GLOAR (Fylde), *v.* to squint.

GLOOR, *v.* to stare fatuously.

COLLIER.
1750.

He *glooart* at it a good while.—*Works : Intro.* p. 38.

BAMFORD.
1840.

He didno come *glooring* at th' chimney reech an' then
maunder back agen. *Life of Radical*, c. xx., p. 134.

WAUGH.
1855.

Aw're forc't dray back a bit, at th' first, he *glooart* so
flaysome.
Lanc. Sketches: Rochdale to Blackstone Edge, p. 130.

GLOPPEN, *v.* to astonish, to surprise.

OLD BALLAD.
1548.

Bounce gus hur hart, an hoo wur so *glopen*
That out o' th' windo hoo'd like fort' lopen.
Warrikin Fair: Gent's. Mag., Sept., 1740.

RAMSBOTTOM.
1864.

Theer aw stoode, an' kept starin' awhoile ;
Aw wur *gloppent* wi' th' sentence they'd passed.
Lanc. Rhymes, p. 21.

B. BRIERLEY.
1868.

Well, i'sted on him bein' *gloppent* when he seed me,
an' beggin' me for t' know nowt, he slapt me on th' back,
an' coed me Old Cockylorum.—*Irkdale*, c. ii., p. 101.

J. P. MORRIS.
(Furness Dialect.)
1867.

What du ye say ? Wos nowte done to stop 'em ?
Why, yes, t' constables tried, but they wer' neā use.
They wer' fairly *gloppen'd*. *Siege o' U'ston*, p. 6.

GLOPPERS (N. Lanc.), *sb. pl.* blinkers for a horse.

GNATTER, *v.* to gnaw, to bite small with the teeth.

COLL. USE.
1881.

He's olus *gnatterin'* at his finger-nails.

GOAD, *sb.* a custom, a way of doing a thing.

> COLL. USE.　　Nay, theau 'll not act i' that *goad*, will to?
> 1881.

GOB, *sb.* a lump of anything, a large piece of meat, a mouthful.

> JOHN SCHOLES.　　Summut ut wur loik lumps o' crud began o' leckin fro
> 1857.　　under hiz hat, un slur'd deawn hiz face e *gobs*.
> 　　　　　　　　*Jaunt to see th' Queen*, p. 28.

GOBBIN, *sb.* an ignorant, clownish person.

> COLLIER.　　Th' *gobbin* ne'er considert o' hongin' wou'd naw be
> 1750.　　cawd good spooart be ony body eh ther senses.
> 　　　　　　　　*Works*, p. 62.

> JOHN SCHOLES.　　Awm noan o thoose awkurt *gobbins* ut nevvur venturn o
> 1857.　　moile off thir own dur-stone.—*Jaunt to see th' Queen*, p. 6.

GOBSLOTCH, *sb.* a glutton ; one who takes his meat in large pieces.

> COLLIER.　　Theaw'rt glenting ot tat flopper-meawth't *gob-slotch*
> 1750.　　Bill o' owd Katty's.　　　　*Works*, p. 72.

GO-BY-THE-WALL, *sb.* a creeping, helpless kind of person.

> COLL. USE.　　Neaw then, owd *go-by-the-wall*, shift eawt o' th' road.
> 1881.

GODDIT, *sb.* Shrovetide.

GODSTONE, *sb.* a small, round, white stone found by children and kept in the pocket as something valuable.

GOD'STRUTH, *sb.* the simple truth ; that which cannot be gainsaid.

> COLL. USE.　　It's *God'struth*, aw tell thi, an' nowt else, whether tha
> 1881.　　believes it or not.

GOIT or
GOYT, } *sb.* **a** watercourse to a mill.

GOLCH, *v.* to swallow ravenously.

GOLDSPINK,
GOWDSPINK, } (Mid. and W. Lanc.), *sb.* a goldfinch.

GOLLIN, *sb.* the marsh marigold. *Caltha palustris.*

GOLLOP, *v.* to swallow hastily or greedily.

> COLL. USE.　　Try him, an' then tha'll see.　Why, he'll *gollop* it up
> 1881.　　i' no-time.

GOMERAL, *sb.* a stupid fellow.

> J. P. MORRIS.　　T' girt *gomerals* hed tacken some brogs on t' sand for
> 1867.　　t' French masts.　　　　*Siege o' Brou'ton*, p. 7.

> DR. BARBER.　　He wos nea *gommeral*, thattan—*Forness Folk*, p. 25.
> 1870.

GONNER,
GONTHUR, } *sb.* a gander.

> BAMFORD.　　'Tis Feargus O'Connor
> 1864.　　I' search of a *gonner*.　　*Homely Rhymes*, p. 147.

> MISS LAHEE.　　"What has tha done wi' th' *gonners* ?"　"*Gonners*,
> 1865.　　says ta ; aw tell thee they're geese."
> 　　　　　　　　*Carter's Struggles*, p. 68.

WAUGH.
1867. It makes me maunder up an' deawn, like a *gonner* wi
a nail in its yed.
Home Life of Factory Folk, c. xvi., p. 142.

B. BRIERLEY.
1868. An''made her squeeal as leawd as a twichelt *gonner*
wi' th' squeeze he gan her. *Irkdale*, c. xii., p. 193.

GONNER-HEAD, *sb.* a stupid person, a gander-head.

GOOD-FOR-NOWT, *sb.* a useless or disreputable person. The
Lancashire equivalent for *Ne'er-do-weel.*

GOOD-WAY, *sb.* a long distance.

COLL. USE.
1881. He went wi' me a *good-way*, an' carried mi things
for me.

GOODE (N. Lanc.), *sb.* the ox-eye daisy. *Chrysanthemum leucanthemum.*

GOOER, ⎱ *sb.* a triangular piece of cloth stitched into a shirt or other
GORE, ⎰ garment when greater width is required at one end
than at the other.

GOOR (W. Lanc.), *sb.* a seagull.

GOOSEGOB, *sb.* a gooseberry.

GOOSEFLESH, *sb.* a term used to describe the skin when roughened
by a shock of cold or by fear.

WAUGH.
1879. But let's not talk about it. It makes me o' *goose-flesh.*
Chimney Corner, p. 204.

GORRISH, ⎱ *adj.* thick and luxuriant, sometimes coarse and
GORRY, ⎰ luxuriant, applied to grass.

GOSTERIN', *adj.* boastful. See GAWSTERIN'.

COLLIER.
1750. I con fettle tits os weel os onny one on um aw, tho'
theaw mey think its *gawstring*. *Works*, p. 71.

WAUGH.
1868. Doesn'to yer what he says, thae *gosterin'* foo?
Sneck-Bant, c. ii., p. 39.

GO-TO, *sb.* beginning of an action; a bout or an attack.

COLL. USE.
1880. Feight! He can feight noan, mon; he wur done up at
th' first *go-to.*

GOUL, *sb.* a yellow secretion in the eyes of children. See GEAWL.

GO-UNDER, *v.* to undergo; to suffer, as in the case of a surgical
operation.

COLL. USE.
1881. Si tha, aw would no' *go-under* it again, not for fifty
pound.

GOWK (W. Lanc.), *sb.* the cuckoo.

GOWK. ⎱ *sb.* a foolish fellow.
GAWK, ⎰

GOWL (W. Lanc.), *v.* to howl, to yell.

GRADELY, *adv.* properly, completely, truly, handsomely. Cf. Icel. *greiðr*, ready ; *greid-liga*, readily, promptly.

OLD BALLAD. 1548.	To Rondle's hoo hied, an' hoo hov' up the latch, Afore th' mon had tied th' mare *gradely* to th' cratch. *Ballads and Songs of Lanc.*, p. 53.
BAMFORD. 1850.	A clothes washing, in those days [Tim Bobbin's time], was never considered to be "*greadly* dun" unless all the woollen things had been thoroughly scoured by the great purifier, and afterwards washed and wrung out of clean hot water. *Intro. to Tim Bobbin*, p. viii.
WAUGH. 1865.	For when hoo's *gradely* donned, hoo'll look As grand as th' queen o' Shayba. *Lanc. Songs : Tum Rindle.*

GRADELY, *adj.* decent, becoming, proper, good, right.

COLLIER. 1750.	Yed's os *greadly* o lad as needs t' knep o'th' hem of a keke [cake]. *Works*, p. 67.
BAMFORD. 1840.	"Why bless yur life, Mesthur Nadin," said George, "yore a *graidley* felley for owt 'at I kno' to th' contrary ; an' I never sed nowt ogen yo' i' my lyve." *Life of Radical*, c. xiii., p. 84.
WAUGH. 1867.	He's had thoose hens mony a year ; an' they rooten abeawt th' heawse just th' same as *greadly* Christians. *Home Life of Factory Folk*, c. xi., p. 105.
IBID. 1867.	Aw go a fishin' a bit neaw an' then ; an' aw cotter abeawt wi' first one thing an' then another ; but it comes to no sense. Its noan like *gradely* wark. *Ib.*, cxvi., p. 142.

GRAIN, *sb.* the prong of a fork.

COLL. USE. 1881.	What's th' owd mon doin' i'th' garden ? Oh he's diggin' up roots wi' an owd three-*grained* fork.

GRAN, *v.* grinned.

COLLIER. 1750.	So I *gran*, on I thrutcht, till meh arms wartcht ogen. *Works*, p. 44.

GRANCH, *v.* to grind up with the teeth ; to eat voraciously.

GRASSED, *part.* discharged from work for a time ; usually for misbehaviour.

COLL. USE. 1881.	What's up wi' yor Jim ? Why, he wur drinkin' ; an' th' mestur *grassed* him for a fortnit.

GRATTER'D, *part. adj.* grated.

BAMFORD. 1840.	A jug of warm ale with some *grattered* ginger in was placed on the table. *Life of Radical*, c. ix., p. 58.

GREAVE OR GREAVE-BY, *phr.* right, or very nearly so. A common saying in the Rochdale district, meaning that anything which may be the subject of dispute is either what it is said to be, or so near as to make no difference.

COLLIER. 1750.	Beleemy mon, I think theaw'rt oather *greave or greave-by*. *Works*, p. 65.
.IBID.	Sed I, is yoar neme Mr. Scar ? Sed he, theaw'r oather *greeof or greeof-by* *Works*, p. 57.

GREAVIN' (N. Lanc.), *v.* delving.

J. P. MORRIS.
1867.

Jinny Dodgon ran into t' garden, whār her āld man was *greavin'*.   *Siege o' Brou'ton*, p. 5.

DR. BARBER.
1870.

Thor off-come chaps seaun began prowlin' about, grubbin' an' *greavvin'* an' pickin'.—*Forness Folk*, p. 20.

GREAWPIN', *sb.* the joining in the binding of a tub.

GREAWT, *sb.* the cheap thin ale drawn off after the first brewing.

GREAWT-NEET, *sb.* a feast of cheap ale. Also called a "Brewin'-main."

B. BRIERLEY.
1868.

They con make tables an' cheears doance abeawt like Little Gorton at a *greawt-neet* stir.
Irkdale, c. vi., p. 140.

GREENEY (N. Lanc.), *sb.* the green grosbeak, or green linnet.

GREEN-SAUCE, *sb.* a kind of sorrel with an acid flavour *(Rumex acetosa).*

WAUGH.
1855.

Gathering on their way edible herbs, such as "payshun docks," and "*green-sauce.*"
Lanc. Sketches: Cottage of Tim Bobbin, p. 50.

GREESE, *sb.* stairs, steps; also a little brow, an ascent. Latimer has "greesings," meaning steps.

GREET, *v.* to weep; past tense, *grat.* A.S. *grétan*, to cry.

GASKELL.
1854.

In Lancashire we sometimes hear it said, when a child is crying, "Give o'er *greetin'*;" and when a person has wept much for another, it is said, "Hoo *grat* sadly."
Lect. Lanc. Dialect, p. 29.

GREVE, GRYEV, *sb.* a division of a district, as the greves or gryevs in the ancient forest of Rossendale.

GREWNT, GRUANT, *sb.* pronunciation of greyhound.

COLLIER.
1750.

Why, yoad'n be os gaunt os o *grewnt*, on welly fammisht.   *Works*, p. 59.

GRIDDLE, *sb.* See GIRDLE.

GRIG, *sb.* a cricket; a lively or restless child.

COLL. USE.
1881.

That's a bonny little *grig* yo'n getten. What's its name?

GRINDLE, GRINDLESTONE, *sb.* a grindstone.

WAUGH.
1870.

Dody's axe wanted grindin', one wark-a-day morn, When there nobry about to gi' th' *grindle* a turn.
Lanc. Songs: The Grindlestone.

GRIP-YARD, GRIP-YORT, *sb.* a platting of stakes and twisted boughs filled up with earth; generally made to confine a water-course, and occasionally to form artificial banks and seats in pleasure gardens.

GRON (as a prefix), *adj.* grand, as *gron-chylt*, a grandchild ; *gron-dad* and *gron-feyther*, grandfather ; *gron-mam* and *gronny*, grandmother.

GROON, *v.* grow.

> WAUGH.
> 1868.
> Little lads o' *groon* into fellys ; don't they, mam ?"
> *Sneck-Bant,* c. iii., p. 53.

GROOP, *sb.* a channel in a shippon behind the cows.

GROO-WEATHER, *sb.* growing-weather.

> WAUGH.
> 1855.
> Wi'n had grand *groo-weather* as week or two. But a sawp o' deawn-fo' 'ud do a seet o' good.
> *Lanc. Sketches: Grislehurst Boggart,* p. 203.

GROYN, *sb.* a swine's snout.

GRUG (Fylde), *sb.* a dandy hen.

GRUMBLE-BELLY, *sb.* a discontented person.

> COLL. USE.
> 1881.
> Neaw then, owd *grumble-belly*, tha'rt at it again— nowt reet, and never satisfied.

GRUMMEL, *sb. pl.* small coal, riddlings.

GRUN-GRON, *adj.* grown on the ground; a native of a given locality ; homespun.

> COLL. USE.
> 1881.
> He's one o' th' owd sort, *grun-gron*—none o' yer new-catcht uns.

GUIDER, *sb.* a tendon.

GULLION, *sb.* a soft, worthless runagate.

GULLOOK, *intj.* begone ; go and look ; see for yourself.

GUMPTION, *sb.* ability combined with good sense. The Lancashire equivalent for *nous.*

> B. BRIERLEY.
> 1868.
> Aw've bin surprist, Dick, ut theau's had no mooar *gumption* abeawt thee nor what theau's shown yet.
> *Irkdale,* c. ii., p. 100.

GURD, *sb.* a fit, as " A gurd o' laughin' " = a fit of laughter.

> COLLIER.
> 1750.
> Th' fly'rin karron seet up o' *gurd* o' leawghin'.
> *Works,* p. 42.

GUTTER, *v.* to make a channel ; applied to a candle when the tallow runs down wastefully.

> COLL. USE.
> 1881.
> Snuff that candle, mon   Doesn't tha see how it's *gutterin'* ?

GYRR, *v.* to purge. A *gyrrd* cauve is a calf purged by having had too rich milk.

H.

HACK (N. Lanc.), *sb.* a pickaxe, a stone-pick or mattock, used by excavators.

HACK, *v.* to shake or knock together.

COLLIER. 1750. Meh teeth *hackt* eh meh heeod ogen.—*Works*, p. 50.

HACKSLAVER, *sb.* an objectionable blockhead; a disgusting and silly fellow.

HADLOONT (E. Lanc.), *sb.* pronunciation of Adlant; the headland of a ploughed field.

HADLOONT-REEAN, *sb.* the gutter, ditch, or space between the head lands and others.

COLLIER. 1750. A tealier i' Crummil's [Cromwell's] time wur thrung pooin' turmits in his pingot, an' fund an urchon i' th' *hadloont-reean*. *Works*, p. 37.

HAFFLE, *v.* to hesitate, to prevaricate.

COLL. USE. 1881. Come, eawt with it mon. We'll ha' noan o' thi *hafflin'* wark here.

HAG (N. Lanc.), *sb.* an enclosure, a wood. A.S. *haga*, what is hedged in, a garden, a field; Icel. *hagi*, a hedged field.

HAG (N. Lanc.), *sb.* a lot or set portion of work, as distinguished from day work.

R. B. PEACOCK. 1869. I wark be t' *hag*, an' not be t' day. *Lonsdale Glossary*, p. 39.

HAG,
HAGGUS, } *sb.* the belly.

HAG-A-KNOWE, *sb.* an ungainly blockhead.

WAUGH. 1866. Sit to deawn, thae gawmbless *hag-a-knowe*, or aw'll kom thi yure for tho.—*Ben an' th' Bantam*, c. v., p. 98.

HAGBERRY (N. Lanc.), *sb.* the bird-cherry (*Prumus padus*).

HAGGUS,
HEYGUS, } *sb.* pottage made of herbs.

HAGUE, ⎫ *sb.* the hawthorn, but especially the hawthorn berry.
HAIG, ⎭ Fruit of *Cratægus Oxyacantha.* A.S. *haga,* a hedge, also haw or hedge thorn ; *hagan,* haws, fruit of the haw, hedge, or white thorn.

B. BRIERLEY.
1868.

"Wilt ha' this bit o' *hague*-blossom ?   Aw geet it eawt o' th' hedge wheer aw seed thee layin' th' clooas eawt," and Joe produced a bunch of hawthorn blossom of a delightful fragrance, and offered it to Mally.

Irkdale, c. iv., p. 116.

HAGWORM (N. Lanc.), *sb.* the common snake ; lit. hedgeworm.

HALA, ⎫ *adj.* shy, bashful.   See AYLA, AYLO, *ante,* p. 20.
HEALO, ⎭

HALCH, *sb.* a noose.   O.E. *halch,* a loop ; *halched,* looped, fastened.

WEST MID. DIAL. (Lanc.) And ȝet hem *halcheȝ* al hole þe halves to-geder.
1320.
Sir Gawayne, l. 1613.

IBID.

A lace lapped aboute, þat louked at þe hede, And so after þe halme *halched* ful ofte.
Sir Gawayne, l. 217.

HALFENDEAL, ⎫ *sb.* a moiety or half.   See also HAUGHENDO.
HALFENDOLE, ⎭

SPENSER.
1586.

Now the humid night was farforth spent, And hevenly lampes were *halfen-deale* ybrent.
Faerie Queene, Bk. III., canto ix., l. 3.

———

1526.

The name of Thomas Smith, vicar of Kirkham, occurs in a lease dated 15th September, 1526, by which he "graunted, demised, sett, and to farme lettyn" to Sir Richard Hoghton, Knt., "the moyte or *hallfendell* and of all profetts, &c., of a certain tacke or bargain belonging to the chappell of Gosenarghe."
Fishwick's Hist. Kirkham, p. 72.

HALIDAY, *sb.* holiday.   A.S. *hálig,* holy.

WEST MID. DIAL. (Lanc.) Er þe *halidayeȝ* holly were halet out of toun.
1320.
Sir Gawayne, l. 1049.

IBID.
1360.

I herde on a *halyday* at a hiȝe masse.
E. Eng. Allit. Poems, C, l. 9.

———

COLL. USE.
1881.

He'll wark none.   It's haliday o' th' year reawnd wi' him.

HALIDAY-JACK, *sb.* a man fond of holidays and of display in clothes.

COLL. USE.
1881.

Look at him neaw.   He's a bonny *haliday-jack*—is n't he ?—wi' his mester's foine shirt on.

HALLIBLASH, *sb.* a great blaze ; something which dazzles.

COLLIER.
1750.

I'st ha set th' how leath on a *halliblash.*
Works, p. 46.

B. BRIERLEY.
1868.

Aw'd ha' sich a blaze as ther hasno bin sin' owd George
o' Jammie's barn wur ov a foyer, for aw'd mak a' *hally-
blash* ov every factory i' Englandshire.
Irkdale, c. i., p. 7.

HAMMIL, *sb.* a hamlet.　A.S. *ham,* a home, dwelling, village.

JOHN SCHOLES.
1867.

Nanny Clegg's peggy-tub, ut goas o reawnd th' *hammil.*
Jaunt to see th' Queen, p. 6.

WAUGH.
1869.

Aw know o' that country-side, deawn as far as Rip-
ponden,—hill an' dale, wood an' wayter-stid, *hamil* an'
road-side heawse.　*Yeth-Bobs,* c. i., p. 30.

HAMMIL-SCOANCE, *sb.* the lantern or light of the village ; the
village Solomon.

COLLIER.
1750.

They look'nt on him as th' *hammil-scoance,* an' thowtn
he'r fuller o' leet than a glow-worm.　*Works,* p. 37.

WAUGH.
1875.

Randle Holt, or "Rondle o' Raunger's," a schoolmaster, who was looked up to by his neighbours as a
kind of " *hamel-scoance,*" or lanthorn of the village.
Old Cronies, c. iii., p. 27.

HAMSHACKLE, *v.* to fasten the head of a vicious animal to one
of its forelegs.

HAMSTERS, *sb. pl.* a kind of knee-breeches ; literally, a covering
for the *hams.*

BAMFORD.
1840.

His *hamsters* were similar in material and condition to
his coat.　*Life of Radical,* Vol. I., p. 50.

IBID.

His *hamsters* of dark kerseymere, grey at the knees.
Ibid., p. 51.

E. RIDINGS.
1845.

Wi' stockins deawn, unteed his shoon,
His *hamsters* loosely hung.
Lancashire Muse, p. 6.

HAN, *v. pl.* have.

WEST MID. DIAL. (Lanc.)
1320.

Þenne he　.　. criande loude,
" Ʒe *han* demed to do þe dede þat I bidde."
Sir Gawayne, l. 1088.

SPENSER.
1579.

It was upon a holiday
When shepheardes groomes *han* leave to playe.
Shepheardes Calender : March.

WAUGH.
1865.

What *han* yo to do wi' me?　Aw want my jackass.
Besom Ben, c. viii., p. 95.

MISS LAHEE.
1875.

" Win gettin' o soarts for yo to-neet, *han*not we
Hannah?"　"We *han,* lad."—*The Charity Coat,* p. 18.

HANCH, *v.* to snap, to bite at.

BAMFORD.
1854.

Th' dog *hancht* at him.—*Dialect of S. Lanc.,* p. 185.

HANCH-APPLE, *sb.* the game of snap-apple, which consists in biting at an apple floating in water or suspended by a cord. It is usually played at Halloween.

HANDY-DANDY, *sb.* a game played by children. Common in Lancashire. Frequently given as "*handy-pandy.*" Something being hidden in one hand, both are presented by the player to his opponent with the words, "*Handy-dandy*, sugar candy, which hand is it in?"

SHAKSPERE.   Hark, in thine ear : change places ; and, *handy-dandy*, which is the justice, which is the thief?
Lear, act iv., sc. vi., l. 157.

HANGMENT, *sb.* mischief. Frequently used as an expletive.

WAUGH.   "Where's that jackass?" cried he, almost out of
1865.   breath. "It's i' th' nook, here," said Twitchel. "What the *hangment* has to sent it up to us for?"
Besom Ben, c. iii., p. 33.

HANKLE, *v.* to twist, to entangle.

HANSEL, *sb.* a gift given to the first purchaser ; also *v.* to have the first use of anything. Icel. *handsal ; hanselling*, the transference of a right or bargain by joining hands. Dan. and Scot. *handsel.*

SPENSER.   That who so hardie hand on her doth lay,
1586.   It dearely shall aby, and death for *handsell* pay.
Faerie Queene, Book VI., c. xi., stanza 15

HAP, *v.* to cover up, to smooth down.

WEST MID. DIAL. (Lanc.)   Ʒe schal not rise of your bedde, I rych yow better,
1320.   I schal *happe* yow here.   *Sir Gawcyne*, l. 1223.

IBID.   For hit watʒ brod at þe boþem, boʒtcd on lofte,
1360.   *Happed* upon ayþer half a hous as hit were.
E. Eng. Allit. Poems, C, l. 49.

1440.   *Happyn* or *whappyn'* yn clopys. Involvo.
Prompt. Parv.

1450.   Lord, what [to] these weders ar cold, and I am ylle
(Yorkshire.)   *happyd*.   *Towneley Mysteries*, p. 98.

WAUGH.   Then hoo geet him to bed, an' hoo *happed* him up weel.
1859.   *Lanc. Songs : Owd Enoch.*

IBID.   He *happed* the clothes about his sleeping wife.
1866.   *Ben an' th' Bantam*, c. i., p. 9.

HAPPEN, *adv.* probably, perhaps, possibly.

WAUGH.   Aw's *happen* be leetin' on tho up Whit'oth Road on
1866.   afore th' next fay-berry time.
Ben an' th' Bantam, c. v., p. 98.

B. BRIERLEY.   Theaw'll *happen* be i' time for th' leeavins, if theaw'll
1868.   be sharp !   *Irkdale*, c. i., p. 46.

HAR, *adj. com.* and *adv.* higher.

HARDSET, *adv.* in difficulties, closely pressed.

> COLL. USE.
> 1881.
>
> He's *hard-set*, aw con tell thi—eawt o' wark an' his woife deawn wi' twins.

HARD-YEDS, *sb.* scabious; also called devil's-bit *(Scabiosa Succisa).*

HARE-GATE, *sb.* an opening in a hedge, sufficient for the passage of hares.

> WAUGH.
> 1879.
>
> The hedge on each side was full of holes and "*hare-gates*," and tunnels, and runs, where the mole, the weazel, and the urcheon wandered at will.
> *Chimney Corner*, p. 5.

> PROVERBIAL SAYING.
> 1880.
>
> "He knows both th' hare an' th' *hare-gate*," *i.e.* he knows both the hare, and the way the hare runs—a proverbial saying commonly applied to a person who is supposed to be thoroughly acquainted with any particular matter.

HARRISHT, *v.* harassed, vexed, tormented.

> WAUGH.
> 1876.
>
> They dunnot know 'at they're wick, Matty,—they dunnot for sure. They mun be *harrisht* an' parisht,
> . . . an' then they'n larn summat 'at 'll last their time. *Chimney Corner*, p. 141.

HARSTONE-TALK, *sb.* boastful talk; promises made at night, and not intended to be kept in the morning.

> COLL. USE.
> 1881.
>
> Dunnot moind 'em, mon. It's o' *harstone-talk*. They'll do nowt i' th' morn.

HATCH-HORN, *sb.* an acorn. See AKRAN, *ante*, p. 7. Icel. *akarn ;* A.S. *æcorn.*

> WAUGH.
> 1865.
>
> Come, aw think o's reet an' square. Reet as a *hatch-horn*. *Besom Ben*, c. i., p. 14.

HATELY, *adv.* hateful, bad tempered. A.S. *hétel, hétol,* fierce.

> WEST MID. DIAL. (Lanc.)
> 1360.
>
> So fro heuen to helle þat *hatel* schor laste.
> *E. Eng. Allit. Poems*, B, l. 227.

> BAMFORD.
> 1850.
>
> Dunno be so *hately*.
> *Gloss. to Tim Bobbin.*

HATTOCK, *sb.* a corn sheaf.

HAUGHENDO,   } *sb.* a half part or half measure. The Rev.
HAUGHENDOLE, } W. Thornber, in his *History of Blackpool*, p. 108, gives "*Haughendo*, seven quarts." See HALFENDEAL.

> POTT.
> 1613.
>
> Iohn Device . . . did covenant with the said Anne [Chattox] that if she would hurt neither of them, she should yearely have one *aghen-dole* of meale.
> *Discoverie of Witches*, p. 23.

JAMES CROSSLEY.
1845.

One Aghen-dole of Meale.—This *aghen-dole*, a word still, I believe, in use for a particular measure of any article, was, I presume, a kind of witches' black-mail. My friend, the Rev. Canon Parkinson, informs me that *aghen-dole*, sometimes pronounced *acken-dole*, signifies a half-measure of anything, from half-hand-dole. Mr. Halliwell has omitted it in his Glossary, now in progress.

Since writing the Note, p. 23, I am indebted to Miss Clegg, of Hallfoot, near Clitheroe, for information as to the exact quantity contained in an *aghendole*, which is eight pounds. This measure, she informs me, is still in use in Little Harwood, in the district of Pendle. The Archdeacon of Manchester [J. Rushton, D.D.] considers that an *aghendole*, or more properly, as generally pronounced, a *nackendole*, is a kneading-dole, the quantity of meal, &c., usually taken for kneading at one time. There can be no doubt that this is the correct derivation.

Notes to Chetham Society's reprint of Potts's
Discoverie of Witches.

HAUT, *sb.* a finger-cover used to protect a cut or wound..

HAVER, *sb.* oats.

HAVER-BREAD,
HAVER-CAKE, } *sb.* a thin cake made of oatmeal.

LANGLAND.
1377.

A few cruddes and creem, and an *haver* cake.
P. Plowman, B, vi., 284.

JOSEPH FIELDING.
1852.

Formerly the bread chiefly eaten by the labouring classes in this parish (Rochdale) was oat-cake; and the same kind of food was in pretty general use in the manufacturing parts of Yorkshire. In the districts where this peculiarity prevailed the people were proud of the distinction; and a regiment of soldiers, raised in the east of Lancashire, and the west of Yorkshire, at the beginning of the French war, took the name of the "Haver-cake Lads;" assuming as their badge an oat-cake which was placed, for the purpose of attraction, at the point of the recruiting sergeant's sword. Oat bread is still eaten here, but its use is by no means general as it was in the latter, and the beginning of the present century.

Rural Gleanings in South Lancashire.

WAUGH.
1865.

Oatmeal porridge, and oatcake, enter largely into the diet of the country people in this part of Lancashire. They used to pride themselves on the name of the *Havercake* Lads. A regiment raised in Lancashire during the war bore this name. This oatcake is baked upon a peculiar kind of stone slab, called a back-stone; and the cry of "*Haver-cake* back-stones" is a familiar sound in Rochdale, and the villages around it, at this day.

Lanc. Sketches: Rochdale to Blackstone Edge, p. 128.

IBID.
1879.

"Here; what's this? Bring me some loaf! I want noan o' thi baked moonshine!" Ay, my lad, thinks I, thou'll be fain of a bit o' *haver-brade* yet afore thou dees!

Chimney Corner, p 285.

HAW (Ormskirk), *adj.* on one side of the perpendicular. "All of a *haw*" = all on one side.

HAWBUCK (N. Lanc.), *sb.* a country clown.

HAWMBARK, *sb.* a horse-collar. See HAWMS.

| COLLIER. 1750. | It slipt o'er his sow, an leet like a *hawmbark* on his shilders. *Works*, p. 52. |

HAWMPLE, *v.* to walk awkwardly, to limp.

B. BRIERLEY. 1870.	"Thank yer, guv'nor," he said, as he *haumpled* eawt. *Ab-o'-th'-Yate in London*, p. 21.
WAUGH. 1876.	He *hawmples* in his walk, like a lame duck. *Hermit Cobbler*, p. 6.
IBID. 1879.	He wur nobbut a *hawmplin'* mak of a walker at th' best. *Chimney Corner*, p. 116.
IBID. 1879.	Thou'll keep *hawmplin'* and slutterin' through it onyhow. *Ibid.*, p. 209.

HAWMS (Ormskirk), *sb. pl.* the hames; the part of the collar by which horses draw. Pronun. of "hame." "Hame and chain maker" common in Manchester.

HAY, *v.* to lay bare; to remove the top earth off gravel. A farmer at Flixton had fetched some gravel and complained of his pay, saying, "I had to *hay* it as well."

HAYBANT, *sb.* a twisted band of hay.

| WAUGH. 1867. | Here, lass, tee this on for mo. It looks like a *haybant*, when aw tee it for mysel'.—*Owd Blanket*, c. i., p. 22. |

HAY-MOO, *sb.* a stack of hay. *Moo* is the pronunciation of *mow*, which means the pile or stack of hay which has been *mowed*. A *mow* is also the loft or chamber in which hay or corn is laid up. The "Barley Mow" is an alehouse sign in Manchester.

| WAUGH. 1866. | He's sprain't his anclif a bit, wi' jumpin' off th' *hay-moo* yesterday. *Ben an' th' Bantam*, c. ii., p. 39. |

HEAD-AN'-HEELS, *adv.* altogether, completely without reserve. The Scottish equivalent is "heels-o'er gowdie." See Burns' *Poem on Life:* "Soon heels-o'er-gowdie! in he gangs."

| COLL. USE. 1881. | 1. His foot slipped, an' in he went, *head-an-heels*. |
| | 2. He's th' reet sort of a chap; when he starts he gwos in for it, *head-an-heels*. |

HEADBOLT (Ormskirk), *sb.* a road over a bog or morass, stopped at one end.

HEARTY-ETTEN, *adj.* hearty, having a good appetite.

| WAUGH. 1867. | The poor woman said that her children were all "*hearty-etten*," especially the lads. *Home Life of Factory Folk*, c. xix., p. 166. |

HEAWSE-MONEY, *sb.* a wife's allowance for house expenditure.

COLL. USE.
1881.

"Does he turn up his wages?" "Nawe, he gies me what he loikes for th' *heawse-money*, an' keeps th' rest for hissel."

HEAWSE-PLACE, *sb.* the living-room in a cottage.

COLL. USE.
1881.

Come, my wench, let's have this *heawse-place* cleaned up.

HEAWSE-PROUD, *adj.* admiringly fond of home.

WAUGH.
1867.

We had some talk with that class of operatives who are both clean, provident, and *heawse-proud*, as Lancashire folk call it.
Home Life of Factory Folk, c. vi., p. 56.

HECK (N. Lanc.) *sb.* a half-door or hatch; a gate.

1735.

Heck, a door, a rack for cattle. North Country.
Bailey's Dict., vol. i., ed. 1735.

HEDGE-BACKIN', *sb.* the bank under or behind the hedge.

B. BRIERLEY.
1870.

We'st ha' nowt to do then i'th' summer nobbut lie in *hedge-backins*, hearkenin' brids sing.
Ab-o'-th'-Yate on Times and Things, p. 94.

HELVE, *sb.* the haft of a spade. A.S. *helf.*

1350.

He hedde an hache uppon heiȝ wiþ a gret *halve*.
Joseph of Arimathie, l. 503.

HEM, *pr.* them. A.S. *hem, heom*, dat. pl. of *hi*, they.

LANGLAND.
1377.

I batered *hem* on þe bakke and bolded here hertis,
And dede *hem* hoppe for hope.
Piers Plowman, B-text, iii. l. 198.

CHAUCER.
1380.

And yif he have nought sayd *hem*, leeve brother,
In o bok, he hath seyd *hem* in another.
Man of Lawes Prologue, l. 51.

SPENSER.
1580.

Wolves, ful of fraude and guile
That often devoured their owne sheepe,
And often the shepheards that did *hem* keepe.
Shepheardes Calender, May, l. 127.

REV. W. GASKELL.
1854.

I believe that "hem," in such phrases as "I'll give it *hem*," is not a contraction of "them," but simply the A.S. dative plural, which we find retained by our poets to a comparatively late period.
Lect. Lanc. Dialect, p. 23.

HEMPLAND (N. Lanc.), *sb.* a small piece of land set apart for growing flax for family use. Mr. J. P. Morris says the practice has fallen into disuse, but the patches of land still retain the name.

HENKY-PENKY, *sb.* trickery; shaffling conduct.

COLL. USE.
1881.

Now mi lad—none o' thi *henky-penky* here; stand up fair.

HENRIDGE,
HAINRIDGE,   } (Ormskirk), *sb.* an outlet for cattle.
HAINING-GROUND,

HEP, *sb.* the fruit of the briar.   Pron. of *hip*, the fruit of the dog-rose.

> CHAUCER.   And sweet is the brambel-flour
> 1380.   That bereth the rede *hepe.*—*Cant. Tales,* l. 13,677.

> WAUGH.   Aw'll keawer me deawn, an' pike a two-thre o' these
> 1869.   *heps.*   *Yeth-Bobs,* c. i., p. 12.

HERBY, *sb.* a shop for the sale of herbs and simples.   The word was used in a paragraph in the *Preston Guardian* during January, 1877.

HE-WITCH, *sb.* a wizard.

HIDDLE, *v.* to hide.   A.S. *hýdan,* to hide; *hýdels,* a den, a hiding-place.   Mr. Skeat (*N. and Q.,* 5th s., vol. vi., p. 209) says: "*Hydels* occurs in the Rushworth MS. of the Northumbrian Gospels, where the phrase 'speluncam latronum (Mark xi. 17) is glossed by 'cofa vel *hydels* ðeafana,' a cove or a hiding-place of thieves. . . . As the word became obsolescent, the false form *hidel* or *hiddel* arose, with a false plural *hideles* or *hiddelis.* Of this there is an example in Barbour's *Bruce* (bk. v., l. 306 of my edition), where Sir James Douglas is said to have lurked 'in *hiddilis* and in prevatè,' that is, in hiding-places and in privacy."   See HIDLANCE.

HIDE, *sb.* skin or body.   *Hide* is the skin of an animal, but used for skin of a man and figuratively for body.   " *Tan* his hide" is used figuratively for " beat his body."

> WAUGH.   Iv ony mon says wrang to me,
> 1859.   Aw'll tan his *hide* to-day !   *Lanc. Songs: Chirrup.*

HIDE, *v.* to beat, to flog.

HIDIN', *sb.* a flogging, beating, or chastisement.

> MISS LAHEE.   Tha desarves a gradely good *hidin',* an tha shall hav
> 1855.   it too afore this job's getten o'er wi'.—*Owd Yem,* p. 22.

HIDLANCE (S. Lanc.),   } *sb.* a place of secrecy or con-
HIDLANDS (Preston and Lonsdale), } cealment.   The word is
HIDLINS (Lancaster),   } always used with the *prep.*
"in," forming an adverbial phrase.   See HIDDLE.

> COLL. USE.   He's not bin seen for mony a month. He's in *hid-*
> 1881.   *lance* somewheer; and has bin, ever sin' he left his
>   woife.

HIG, *sb.* passion ; pettish anger.

> COLLIER.   Wi' that I leep off th' tit in a great *hig.*—*Works,* p. 61.
> 1750.

> BAMFORD.   He's in a great *hig.*   *Dialect of S. Lanc.,* p. 187.
> 1854.

HIGH TIME, *sb.* time fully arrived.

BIBLE.
1610.

And that, knowing the time, that now it is *high time* to awake out of sleep. *Romans* xiii. 11.

COLL. USE.
1881.

Aw'm feart for yon lad : it's *high-time* he were back.

HILL, ⎫ *v.* to cover. A.S. *helan,* to cover, conceal; Icel. *hylja,*
HULL, ⎭ to hide, cover; O.H.G. *huljan;* Germ. *hüllen;* Dan. *hylle* and *hæle.*

NORTHUMB. PSALTER.
Before 1300.

Depnes als schroude his *hiling* alle.—*Psalm* ciii., l. 6.

SPENSER.
1586.

Else would the waters overflow the lands,
And fire devoure the ayre, and *hell* them quight,
But that she holds them with her blessed hands.
Faerie Queene, iv. x. 35.

COLLIER.
1750.

Sitch a floose o hay follud meh, at it drove meh sheer deawn, an Seroh atop o meh, an quite *hill'd* u booath.
Works, p. 68.

REV. W. GASKELL.
1854.

A Lancashire man, when he wishes to be covered up, as with bed-clothes, says "*hill* me up." And he calls the husk or covering of the pea "a pea-*hull,*" and removing it is "*hullin'*" it.
Lect. Lanc. Dialect, p. 15.

B. BRIERLEY.
1870.

Th' owd lad wur *hillin'* hissel up nicely.
Ab-o'-th'-Yate on Times and Things, p. 121.

HINDER-END, *sb.* the back part of a thing; the posterior.

WAUGH.
1869.

He let wi' his *hinder-end* thump o' th' top-bar, an' then roll't deawn upo' th' har'stone.
Lanc. Sketches, p. 30.

HINDERSOME, *adj.* obstructive.

HIPPIN' or ⎫ *sb.* a napkin, a cloth in which something is
HIPPIN'-CLOUT, ⎭ "happed" or folded.

WAUGH.
1867.

Mary, reach me yon *hippin'* off th' oon-dur.
Home Life of Factory Folk, c. xix., p. 165.

IBID.
1876.

He caps me ! A mon o' three score gettin' wed to a bit of a snicket that's hardly done wearin' *hippins !*
Hermit Cobbler, p. 44.

HIPPINGS, ⎫ *sb. pl.* stepping-stones in a brook. Bungerley
HIPPING-STONES, ⎭ *Hipping-stones,* across the Ribble, near Clitheroe, so called to this day, are mentioned in *Warkworth's Chronicle,* A.D. 1470, where the word is spelt "*hyppyngstones.*" *Hipping* is a form of *hopping :* "That *hippe* aboute in Engelonde" (*Piers Plowman,* B, xv. 557).

1879.

Pendle Forest district may almost be said to be shut up from the people of Burnley, so far as a field-walk is concerned. For, by far the greatest portion of the year, there is no passing whatever for foot passengers for the whole length between Padiham and Pendlebottom

bridges. There are two sets of stepping-stones—one known as the "Pendle *Hippings*," the other as the "Duckpit *Hippings*." The public have an undoubted right to travel over both these places ; but, in the case of Pendle *Hippings*, there is no passing at all for travellers except through the water ; and, in the other case, they can only be crossed at the dryest seasons of the year.
Burnley Gazette.

HIS-SEL, *pr.* himself.

WAUGH.
1876.

He's as poor as a crow *his-sel.*
The Chimney Corner, p. 144.

HOAST, *sb.* a cough.   Icel. *hostr*, the throat ; *hosti*, a cough.

1440.

Hoose, or cowghe (host or hoost).   *Prompt Parv.*

___

WAUGH.
1876.

Eh, I have sich a *hoast !* My throttle's as reawsty as a bone-house-dur lock. *Chimney Corner*, p. 169.

HOBBIL, *sb.* a dunce, an idiot.   See *hob*, a clown, a rustic, a fairy, in Skeat's Etym. Dict. : "*Hob*, strange as it may appear, was a popular corruption of *Robin*.   The name *Robin* is French, and, like *Robert*, is of O.H.G. origin ; Littré considers it as a mere pet corruption from *Robert*, a name early known in England, as being that of the eldest son of William I."

NICH. UDELL.
1550.

Ye are such a calfe, such an asse, such a blocke,
Such a lilbúrne, such a *hoball*, such a lobcocke.
Roister Doister, act iii., sc. 3, l. 17.

HOBTHURST, *sb.* an ungainly dunce.   In Tim Bobbin's time, a wood goblin—Hob o' th' Hurst, or Hob of the Wood. Cf. Shakspere, *Lear* IV. i. 62 : " Hobbididance," a dumb fiend or goblin.

COLLIER.
1750.

Th' goblin wur awtert when they poodn him eawt, an' whot a *hobthurst* he lookt wi' o' that berm abeawt him.
Works, p. 53.

BAMFORD.
1854.

Theau great *hobthurst*. Tim Bobbin describes it as an apparition "haunting only woods" [*i.e.* Hob o' th' hurst], but in that sense it is not now understood.
Dialect of S. Lanc., p. 188.

HOG, *v.* to cover a heap with earth or straw.

PARSON WALKER.
1730.

I put off at present, being throng *hogging* up some of my potatoes.   *Diary*, p. 23.

HOG-MUTTON, *sb.* a year-old sheep.

HOLE, *v.* to hide, or get under cover.

WAUGH.
1879.

" How leets thou didn't *hole ?*"   "*Hole !* wheer mut I *hole*, at th' top o' Rooly Moor, where o's as bare as a bakstone for five mile round ?"
Chimney Corner, p. 169.

HOLLIN, *sb.* the holly. A.S. *holen, holegn.* The spellings *holin, holie* both occur in the Ancren Riwle, p. 418. See *holly* in Skeat's Etym. Dict.

| WEST MID. DIAL. (Lanc.) 1320. | Bot in his on honde he hade a *holyn* bobbe [*i.e.* a holly bough]. *Sir Gawayne*, 1. 206. |

| COLLIER. 1750. | Meh carkuss wur pratty yeasy, boh meh mind moot os well ha line in o rook o' *hollins* or gorses. *Works*, p. 54. |

HOMER (Fylde), *v.* to incommode.

HOND-RUNNIN' (hand-running), *adv.* consecutively, quickly.

| COLL. USE. 1881. | He'd feight the whole lot on 'em, *hond-running*, as easy as ninepence. |

HOND'S-TURN, *sb.* a small service.

| WAUGH. 1876. | Folk 'at never did a *hond's-turn* for theirsels sin they wur born into th' world. *Chimney Corner*, p. 141. |

HONISHT (N. Lanc.), *p. adj.* wearied, tired out. See three capital illustrations of this remarkable word in Skeat's Notes to P. Plowman, pp. 237, 238. The etymology there suggested is wrong; it is not allied to *hunch*, but derived from O.F. *honnir, honir*, to disgrace (as in *honi soit*).

HONTLE, *sb.* a handful.

| E. RIDINGS. 1845. | A *hontle* o' woise saws Or moral rules an' laws. *Lancashire Muse*, p. 11. |

HOO, *pr.* she. A.S. *heo.* Dr. R. Morris, in his *Historical Outlines of English Accidence*, p. 120, says: "*She*, in the twelfth century, in the Northern dialects, replaced the old form *heo*. The earliest instance of its use is found in the *A. Sax. Chronicle*, 1140 (Stephen): 'Dær efter *scæ* ferde ofer *sæ*.' In the thirteenth century, the ordinary form of *she* is *sco*, found in Northern writers; *sche (scæ)* is a Midland modification of it."

WEST. MID. DIAL. (Lanc.) Into a comely closet coyntly *ho* entreȝ.
1320. *Sir Gawayne and G. K.*, 1. 935.

WEST MID. DIAL. (Lanc.) *Ho* profered me speche.
1360. *E. Eng. Allit. Poems*, A, l. 235.

| LANCASHIRE. 1548. | Bounce gus hur hart, an *hoo* wur so glopen That out o' th' windo *hoo'd* like for t' lopen. *Hoo* staumpdt, an *hoo* star'dt, an down stairs *hoo* run. *Warrikin Fair: Gentleman's Mag.*, Sept., 1740; and *Ballads and Songs of Lanc.*, p. 53. |

| About 1815. | *Hoo's* nout agen th' king, Bur *hoo* loikes a fair thing, Un *hoo* says *hoo* con tell when *hoo's* hurt. *Ballads and Songs of Lanc.: Jone o' Grinfilt Junior*, p. 169. |

WAUGH.
1859.

An' aw kiss'd her agen ; but *hoo* said
At *hoo* wanted to kiss thee an' o'.
Lanc. Songs : Come Whoam to thi Childer.

IBID.
1867.

When *hoo'd* getten o' reet, *hoo* set off after a place ;
and when *hoo* geet theer, th' mistress said *hoo* thought
hoo'd suit 'em, but *hoo* wur to co' again at six o'clock.
Owd Blanket, c. iii., p. 72.

HOPPET, *sb,* a small basket.

JOHN SCHOLES.
1857.

Hoo put hur hont deawn fur hur *hoppet ;* boh th'
hoppet, wi' Peg's fewtrils in, wur gwon.
Jaunt to see th' Queen, p. 29.

HOPPLE (Fylde), *v.* to fetter.

HOP-SHACKLE'T, *p. adj.,* cumbered or hindered in walking, by
some natural or other impediment or defect.

WAUGH.
1879.

"Well ; come on then ! What's to do witho ? Thou
walks as if thou were *hop-shackle't !*" "Thou'd be
hop-shackle't too, if thou'd as mony corns o' thi toes as I
have." *Chimney Corner,* p. 17.

HORN, *sb.* a comb for the hair.

WAUGH.
1879.

Here ; tak how o' this *horn,* an' ready thi yure a bit—
for thou'rt moore like a corn-boggart nor aught belungin'
this world. *Chimney Corner,* p. 168.

HORSE-NOP (N. Lanc.), *sb.* the knap weed *(Centaurea nigra).*

HORSE-STANG (N. Lanc.), *sb.* the gad-fly.

HOTFOOT, *adv.* in great haste. The same as *fut-hate* (foot-hot) in
Barbour's *Bruce,* iii. 418, xiii. 454. See note in Skeat's edition,
p. 557. Also *foot-hoot* in Chaucer, Man of Lawes Tale, l. 340.

COLL. USE.
1881.

He coom deawn *hot-foot,* bent on havin' a quarrel.

HOTTERIN', *v.* fidgetting, or trembling with emotion.

JOHN SCHOLES.
1857.

Hoo'd o face loik o turkey-cock, un hoo wur fayr
hotterin' wi' vexashun. *Jaunt to see th' Queen,* p. 28.

HOTTERIN'-MAD, very angry.

HOWLE, *adj.* hollow. A.S. *hol,* a hole.

CHAUCER.
1380.

And he was not right fat, I undertake,
But lokede *holwe,* and therto soburly.
Prologue, C. T., l. 288.

———

WAUGH.
1874.

"He must be varra *howle* when he's hungry," said the
landlady. "*Howle !*" said Adam, "why he'll be like
a two-legged drum, about t' middle o' t' forenoon.
Jannock, c. iv., p. 30.

HOYT, *sb.* a long road.

HUBBONS, } *sb. pl.* the hips. In the Lincolnshire dialect this word
HUGGINS, } appears as "huck." See Tennyson's "Northern
Cobbler"—"I slither'd and hurted my *huck.*"

> JOHN SCHOLES. Aw shud o shaumt wur nur o thief when aw're o lass
> 1857. t' ha' bin sin wi mi cooatts brad eawt o yard un o hauve
> across th' *hubbons.* *Jaunt to see th' Queen,* p. 23.

HUCKLE, *v.* to stoop, to bend from weakness or age.

> REV. W. GASKELL. In Lancashire, a person who stoops is said to "*huckle;*"
> 1854. and "hunch-backed" is expressed by "*huckle-backed;*"
> this may come from the A.S. *hóc,* a hook ; or from what
> seems more like it, the Welsh *hwca,* hooked.
> *Lect. Lanc. Dialect,* p. 13.

HUD, *v.* to hide ; also hid or hidden.

> MISS LAHEE. Mi feyther coom back wi' a greyt top-quot on ut welly
> 1875. *hud* him eawt o' seet. *The Charity Coat,* p. 9.

> WAUGH. *Hud* thisel' i' th' buttery theer, till hoo's gone.
> 1879. *Chimney Corner,* p. 186.

> IBID. He ga' me howd of a greight stang, about twelve fuut
> 1879. lung, at they had *hud* in a nook.
> *Chimney Corner,* p. 172.

HULL, *v.* to cover. See HILL.

HULL, *sb.* a husk ; used especially for the husk of the pea, which
is called a pea-*hull.*

HULLET, *sb.* an owl. See also ULLET.

> J. P. MORRIS. Folk used to say it wod screeàm like a *hullet.*
> 1867. *Lebby Beck Dobby,* p. 4.

HULLY-BUTTERFLEE (N. Lanc.), *sb.* any heavy-bodied night-
flying moth.

HUMBUGS, *sb.* an old-fashioned sweetmeat, made of mint and
sugar.

> WAUGH. I remember gooin' wi' him once into owd Nanny
> 1879. Shackleton's toffy-shop, a-buyin' a hawporth o' *hum-
> bugs ;* an' as soon as he'd getten th' *humbugs,* he popt
> one into his mouth, an' tother into his pocket.
> *Chimney Corner,* p. 240.

HUMMABEE, *sb,* the common field bee ; *i.e. hummer-bee.*

> COLLIER. As thick as wasps in a *hummobee*-neest.—*Works,* p. 43.
> 1750.

> JOHN SCHOLES. O th' folk i' th' hammil wur huzzin' abeawt loik a
> 1857. swarm o' *hummobees.* *Jaunt to see th' Queen,* p. 15.

> B. BRIERLEY. Theere they're at it, pell-mell, like wasps in a
> 1870. *hummabee* neest.
> *Ab-o'-th'-Yate on Times and Things,* p. 64.

HUMP-BACK, *sb.* a person with a hunched back.

HUMP-STRIDD'N, *adv.* astride a person's back.

> COLLIER. Nick may ride *hump-striddn* a' beggin.
> 1750. *Works,* p. 34.

HURE, *sb.* hair.　See also YURE.

COLLIER.
1750.

Aw find teaw con tell true to o *hure.—Works,* p. 55.

JOHN SCHOLES.
1857.

Aw con clog mi own clogs, pow *hure,* fettle clocks.
Jaunt to see th' Queen, p. 6.

HURKLE (N. Lanc.), *v.* to stoop or squat.　Du. *hurken,* to squat;
cf. M.E. *rouke,* to squat.

WEST MID. DIAL. (Lanc.)
1360.

Ouer þe hiȝest hylle þat *hurkled* on erþe.
[Over the highest hill that rested on earth.]
E. Eng. Allit. Poems, B, l. 406.

HURR, *v.* to snarl like a dog.　Cf. Lowland Scotch *hur,* to snarl.
See *hurdy-gurdy* in Skeat's Etym. Dict.

HURRY (Oldham), *sb.* a spasm, a fit, a sharp attack of illness, or
even an outburst of temper.

COLL. USE.
1881.

Hoo's had a bad cryin' *hurry* (said of a passionate
child).

HUTCH (Fylde), *v.* to hoard.

HUTCH, *v.* to sit close, to get nearer.

MISS LAHEE.
1855.

Hoo never offer't to *hutch* up to make reawm for me
bi th' side on her.　　　　　*Owd Yem,* p. 20.

WAUGH.
1865.

Come, Dimple, let's be *hutchin'* a bit nar whoam !
Besom Ben, c. i., p. 10.

IBID.
1875.

"We're o' reet," said Jone o' Gavelock's, "if I can get
Craddy, here, to *hutch* a bit fur off." "Craddy," said
Giles, "*hutch* up lower, mon."
Old Cronies, c. iii., p. 33.

HUZZY, *sb.* a daughter, a female child.　See *hussy* in Skeat's Etym.
Dict.

B. BRIERLEY.
1868.

They co'en me odd, aw know, an a mon may well be
when he con see other folk wi' ther bits o' *huzzies* reawnd
'em an' noane o' ther own for t' mak 'em even.
Irkdale, c. i., p. 55.

I.

ICCLE, *sb.* an icicle.   A.S. *ísgicel.*

COLLIER.
1750.
Beside, yoad'n be os cowd os *iccles.—Works*, p. 49.

WAUGH.
1855.
An' feel at it nose; it's as cowd as *iccles.*
Lanc. Sketches: Birthplace of Tim Bobbin, p. 80.

JOHN SCHOLES.
1857.
Mi hure stood up in o minnit us stiff us *iccles,* streyt
up, loik o rush cap.   *Jaunt to see th' Queen,* p. 60.

GASKELL.
1854.
The Anglo-Saxon for what was "cel," chill, or con-
gealed, was *gicel,* and the Lancashire for an icicle is only
another form of the same word, *iccle.* We meet with it
in the time of Charles II. in some lines by Cotton, who
wrote a continuation of Walton's *Complete Angler.* He
says:—

> Be she constant, be she fickle,
> Be she firm, or be she *ickle.*
> *Lect. Lanc. Dialect,* p. 19.

I'GADLIN,
I'GODLIN, } *interj.* a petty oath.

WAUGH.
1874.
"He says I'm to clear t' table." "Clear t' table, eh!
I'godlin, he's done a good stroke at that, hissen!"
Jannock, c. iv., p. 28.

IBID.
1875.
"Hello, Snip!" said Giles. . . "A merry Christmas
to tho, owd craiter! *I'gadlin,* we's never look beheend us
after this."   *Old Cronies,* c. iii., p. 29.

IGNAGNING (Fylde), *sb.* the name given to a morris or sword-
dance, common in the Fylde some fifty years ago.

REV. W. THORNBER.
1837.
Others performed a kind of morris-dance or play,
known by the name of *ignagning,* some mystery in
honour of St. Ignatius, but more probably its derivation
is from ignis Agnæ, who suffered martyrdom at the stake.
Ignagning has almost fallen into disuse, and a band of
boys, called Jolly Lads, has succeeded.
History of Blackpool, p. 92.

I'GODDIL, *interj.* if God will.

COLLIER.
1750.
Tim. I think lunger ot fok liv'n an th' moor mis-
choances they han.
Mary. Not awlus, *o Goddil.*   *Works,* p. 40.

I'GODSNAM, *interj.* in God's name; a petty oath.

COLLIER.
1750.
Let um speyk greadly, os we dun, *i'godsnum.*
Works, p. 35.

WAUGH.
1876.
Get some'at into tho lad, *i God's-nam,* for thou'll
need it.   *Hermit Cobbler,* p. 16.

IKE, *sb.* abbreviation of Isaac.

ILL-DOIN', *adj.* in bad condition ; sickly.

ILL-DONE-TO, *adj.* badly treated ; ill used.

ILL-GETTEN, *adj.* dishonestly obtained.

IN-FOR-IT, *ad.* in circumstances of danger or difficulty ; overtaken by calamity.

> COLL. USE. 1881.
> Tha'rt *in-for-it*, neaw, owd mon ; aw wouldn't be i' thy shoes for summut (something).

INGLE-NOOK, *sb.* the corner of a fire-place.

INGLUN-SHIRE, *sb.* England.

INKLE-WEAVER, *sb.* a tape weaver. See BEGGAR-INKLE, *ante*, p. 34.

> WAUGH. 1868.
> Thick ! We're as thick as a pair o' owd reawsty *inkle-weyvers*. *Sneck-Bant*, c. i., p. 11.

INSENSE, *v.* to convey a meaning ; to make a stupid person comprehend.

> O. ORMEROD. 1862.
> It's no mak o use me troyin' for to *insens* yo into o us aw seed. *Felley fra Rachde*.

INSIDE, *sb.* the stomach or bowels.

> WAUGH. 1876.
> Th' lad had bin wrang in his *inside* a while, an' one day he says to his faither, "Eh, faither, I do like th' bally-warche !" "Thou likes it ? Why, what for ?" "Becose it's so nice when it gi's o'er !" *Manchester Critic*.

INTACK, *sb.* an enclosed piece of common. Cf. Icel. *itak.*

IR, *pron.* of our.

> WAUGH. 1869.
> There wur *ir* Jammy lad, an' me, an' some moor on us. *Lanc. Sketches*, p. 206.

IRNIN', *sb.* cheese-making. A farmer when he has begun to make curd for cheese is said to have begun *irnin'*. An *irnin'-tub* is the tub in which the milk is placed for curding. A.S. *yrnan*, to run, *i.e.* to coagulate. See *Rennet* in Skeat's Etym. Dict.

I'ST, *pro.* and *v.* I should, or I shall.

> COLLIER. 1750.
> *Tim.* Neaw, Meary, whot cou'd onny mon doo ? *Mary.* Doo ! *I'st* o gon stark woode [*i.e.*, mad]. *Works*, p. 42.

> IBID.
> *I'st* naw have one boadle t' spare. *Works*, p. 55.

IT, *pron.* used for " its." Prof. Skeat in his Etym. Dict. says " the genitive case *its* was just coming into use in Shakspere's time, but we find *it* (with the sense of *its*) in the first folio, in thirteen passages."

WAUGH.
1869.

An' look at *it* een ; they're as breet as th' north-star ov a frosty neet ! *Lanc. Sketches*, p. 80.

COLL. USE.
1881.

If he can catch howd o' that dog he'll have *it* life, as what comes on it.

I'TAW, ⎫
I'TEAW, ⎭ compound ; in two, or in two pieces.

WAUGH.
1859.

An' bith light in her een,
It were fair to be sin,
That hoo're ready to rive me *i'teaw.*
Lanc. Songs : Jamie's Frolic.

IVIN, *sb.* ivy.

B. BRIERLEY.
1869.

"Isn't your name over the door?" "Ay, but yo couldno' see it; for it's groon o'er wi' *ivin*, an' has bin mony a year." *Red Windows Hall*, c. ii., p. 12.

J.

JACKSTONES, *sb.* a child's game, played with a large marble and the knuckle-bones of a sheep ; also with small white pebbles or jackstones. The same game is also known as " Bobber and kibs ;" the kibs being the sheep's bones.

JAMBLES, *sb.* the hames ; the part of the collar by which horses draw.

JAMMY-CRANE (N. Lanc.), *sb.* the heron.

JAMRAGS (N. Lanc.), *sb.* anything overcooked.

JANNOCK, *sb.* a dark-coloured bread or cake made of oatmeal, or of coarse wheat-meal ; also, metaphorically applied to anything or any action that is honest or thorough.

> REV. P. WALKDEN.　　Paid 1/- for a new cheese and a *janocke.*—*Diary,* p. 44.
> 1725.
>
> REV. W. THORNBER.　　[At Easter] *jannock,* introduced by the Flemish
> 1837.　　refugees, [was] eaten with zest by the hungry labourer.
> 　　*Hist. of Blackpool,* p. 93.
>
> WAUGH.　　The thick unleavened oatcake, called *jannock,* is
> 1855.　　scarcely ever seen in South-east Lancashire now ; but it
> 　　used to be highly esteemed. The common expression,
> 　　" That's noan *jannock,*" applied to anything which is
> 　　not what it ought to be, commemorates the fame of this
> 　　wholesome old cake of theirs.
> 　　*Lanc. Sketches: Rochdale to Blackstone Edge,* p. 129.

JAWMS, *sb. pl.* pronun. of jambs, the side-posts of a window, fire-place, or other portion of a house.

JERRY, *v.* to cheat.

JERRY, *adj.* bad, defective, and deceptive ; *i.e.* a *jerry* building is one that is badly built, although it may look well outwardly.

JERRY,
JERRY-SHOP, } *sb.* a public-house.

JIDDY, *v.* to agree.

> COLL. USE.　　They never *jiddy* together. (Heard in Bolton and Bury.)
> 1880.

JILLIVER, *sb.* a termagant.

JIMP, *adj.* neat, spruce, tidy, slender. Burns has—

> I see thee dancing o'er the green,
> Thy waist sae *jimp,* thy limbs sae clean.

And see also Scott's Minst. Border (" Lord Thomas and Fair Annie ")—

> She maun lace on her robe sae *jimp*
> And braid her yellow hair.

JIMPLY (Ormskirk), *adv.* smoothly.

JINDERIN' (Ormskirk), *v.* seeking a mate.

JINNY-GREEN-TEETH, *sb.* literally the green scum on ponds, but supposed to imply the presence of a water-sprite or "boggart;" a terror to children as they pass the pond on which the appearance is seen.

JINNY-SPINNER (N. Lanc.), an insect, *Tipula.*

JOBBERNOWL, *sb.* a dunce or dolt. Cf. *nowl* in Mids. N. Dream, iii. ii. 17.

JOHNNY-RAW, *sb.* a foolish or stupid person.

COLL. USE.
1881.
What a *Johnny-raw* he must be, to swallow a tale o' that soart !

JORUM, *sb.* a large quantity.

REV. W. THORNBER.
1837.
A *jorum* of "browess," and roasted wheat or frumenty, for dinner, was the treat of Good Friday.
Hist. of Blackpool, p. 93.

COLL. USE.
1881.
Neaw lads, set-to—there's a *jorum* o' porridge for you ; in wi your spoons an' start fair.

JOW, *v.* to jog ; to push or knock against. See *jowl* in Shakspere—
"They may *jowl* horns together :" As You Like It, i. iii. 59 ;
"How the knave *jowls* it to the ground :" Hamlet, v. i. 84.

B. BRIERLEY.
1868.
It'll end i' folk *jowin'* ther yeds t'gether till they'n be fain o' quietness at any price. *Irkdale,* p. 23.

WAUGH.
1867.
"Who are yo ? For yo're not mich to look at." "Reet again, owd craiter," answered Tim, "Reet again !—*jow* thi yed !" "What mun aw *jow* mi yed for, yo greight starin' rack-an-hook ?" replied Betty. "*Jow* yo'r own yed ! It's o' at it's good to."—*Owd Blanket,* c. i. p. 9.

IBID.
1868.
Then, th' wife an' him *jowed* their yeds together, as they wur bendin' deawn to reitch their stockin's up.
Sneck-Bant, c. ii. p. 36.

JOYST, *sb.* pasturage for cattle let out to farmers or others for a consideration. A corruption of *agist.*

REV. P. WALKDEN.
1725.
Received from Seath Jolly off half *joyst,* £4. 0. 0.
Diary, p. 161.

JUD, *sb.* familiar substitute for *George.*

JUMP, *sb.* a Sunday coat, gown, or other outer garment ; probably a well-fitting coat. In Shakspere the word means *just, exactly,* also *to tally.* See Hamlet, act i., sc. i., l. 65 ; Othello, act ii., sc. 3, l. 392.

COLLIER.
1750.
Soh I donn'd meh Sunday *jump,* o top o meh singlet.
Works, p. 41.

JUST-NOW, *ad.* in a short time ; after a little interval, as "e'en-now" means without interval, immediately. Also a little while before the present time.

K.

KALE (N. Lanc.), *sb.* broth or pottage.

WAUGH.
(Furness Dialect.)
1874.

"I never had mich traffic o' that mak." "Nor me nawther; mine's bin chiefly poddish an' peas-*kale*, an' blue-milk cheese." *Jannock*, c. ix., p. 97.

KALE, *sb.* a turn in rotation. See CALE, *ante*, p. 66.

B. BRIERLEY.
1868.

Yo'st o' be wed when yor *kale* comes.
Irkdale, p. 225.

WAUGH.
1879.

They keepen droppin' off, an' comin' on. It's once a-piece for us, o' round. It'll be our *kale* in a bit, Snaffle. *Chimney Corner*, p. 231.

KALES, *sb.* the game of ninepins, See *kails* in Skeat's Etym. Dict. Of Old Low German origin; Du. *kegel*, "a pin, kail; *mid kegels spelen*, to play at ninepins: Sewel."

KAME, *sb.* a comb. A.S. *camb;* Icel. *kambr;* Dan. *kam.*

KAYTHUR or }
KEYTHER, } *sb.* a cradle.

COLLIER.
1750.

Whether it lawmt [lamed] th' barn ot wur i' th' *keather*, I know naw. *Works*, p. 66.

BAMFORD.
1840.

I'll put th' chylt i' th' *keyther* an' set at yon wark.
Life of Radical, c. ix., p. 61.

WAUGH.
1859.

Keep th' *keyther* stirrin' gently; an'
Make very little din. *Lanc. Songs:* "Neet-fo'."

B. BRIERLEY.
1868.

If theaw hasno' bin rocked enough i' thy younger days, it's time theaw'd a new *kaythur* made for thee.
Irkdale, p. 74.

KAYVE, *vb.* to overturn, to upset. *Kayvt*, upset, turned over.

KEAWER, *v.* pron. of *cower;* to shrink, to crouch, to squat.

COLLIER.
1750.

Let's *keawer* us deawn o' th' yeoarth o bit.
Works, p. 41.

B. BRIERLEY.
1868.

He'd *keawer* up th' stairs o' day if aw did no fotch him by th' skuft o' th' neck. *Irkdale*, p. 47.

WAUGH.
1876.

I wonder how thou can for shame o' thi face sit *keawerin'* theer hutch't of a lump. *Critic.*

KEAWL, *v.* to crouch, to quail.

KEAWLT, *part.* repulsed, intimidated.

KEAWNT, *sb.* account; as "Aw ma no *keawnt* of it."

KEBBIN' (Morecambe), *part.* fishing for flat fish with four hooks hanging from the ends of a weighted wooden cross.

KECK, *v.* to upset. A variant of *kick.*

DR. BARBER.
1870.

Lads wos . . . bringin' girt clogs o' stuff to t' chaps i' thor shades as they co' ryvers, to be *keckt* up reet in front o' them. *Forness Folk*, p. 10.

COLL. USE.
1881.

" Who's spilt this milk ?" "Me, mother : aw couldn't help it ; aw *keckt* it o'er wi' my sleeve."

KECKER (Ormskirk), *sb.* the bar which connects the body of the cart with the thills.

KECKIN' (N. Lanc.), *part.* spying. Cf. Icel. *kaga, kikja,* to peep; Scot. *keek,* to look with prying eye, or with stealth.

KECKLE, *sb.* prate, cackle, idle or foolish talk.

KECKLE (N. Lanc.), *v.* to giggle, to laugh.

KECKLE, *adj.* pert.

KECKLETY,
KECKLY, } *adj.* unsteady, likely to topple over.

JOHN SCHOLES.
1857.

Aw'm as *keklety* us o owd waytur tub after o twel-munth's drouth. *Jaunt to see th' Queen*, p. 20.

WAUGH.
1879.

" What's to do wi' tho ? Thou stonds very *keckley*." " Rheumatic or summat. I've never bin reet o' mi pins sin' Rushbearin." *Chimney Corner*, p. 112.

KECK-MEG, *sb.* a pert, meddling woman.

KECKS,
KEX, } *sb. pl.* the hollow stems of the common hemlock; used by lads to shoot peas with, also for making a rude flageolet.

SHAKSPERE.
1599.

Nothing teemes
But hatefull dockes, rough thistles, *keksyses*, burres,
Loosing both beautie and utilitie.
Henry Fifth, act v., sc. ii., l. 51.

TENNYSON.
1850.

Tho' the rough *kex* break
The starr'd mosaic. *The Princess*, iv. 59.

B. BRIERLEY.
1868.

Thoose . . . wi' texts o' Scriptyer i' ther meawths ut they con shoot eawt as readily as paes eawt of a *kex*.
Irkdale, p. 48.

REV. W. GASKELL.
1854.

As boys, the name we gave to the stalks of the wild hemlock, which we used for pea-blowers, was *kecks*. I am not aware that this is to be found in the Gothic with any similar meaning ; but in Welsh we have *cecys*, plants with hollow stalks ; and in Cornish *kegaz* means hemlock ; and I see no reason why this should not be regarded as a genuine British relic.
Lect. Lanc. Dialect, p. 9.

COLL. USE.
1881.

As dry as a *kex* (meaning *thirsty*).

KEDDLE-DOCK, *sb.* common ragwort. *Senecio Jacobæa.*

1776.
July 30. This summer is remarkable for the great quantity of *keddledocks.—A Middleton Farmer's Diary in Manchester Guardian,* Feb. 26, 1877.

1877.
In the rural part of Mid-Lancashire (near Goosnargh), where I was reared, the word was pronounced "*kettle-dock.*" It is the broad-leafed common dock, and the name is used in contradistinction to sour dock and patience dock ; it is totally different to the "ketlock" (*Sinapis arvensis.*)
Edward Kirk, in Manchr. Guardian, March, 1877.

KEEL, *v.* to cool, to assuage, to allay, to moderate. A.S. *célan,* to chill ; formed from *cól,* cool, by the usual mutation of *o* to *e.* See Skeat's Notes to *Piers the Plowman,* p. 434.

About 1370.
Then downe on knees ful humbly gan I knele,
Beseeching her my fervent wo to *kele.*
Court of Love (Aldine Chaucer), l. 774.

1440.
Kelyn, or make cold. Frigefacio.—*Prompt Parv.*

SHAKSPERE.
1598.
While greasie Jone doth *keele* the pot.
Love's Labour Lost, act v., sc. ii., l. 930 and 939.

COLLIER.
1750.
Fear me not, sed I, for I'm as hungry as a rott'n. . . .
Yo mey come on' begin, sed hoo, for they need'n no *keelin'.* *Works,* p. 68.

KEEMIN'-COMB, *sb.* a small tooth comb.

KEEN, *v.* to kindle.

COLL. USE.
1881.
What, is ther no foire *keen'd* yet ? Aw mun have yo' wenches eawt o' bed afore this toime in a mornin'.

KEEN-BITTEN, *adj.* eager, sharp, hungry; ready to take advantage.

COLLIER.
1750.
I'r so *keen-bitt'n* I mede no bawks at o heyseed.
Works, p. 68.

WAUGH.
1865.
There were no symptoms of indigestion about Ben. He was as *keen-bitten* as a starved ostrich.
Besom Ben, c. i., p. 6.

IBID.
1876.
It wur Dody o' Joseph's, a joiner by trade,
A comical cowt, an' a *keen-bitten* blade ;
He're as fause as a boggart.
Lanc. Songs: The Grindlestone.

KEEP, *sb.* food, board, maintenance.

COLL. USE.
1881.
"What does he get ?" "Nine shillin' a-week an' his *keep;* an' noan bad wages, noather."

KEEPIN' COMPANY, *part.* courting, being betrothed.

COLL. USE.
1881.
"How lung does ta say they *kept* company ?"
"Why, for seven years ; an' walked many a thousand mile, mon, while they were at it."

KEEVIL (Lytham), *sb.* a candle.

KEEVIL, *sb.* the person who stands on the centre of a sway-plank.

KEIGH-NEIGHVT, *adj.* = key-fisted, malformed, applied to the hand, and referring to a hand chronically shut or half-shut.

WAUGH.   "Had he a hair-shorn lip?"   "Ay, he had ! An' he
1865.   wur *keigh-neighvt!*"   *Besom Ben,* c. vii., p. 90.

KEISH (N. Lanc.), *sb.* the hollow stem of the hemlock. See KEX.

KELCH (Ormskirk), *sb.* a sprain. See KENCH.

KELK (N. Lanc.), *v.* to strike.

KENCH, *sb.* a sprain.

KENCH, *v.* to sprain.

COLL. USE.   1. "What's up Ned?"   "Nowt mich—a bit of o'
1881.   *kench* i' my back."

               2. Aw slipp'd off th' kerb-stone an' *kench'd* my ankle.

KENNED, }
KENT,   } (N. Lanc.), *v.* knew.

DR. BARBER.   "That's a bit o' aad Bat's wark."   "Whā's he?" I ext.
1870.   "I sud ha' thowte ivvery body *kent* aad Bat."
                          Forness Folk, p. 13.

KENSPAK (N. Lanc.), *adj.* easy to know.

DR. BARBER.   It's t sleatts et gev that bye-neamm to t' spot, 'cos
1870.   the'r *kenspak* amang udder sooarts.
                          Forness Folk, p. 11.

KENSPECKLE, *adj.* conspicuous from some oddity of person or attire; easy to recognize. Icel. *kenni-speki,* the faculty of recognition.

WAUGH.   He's a *kenspeckle* mak of a face, as far as I can judge.
1879.   *Chimney Corner,* p. 127.

KEP (N. Lanc.), *v.* to catch.

KERSEN, }
KESSEN, } *v.* to christen.

COLLIER.   Eh, truth, Meary, I never lee eh sitch bed sin eh wur
1750.   *kersunt.*   *Works,* p. 54.

WAUGH.   Did'n yo never hear tell on 'em gooin *a-kessunin'*
1879.   that chylt o' theirs?   *Chimney Corner,* p. 32.

KESMAS,   }
KERSMUS (N. Lanc.), } *sb.* Christmas.

WAUGH.   Aw's be seventy-one come *Kesmas* mornin'.
1867.   *Owd Blanket,* c. iii., p. 62.

KEST (N. Lanc.), *sb.* a ride; a lift on the way.

J. P. MORRIS.   I gat a *kest* in a coup er I wod a' bin teer't.
1869.   *Furness Glossary,* p. 52.

KESTER, *sb.* Christopher.

KESTLIN, *sb.* a calf dropped before its time.

KESTREL, *sb.* a flawed and inferior earthen vessel.—Whittaker.

KET (Fylde and Lonsdale), *sb.* carrion.

KET-CROW (Fylde and Lonsdale), *sb.* the carrion crow.

KEEVILLY, *adj.* unsteady.

KIB, *sb.* a small bone in the sheep's foot, used in playing the game called " Bobber and kibs."

KIBBLE (Fylde), *sb.* a stick.

KIBBLER (Fylde), *sb.* a bad walker.

KIBBO, *sb.* a long stick.

> COLLIER. Aw' th' rest on um had hoyts, or lung *kibboes*, like.
> 1750. swinging sticks or raddlins. *Works*, p. 43.
>
> IBID. A felly with a wythen *kibbo* in his hont.—*Works*, p. 52.

KIBE, *v.* to pout the lip in scorn, to gibe, to mock.

KILL, *sb.* a kiln.

> REV. W. GASKELL. In the Welsh word for a furnace, we have that which
> 1854. is constantly used in Lancashire ; not *kiln*, with the *n*
> at the end, but *cyl*, as a lime*kill*, a brick*kill*.
> *Lect. Lanc. Dialect*, p. 10.

KIM-KAM, *adv.* to walk with a throw of the legs athwart one another. Whittaker.

KIN-COUGH, *sb.* the whooping-cough. See CHINCOUGH, *ante* p. 74.

KINDLE, *v.* to bring forth ; chiefly applied to rabbits.

> SHAKSPERE. The cony that you see dwell where she is *kindled*.
> 1600. *As You Like It*, iii. ii. 358.

KINGDOM-COME, *sb.* heaven ; a state of happiness.

> COLL. USE. Poor owd lad ! He's gone to *Kingdom-come* at last.
> 1881.

KINK, *v.* to lose the breath with coughing or laughing. See CHINK, *ante*, p. 74.

> JOHN SCHOLES. Hoo set Throddy agate o laffin at hur till e *kinkt*
> 1857. ogen. *Jaunt to see th' Queen*, p. 57.

KINK (N. Lanc.), *sb.* a crease.

KINK-HAUST, } *sb.* a violent cough or cold. See CHINCOUGH,
KINK-HOOST, } *ante*, p. 74.

KINKIN' (N. Lanc.), *part.* laughing.

KIPE (N. Lanc.), *v.* to retort.

KIPPER, *adj.* amorous.

KIPPLE, *v.* to lift a weight from the ground on to the shoulder without help or stay.

KIST, *sb.* a chest. A.S. *cist;* Icel. *kista;* Dan. *kiste.*

WEST MIDLAND DIALECT. And he with keyes uncloses *kystes* ful mony.
1360. *Allit. Poems,* B, 1438.

BAMFORD. If it were during winter, or in broken cold weather,
1850. the great oaken *kist* would have to yield up its most substantial article of attire.—*Intro. to Tim Bobbin,* p. vii.

JOHN SCHOLES. Aw stare't at him, un weel aw met, fur aw thowt o'
1867. th' meyl *kist.* *Jaunt to see th' Queen,* p. 41.

DR. BARBER. Fellas wos runnin' abowt as rank as mice in a meeal
1870. *kist.* *Forness Folk,* p. 12.

KITE (N. Lanc.), *sb.* the belly.

WAUGH. Noo an' then I've starken't my *kite* wi' bacon an'
(Furness Dialect.) cabbish. *Jannock,* c. ix., p. 97.
1874.

KITTER (S. Lanc.), ⎫ *adj.* delicate.
KITTLE (N. Lanc.), ⎭

KITTLE, *v.* to miss, to fail in an attempt.

KITTLE, *v.* to tickle. Icel. *kitla.*

KITTLE, *adj.* ticklish, nicely-balanced.

KITTLE, *v.* to bring forth, applied to cats.

WAUGH. Owd Ben had a daughter wed, an' a keaw cauve't, an'
1875. a mare foal't, an' a cat *kittle't,* o' in one day.
Old Cronies, c. vi., p. 56.

KITLIN', *sb.* a kitten. Professor Skeat in his Etym. Dict., art. Kitten, says: "The true English form is kit-ling, where-ling (= — *l* + *ing*) is a double diminutive suffix."

ROBERT HERRICK. The brisk mouse may feast herself with crums,
1648. Till that the green-ey'd *kitling* comes.
A Country Life.

WAUGH. Aw connot ston it. Aw'm as wake [weak] as a *kitlin'*
1867. this minute.—*Home Life of Factory Folk,* c. xxii., p. 194.

KIZEN'T (N. Lanc.), *adj.* parched, dried up.

KNAP (N. Lanc.), *sb.* a blow.

KNOBLUCKS, *sb. pl.* small lumps.

KNOCKUS, *sb. pl.* knuckles.

COLLIER. Hal o' Nabs had his *knockus*-lapt in his barmskin.
1750. *Works,* p. 43.

KNOGGY, *adj.* knotty.

KNOWE, *sb.* pronun. of knoll.

> WAUGH.
> 1879.
> I went out at th' town-end till I geet at th' top of a bit of a *knowe.* *Chimney Corner,* p. 252.

KNUCKLE-DOWN, *v.* to submit, to consent to indignity.

> COLL. USE.
> 1881.
> Aw shall never *knuckle-down* to that chap, aw con tell thi'.

KNUCKLE-UNDER, *v.* to humiliate oneself ; to take the second place.

> COLL. USE.
> 1881.
> If hoo once gets thee to *knuckle-under* tha's done for.

KOBNOGGLE (Fylde), *v.* to pull the hair and then hit the head with the knuckles.

KRINDLE, *sb.* kernel.

> WAUGH.
> 1879.
> Onybody may ha' th' shell, Mary, if they'n lev me th' *krindle.* *Chimney Corner,* p. 203.

KUSS,) *sb.* a kiss. A.S. *coss ;* Mid. Eng. *cos, kos, kus ;* Icel.
KUSSIN',) *koss ;* Du. *kus,* sb., whence *kussen,* vb. See *Kiss* in Skeat's Etym. Dict. "The form *kusse* is as late as Skelton, Phylyp Sparowe, 361."

> WAUGH.
> 1868.
> Aw could just like to *kuss* tho once, afore we starten, iv thae's no objection, for thae looks hondsomer nor ever this mornin'. Let's just ha' one *kuss,* lass.
> *Sneck-Bant,* p. 59.

> IBID.
> 1875.
> "Give us a *kussin' !* " And hoo gave him one.
> *Old Cronies,* c. iv., p. 43.

KYE, *sb. pl.* cows, kine. A.S. *cú,* a cow ; *cý,* cows.

> WEST MIDLAND DIALECT.
> 1360.
> Bothe to cayre [drag] at the kart and the *kuy* mylke.
> *Allit. Poems,* B, 1259.

> BURNS.
> 1786.
> The *kye* stood rowtin' i' the loan.—*The Twa Dogs.*

> REV. W. GASKELL.
> 1854.
> Another relic of an Anglo-Saxon plural we have in the word which Wickliffe uses when he says, "And thus we blame *childre.*" In A.S. this was *cildru.* Our word "children" is a double plural, and really not so good a form as "childre." And so with "kyne," the A.S. being *cý,* to which the Lancashire *kye* answers.
> *Lect. Lanc. Dialect,* p. 24.

KYSTY (N. Lanc.), *adj.* dainty.

> J. P. MORRIS.
> 1867.
> Some weshed out the'r chammer-pots—ye may be suer they worn't *keisty*—an' hed 'em filled.
> *Invasion o' U'ston,* p. 5.

> DR. BARBER.
> 1870.
> Ooer *kysty* to be amang dacent foke.
> *Forness Folk,* p. 31.

L.

LACE (S. Lanc.), } *v.* to beat, to castigate. Literally to strike
LEÁCE (N. Lanc.), } with a leather thong.

THOMAS WILSON. Hoo towd me hoo'd get me weel *laced*,
1842. If aw didna' that minute goo whom.
Songs of the Wilsons, p. 45.

LAD, *v.* led.

WAUGH. It'll do noan ! I'll not be *lad* into temptation wi' yo.
1879. *Chimney Corner*, p. 277.

LADSAVVUR, } *sb.* southernwood. *Artemisia Abrotanum.*
LADS-LOVE, }

LADYBIRD, } *sb.* the small scarlet beetle with black spots. *Cocci-*
LADYCOW, } *nella punctata.* Lancashire children sing the
following song :—

Lady-cow, lady-cow, fly away home,
Your house is on fire and your children all gone.

LADY-SMOCK, *sb.* the plant cuckoo-flower. *Cardamine pratensis.*
Most commonly known in Lancashire as the " May-flower."

SHAKSPERE. Daisies pied and violets blue
1597. And *lady-smocks* all silver-white.
Love's L. L., act v., sc. ii.

LAFTER (N. Lanc.), *sb.* one brood of chickens; the eggs which a
hen sits upon during incubation. Cf. Icel. *látr*, the place where
animals lay their young (which Mr. Vigfusson wrongly identifies
with E. *litter*).

LAGS, } *sb. pl.* the staves of a tub or cask.
LAGGINS, }

B. BRIERLEY. The fence, his own making, was but a rickety fabric of
1867. " *laggins*," worn-out treadles, and discarded weight
ropes. *Marlocks of Merriton*, p. 68.

LAIGH, *v.* to laugh; *laighin*, laughing; *laighless*, laughless, without
laughter.

LAITH, *v.* to laugh.

B. BRIERLEY. "Aw da'say," said Jacob, "hoo'll want summat to
1868. *laith* abeawt." *Irkdale*, c. xvii., p. 241.

LAITH, } *sb.* a barn or storehouse. Icel. *hlaða*, a barn, a store-
LEATH, } house.

CHAUCER. Why nad thou put the capul [horse] in the *lathe?*
1380. *Reeves Tale*, l. 168.

___

COLLIER. Just as I'r gett'n to th' *leath* dur. *Works*, p. 67.
1750.

LAITHE, *v.* to invite. A.S. *lathian*, to invite, bid, send for, assemble. Icel. *laða*, to bid, to invite a guest.

A.D. 995.

"Ða se sunder-halga, þe hine *in-gelaðode*,"—when the Pharisee, who had invited him.
A.S. Gospels, Luke vii. 39.

WAUGH.
1855.

" Come, poo a cheer up," he said, " an' need no moor *laithein'*."—*Lanc. Sketches: Cottage of Tim Bobbin*, p. 53.

IBID.
1859.

Aw'll *laithe* a rook o' neighbour lads,—
Frisky cowts, an' bowd uns.
Lanc. Songs : Tum Rindle.

B. BRIERLEY.
1868.

O' th' folk i' Irkdale wur *laithe* to th' buryin'.
Irkdale, c. i., p. 30.

LAKE, *v.* to play. A.S. *lác*, play ; *læcan*, to play. Icel. *leika*.

1440.

Laykyn, or thynge that chyldryn pley wythe.

Promp. Parv.

J. P. MORRIS.
1867.

A lot of us lads wer' *lakin* down èt t' lā end o' Brou'ton.   *Siege o' Brou'ton*, p. 3.

LAM, *v.* to beat soundly. Icel. *lemja*, to thrash, flog, beat, so as to lame or disable ; A.S. *lemian*.

LAMMAS, *v.* to run, to disappear quickly.

WAUGH.
1859.

Thae'm mind te hits, an' when aw sheawt
Be limber-legged, an' *lammas* eawt.
Lanc. Songs : Margit's Comin'.

B. BRIERLEY.
1868.

Aw'm noane feart on thee gooin' back. Theau con *lammas* off agen, if t' thinks theau con do better some-wheere else.   *Fratchingtons*, p. 62.

LANGEL (N. Lanc.), *v.* to tie the forelegs of cattle to prevent them from straying.

1440.

Langelyn, or byynd to-geder.   *Prompt. Parv.*

LANG-LENGTH (N. Lanc.), }
LUNG-LENGTH (S. Lanc.), } *adv.* at last ; ultimately.

COLLIER.
1750.

Yoan pood truth eawt ov a dirty pleck at *lung-length*.
Works, p. 65.

WAUGH.
1859.

At th' *lung-length* aw geet 'em laid still.
Lanc. Songs : Come Whoam to thi Childer.

IBID.
1869.

Well, at th' *lung-length* we geet to th' White Heawse.
Yeth-Bobs, c. ii., p. 33.

LANKISTER-LOWP, *sb.* leap-frog.

LANT, *v.* to beggar, to disappoint. Cf. Icel. *hlanna*, to pilfer.

LANT, *sb.* stale urine. Generally spoken of as " owd lant." Formerly much used by Lancashire cottagers for scouring or cleaning blankets and other woollen cloths; also for sundry medicinal purposes. In every yard or garden would have been found a receptacle for storing it. Icel. *hland.*

LATCH, *v.* to take, to catch; as "to *latch* a distemper." A.S. *læccan*, to catch.

LATE, *v.* to seek. Icel. *leita*, to seek, to search. See *Laitand* in Spec. of Eng., ed. Morris and Skeat.

> B. Brierley.
> 1867.
> There's a gentleman at th' back ut aw dar say yo' known; so aw'll leeave yo to *lait* up owd acquaintance while aw get ready.—*Red Windows Hall*, c. iv., p. 22.

> Dr. Barber.
> 1870.
> They heven't time to *lait* thér lost sheep.
> *Forness Folk*, p. 23.

LATHER, *sb.* a ladder (sometimes pronounced *ladther*).

LATTER-END, *sb.* death, the time of death.

> Coll. Use.
> 1881.
> It's toime for thee to begin o' thinkin' o' thi *latter-end*, owd mon.

LAWRENCE, *sb.* used figuratively for idleness.

> Coll. Use.
> 1881.
> "Is he poorly?" "Not him, belike. He's getten *Lawrence* on his back—that's his ailment."

LAYERS-FOR-MEDDLERS, *sb.* anything which it may not be desirable to describe; a term used in answer to the impertinent or inconvenient question of a child.

> Coll. Use.
> 1881.
> "What hav yo' getten i' that bag?" "*Layers-for-meddlers*—does ta want to know?"

LAYROCK, } *sb.* the lark. Icel. *lævirki*. Chaucer in *Cant. Tales*
LEAROCK, } has *laverock; Romaunt of Rose*, l. 662, *laverokkes ;* Burns, *Holy Fair*, st. i. See *Lark* in Skeat's Etym. Dict.

> Bamford.
> 1840.
> A climb of about two miles brought us upon the level of the hill at Ashworth Moor, soon after which we came in sight of *Learock* Hoyle, in modern English, "Lark's Hole," a substantial hostel and farm house.
> *Life of Radical*, vol. i., c. viii., p. 53.

> Ramsbottom.
> 1864.
> Yo'll ne'er find swallows uppo th' wing,
> Nor hearken th' bonny *layrock* sing,—
> A dark spot ditherin' i' th' blue sky.
> *Lanc. Songs: Lancashire Emigrants*, p. 100.

> Waugh.
> 1867.
> The inhabitants of Dean valley are so notable for their love of music, that they are known all through the vales of Rossendale as "Th' Deighn *Layrocks*," or "The larks of Dean."
> *Home Life of the Factory Folk*, c. xxiii., p. 199.

LEA (N. Lanc.), *sb.* a scythe. Icel. *lé, ljár.*

LEAF, *sb.* the inner fat of the pig, which, when melted, is called lard.

LEAN-TO, *sb.* a building erected against another; also used as an adj., and applied to a roof, as—"a lean-to roof."

LEASE, }
LEECE, } *sb.* the dividing of the thread in a warp.

LEATHER, *v.* to beat, to thrash.

MISS LAHEE.
1865.

As for Ned Buttereth, bith' mass, aw'll *leather* him i' th' seet ov himsel, when aw see him again.
Carter's Struggles, p. 52.

LEATHERIN', *adj.* large.

J. P. MORRIS.
1867.

Ther' wer' some gert *letherin'* young chaps (fell-bred, I'se uphod 'em), stackerin' abowt.
Siege o' Brou'ton, p. 3.

LEATHERIN', | *part.* going at a great rate or with much
LEATHERIN' AWAY, | vigour.

B. BRIERLEY.
1870.

Leatherin' away at one's loom as if it we'rn feightin' a battle. *Ab-o'-th'-Yate on Times and Things*, p. 14.

S. LAYCOCK.
1870.

He sprang eawt o' th' heawse witheawt jacket or hat; went *leatherin'* deawn th' street to an uncle o' mine.
Lanc. Songs, p. 45.

LEATHER-YED, *sb.* a blockhead, a stupid person.

B. BRIERLEY.
1870.

When I come for t' calkilate heaw mony scamps it tak's for t' keep one o' these *leatheryeds* i' concait wi' hissel, I break eawt in a cowd swat.
Ab-o'-th'-Yate on Times and Things, p. 34.

WAUGH.
1875.

"I can't say that I quite understand what it is that you want, exactly." "Well, then," said he, "thou'rt a *leather-yed*." *Old Cronies*, c. vii., p. 70.

LEAVIN'S, *sb.* anything left; remnants; also offal. Icel. *leifar*, leavings, remnants, esp. of food.

COLL. USE.
1881.

Nay, aw'st ha' noan o' thy *leavin's*—tha mun ate 'em thisel'.

LEAWK, *v.* pron. of *lowk;* to beat, to thrash.

LEAWK, | *sb. pl.* tufts of barren dry grass; locks of hair.
LEAWKS, |

JOHN SCHOLES.
1857.

Theaw mun recollect ut Jim wur browt up omung th' *leawk* ut top o' Breawn Wardle.
Jaunt to see th' Queen, p. 40.

LEECE-ROD, *sb.* a rod to divide the threads of a warp.

LEECH, *sb.* a pond or pool of water; water lying in the hollow of a road. In old Lancashire deeds and inquisitions the word appears frequently as *lache,* as in Blake-*lache,* Brad-*lache,* Grenelow-*lache,* Gos-*lache,* and Melshaw-*lache,* always indicative of a marshy locality. See Chetham Society's Publications.

COLL. USE.
1881.

Comin' tearin' alung i' th' dark, aw went reet through a *leach* o' watter, an' o'er my shoe-tops.

LEEM (N. Lanc.), *v.* to free nuts from their husks.

LEEMERS (N. Lanc.), *sb.* ripe hazel nuts.

LEET,
LEETEN, } *v.* to alight ; *let,* alighted ; also to happen, and to find.

WAUGH.
1859.

One *leets* o' few sich nooks as this,
An th' journey ends i' th' gravel.
Lanc. Songs : Come, Limber Lads.

IBID.
1868.

His een *let* upo' th' tow-bar.—*Sneck-Bant,* c. ii., p. 35.

IBID.
1879.

" How did yo sattle it ? " " He tanned my hide for
me." " Well, come ; that's done wi'—till we *leeten* o'
one another again." *Chimney Corner,* p. 182.

COLL. USE.
1881.

1. We'll see how it *leets* (happens).
2. If aw *leet* on him (find him), aw'll tell thi.

LEET, *sb.* pron. of light, as in day-*leet ; leeter,* lighter ; *leetnin',*
lightning.

LEET-LOOKIN', *adj.* light, in full daylight.

WAUGH.
1879.

To goo an' come straight out o' thi looms, an' walk
three mile, i'th *leet-lookin'* day, to feight a battle.
Chimney Corner, p. 153.

LEETSOME, *adj.* light, cheerful, pleasant-looking.

WAUGH.
1859.

Th' cat pricks up her ears at th' sneck,
Wi' mony a *leetsome* toot. *Lanc. Songs : Neet-fo.*

MISS LAHEE.
1870.

One *leetsome* neet, abeawt hay-time.—*Owd Yem,* p. 5.

LEG-DOWN, *v.* to cause to fall or stumble by putting forward the
leg in the way of another ; figuratively, to bring into trouble.

LEISTER (N. Lanc.), *sb.* a fish-spear. Icel. *ljóster.*

LENNOCK, *adj.* pliant, nimble ; also long, pendulous.

REV. W. GASKELL.
1854.

Another word, not so often heard, which he [the Rachda
Felley] makes use of, is *lennock.* I can only charge my
memory with having heard this once, and that was some
years ago ; it means limber or pliant.
Lect. Lanc. Dialect, p. 21.

WAUGH.
1869.

Thae's a fuut like a angel, Ben ; an, by th' mon, thae'rt
as *lennock* as a snig. *Yeth-Bobs,* c. i., p. 29.

LEP (Fylde), *v.* to steep.

LET, *v.* lighted.

WAUGH.
1879.

He took me into a long, dark room, wheer there wur
a hawp'ny candle *let.* *Chimney Corner,* p. 245.

LET-ON, *v.* to tell a secret ; to admit knowledge of a thing.

COLL. USE.
1881.

Whatever he says, dunnot thee *let-on* 'at tha knows
owt about it.

LEY, *sb.* the carnation.

WAUGH.
1855.

She was the queen of all flower-growers in humble life
upon her native ground ; especially in the cultivation of
the polyanthus, auricula, tulip, and " *ley,*" or carnation.
Lanc. Sketches : Heywood and Neighbourhood, p. 184.

LEY, *sb.* pasture or grass land, as distinguished from plough land or such as is kept under tillage.

LICK, *v.* to beat; also to excel, to surpass.

WAUGH.
1879.

I could ha' *lickt* him mysel'—wi' one hont teed beheend mo !   *Chimney Corner,* p. 153.

COLL. USE.
1881.

Tha'll not *lick* (excel) that, if tha' tries for a week ; so tha' may as weel give in.

LICK,
LICKIN', } *sb.* a beating.

B. BRIERLEY.
1868.

Theau'd want byettin' [beating] twice a-day wi' an odd *lick* extry neaw an' agen.   *Fratchingtons,* p. 68.

LICKIN', *sb.* provender for cattle.

LIEF, *adv.* soon, in the sense of willingly or preferably.

SHAKSPERE.
1600.

I had as *lief* have been myself alone.
                              As You Like It, iii. ii. 269.

WAUGH.
1868.

Iv it's o' th' same to yo, aw'd as *lief* yo wouldn't co' me no mak o' nick-names.   *Sneck-Bant,* c. iv., p. 73.

B. BRIERLEY.
1868.

Aw'd as *lief* goo to a comfortable corner o' th' tother shop.   *Irkdale,* c. i., p. 49.

LIEFER,
LEVER (N. Lanc.), } *adv.* rather, sooner.

TENNYSON.
1859.

Myself would work eye dim, and finger lame,
Far *liefer* than so much discredit him.
                        Idylls of the King: "Enid."

COLLIER.
1750.

I'd *leefer* ha' taen forty eawls.   *Works,* p. 72.

WAUGH.
1859.

But, he that would *liefer* drink wayter,
    Shall never be stinted by me.
          Lanc. Songs: God Bless these Poor Folk.

MISS LAHEE.
1865.

Nawe, aw'd *liefer* wait till they com'n.
                          Betty o' Yep's Tale, p. 12.

LIEW, *adj.* thin, poor, diluted.

LIG, *v.* to lie. A.S. *licgan* ; Icel. *liggja.*

SPENSER.
1580.

Tho gan shepheards swaines to looke aloft,
And leave to live hard, and learne to *ligge* soft.
              Shepheardes Calender: May, l. 124.

REV. W. GASKELL.
1854.

Another word retaining the Anglo-Saxon form, which occurs in our older poets, and also prevails in the Lancashire dialect, is the verb to "*lig,*" which has now become *lie.* A medical friend of mine, being once sent for to visit a person who was ill, asked the messenger, by the way, whether the person he was going to see was a respectable man. He wanted to know what was the rank of his patient. The answer was, "Aw dunnot knoa disaktly what yo koen 'respectable,' but he wears a watch an' *ligs* aloan." *Lect. Lanc. Dialect,* p. 16.

MISS LAHEE. 1865.	"Aw could do neaw to *lig* me deawn a bit." "Humph," aw ses, "aw shouldn't wonder iv tha *ligged* deawn an' brast, for aw ne'er see'd a woman eyt so mich." *Betty o' Yep's Tale*, p. 7.
DR. BARBER. 1870.	He *ligged* i' bed a lang while afooar he deed. *Forness Folk*, p. 13.

LIKE, *adv.* used in a curious manner for the purpose of intensifying an expression—as, "I'm all of a dither, *like*," meaning, "I am trembling violently."

LIKED, *v.* obliged, compelled, almost.

COLL. USE. 1881.	1. "Tha'rt never gooin to make that journey to-neet, surely." "Yea, aw am : aw'm *liked*." 2. "What did tha hit him for ?" "Aw couldn't help it : aw felt as if aw wur *liked* to do it." 3. Get out o'th' way, aw'd *liked* to knock'd thi deawn.

LILE (Ormskirk and N. Lanc.), *adj.* little. Dan. *lille*, little.

DR. BARBER. 1870.	He meadd a deeal o' fancy things i' his aan *lile* smiddy. *Forness Folk*, p. 13.

LILT, *v.* to step lightly.

WAUGH. 1859.	Come, Mary, link thi arm i' mine, An' *lilt* away wi' me. *Lanc. Songs.*

LIMB, *sb.* a wild or frolicsome or over-clever person.

COLL. USE. 1881.	What a *limb* that wench is !

LIMBER, *adj.* supple, flexible.

WAUGH. 1859.	He're straight as ony pickin'-rod, An' *limber* as a snig. *Lanc. Songs: Chirrup.*
IBID. 1879.	Th' cowt's as pratty a *limber*-legged craiter as ever I clapt een on. *Chimney Corner*, p. 157.

LIME-GAL, *sb.* a pony used for the carrying of lime ; *gal* is probably a contraction of "galloway."

About 1860.	Clitheroe, in the reign of Henry the Eighth, was a paltry, poverty-stricken borough, its staple, and indeed its only, commodity being lime, which was brought from the neighbouring kilns upon the backs of small, shaggy-coated ponies (there denominated "*lime-gals*"), and disposed of in the adjacent country. *Ned of the Fell*, p. 12.

LIN, *sb.* linen. A.S. *lin*, flax. Prof. Skeat in his Etym. Dict. has "Linen, used as a *sb.*, but really an adj. with adj. suffix -*en*, as in *wooll-en*, *gold-en ;* the original sb. was *lin*, preserved in *lin-seed*. Mid. Eng. *lin*, sb. ; *linen*, adj."

WAUGH. 1865.	It's a quare thing about ghosts comin' back, wi' their clooas on, too ! That caps me ! Think o' th' ghost of a *lin* sheet ! *Sexton's Story*, p. 25.
IBID. 1874.	I can see him sittin' there . . . drest in a check *lin* shirt, wi' a strap round his neck for a stock. *Jannock*, c. viii., p. 82.

LINDRINS, *sb. pl.* ropes put round a weaver's beam when the woof is nearly finished.

B. BRIERLEY.
Wi' mi pickers an' pins,
An' mi wellers to th' shins,
Mi *linderins*, shuttle, and yeald-hook.
Wayver o' Wellbrook.

LINES, *sb.* a marriage certificate.

LINTHER, *v.* to make fast the end of a warp so that it can be woven close and finished.

LIPPEN, *v.* to expect, to calculate.

COLLIER.
1750.
Hoo towd me hoo *lipp'nt* hur feythur wur turnt stracklin'.   *Works*, p. 68.

WAUGH.
1859.
Eawr Tummy's at th' fair, where he *lippens*
O' swappin' his cowt for gowd.
Lanc. Songs : Yesterneet.

IBID.
1868.
Aw *lippen* on him breighkin' his neck some o' these days.   *Sneck-Bant*, c. ii., p. 25.

IBID.
1879.
Hoo *lippen't* o' bein' wed, yo known—but it fell through.   *Chimney Corner*, p. 27.

LISH (Fylde and N. Lanc.), *adj.* smart, active, nimble. Cf. E. *lithe.*

DR. BARBER.
1870.
Afooar t' men gat down, a *lish* young fella hed setten off on horseback to tell 'im.   *Forness Folk*, p. 48.

LISK (N. Lanc.), *sb.* the groin.

LITHE, *v.* to thicken broth or soup with oatmeal or flour.

WAUGH.
1865.
There'll be broth to-morn, weel *lithe't*, an plenty o' pot-yarbs in 'em.   *Besom Ben*, c. i., p. 15.

B. BRIERLEY.
1867.
The old woman was engaged in "*lithing*" the broth, when her spouse rushed in to tell her dreadful tidings. "Whatever's to do neaw?" she exclaimed, hurriedly placing the *lithing* bowl on the hob.
Marlocks of Merriton, p. 69.

LITHER, *adj.* idle, lazy.   See *Lither* and *Luther* in Spec. of English.

MISS LAHEE.
1875.
Theyr'n too farrently *lither* to give a gradely deawnfo' an' be done wi' it.
Robin o' Dick's Charity Coat, p. 12.

WAUGH.
1879.
Well, thou knows, Ben were olez to *lither* to wortch, fro bein' a lad.   *Chimney Corner*, p. 278.

IBID.
Lither folk wi' their stomachs so dainty,
They wanten their proven made fine.
Ibid., p. 234.

LIVEN, *v.* plural of *live.*

WAUGH.
1859.
Thae's wit enough to know
That daisies *liven* weel
Where tulips connot grow.
Lanc. Songs: God Bless thi Silver Yure.

IBID.
1868.
"Little lads o' groon into fellys ; don't they, mam?"
"Ay, if they *liven*, my love," answered Betty, in a quiet tone.   *Sneck-Bant*, c. iii., p. 53.

LOADEN, *v.* to load.

LOANE, *sb.* a lane.   A.S. *láne, lone.*

> 1681.   William Hunt fined one shilling for keeping geese in the *loanes.—Bailiff's minute-book, Fishwick's Hist. of Kirkham,* p. 20.

> B. BRIERLEY.   His shirt no lad would ha punced if he'd seen it lyin'
> 1869.   i' th' *loane.*   *Ab-o'-th'-Yate in London,* p. 19.

LOAVE (N. Lanc.), *v.* to offer.

LOB, *sb.* a clown, a clumsy fellow.   W. *llob,* an unwieldy lump ; also a blockhead.

> REV. W. GASKELL.   We sometimes hear a heavy clumsy man called "a
> 1854.   great *lob* of a felley."   *Lect. Lanc. Dialect,* p. 13.

LOB (Ormskirk), *sb.* an assistant gamekeeper.

LOB, *v.* to run with a long and irregular stride.   Cf. Dan. *löbe,* to run.

LOBCOCK, *sb.* a great, idle, young person.

LOBSCOUSE, *sb.* a dish consisting of hashed meat, cooked with potatoes and onions.

> WAUGH.   Aw'm partial to butcher's chips ; aw wish they wer'n
> 1865.   abeaut twopence a peawnd ; we'd oather ha' *lobscouse,* or beef-bo', every day, bi go !   *Besom Ben,* c. i., p. 15.

LOBSIDED, *adj.* on one side, out of proportion.

> COLL. USE.   He's a *lobsided* sort of a chap—body an' moind,
> 1881.   booeth (both).

LOCK (N. Lanc.), *sb.* a quantity.

LOIT, *adj.* few.

> WAUGH.   "It's close upo' puddin' time," said the old man.
> 1869.   "It'll be within a *light* minutes o' noon, aw'll be bund."
> *Yeth-Bobs,* c. iii., p. 47.

> B. BRIERLEY.   If anybody had axt me heaw mony friends I had, I
> 1870.   should ha' bin bothered to ha' said how *loit.*
> *Ab-o'-th'-Yate on Times and Things, p.* 48.

LOLLOPIN', *part.* loose, hanging, limp.

> WAUGH.   Thou greight, o'er-grown, idle, *lollopin'* hount (hound) !
> 1879.   *Chimney Corner,* p. 153.

LOMPER, *v.* to walk heavily.

LONDON-BOBS (Calder Vale, near Garstang), *sb.* Sweet William.

LONG-SETTLE, } *sb.* a sofa with a high wooden back.   A.S. *setl,*
LUNG-SETTLE, } a seat.

> WAUGH.   Old Sam, the landlord, sat quietly smoking on the
> 1855.   *long-settle,* in a nook by the fireside.
> *Lanc. Sketches,* p. 23.

> IBID.   Come thi' ways to th' fire.   There's plenty o' reawm
> 1876.   [room] upo' th' *lung-sattle* here.—*Hermit Cobbler,* p. 32.

LONK, *sb.* a Lancashire-bred sheep.

LOOK-AFTER, *v.* to watch, to attend to.

> COLL. USE. 1881.　　Aw'll *look-after* thi, my lad; tha'll not get so far without me knowin'.

LOPE, *v.* leapt.　See *Leop* in Spec. of Eng.

> WAUGH. 1859.　　Tum Rindle *lope* fro' th' chimbley-nook.
> *Lanc. Songs: Tum Rindle.*

LOPPER, *v.* to boil slowly.

LOPPERIN'.

> WAUGH. 1879.　　I've bin wheer there's roast an' boiled—an' a *lopperin'* stew, that it would make a mon's yure curl to smell at.
> *Chimney Corner,* 126.

LOPPERT-MILK, *sb.* boiled milk or curdled milk.

LOPPERT, *part.* coagulated, clotted.

LORRY or LURRY, } *sb.* a long cart, without sides, and with four wheels.

LORRY, *v.* to pull or drag a person along against his will.

> COLL. USE. 1881.　　Aw'l not be *lorried* in that way oather by thee or onybody else.

LOSSY, *adj.* unprofitable, causing waste.

> COLL. USE. 1881.　　These potatoes are very *lossy;* aw have to cut haaf on 'em away.

LOTCHIN', *v.* limping.

LOUND (N. Lanc.), *adj.* calm, or out of the wind.　Icel. *logn,* Swed. *lugn,* calm, said of weather.

LOUNDER (N. Lanc.), *v.* to lounge idly about.

LOUP, *v.* to leap.

LOVER, LOOVER, } *sb.* a chimney.

LOW, *sb.* a flame.　Icel. *log,* a flame.

LOWK (Fylde and N. Lanc.), *v.* to weed.　Icel. *lok,* a weed; A.S. *lyccan,* to pull, weed.

LOWMOST, *adj.* lowest.

> WAUGH. 1865.　　The fire was dying out in the *lowmost* bars of the grate.　　*Besom Ben,* c. ix., p. 110.

LOW-SIZED, *adj.* little, short of stature.

LOZZUCK, *v.* to loll, to rest idly.

LUG, *sb.* the ear. Cf. Swed. *lugg*, the fore-lock.

LUG, *v.* to pull the hair. Swed. *lugga*, to pull by the hair; *lugg*, the fore-lock.

> JOHN SCHOLES. 1857.
> Hoo pood his ears for him, an *lugged* him reet weel when hoo found eawt. *Jaunt to see th' Queen*, p. 61.

> WAUGH. 1867.
> "That big un's gone an' cut every smite o' th' lad's toppin' off." "Well," said the elder lad, "Aw did it so as nobody could *lug* him." And it certainly was a close clip. *Home Life Factory Folk*, c. xx., p. 178.

LUM, *sb.* a chimney.

LUM, *sb.* a deep pool.

LUMBER, *sb.* mischief.

> B. BRIERLEY. 1869.
> I begin to think I shall never see Walmsley Fowt no moore, for if I dunno' get lost, or kilt, or takken up for dooin' summat I never intended dooin', I shall be i' *lumber* o' some sort.—*Ab-o'-th-Yate in London*, p. 49.

> WAUGH. 1876.
> "What's keepin' Robin till this time o'th' neet?" I hope he hasnt getten into *lumber*, for he's hardly to be trusted on a market day—as owd as he is. *Hermit Cobbler*, p. 12.

LUNGE, *v.* to strike heavily.

> COLL. USE. 1881.
> He *lunged* out wi' his fists to some tune, aw con tell yo.

LUNGEOUS, *adj.* rough and clumsy. See *Lounge* and *Lunge* in Skeat's Etym. Dict.

> JOHN SCHOLES. 1857.
> Weft into th' yung rascot. Maw hont's raythur too *lunjus*, or aw'd ge'et him to some bant. *Jaunt to See th' Queen*, p. 29.

> WAUGH. 1879.
> He leet fly at Antony wi' a greight strap 'at he had, an' he said, "Hasto catched that?" "Come, give o'er!" said Antony, "give o'er; yo're too *lungous!*" *Chimney Corner*, p. 161.

LUNG-LENGTH, *adv.* See LANG-LENGTH.

LURCHER, *sb.* one who lurks; also a kind of dog.

LURDEN, *sb.* an idle fellow.

> About 1390.
> He loketh al louryng, and *lordein* hym calleth. *P. Plowman*, c. vi. 163.

LURRY, *v.* to drag, to pull; *lurried*, dragged along. See LORRY.

LUTCH, *v.* to pulsate; *lutchin'*, pulsating painfully, as in a tumour, or in tooth-ache.

> WAUGH. 1879.
> It steawnges an' *lutches* to that degree that I sometimes wish my yed would fly straight off. *Chimney Corner*, p. 143.

M.

MACK (N. Lanc.), *sb.* a maggot. Mid. Eng. *mawk.* See *Mawkish* in Skeat's Etym. Dict.

MADDLE, *v.* to confuse, to irritate; parallel to *madden.*

WAUGH.
1867.
Make a less din, childer, win yo: for my yed's fair *maddle't* wi one thing an' another.
Home Life of Factory Folk, c. xix., p. 165.

DR. BARBER.
1870.
They wor fairly *maddlet* amang it, an' gev it up as a bad job. *Forness Folk,* p. 20.

MADLIN', *sb.* a flighty, extravagant person.

MADLOCK, *sb.* a wild, giddy person. From *mad.*

MAES, *v.* makes. See MAY.

MAFFLE, *v.* to hesitate, to falter, to stammer, to mumble.

MAFFLE, MAFFLEMENT, } *sb.* hesitation, dilatoriness.

WAUGH.
1855.
He're a fine, straight-forrud mon, wi' no *maffle* abeawt him, for o' his quare, cranky ways.
Lanc. Sketches: Cottage of Tim Bobbin, p. 55.

IBID.
1874.
"Come noo," said the landlord, "I like that! There's nae *mafflement* aboot it."—*Jannock,* c. v., p. 34.

MAFFLEHORN, *sb.* an incapable, blundering, inefficient person.

MAID (N. Lanc.), **MAIDEN** (S. Lanc.), } *sb.* a clothes-horse. See *Tamsin* in Pegge's *Kenticisms.*

WAUGH.
1859.
Aw iron't o' my clooas reet weel,
An' aw hanged 'em o' th' *maiden* to dry.
Lanc. Songs: Come Whoam to th' Childer.

MAIKIN (N. Lanc.), *sb.* the common yellow iris. *Iris pseudacorus.*

MAIN-SHORE, *sb.* the principal sewer in a street.

MAK, *sb.* sort, kind, appearance.

B. BRIERLEY.
1866.
What sort o' sons an' dowters-in-law hast getten? Are they of a farrantly *mak?*
Red Windows Hall, c. xiv., p. 107.

WAUGH.
1867.
Th' shopkeepers an' th' ale-heawses are in for it as ill as ony *mak.*—*Home Life of Factory Folk,* c. ii., p. 21.

MAKE, *v.* to fasten. Shakspere uses the word in this sense : *Com. Errors*, iii. i. 93 ; *As You Like It*, iv. i. 162.

> COLL. USE.
> 1881.
>
> It's toime we wur gooin' to-bed. Hasto *made* aw t' durs (doors)?

MAM, *sb.* mother. W. *mam.* See *Mamma* in Skeat's Etym. Dict.

> B. BRIERLEY.
> 1868.
>
> Well, an' heaw lung's thy *mam* bin deead ?
> *Irkdale*, c. i., p. 42.

MANGY (Ormskirk), *adj.* ill-tempered, peevish.

MANIGATE (Ormskirk), *sb.* a straight road over bog or moss land.

MANK, *sb.* a sportive trick.

> WAUGH.
> 1865.
>
> " Neaw for a *mank!* " said Ben, as he drew the patient companion of his wanderings under the rope.
> *Besom Ben*, c. ii., p. 21.

MAPMENT (N. Lanc.), *sb.* nonsense.

> A. C. GIBSON.
> (High Furness Dialect.)
> 1868.
>
> *Mapment*, Martha, *mapment!* Thow kna'sn't what thow says.—*Folk-Speech of Cumberland, &c.*, p. 86.

MAPPEN (N. Lanc.), *adv.* perhaps, possibly. See MEBBE and HAPPEN.

> DR. BARBER.
> 1870.
>
> He seed a woman liggin deead, which put him in a sad pucker, for she'd *mappen* bin murder'd or summat o' t' mak.
> *Forness Folk*, p. 31.

MARKET-FRESH, *sb.* a stage of inebriation.

MARLOCK, *sb.* a playful trick, a prank, a game, a joke, fun, mischief. Probably = merry lark.

> COLLIER.
> 1750.
>
> He made sitch *marlocks* that if I'd naw bin i' that wofo pickle I'st a bross'n wi' laughin'.—*Works*, p. 70.

> WAUGH.
> 1865.
>
> Aw'll bet tho a hawpenny he's done it for a *marlock*.
> *Besom Ben*, c. ii., p. 28.

> B. BRIERLEY.
> 1868.
>
> He'd be makin' o' sooarts o' *marlocks* wi' th' bedclooas an' cheers an' drawers, tumblin' 'em o' of a rook like an' owd goods-shop.
> *Irkdale*, c. i., p. 47.

MARLOCK, *v.* to play. The suffix *-lock* is clearly the same as *laik* or *lake*, to play. South E. *lark*.

> RAMSBOTTOM.
> 1864.
>
> Ther'll nob'dy tak yo into th' cloof,
> An' let yo romp an' *marlock* theer.
> *Lanc. Rhymes*, p. 99.

> WAUGH.
> 1866.
>
> He's been *marlockin'* at th' front, wi' two or three more from Littlewood Schoo'.
> *Ben an' th' Bantam*, c. iv., p. 84.

MARRIAGE-LINES, *sb.* the certificate of marriage.

MARROW, *sb.* a match, a mate, an equal ; also likeness, resemblance.

> 1440.
>
> *Marwe*, or felawe yn travayle or mate.
> *Promp. Parv.*

TUSSER.
1573.

Though buieng and selling doth woonderful well,
To such as have skill how to buie and to sell:
Yet chopping and changing I cannot commend,
With theefe and his *marrow*, for fear of ill end.
                                        Chap. 57, st. 40.

WAUGH.
1859.

Hoo'll never meet thy *marrow*,
For mony a summer day.
                    Lanc. Songs: What Ails Thee.

IBID.
1868.

Eh, Ben, onybody may know who's chylt this is. He's
just thy *marrow* to nought, temper, an' o'.
                            Sneck-Bant, c. iii., p. 51.

MISS LAHEE.
1870.

His curls lay quite flat, like a parson, so ut he wor th'
marrow ov his brother Dick.   *Owd Yem*, p. 15.

MASH (Ormskirk), *sb.* a large quantity.

MAULP, } *sb.* a bullfinch.   The low, plaintive cry of the wild
MAWP, } bullfinch sounds not unlike *mope* or *moup*.   In the
Fylde district, *maup* is the common name for the blue-tit, and
spink for that of the bullfinch.

1673.

Payd for *maulpp* taken 38 in Rostherne, 79 in High
Leigh, 63 in Overtabley; for every *malpe* 1d.; the whole
number 180: 0. 15s. od.
                    Rostherne Churchwardens' Accounts.

MAWKIN, *sb.* a scarecrow.   *Rob-mawkin* is a poor fellow who
exchanges his hat or coat for that which has been used for a
scarecrow.

MAWKIN, *sb.* a slattern.   See *Grimalkin* in Skeat's Etym. Dict.

WAUGH.
1876.

He co'de her a mismanner't daggle-tail an' a *mawkin'*.
                            Manchester Critic, March 31.

MAY, *v.* make.   See MAES.   Hampole (A.D. 1340) has *mas* for
makes, *Pricke of Conscience*, lines 255 and 702, and *mase*, l. 242.
See also *Sir Gawayne* (A.D. 1320), l. 106, "Much mirthe he
mas with alle."

WAUGH.
1867.

Thae *mays* mo war [worse] nor aw am, wi' thi talk.
                            Owd Blanket, c. i., p. 18.

MAY-FLOWER, *sb.* the lady-smock.   *Cardamine pratensis.*

MAZZERT, excessively vexed.

COLL. USE.
1880.

He'd his best Sunday black on, and he came smack
i'th' slutch and he wur *mazzert*, I'll a-warnt yo.

MAZZLIN', *adj.* confused, foolish.   See *Maze* in Skeat's Etym. Dict.

MEAWNGE or } *v.* to chew, munch.
MUNGE,   }

MEBBE (may-be), *adv.* perhaps.

MEEMAW, *sb.* an antic or grotesque action or expression of face ; an affected manner.   See *Mow* (3), a grimace, in Skeat's Etym. Dict.

> Yf þon make *mawes* on any wyse,
> A velany þon kacches or euer þon rise.
> > *Book o Curtasye*, Sloane, 1986 (Furnivall's Manners
> > and Meals, p. 300).

WAUGH.
1864.
"A'wm noather partial to th' teawn nor teawn's folk," said Randal. "Nor me noather," replied Ben. "They'n too mony *meemaws* abeawt 'em for me."
Sneck-Bant, c. ii., p. 34.

MEETEN, *v.* pl. of meet.

WAUGH.
1879.
I'll tell tho moore when we *meeten* again.
Chimney Corner, p. 200.

MEETERLY, *adv.* tolerably well, comfortably.   Literally "measurably," from the verb to *mete.*

COLLIER.
1750.
Mary : That wur clever too ; wur it naw? *Thomas :* Yigh, *meeterly.*   *Works*, p. 47.

B. BRIERLEY.
1860.
"Well, Mary, heaw art ta wench?" "*Meeterly*, Jone ; heaw art theaw?" was the widow's response. "Well, a'wm *meeterly* as theaw ses, considerin' like."
Lanc. Tales and Sketches, p. 127.

WAUGH.
1867.
They'n getten *meeterly* weel sarv't this time.
Owd Blanket, c. iii., p. 52.

MEEVERLY, *adv.* modestly, gently, handsomely.

COLLIER.
1750.
Aw carrid mesell meety *meeverly* too, an' did as yo bidd'n meh.   *Works*, p. 37.

JOHN SCHOLES.
1857.
Aw thowt aw'd nare sin hur lookin' more *meeverly.*
Jaunt to see th' Queen, p. 14.

MEIGHT, *sb.* meat.

WAUGH.
1879.
Fat ! Yo connot ha' good *meight* bcawt fat.
Chimney Corner, p. 221.

MELCH, *adj.* moist and warm.

WAUGH.
1879.
"Nice *melch* mak o' a mornin'." "Grand grooweather, for sure. Weet an' warm, like Owdham brewis."   *Chimney Corner*, p. 113.

MELDER (N. Lanc.), *sb.* a quantity.

J. P. MORRIS.
1867.
Under a pile o' hay they fand a *melder* o' meeal—girt secks full.   *Invasion o' U'ston*, p. 5.

MELL, *v.* to meddle, to have to do with.   The M. E. verb *medlen*, often spelt *mellen*, means " to mix."   See *Meddle* in Skeat's Etym. Dict.

CHAUCER.
1386.
Now let me *melle* therwith but a while.
Chanoune Yemannes Tale, l. 173.

SHAKSPERE.
1597.

And say a soldier, Dian, told thee this,
Men are to *mell* with, boys are not to kiss.
Love's L. L., iv. iii. 257.

About 1400.

In Whalley Church there are eighteen antique oak
stalls from the dismantled abbey, each with its quaintly-
carved " miserere " or folding seat, under which, in
admirable workmanship, grotesque figures are sculptured,
with ludicrous jokes—for which the holy men seem to
have had a remarkably keen appetite. Among the most
noticeable is one representing a man forcibly shoeing a
goose, with the inscription

Woso *melles* of wat men dos,
Let him cum hier and shoe the ghos.

MELL (Fylde and N. Lanc.), *sb.* a mallet.

MENSEFUL, *adj.* managing, creditable.

WAUGH.
1874.

It'll be a sham [shame] if we connot find him a *menseful*
bit of a dinner. *Jannock*, c. ii., p. 13.

MET, *v.* might.

WAUGH.
1867.

Ben kissed her again. " Eh, Ben," said she, "do
give o'er ! Thae *met* be sweetheartin'."
Owd Blanket, c. i., p. 24.

MEXEN, *v.* to cleanse a stable or shippon. Literally to clean a
mixen, as it is called. Tennyson uses *mixen* for a midden : " And
cast it on the *mixen* that it die."—*Enid*, l. 672.

COLLIER.
1750.

I think t' be an ostler, for I con *mex'n*, keem, or fettle
tits as weel as ony one on um. *Works*, p. 71.

MEZZIL-FACE, *sb.* a fiery face, full of red pimples.

**MICKLE,
MICKLETH,** } *sb.* size, bulk. A.S. *mycel*, great.

BAMFORD.
1840.

" That wur indeed a strange brid," said Bangle; "but
wot *mickle* wur it, and wot wur it like i' shap?"
Life of Radical, vol. i., p. 133.

B. BRIERLEY.
1866.

That's just th' length an' bradth on't to th' *mickleth* of
a yure. *Red Windows Hall*, c. v., p. 38.

MIDDEN, *sb.* a heap of dung or refuse; the ashpit at one time
commonly attached to most houses in Lancashire. Dan. *mödding*,
a dunghill.

HAMPOLE,
1340.

A fouler *mydding* saw thow never nane.
Pricke of C., l. 628.

PALLADIUS.
1420.

The *myddyng*, sette it wete as it may rote,
And saver nought eke sette it ought of sight
The sede of thorn in it wol dede and dote.

WAUGH.
1879.

He leet go th' rope, an' roll't off th' slate into a
midden at th' back o' th' house.
Chimney Corner, p. 297.

MIDDEN-HOLE, *sb.* the receptacle for dung.

MIDDEN-STID, *sb.* a place for dung.

MIDDLE, *sb.* the waist, the middle part of the body.

> COLL. USE. 1. He wur up to his *middle* i' watter (water).
> 1881. 2. He geet him by th' *middle* an' pitch'd him upo' th' floor.

MIDGE, *sb.* anything very small.

> COLL. USE. "Jone wur married o' Monday. Hasto seen his
> 1881. woife?" "Aye, hoo's nowt but a *midge*." "Hoo is a little un, for sure."

MIMP, *adj.* prim, precise, affected.

MINDER, *sb.* the name given to one of the workers in a spinning mill.

MISTAL, *sb.* a cowhouse = mist-stall ; mist = dung.

MITS, *sb. pl.* a woollen covering for the hands which leave the fingers and half the thumb bare ; also strong leathern gloves without partitions for the fingers, used when handling thorns and prickly shrubs, or repairing fences. See *Mittens* in Skeat's Etym. Dict.

MIZZY, *sb.* a soft, boggy place ; allied to *mist* in mist-stall.

MOIDER, }
MOITHER, } to embarrass, to confuse, to perplex.

> COLLIER. Neaw aw'r so strackt woode, I'r arronly *moydert*.
> 1750. *Works*, p. 58.
>
> WAUGH. Aw declare it's enough to *moighder* a stoo'-fuut (the
> 1868. leg of a stool). *Sneck-Bant*, c. iii., p. 50.
>
> B. BRIERLEY. Aw begun o' thinkin' till aw're welly *moidert*.
> 1868. *Irkdale*, c. i., p. 50.
>
> DR. BARBER. At t' end of o' they wor fairly *moidert* amang it, and
> 1870. gev it up as a bad job. *Forness Folk*, p. 20.

MOLLART, *sb.* a mop for a baker's oven. Cf. *malkin*, the old name.

MOO, }
MOOF, } *sb.* a hay-mow. See *Mow* (2) in Skeat's Etym. Dict.

MOO'D, crowded, stowed to an inconvenient pitch, put away. Articles laid by to be out of the way are said to be *mooed* up.

MOOIN', putting hay on the mow.

MOONLEET-FLITTIN', *sb.* the stealthy removal of household furniture in the night to avoid payment of rent.

> COLL. USE. Aw met a cart i' th loan—they wouldn't speyk (speak)—
> 1881. it wur some'dy makkin a *moonleet-flittin'*.

MOOT, }
MUT, } *v.* might.

> COLLIER. That *moot* be, sed I, for after theau laft me eawr
> 1750. Seroh browt me meh supper, an' hoo *moot* leave it oppen. *Works*, p. 70.

MOOTER, *sb.* mill-toll; a quantity of meal or flour taken by the miller as his due for grinding. Latin *molitura;* Fr. *mouture,* speÏt *moulture* in Cotgrave.

MOPSY, *sb.* a slattern.

MORNIN'-PIECE, *sb.* a small piece of bread taken before going to work in the morning.

> COLL. USE.
> 1881.
> When aw come deawn stairs aw awlus foind mi *mornin'-piece* on th' table; mi mother puts it eawt before hoo goos to bed.

MORRICE,
MORRIS, } *sb.* a rustic dance.

> BAMFORD.
> 1849.
> My new shoon they are so good,
> I could dance *Morris* if I would;
> And if hat and sark be drest,
> I will dance *Morris* with the best. *Early Days.*

MORT, *sb.* a lot, a quantity.

> REV. W. GASKELL.
> 1854.
> We sometimes hear a Lancashire man talk of a "*mort* of people," or a "*mort* of things."
> *Lect. Lanc. Dialect,* p. 30.

MOSS-CROP, *sb.* cotton-grass. *Eriophorum.*

> WAUGH.
> 1867.
> Three neet-geawns o'th best gray calico, an' they wur eawt i' eawr yard, bleachin', nearly a fortnit, till they wur as white as a *moss-crop.—Owd Blanket,* c. iii., p. 72.

MOT (N. Lanc.),
MOTTY (S. Lanc.), } *sb.* a word. Fr. *mot,* the same word as Ital. *motto.*

> WAUGH.
> 1879.
> He couldn't bide a minute longer beawt puttin' his *motty* in. *Chimney Corner,* p. 355.

MOTHERIN', *part.* the visiting of parents by their children on Mid-lent Sunday—an ancient custom. Mid-lent Sunday is also called "Motherin' Sunday."

MOTH-ULLET (Lytham), *sb.* a small butterfly = moth-owlet.

MOTTY, *sb.* an aggregate of small deposits of money; a kind of small money club.

MOW, *v.* to cover up, to heap together. See MOO and MOO'D.

MOWDYWARP, *sb.* the mole. Icel. *moldvarpa.*

> COLLIER.
> 1750.
> Hoo's as fat as a snig, an' as smoot as a *mowdywarp.*
> *Works,* p. 57.

> WAUGH.
> 1867.
> Eh, he has bin gooin' on! He's getten a *mowdiwarp* in his pocket. *Owd Blanket,* c. iii., p. 76.

MOZZLY (Oldham), *adj.* Equivalent to *muggy:* damp, warm, and heavy. Used as follows: Butcher says "he never knew such bad-keeping weather as there has been this back-end, it has been so moist and *mozzly,* and it turns the meat foist."

MUCK, *v.* to manure.

> WAUGH. 1879.   Like Jerry o' th' Knowe, 'ut *muck't* wi' sond, an' drain't wi' cinders. *Chimney Corner*, p. 195.

MUCKOT (Rossendale), *sb.* a tub or vessel carried between two men, and used for bearing manure to hilly ground. Also, a name given in derision to a naughty boy.

MUCK-SWEAT, *sb.* a state of great anxiety.

> COLL. USE. 1880.   I wur o' of a *muck-sweat* to know what'd coom ov her.

MULL (N. Lanc.), *sb.* dust. Swed. *mull.*

MULL, MULLOCKS, } (Fylde), *sb.* broken turf.

MULLOCK (Ormskirk), *sb.* a bundle of dirty clothes.

MUMP, *v.* to thump, to beat.

MUMPS, *sb.* sulkiness. See *Mump* in Skeat's Etym. Dict.

MUN (N. Lanc.), *sb.* the mouth. Icel. *munnr.* See *Mouth* in Skeat's Etym. Dict.

MUN, MUNT, } *v.* must. Icel. *munu.*

> COLLIER. 1750.   I asht 'im whot way eh *munt* gooa? On he towd meh. *Works*, p. 47.

> WAUGH. 1867.   It will not do, my lass! Go aw *mun!* *Home Life of Factory Folk*, c. xxii., p. 195.

MUNGE, *v.* See MEAWNGE.

MURTH, *sb.* a large quantity or number. Another form of *mort.*

MUSE, *sb.* a gap for game; a run in a hedge for rabbits or other game. Old Fr. *mussette.* Shakspere, *Venus and Adonis*, line 683, referring to the hare, speaks of "the many *musets* through the which he goes."

MUSICIANER, *sb.* a musician; one who plays upon an instrument.

> WAUGH.   An' thee, too, owd *musicianer,*—
> Aw wish lung life to thee,—
> A mon that plays a fiddle weel
> Should never awse to dee!
> *Lanc. Songs: Eawr Folk.*

MUT, *v.* must.

> WAUGH. 1879.   If I *mut* ha my mind, you would ha' to dangle at th' end of a bant. *Chimney Corner*, p. 30.

MUZZY, *adj.* sleepy, dull; also bemused with liquor.

MYCHIN, *part.* pining, out of humour. The same, probably, as Shakspere's *miching.* See *Mich*, to skulk, hide, play truant, in Skeat's Etym. Dict.

N.

NAG, *v.* to torment or irritate with the tongue, to scold incessantly. Icel. *naga,* to gnaw.

> DR. BARBER.
> 1870.
>
> T' aad fella said she was olas terble reedan; he let her *knag* away. *Forness Folk,* p. 37.

> COLL. USE.
> 1881.
>
> He's awlas *naggin'* at me; aw 've no peace o' mi loife.

NAGAS (N. Lanc.), *sb.* a greedy, stingy person.

NAGGLE, *v.* to gnaw. Icel. *naga,* to gnaw.

NAGNAIL, *sb.* a sore, caused by the peeling of the skin from the roots of the finger nail.

NANGNAIL (Ormskirk), *sb.* a tyrant; an ill-tempered, troublesome person.

NANNY, *sb.* a she-goat; generally takes the form—"Nanny-goat."

NAP-AT-NOON (N. Lanc.), *sb.* the purple goat's-beard (*Trapogon porrifolius,* Linnæus), which opens its flowers only in the forenoon, after which they close.

NAPLINS, *sb. pl.* small round coal, as distinguished from the cob and slack or dust. Also, "Nibblins."

> WAUGH.
> 1866.
>
> These coals are noan so good as t'other. We's ha to try another pit th' next time. Put some *naplins* under that pon. *Ben an' th' Bantam,* c. ii., p. 30.

NAPPERN, *sb.* an apron (Whittaker). See APPERN.

> SPENSER.
> 1590.
>
> And put before his lap a *napron* white. *F. Queene,* Bk. V., c. v., st. 20.

NAPPY, *adj.* merry, joyous, under the influence of liquor.

NAR, *adj.* and *adv.* nearer; superl. *narst.*

> SPENSER.
> 1579.
>
> To Kirke the *narre,* from God more farre, Has bene an old-sayd sawe. *Shepheardes Calender:* July.

> JOHN SCHOLES.
> 1857.
>
> Aw hardly know iv aw awt to ventur ony *narr,* yor look'n so smart. *Jaunt to See th' Queen,* p. 19.

> WAUGH.
> 1867.
>
> "It's o' reet!" said th' singers, in a whisper. "He's better nor expectation!" an' they begun a-drawin' *nar* to th' heawse. *Owd Blanket,* c. iv., p. 95.

B. BRIERLEY.
1868.

If eaur Dick wur t' dee, aw should feel as if aw wanted to goo i' th' coffin wi' him, isted o' letten somb'dy else be *nar* to him nor me.   *Irkdale*, c. xiii., p. 198.

WAUGH.
1867.

"By th' mon," cried one of them, "aw believe that chap 's th' *narst* ov ony on us."   *Dulesgate*, p. 24.

NATTER, *v.* to nibble, to bite; also to tease, to irritate. Icel. *gnadda*, to murmur, to vex; also, *knetta*, to grumble; see Appendix to Vigfusson's Icelandic Dictionary.

COLL. USE.
1881.

1. Hello, there's bin a mouse i' th' bread-mug; sitho heaw this loaf's *nattered*.

2. Aye he's a *natterin'* soart of a chap—they'll nobody ha' mich rest as is near him.

WAUGH.
1875.

Hoo're as hondsome a filly as mortal e'er see'd,
But hoo coom of a racklesome, *natterin'* breed.
        Old Cronies, c. v., p. 50.

NATTLE, *adj.* irritable, touchy, cross.

WAUGH.
1859.

But aw're mazy, an' *nattle*, an' fasten't to tell
What the dule it could be, that're ailin' mysel'.
        Lanc. Songs: Jamie's Frolic.

IBID.
1867.

"Eh, Sam," I said, "thou's never bin nettlin' of a Sunday again, hasto?" "Why, what for?" he said, as *nattle* as could be. "They groon on a Sunday, donnot they?"   *Tattlin' Matty*, c. i., p. 14.

IBID.
1868.

He's a quare un, is tat. Terrible *nattle* betimes; but noan o' th' warst mak for o' that.
        Sneck-Bant, c. ii., p. 25.

MISS LAHEE.
1865.

Jinny begun, for th' first toime, to think at folks had bin laughin' at her, an' hoo geet rayther *nattle*, an' wouldn't eyt no moor. *Betty o' Yep's Tale*, p. 27.

NATTY, *adj.* neat, handy.

TUSSER.
1580.

How fine and how *nettie*
Good huswife should iettie,
From morning to night.   *Husbandrie*, 68, 1.

COLL. USE.
1881.

He's a rare mon to have abeawt th' heawse—he's so *natty* at a bit o' joinerin' an' that soart o' wark.

NATURE, *sb.* softness, kindliness, when applied to the texture of cloth; nutritive quality, when applied to food.

COLL. USE.
1881.

1. It's a noice bit o' cloth this, mon; there's some *nature* in it.

2. Aw wouldn't gi' tuppence a pound for stuff loike that. It'll fill no ballies (bellies); there's no *nature* in it.

NAYTHER (N. Lanc.), } *pro.* neither.
NOATHER (S. Lanc.), }

WAUGH.
1867.

Hoo's *noather* feyther nor mother.
        Home Life of Factory Folk, c. xxi., p. 185.

NAZZY, *adj.* peevish, cross, short-tempered.

> COLL. USE.
> 1881.
>
> Dunnot speyk to him—he's as *nazzy* as he can hutch (as peevish as it is possible for him to be).

NEATRIL, *sb.* a born fool, a *natural.* "He's a *nattral* foo'" is a common phrase.

> COLLIER.
> 1750.
>
> *Mary:* "Eh, Tummus! Aw deawt tearn mayin' a parfit *neatril* on yo." *Thomas:* "A *neatril?* Eigh, th' big'st at ever wur made sin Cain kilt Abel."
> *Works,* p. 58.

> IBID.
>
> I stoode like a gawmblin or a parfect *neatril* till welly day. *Works,* p. 69.

> JOHN SCHOLES.
> 1857.
>
> He mun be o pure *neatril,* hoo sed; did he think ut a pow [pole] could stond on th' woint [wind].
> *Jaunt to See th' Queen,* p. 25.

NEAVE (S. Lanc.),
NEYVE "
NEÂF (N. Lanc.),
sb. the fist. Icel. *hnefi,* the fist; Swed. *näfve;* Dan. *næve.* The word is not found in A.S. or Ger.

> SHAKSPERE.
>
> Give me your *neaf,* Mounsier Mustardseed.
> *Mid. N. Dream,* iv. i. 20.

> COLLIER.
> 1750.
>
> I up weh meh gripp'n *neave,* on hit him o good wherrit o' th' yeear [in the ear]. *Works,* p. 59.

> SHAW.
> 1853.
>
> My *kneoves* wurn gript, my yure stood still,
> Aw durst na hardly look.
> *Lancashire Muse: Sequel to Tim Bobbin's Grave.*

> JOHN SCHOLES.
> 1857.
>
> Aw giv hur sich o grip o' mi *neyve* as hoo never feldt afore. *Jaunt to See th' Queen,* p. 12.

> MISS LAHEE.
> 1865.
>
> Tha's nare bin bout nother sugar nor butter; nor tha nare shall be whol aw've *kneaves* o' th' end o' mi arms.
> *Carter's Struggles,* c. vi., p. 39.

> DR. BARBER.
> 1870.
>
> He darted his *neeaf* down aside on it, to bring out a girt slapper. *Forness Folk,* p. 40.

NEB, *sb.* the nose. A.S. *nebb,* the face, John xi. 44; Du. *neb,* bill, beak, nib, mouth.

> WAUGH.
> 1867.
>
> "Will ye bring me some?" said a little, light-haired lass, holding up her rosy *neb* to the soup-master.
> *Home Life of Lancashire Factory Folk,* c. vii., p. 62.

NEB, *sb.* the peak of a hat, cap, or bonnet, the edge of a cake. In Shakspere, the bill of a bird—"Go to, go to! How she holds up the *neb,* the bill to him!"—*Winter's Tale,* i. ii. 182.

> COLL. USE.
> 1881.
>
> What soart of a cap had he on? Blue cloth, wi' a shoiny *neb.*

NECK (Fylde), *v.* to beat, as a watch.

NECK-HOLE, *sb.* the nape of the neck.

> COLL. USE.
> 1881.
>
> Put that umbrella deawn—th' waater's runnin' into mi *neck-hole.*

NECKLIN', *part.* to clatter, as with iron pattens on a stone floor.

> B. BRIERLEY.
> 1868.
> Nanny's pattens were heard "*neckling*" over the kitchen flags. *Irkdale*, c. ii., p. 73.

NECK-OR-NOWT, *ad.* entirely, altogether. Literally up to the neck or not at all.

> COLL. USE.
> 1881.
> Aw'm in for it neaw—*neck-or-nowt*.

NED, *v.* needed.

> BAMFORD.
> 1854.
> I hanno *ned* it=I have not needed it; *nedno*, needed not; *nedn*, we needed; *nednno*, we needed not. *Dialect of S. Lancashire*, p. 205.

> RAMSBOTTOM.
> 1864.
> We took no thowt wi' th' childher ill,
> Bo geet em what they *ned* fro' th' teawn.
> *Lanc. Rhymes*, p. 51.

NEE, *adv.* near. A.S. *neáh, néh;* Mid. Eng. *neh, neih, ney, nigh.*

NEELD, *sb.* a needle.

> JOHN SCHOLES.
> 1857.
> Hur hussif [her needle-case, called a "housewife"] wur eawt, un hur *neeld* thredud e quick toime. *Jaunt to See th' Queen*, p. 47.

> RAMSBOTTOM.
> 1864.
> Well, want yo pins or *neelds* to-day,
> Or buttons, threed, or hooks an' eyes? *Lanc. Rhymes*, p. 54.

NEET, *sb.* pron. of night.

> WAUGH.
> 1867.
> "Good *neet*, Matty," said I, walking out of the garden gate. "Good *neet*, to yo!" replied the old woman. *Tattlin' Matty*, c. ii., p. 27.

NEET-CROW, *sb.* a night-bird. Figuratively a person fond of staying up late.

> COLL. USE.
> 1881.
> What a *neet-crow* thou art! Get thee to bed; tha'll never grow if ta stops up o' this way.

NEET-GLOOM, *sb.* the gloaming.

NEET-HAAK (N. Lanc.), *sb.* the night-jar. *Caprimulgus Euro pæus.*

NEMINIES, *sb.* the wind-flower. *Anemone nemorosa.* In Tennyson's "Northern Farmer" the flower is called "Enemies"—"Doon i' the woild *enemies.*"

NEPS, *sb. pl.* the dried flower-buds of lavender.

> B. BRIERLEY.
> 1867.
> "Dost keep thy clooas i *neps?*" "Ay; aw awlus do." *Red Windows Hall*, c. xiv., p. 111.

> IBID.
> 1868.
> Ther Sunday clooas boxed up nicely wi' *neps* t'keep 'em sweet. *Irkdale*, c. x., p. 48.

> COLL. USE.
> 1881.
> Aw've awlus a bunch o' *lavender neps* i' mi clooas drawer to keep th' moths away.

NESH, *adj.* tender, weak, delicate, soft. A.S. *hnesc,* tender ; cf. Icel. *hnjóskr.*

GASKELL.
1854.

A very expressive adjective (of which the current word "nice," in the sense of "dainty," has only half the force) is *nesh,* meaning weak and tender, not able to bear pain; in Anglo-Saxon, "nesc" [correctly, *hnesc*]. Thomas Wilson, in his *Art of Rhetoric,* perhaps the earliest writer on any such subject in the language, uses the Lancashire noun, and writes, "To be born of woman declares weakness of spirit, *neshnese* of body, and fickleness of mind." *Lect. Lanc. Dialect,* p. 20.

COLL. USE.
1881.

Oh, he's too *nesh* for owt; they'n browt him up that way.

NEST-EGG, *sb.* an egg left in the nest for the purpose of inducing the bird to lay. Figuratively a small sum of money kept back or saved to induce further savings.

COLL. USE.
1881.

Yore Jim's getten a *nest-egg* somewheer, aw'll be bound; he's a saving chap.

NESTLE-COCK, *sb.* the nestling, the last child.

WAUGH.
1869.

My young'st brother, eawr Joe, deed wi' Nelson, at Trafalgar. Eh, aw thought my mother would ha' brokken her heart ! He're like th' *nestle-cock* at eawr heawse.
Yeth-Bobs an' Scaplins, c. i., p. 21.

IBID.
1869.

It seems that this lad—bein' th' *nestle-cock*—had been much marred when he wur yung, both bi his feyther an' mother. *Ibid.,* c. ii., p. 37.

NETTLIN', *sb.* the act of gathering nettles.

WAUGH.
1867.

Thou's never bin *nettlin'* of a Sunday again, hasto ?
Tattlin' Matty, c. i., p. 14.

NEVER-HEED, *v.* don't notice, take no care.

COLL. USE.
1881.

1. Tha mun *never-heed* what *he* says to thi. If ta does tha'll goo wrung.

2. Its roof (rough) wark, aw know; but jog on, an' *never-heed.*

NEW-CATCH'D, *adj.* raw, inexperienced.

COLL. USE.
1881.

They'll make him believe owt. He's a *new-catch'd* un.

NEW-COME, *adj.* fresh, newly arrived.

SHAKSPERE.
1596.

A messenger with letters from the doctor
New-come from Padua. *Merchant,* iv. i. 108.

NEW-ON, *adj.* new, fresh. Applied to clothes.

COLL. USE.
1881.

He's got everythin' *new-on*—it met be Ayster (Easter) Sunday.

NIBBLINS. See NAPLINS.

NIGGERT (N. Lanc.), *sb.* a piece of iron placed at the side of a fire grate to contract its width and save coals.

NINNYHAMMER, *sb.* a blockhead.

> COLLIER. 1750.   Yo'ar a *ninnyhommer* t'heed hur.   *Works*, p. **72.**

NIP, *sb.* a small portion of food or drink taken between meals.

NIPPER, *sb.* a carter's assistant; a lad who accompanies a lurry or cart.

NIT, *sb.* a small louse. A.S. *hnitu,* Icel. *nitr,* a louse.

> TUSSER. 1580.   Let season be drie when ye take them to house;
> For danger of *nittes,* or for fear of a louse.
> *Husbandrie*, 21, 23.

NOAG, *v.* to hit the knuckles by flirting a marble against them.

NOAG-HOLE, *sb.* a game at marbles.

NOÁGUR, *sb.* an auger. A more correct form; the *n* being original. A.S. *nafegár,* an auger.

NOAN, *adj., adv.,* and *pro.* pronun. of none.

> WAUGH. 1879.   Eh, that'll do *noan,* lass.—*Chimney Corner,* p. 143.

NOAN, *sb.* an aunt.

NOATHER. See NAYTHER.

NOBBIN', *part.* striking the head.

NOBBUT, *con.* but, only, nothing-but (naught-but), a peculiar negative or emphatic form of the conjunction *but.*

> B. BRIERLEY. 1868.   If th' rain'll *nobbut* keep off a bit, we'st get whoam beawt havin' a fither [feather] turnt.
> *Irkdale*, c. i., p. 36.

NOBRY, *sb.* nobody.

> WAUGH. 1879.   Wi' a lot o' little childer yammerin' round tho, an' *nobry* to feight and fend for 'em nobbut thisel'.
> *Chimney Corner*, p. 144.

NODDLE-YED, *sb.* a person of loose, unsteady head or brain. A curious instance of the duplication of a word. Wedgewood says " the *noddle, noddock,* or *niddock* is properly the projecting part at the back of the head, the nape of the neck, then ludicrously used for the head itself."

NOGGIN, *sb.* a measure of liquid—the quarter of a pint. What is called a "gill" is not in Lancashire the fourth part of a pint, but the half of a pint. There are therefore two *noggins* to the gill.

> COLL. USE. 1881.   " What does ta say to a drop o' rum in us (our) tay?"
> " Aye sure, let's have a *noggin* between us."

NOMINY, *sb.* a long, wordy, and tiresome speech.

NOMPION, *sb.* a leader, a great man.

NONSUCH, *sb.* one who is not to be equalled. Generally used in irony—a "superior" person.

NOONIN', *sb.* the rest from labour at noon.

NOONSCAWPE, *sb.* rest taken at noon. See NOONIN'.

NOPE (Fylde), *sb.* a small blow.

NOR, *con.* than.

> REV. W. GASKELL.
> 1854.
>
> Lancashire people almost invariably use *nor* for than. I have never been able to make out satisfactorily the derivation of this; but it seems to me not improbable that it may have been originally the same as the Welsh *no* or *nog*, which means "than." I give that very doubtfully.
> *Lect. Lanc. Dialect*, p. 11.

> WAUGH.
> 1865.
>
> Let thoose chaps go their ways whoam; it would seem 'em better *nor* sittin' slotchin' theer.
> *Sexton's Story*, p. 12.

NOTCHEL, *sb.* a warning ; to cry "notchel" is to give notice that a certain person or persons will not pay the debts of another person.

NOTCHELS, *sb. pl.* fragments, broken meats, leavings of a feast.

NO-TIME, *sb.* a short time.

> COLL. USE.
> 1881.
>
> Come, be sharp wi that baggin; thi fayther 'ill be here i' *no-time*.

NOUS, *sb.* sense and ability, combined with quickness of apprehension; cleverness, combined with common sense. A word of various import, and almost untranslatable. Similar in meaning to the word *gumption*. Gk. νοῦς, mind; a piece of university slang.

NOW, *adv.* pron. of no. Sometimes the sound is nearer to that of *nawe*.

NOWMUN, *sb.* a term of contempt : possibly = no-man.

> WAUGH.
> 1855.
>
> Get tee forrud, wilto, *nowmun;* thae met ha' bin deawn again by neaw.
> *Lanc. Sketches: Bury to Rochdale*, p. 29.

> IBID.
> 1859.
>
> An' there's mony a miserly *nowmun* At's deed ov a surfeit o' gowd.
> *Lanc. Songs: Tickle Times.*

> B. BRIERLEY.
> 1868.
>
> Peggy, after giving a glance at the stairs: "Theau great *knowman!* Dost co this cleanin'?"
> *Fratchingtons*, p. 19.

NOWT, *sb.* nothing.

NOWT, *adj.* bad.

NOWTY, *adj.* naughty.

> BAMFORD. 1864.　　An' though he shift, unless he mend,
> He's still a *nowty* felley. *Homely Rhymes*, p. 135.

NOZZLE, *sb.* the nose.

NOZZLE, } *v.* to nestle, to lie close to. See NUZZLE in Skeat's
NUZZLE, } Etym. Dict.

NUMB, *adj.* stupid.

> COLL. USE. 1881.　　He's oather new at his job, or a bit *numb*.

NUMSKULL, *sb.* a stupid person.

> COLL. USE. 1881.　　Yo'll make nowt on him chuz what yo do. He's a
> regglar (regular) *numskull*.

NURR, *sb.* the ball beaten to and fro in the game of bandy. M.E. *knor*, a knot in a tree ; O.Du. *knorre*, a knot in wood, a hard swelling, hence a hard ball. Similarly, Icel. *knottr*, a ball (perhaps the same as *nurr*) is allied to Icel. *knütr*, a knot.

NYFLE, *sb.* a delicacy, a dainty.

> WAUGH. 1865.　　Aw guess thae's bin wearin' [spending] thi brass o' bits
> o' dainty *nifles* i' th' teawn.—*Besom Ben*, c. ix., p. 105.

> IBID. 1868.　　She took Betty's basket and crammed it with fruit,
> and with all sorts of sweet "*nifles*," to the great delight
> of Billy. *Sneck-Bant*, c. iv., p. 89.

O.

O, *adj.* pron. of all.

WAUGH.]
1866.

" Is this *o'* aw mun have?" said the lad, looking at the shilling. "It's *o'* thae mun have, my lad," said the landlord. *Ben an' th' Bantam,* c. iv., p. 81.

B. BRIERLEY.
1868.

Aw da' say hoo's gooin' t' leave him *o'* her brass.
Irkdale, c. xvii., p. 235.

O', *prep.* on or upon ; also of.

COLLIER.
1750.

I towd a parcil *o* thumpin' lies *o* purpose.
Works, p. 73.

OANDURTH, *sb.* afternoon. Icel. *undorn.*

COLLIER.
1750.

He sowd it et Owdham that *oandurth* for twopence hawpenny o peawnd. *Works,* p. 43.

OATHER, *pro.* pron. of either.

WAUGH.
1859.

Iv aw'd th' pikein' o' th' world to mysel',
Aw'd *oather* ha' Jamie or noan.
Lanc. Songs: The Dule's i' this Bonnet.

IBID.
1868.

They were'n o' on em *oather* yarb doctors or planet rulers. *Sneck-Bant,* c. ii., p. 29.

B. BRIERLEY.
1868.

" *Oather* 'll do," said the joiner. *Irkdale,* p. 236.

COLL. USE.
1881.

"Which is the right pronunciation of *either*—is it *eethe,* or *eyether?*" " *Oather* will do." (Said to have been a Lancashire schoolmaster's answer to the question of his pupil.)

OBBUT, *conj.* but, except. See NOBBUT, which has the same meaning.

B. BRIERLEY.
1868.

What right has theau t' think abeawt her, *obbut* as a brother should think abeawt a sister ?—*Irkdale,* p. 74.

IBID.

" Aw've finished," said Dick, " *obbut* polishin' off wi' summut ut'll mak it feel smoot i' th' meawth.
Ibid., p. 244.

ODDMENTS, *sb. pl.* scraps, fragments, trifles, remnants, pieces of furniture.

RAMSBOTTOM.
1864.

Un hoo said,
Ut if th' wust coom to th' wust we should then
Ha' for t' turn some o' th' *oddments* to bread.
Lanc. Rhymes, p. 16.

WAUGH.
1876.

An' I bought a two-thre *oddments* 'at we wanten a-whoam.—*Chimney Corner: Manchr. Critic,* March 31.

ODD-OR-EVEN, *sb.* a child's game, played by holding in the closed hand one or two small articles, the opposing player having to guess the number.

ODDS-BOBS-AN'-BUTTYCAKES, *interj.* a humorous expression of surprise.

> COLL. USE.
> 1881.
> *Odds-bobs-an'-buttycakes*, here's a bonny mess !

OD-ROT-IT, *interj.* a corrupted oath.

O'ER-LAY, *v.* to kill by lying upon, as in the case of a child.

> COLL. USE.
> 1881.
> "Is th' chylt dead?" "Aye, hoo wur drunk, an' *o'erlaid* it."

O'ER-TH'-LEFT, *adv.* not at all; by the rule of contrary.

> COLL. USE.
> 1881.
> "Has he raised thi wages?" "Aye, *o'er-th'-left*— he's bagg'd me" (discharged me).

OF, *prep.* used in place of *for.*

> HOLLINGWORTH.
> About 1650.
> Which could not be done *of* some months after the consecration. *Chronicle of Manchester.*

> COLL. USE.
> 1881.
> He's not been here *of* ever so lung (for a long time).

OFF-AN'-ON, *adv.* in an irregular manner.

> COLL. USE.
> 1881.
> He's bin courtin' that lass *off-an'-on*, now, for ten year. It's a shame to see it. Aw'd scawd (scauld) him if he were comin' to eawr heawse.

OFF-COME (N. Lanc.), *sb.* a stranger; not a native.

> DR. BARBER.
> 1870.
> T' landlord thenk't him, . . . praisin' t' *off-cum* chap o' t' while, cos he wos sewer he wos gaan to stop a week at t' varra leeast. *Forness Folk*, p. 58.

> J. STANYAN BIGG.
> 1860.
> Morkim Bay ye *off-comes* ca' t'. *Alfred Staunton*, p. 6.

OFF-HIS-YED (head), *adj.* mad.

> COLL. USE.
> 1881.
> He's graidly *off-his-yed*, mon—they'll ha' to send him to th' 'sylum (asylum).

OFF-IT, *adj.* insane; also, mistaken, having missed the mark.

> COLL. USE.
> 1881.
> 1. He's gooin' *off-it*, sure enough—tha should yer (hear) him talk.
>
> 2. Nay, tha'rt *off-it* this toime—tha mun try again.

OGREATH, *adv.* right, straight, perfect.

> COLLIER.
> 1750.
> So I seet eawt, on went *ogreath* till aw welly coom within a mile o' th' teawn. *Works*, p. 41.

OLEZ, *adv.* always.

> WAUGH.
> 1867.
> Aw *olez* fund tho a mon o' thi wort, Ben. *Owd Blanket*, c. i., p. 20.

> IBID.
> 1879.
> We're *olez* pincht for coverin', thou knows, when winter comes on. *Chimney Corner*, p. 143.

O-MAKS, *sb. pl.* all kinds, all sorts or makes. See AWMAKS, *ante*, p. 18.

ON, *prep.* used for *of.*

B. BRIERLEY. 1868.	"Eh, whatever will be th' upshot *on* it?" exclaimed Nanny. *Irkdale*, c. viii., p. 164.
COLL. USE. 1881.	He makes nowt *on* him (makes nothing *of* him; *i.e.*, does not consider him of any consequence).

ONELY, *adj.* lonely, solitary.

WAUGH. 1859.	When aw'd mended thi stockin's an' shirts, Aw sit deawn to knit i' my cheer, An' aw rayley did feel rather hurt— Mon, aw'm *onely* when theaw artn't theer. *Lanc. Songs: Come Whoam to thi Childer.*
IBID. 1865.	Sich a *onely* place as this is.—*Besom Ben*, c. ix., p. 104.

ON-FOR, *compound prep.* about, near to.

COLL. USE. 1881.	1. He's *on-for* a spree, aw con see that. 2. What's that lad *on-for* neaw? Some mak o' mischief.

ONNY-BIT-LIKE, *adv.* in tolerable condition.

COLL. USE. 1881.	"Will ta be comin' across to-morrow?" "Aye, if th' weather's *onny-bit-loike.*"

ON-SETTER, *sb.* ancestor.

WAUGH. 1855.	They liv't i' th' heawse 'at he's speykin' on; an' so did their *on-setters* afore 'em. *Lanc. Sketches: Birthplace of Tim Bobbin*, p. 93.

OON, *sb.* oven.

WAUGH. 1859.	There's some nice bacon collops o' th' hob, An' a quart o' ale-posset i' th' *oon.* *Lanc. Songs: Come Whoam to thi Childer.*
IBID. 1867.	"Hasto a pair o' leather breeches cookin' i'th *oon*, Mary?" "Nay," said Mary, opening the oven-door, "there's nowt at o' i' th' *oon.*" *Owd Blanket*, c. iv., p. 105.
B. BRIERLEY. 1867.	Win yo just shift back a bit, while aw put a bit o' fire under th' *oon*? *Red Windows Hall*, c. xiv., p. 111.

OON-CAKE, *sb.* a loaf baked without a tin or dish; would be described as "baked on the oven-bottom."

WAUGH. 1868.	"Ben," said Betty, "wilto ha' loaf-brade, or thae'll ha' *oon-cake*?" "*Oon-cake* for me," replied Ben. *Sneck-Bant*, c. i., p. 11.
IBID. 1875.	Eh, mother, couldn't yo' gi' me a lump o' *oon-cake* to be gooin' on wi'? *Old Cronies*, c. iii., p. 29.

OSS, *v.* to offer, to try, to attempt. See AWSE, *ante*, p. 18.

COLLIER. 1750.	His scrunt wig fell off, on when he *os* t' don it, on unlucky karron gan it o poo. *Works*, p. 52.
IBID.	I'r ot heawse in o crack, on leet o' th' owd mon i' th' fowd, *ossin'* t' get o tit-back. *Works*, p. 57.
RAMSBOTTOM. 1864.	They'd gether reawnd some choilt wi' mayt, An' every bit it *ost* to-tak Their little meawths ud oppen too. *Lanc. Rhymes*, p. 67.

OTHERGATES, *adv.* otherwise.

OTHERSOME, *compound sb.* others, other persons.

| SHAKSPERE. 1599. | How happy some o'er *other some* can be !
Mid. N. Dream, act i., sc. i., l. 226. |

| WAUGH. 1868. | Thae looks hondsomer nor ever this mornin' ! Weddin' becomes some folk better nor *othersome.*
Sneck-Bant, c. iii., p. 59. |

| IBID. 1879. | They chargen moor at some places than ut *othersome.*
Chimney Corner, p. 53. |

OUMER (Fylde and Lonsdale), *v.* to shadow.

OUSEN, *sb. pl.* oxen.

OUT-AN-OUT, *adv.* altogether, entirely, extreme.

| COLL. USE. 1881. | He's *out-an-out* th' best hand at puncin', as we'n getten i' this shop (place). |

OUT-COMLIN', *sb.* a stranger. See EAWT-CUMLIN, p. 115.

OUT-RAKE (N. Lanc.), *sb.* a common near enclosed land.

OUZEL, *sb.* the blackbird.

| SPENSER. 1595. | The *ouzell* shrills; the ruddock warbles soft.
Epithalamion, st. 4. |

| SHAKSPERE. 1599. | The *ousel* cock so black of hue.
Mid. N. D., iii. i. l. 128. |

| COLLIER. 1750. | Now th' *ouzel* whistles, wheet-wit, wheet-wit, whee'u.
Works (Poem : The Blackbird), p. 413. |

| BAMFORD. 1840. | It wur nother gorse-cock, *ouzle*, nor dunnock.
Life of a Radical, vol. i., p. 133. |

OWD, *adj.* pron. of old. See ALD, *ante*, p. 7.

| RAMSBOTTOM. 1864. | While th' *owd* folk bear as best they con,
An' th' young uns o' forget to play.
Lanc. Rhymes, p. 42. |

| IBID. | Some *owdest* son may stayle for bread,
Some *owdest* dowther sink to shame.
Lanc. Rhymes, p. 43. |

OWD-LAD, *sb.* the devil (generally used with the definite article).

| COLL. USE. 1881. | If th' *owd-lad* were in him, he couldna be worse. |

OWLER, *sb.* the alder ; alder timber.   Also, used metaphorically as a synonym for clogs, the soles of which are made of alder ; as, " He up wi' his foot an' gan him some *owler*"—*i.e.* kicked him.

| B. BRIERLEY. 1868. | Aw could mak one eawt of a lump o' *owler* any day.
Irkdale, p. 198. |

| WAUGH. 1874. | I'd some'at to do to bant him, but I leet him taste o' mi *owler*, now an' then.
Chimney Corner: Manchr. Critic, August 14. |

OWL-LEET, *sb.* twilight.

> WAUGH.
> 1879.
>
> An' th' *owl-leet's* comin' on too. It's getten to th' edge-o'-dark, an' there 'll be boggarts abroad in a bit.
> *Chimney Corner*, p. 359.

OWT, *sb.* aught, anything.

> COLLIER.
> 1750.
>
> Too mitch of *owt's* good for nowt.   *Works*, p. 35.

> B. BRIERLEY.
> 1868.
>
> " Is thy feyther hearty, an' thy moather?"   "Ay, for *owt* aw know."   *Irkdale*, c. ii., p. 94.

> COLL. USE.
> 1881.
>
> The following is said to be a common laconic morning colloquy in the Oldham district:—"Mornin'" (good morning). "Mornin'" (the reply). "*Owt?*" (is there anything new)? "Nowt" (not anything). "Mornin'" (the farewell). "Mornin'" (the reply).

OWT-LIKE, *adj.* satisfactory, in fair quantity. *Nowt-like* is used to express the opposite meaning.

> COLL. USE.
> 1881.
>
> ' " Is it *owt-like* of a job?" "Aye, it'll pay weel enoof" (enough).

OYTCH (S. E. Lanc.), *pron.* of each.

> COLLIER.
> 1750.
>
> *Oytch* public trust is choyng'd into a job.
> *Works*, p. 33.

> T. WILSON.
> 1814.
>
> They wur men wi big cooats an' a stick i' *oytch* hond.
> *Songs of the Wilsons*, p. 35.

> WAUGH.
> 1859.
>
> Says he, " I thought *oitch* body knowed
>   Gentle Jone."
> *Lanc. Songs: Gentle Jone.*

P.

PAAMAS (N. Lanc.), *comp. v.* palm us, *i.e.* give us alms. See AAMAS, *ante*, p. 2.

PACE-EGG, *sb.* a hard-boiled egg, dyed or stained, and presented as an Easter offering. Pace = Pasque, Old French form of *Pascha.*

> REV. W. THORNBER. 1837. Easter introduced a change. The slothful now demanded his "*pace-egg*" (Paschal-egg) as a privileged dole ; the young of both sexes, on the afternoon of Easter Sunday, amused themselves in the meadows with eggs dyed by the yellow blossoms of the "whin."
> *History of Blackpool*, c. iv., p. 92.

PACE-EGGERS, *sb. pl.* mummers, who go about in bands at Easter-time, usually performing the old masque of *George and the Dragon.*

PADDOCK, *sb.* the toad or frog. Icel. *padda.*

PADDOCK-STOOL, *sb.* a fungus, a toad-stool.

PAN (N. Lanc.), *v.* to fit or tally.

PANBINDIN' (Cartmel), *sb.* a payment or compensation for an injury.

> COLL. USE. 1870. I'se gi' thee money to pay th' *panbindin'.*

PANCAKE-TUESDAY, *sb.* Shrove Tuesday.

PANT (Cartmel), *sb.* mud.

PANTLE (Fylde), *sb.* a bird-snare made of hair. O.F. *pantiere*, a kind of snare for birds. See PAINTER, a rope for mooring a boat, in Skeat's Etym. Dict.

PANTLE (Ormskirk), *v.* to snarc for snipes.

PAPPER, *sb.* pron. of paper. Icel. *pappir.*

> WAUGH. 1879. "My advice to thee is this—deet no *papper*." "Bi th' heart, Bill ; I connot do that, except I fling th' ink-bottle at it,—for I con noather read nor write."
> *Chimney Corner*, p. 210.

PARISH, PERISH, } *v.* to starve with cold or hunger.

> WAUGH. 1879. Come, Sally, let's poo up to th' fire a bit. I'm gettin' quite *parisht*. *Chimney Corner*, p. 30.
>
> IBID. They mun be harrish't, an' *parish't*, an' hamper't, an' pincer't, an' powler't about th' cowd world a while.
> *Ibid.*, p. 141.

PARITOR, *sb.* the name always applied to a verger ; an apparitor.

SHAKSPERE.
1597.

Sole imperator and great general
Of trotting *'paritors.*   *L. L. L.*, iii. i. 188.

PARLISH (N. Lanc.), *adj.* very great, terrible.   Same as *parlous*, *i.e.* perilous.

J. P. MORRIS.
1867.

Ther's *parlish* lile I du believe in.
Lebby Beck Dobby, p. 4.

DR. BARBER.
1870.

Ned hed bin lectur't be t' maister for not gangin' tul a church, a *parlish* lock o' times.   *Forness Folk*, p. 23.

PARROCK (N. Lanc.), *sb.* an enclosure.   A.S. *pearroc.*   Prof. Skeat in his Etym. Dict., Art. Paddock (2), says it is tolerably certain that *paddock* is a corruption of parrock, another form of *park.*

PART-AN'-PARCEL, *adv.* belonging to, being of the same kind.

COLL. USE.
1881.

He may say what he loikes ; but he's *part-an'-parcel* o' th' same lot.

PARTLY-WHAT, *adv.* partially, imperfectly.

DR. BARBER.
1870.

T' captin *partly-what* kent t' fella.
Forness Folk, p. 21.

COLL. USE.
1881.

" Does ta know him ?"   " *Partly-what.*"

PASH, *sb.* a sudden gush ; a fall ; a blow.   Shakspere in *Tr. and Cressida* (act ii., sc. iii., l. 213) uses it as a verb in the sense of to strike : " If I go to him, with my armed fist I'll *pash* him o'er the face."   It is similarly used by Langland in *P. Plowman*, Text A., v. 16, B. xx. 99, and by North in his translation of Plutarch.

WAUGH.
1867.

" Fine weather for yung ducks," said Ben.   " It's come'n wi' a gradely *pash* this time.   Aw'm wringin' weet."   *Owd Blanket*, c. iii., p. 52.

PAYSHUN-DOCK, *sb.* patience-dock or passion-dock ; called also poor-man's cabbage.

WAUGH.
1855.

Gathering on their way edible herbs, such as " *payshun-docks*," and " green-sauce," to put in their broth.
Lanc. Sketches : Cottage of Tim Bobbin, p. 50.

PEART, *adj.* cheerful, lively, smart, self-confident.   This word in its provincial sense is a curious variation on the literary meaning of *pert.*

WAUGH.
1867.

He walks by me i'th street as *peart* as a pynot, an' never cheeps.   But he's no 'casion.
Home Life of Factory Folk, c. xi., p. 106.

COLL. USE.
1881.

(Applied to a baby.)   It's a little un, for sure, but it's *peart* enough.

PEA-SWAD, *sb.* the hull or husk of a pea.

WAUGH.
1879.

He wur badly clemmed. I've sin him pike *peigh-swads* out o' th' swillin'-tub mony a time.
Chimney Corner, p. 225.

PEAWK or POUK, } *sb.* a small boil or swelling resulting from inflammation, a pimple. A.S. *poc*, a pustule.

COLL. USE.
1881.

He does na need to mak sich a greyt to-do abeawt it ; it's nobbut a bit of a *peawk*.

PEED (Cartmel), *adj.* blind of one eye.

PEEDLE (Cartmel), *v.* to look slyly about.

PEET-LARK, *sb.* the meadow-pipit or titlark. *Anthus pratensis.*

PEG, *v.* to walk; also to proceed with determination.

B. BRIERLEY.
1869.

"Nay," I said, "I'll trust yo' no furr, I'll *peg* it." An' I did *peg* it ; an' a weary treaunce it wur.
Ab-o'-th'-Yate in London, p. 80.

PEGGY, *sb.* a wooden instrument used in the washing of clothes.

B. BRIERLEY.
1860.

How well she looked at a tub—how dexterously she twisted her fat arms about when plying the "peggy."
Tales of Lanc. Life: Traddlepin Fold, p. 144.

PEG-LEG, *sb.* a wooden leg.

WAUGH.
1868.

When Billy heard the sound of Dody's wood leg upon the kitchen floor, he looked down at it very earnestly, and then turning to Ben he said, "Dad, he's getten a table-leg." "Theer, Dody," said the landlady, laughing, "it's thy turn this time. Thae'd better tak that *peg-leg* o' thine eawt o' seet, or else he'll be at it again."
Sneck-Bant, c. iv., p. 91.

PEIGHL, *sb.* hurry.

WAUGH.
1869.

"Twelve o'clock's my time," said Ben, "an' it wants an hour yet." "Well, then," said the fiddler, "thae'rt i' no *peighl*. So come an' sit tho deawn."
Yeth-Bobs, c. i., p. 17.

PELT, *sb.* speed, rate.

WAUGH.
1879.

Now then, Bob, doesto yer ? Wheer arto for at sich a *pelt* ?

PEN-FED (N. Lanc.), *adj.* stall-fed.

PENK, *v.* to strike a small blow ; also to work ineffectually, to make a feeble attempt.

WAUGH.
1875.

Judd nipt up a knobstick, an' began a weltin' at th' seck as he said, to *penk* th' dust out on't a bit.
Old Cronies, c. iv., p. 46.

IBID.
1879.

Two foos,—stonnin' up, an' *penkin'* at one another's faces, like a couple o' nailmakers.
Chimney Corner, p. 154.

PENKLE, *v.* to trifle; to waste time on things of small consequence. See **PENK.**

B. BRIERLEY.
1868.

If they'd lemmi goo to ther heawse neaw an' agen, an' be a brother to her—*penklin'* abeawt th' heawse an' garden, an' doin' bits o' jobs for 'em—aw could be content. *Irkdale*, c. ii., p. 102.

PENNORTH, *sb.* a penny's worth.

PERCH (Lytham), *sb.* a pole surmounted by a barrel and set up to mark a shoal.

PERRY, *v.* to scatter money or other objects amongst a crowd.

THORNBER.
1837.

At the church-door, an idle crowd was always ready for the "*perry*," *i.e.*, to contest for the scattered half-pence. *History of Blackpool*, c. iv., p. 97.

PESTIL, *sb.* the shank of a ham.

COLLIER.
1750.

Hoo browt meh some hog-mutton, an' as prime veeol an' *pestil* as need be toucht. *Works*, p. 53.

PETTLE (Cartmel), *v.* to coax; also to play with.

PEYL, *v.* to beat severely.

B. BRIERLEY.
1869.

Eawt we tumbled, th' owd woman o' th' top o' me, *palin'* me abeaut th' yead wi' her empty reticule. *Ab-o'-th'-Yate in London*, p. 12.

MISS LAHEE.
1870.

Aw'd getten Bob deawn, an' wur *peylin* him i' gradely Lancashire style. *Owd Yem*, p. 7.

PICKIN'-PEG, PICKIN'-ROD, PICKIN'-STICK, *sb.* a wooden rod or handle by which the shuttle is thrown in weaving.

WAUGH.
1859.

He're straight as ony *pickin'-rod*,
An' limber as a snig. *Lanc. Songs: Chirrup.*

IBID.
1855.

When the horn sounded, the weaver lads used to let go their *pickin'-pegs*, roll up their aprons, and follow the chase afoot.
Lanc. Sketches: Rochdale to Blackstone Edge, p. 127.

PICKLE, *sb.* a condition of difficulty or disgrace; confusion.

COLL. USE.
1881.

Tha's getten into a bonny *pickle* this toime, lad.

PICKS (Cartmel), *sb. pl.* diamonds at cards. See **PIP** (3), a spot on cards, in Skeat's Etym. Dict.

PIECE, *sb.* a recitation.

COLL. USE.
1881.

"What are yo for neaw?" "We're gooin' a-sayin' *pieces* at schoo'."

PIECE-POKE (Eccles), *sb.* a weaver's work-bag.

PIG, *v.* to crowd together.

COLL. USE.
1881.

They *pig* o' of a rook i' one room.

PIGGIN, *sb.* a small wooden pail. W. *picyn.*

WAUGH.
1879.

I'll have a penk at her *piggin'*, if I have to pay for th' garthin' on't." *Chimney Corner*, p. 154.

PIGNUT, *sb.* the earth-nut. *Bunium flexiosum.*

SHAKSPERE.
1610.

I with my long nails will dig thee *pignuts.*
Tempest, ii. ii. 172.

PIKE, *v.* to choose, to select; also to pick one's way; to gather one's-self together. A word of peculiar use, for which it is difficult to find a literary synonym.

WAUGH.
1865.

When we'n getten fairly off, thae mun lock th' durs, an' *pike* eawt at th' back after us as nicely as thae con.
Besom Ben, c. iii., p. 34.

B. BRIERLEY.
1869.

That wur enoogh, for they *piked* thersel's off.
Ab-o'-th'-Yate in London, p. 12.

WAUGH.
1879.

If I had ony company, I'd *pike* somebry 'at wur some bit like daycent. *Chimney Corner*, p. 155.

PIKE-FORK, *sb.* a pitch-fork.

WAUGH.
1869.

Aw tell yo what, maister, yo're gettin new things fast! Posies an' o'! Eh, dear! there'll be no touchin' yo wi' a *pike-fork* in a bit. *Yeth-Bobs*, c. i., p. 8.

PIKEIN', *sb.* picking, gathering, getting.

WAUGH.
1867.

It's thin *pikein'* for poor folk just neaw.
Home Life of the Factory Folk, c. ii., p. 21.

PIKEL, *sb.* a pitchfork; a hay-fork.

B. BRIERLEY.
1870.

Her clooas same as if they'd bin tossed on her back wi' a *pikel.—Ab-o'-th'-Yate on Times and Things*, p. 38.

PIKELET (gen.),
PIKELIN (Cartmel), } *sb.* a kind of thin cake or muffin; in Scotland called a *scone.*

PIKETHANK (Cartmel), *sb.* a hanger-on.

PILDER, *v.* to wither, to shrivel.

B. BRIERLEY.
1870.

[Hoo] had waited for a fine husbant till hoo're as *pildert* as an owd apple ut's been tumblet abeawt in a drawer a year or two.
Ab-o'-th'-Yate on Times and Things, p. 36.

PILGARLICK, *sb.* a term used to describe a pitiable or distressed person.

COLL. USE.
1881.

He's a poor *pilgarlick* as ever crept upo' two legs.

PILL-GILL (Cartmel), *sb.* a raree show or any kind of itinerant or public entertainment.

PINCER, *v.* to pince with pincers—metaphorically to torment, to harass.

B. BRIERLEY.
1868.

Aw should be soory for anybody ut were *pincert* wi' two [wives] at once't. *Irkdale*, c. xii., p. 192.

PINDER, *v.* to burn, to over-roast meat.

> COLL. USE.   Nay, tha mun tak that back ; aw'st ate none on it ;
> 1881.   it's *pinder't* to a cinder.

PINGERT, }
PINGOT, } *sb.* a small inclosure of land.

> COLLIER.   A tailor wur thrung pooin' turmits in his *pingot*.
> 1750.   *Works, p.* 37.

PINAFORE,)
PINNER, } *sb.* a large linen apron worn by childen and used as
PINNY,) a covering for the ordinary clothes. See BISHOP,
ante, p. 40.

> THOMAS HARDY.   Honest travelling have been so rascally abused since I
> 1876.   was a boy in *pinners.—Hand of Ethelberta*, chap. xlvi.

PINS-AND-NEEDLES, *sb.* the sensation of pricking felt in the
limbs when the circulation is stopped.

PISSABED, *sb.* the dandelion flower.

PISMOTE, *sb.* an ant. Cf. A.S. *maða*, a maggot, a bug.

PITCH-AN'-TOSS, *sb.* a game played with coins, a form of gambling.

> BAMFORD: There's a deal o' sin committed thereabeawts ; *pitchin'*
> 1859.   *an' tossin'*, an' drinkin', an' beawlin', i' Summer time."
>   *Early Days*, p. 169.

PLACE, *sb.* occupation, work.

> COLL. USE.   "He's lost his *place*."   "What for ?"   "Fuddlin'
> 1881.   again."

PLANTIN', *sb.* a plantation.

PLAYIN', *part.* being out of work.

> COLL. USE.   Aye, they're in a bad way, poor childer—thur fayther's
> 1881.   been *playin'* for nearly a twelvemonth.

PLECK, *sb.* a place. The A.S. *plæc*, cited by Mr. Gaskell in the
passage quoted below, is only found in the O. Northumbrian
version of Matt. vi. 5.   See PATCH (1) in Skeat's Etym. Dict.

> COLLIER.   He cudno be i' two *plecks* at one time, yo known.
> 1750.   *Works,* p. 65.

> REV. W. GASKELL.   Instead of "place," the old Anglo-Saxon word *plæc* is
> 1854.   still used unchanged.   I have heard of a raw recruit from
>   this neighbourhood, who, in his first battle, as soon as
>   the firing began, cried out, "I say, Cap'n, yo mun move
>   us from this *plec*, or we's some on us be hurt !"
>   *Lect. Lanc. Dialect*, p. 19.

> B. BRIERLEY.   Owd Tummy Trotter creepin' abeawt th' *pleck*, wi' a
> 1869.   roll o summat in his hont.
>   *Red Windows Hall*, c. v., p. 38.

PLOG, *v.* to plug, to close. Gaelic *ploc*. See PLUG in Skeat's
Etym. Dict.

> WAUGH.   Sit tho still ; an' *plog* thi ears up !
> 1879.   *Chimney Corner*, p. 151.

PLUCK, *sb.* the lungs of a sheep, cow, or other animal.

PLUG, *v.* to pull the hair, to lug.

POBBIES, } *sb.* a child's dish of bread and warm milk.   Welsh *pobi,*
POBS,   }   to bake.

> REV. W. GASKELL.   The word generally used by Lancashire people for
> 1854.   young children's food, bread soaked in milk or water by
>   the fire, is "*pobs*" or "*pobbies;*" and the most probable
>   derivation of this which I have been able to find is from
>   the Welsh *pob,* which means a baking; *pobi* being to
>   bake or roast.   *Lect. Lanc. Dialect,* p. 9.

> LAYCOCK.   Toimes are bad ;
> 1866.   We're short o' *pobbies* for eawr Joe,
>   But that, of course, tha didn't know,
>   Did ta, lad ?
>   *Lanc. Songs : Welcome, Bonny Brid.*

POCK-ARR, *sb.* a pock-mark.

POD (Ormskirk), *v.* to sulk.

PODGY, *adj.* stout and of short stature.

POLLYWOG (Preston), *sb.* a tadpole.

POOT, *sb.* a young hen just ready for or beginning to lay.   Applied
metaphorically also to a young, inexperienced person.   Poot =
poult.   See POULT in Skeat's Etym. Dict.

> B. BRIERLEY.   Aw'm nobbut a *poot* yet, an' happen a bit gawmless.
> 1868.   *Irkdale,* c. ii., p. 102.

PORRIDGE-STICK, *sb.* a piece of hard wood, used for stirring
oat-meal porridge in the pan.

POSSET, *sb.* a warm drink, usually made of milk and ale.

> WAUGH.   The country people in Lancashire have great faith in
> 1855.   simples, and in simple treatment for their diseases.   One
>   of their receipts for a common cold is "a whot churn-
>   milk *posset,* weel sweet'nt, an' a traycle cake to't, at bed-
>   time."   *Lanc. Sketches: Bury to Rochdale,* p. 22.

POSSET, *sb.* the flower of the meadow-sweet.

> WAUGH.   That tall, white flower, which country folk call
> . 1855.   "*posset,*" spread out its curdy top among the elegant
>   summer grasses.
>   *Lanc. Sketches: Heywood and Neighbourhood,* p. 163.

POST-AND-PATRIL WALL (Ormskirk), *sb.* a mud wall.

POSY, *sb.* any single flower ; not a bunch of flowers, as in literary
English.   *Clock-posy* is the flower of the dandelion.

> COLL. USE.   "What a pratty *posy* tha's getten.   What is it?"
> 1881.   "Oh, it's nobbut a woild un—a bit o' honeysuckle 'at
>   aw geet i' th' cloof."

POT-BO' (pot-ball), *sb.* a dumpling.

> COLLIER.   What wofo' times are theese !
> 1750.   *Pot-baws* are scant, an' dear is seawl an' cheese.
>   *Works,* p. 33.

POTE, *v.* to push with the feet.   A variation of *poke.*   See POKE (2) in Skeat's Etym. Dict.

B. BRIERLEY.
1870.

> A choilt looks forrad when it *potes* i' th' gooin-cheear, an' feels itsel' gettin' o'er th' floor for th' fust time.
>
> *Ab-o'-th'-Yate on Times and Things,* p. 80.

WAUGH.
1879.

> I've had th' young'st lass sleepin' wi' mo, an' th' little thing *potes* clooas off i' th' neet-time.
>
> *Chimney Corner,* p. 143.

POT-MARJORAM, *sb.* a savoury herb used to season broth.

POTTER, *v.* to make a feeble attempt ; to meddle and muddle ; to vex, puzzle, confuse, or perplex.   A frequentative form of *pote.* Old Dutch *poteren,* "to search one throughly," from the notion of poking a stick into every corner.   See POTHER and POTTER in Skeat's Etym. Dict.

BAMFORD.
1840.

> It wur as mitch a wagtail as theaw'rt a dagtail, an' theaw'd be *pottert* if onybody co'd the' so.
>
> *Life of a Radical,* vol. i., p. 134.

REV. W. GASKELL.
1854.

> There are many forms of speech and peculiarities of pronunciation in Lancashire, that would sound strange, and, to use a Lancashire expression, "*potter*" a Southern.
>
> *Lect. Lanc. Dialect,* p. 13.

IBID.

> When a Lancashire man is a little vexed or excited, he says he's "*pottert,*" and "it's enough for't *potter* ony mon's plucks." I do not know any Anglo-Saxon word from which this can come ; but the Dutch *poteren,* to stir, yields a not inappropriate meaning.—*Ibid.,* p. 27.

LAYCOCK.
1866.

> An' aw felt rarely *potter'd* at th' trick aw'd bin sarved.
>
> *Lanc. Songs : John Booth an' th' Vicar.*

WAUGH.
1876.

> Thou's bin a long time *potterin'* about yon stables. Whatever hasto bin doin' ?   *Hermit Cobbler,* p. 24.

POTTER-OUT, *v.* to pay, to deliver.

COLL. USE.
1881.

> Come, *potter-out* thi brass—tha's had it, an' tha mun pay for't.

POW, *v.* pron. of *poll ;* to cut the hair.

RAMSBOTTOM.
1864.

> Aw had t' begin an' shave mysel',
> An' get mi wife to *pow* my yure.
>
> *Lanc. Rhymes,* p. 47.

WAUGH.
1867.

> The mother, seeing us laugh at the lads, said, "That big un's been *powin'* tother, an' th' little monkey's gone an' cut every smite o' th' lad's toppin' off."
>
> *Home Life of Factory Folk,* c. xx., p. 177.

B. BRIERLEY.
1868.

> Aw'd ate my yed, an' have it *powd* o' purpose.
>
> *Irkdale,* c. iv., p. 118.

POWFAG, *v.* to tire.

POWFAGGED, *part.* wearied, worn out, distressed.

COLL. USE.
1881.

> "Joe, tha looks terribly *powfagg'd.*"   "Aye, aw've been wanderin' abeawt seechin' for wark for weeks."

POWLER, *v.* to live in a state of exigency and vicissitude ; to go about in a shiftless or confused way.

COLLIER.
1750.

Wi' mich *powlerin'* I geet eawt o' th' poo.
Works, p. 69.

BAMFORD.
1843.

A person who leaves his work and goes spreeing and fuddling about the country is said to "be *powlerin'*." A rambling, unsettled, dissipated person is said to "*powler* through the country." The hooters, shouters, clappers, and other noisy rabble described by Tim Bobbin at the Eawl-takin' were *powlerers*.—*MS. Glossary*, p. 139a.

WAUGH.
1868.

Billy an' th' wife wur *powlerin'* abeawt i' th' dark.
Sneck-Bant, c. ii., p. 37.

POWLERT, *part.* distressed, broken down, impoverished.

BAMFORD.
1843.

He's sadly *powlert*. He's bin off a week an' has comn whoam quite *powlert*. *MS. Glossary*, p. 139a.

POWSE,
POWSEMENT, } *sb.* something worthless, waste, rubbish; often applied metaphorically to a mischievous or dirty child.

COLLIER.
1750.

I'd scorn t' touch sich *powsments* wi' tungs.
Works, p. 33.

REV. W. GASKELL.
1854.

A strong and expressive word, as many of these are in the mouths of the Lancashire people, is "*powse*," denoting dirt that is thrown out, generally into a heap; and as a term of contempt applied to a person, though in that case it is more frequently converted into "*powsement*" or "*powsedurt*." The only origin which I have been able to discover of this word is the Welsh *pws*, which means what is expelled or rejected, refuse. This agrees very closely with the Lancashire signification.
Lect. Lanc. Dialect, p. 11.

WAUGH.
1867.

"Come," said the mother, "yo two are makin' a nice floor for mo. . . Go thi ways, an' dry thisel', thae little *pouse*, thae."
Home Life of Factory Folk, c. xx., p. 178.

IBID.
1867.

Neaw, Sammul, thaew'll ha' that pot upo' th' floor eenneaw—thae little *pousement*, thae ! Do keep eawt o' mischief. *Ibid.*, c. xix., p. 165.

POWSE-DIRT, *sb.* a worthless person.

WAUGH.
1867.

Ger off my dur-stone, aw tell yo ! Yo'r a *pouse-dirt* o' somebory's ! Aw'll not have him lad [led] off wi' noan sich like wastrels. *Owd Blanket*, c. i., p. 10.

PREASE (Cartmel), *v.* to invite.

PRIAL, *sb.* three, a trio, *i.e.* pair-royal. See PRIAL in Skeat's Etym. Dict.

WAUGH.
1865.

He closed the door upon the merry *prial* of conspirators. *Besom Ben*, c. vi., p. 82.

PRICKET (Ormskirk), *sb.* six sheaves of corn.

PRICK-METE, *adv.* neither more nor less; exactly the complement or measurement of anything.

> WAUGH. 1869. — Their mother's just *prick-mete* their dur-hole full, to an inch; an' hoo has to bend deawn, and come eawt sideways. *Yeth-Bobs,* c. iii., p. 45.

PRIMILY, *adv.* excellently.

PRISON-BARS, *sb.* a rustic game, in which the players on each side run after each other and wait their turn in enclosures called *prisons.*

PRITTLE-PRATTLE, *sb.* small talk; also childish conversation.

> PHILLIP STUBBES. 1583. — *Prittle-prattle* and tittle-tattle, the evils of 'em. *Anatomy of the Abuses in England,* pt. i., p. 93.

PROD, *v.* to poke, to prick, to stab.

PROUD-FLESH, *sb.* diseased flesh surrounding a wound.

PROVVEN,) *sb.* food, provender. Shakspere in *Coriolanus* (act ii.,
PROVVIN,) sc. i., l. 267) has *provand:*—

> Camels in the war, who have their *provand*
> Only for bearing burdens.

Prof. Skeat, in his Etym. Dict., Art. Provender, says the final *r* is an English addition, just as in *lavender.* Shakspere's *provand* is, strictly, the better form of the word.

> COLLIER. 1750. — Theaw may sleep if t'l lay th' *proven* ready. *Works,* p. 67.

> JOHN SCHOLES. 1857. — Awl giv onybody leeov to pack mi i barrels fur winter *proven.* *Jaunt to see th' Queen,* p. 46.

PROWSE, *v.* to stir.

> WAUGH. 1865. — By th' mon, it has *prowst* my inside up—to some guage. *Sexton's Story,* p. 14.

PROWT, *sb.* worthless, trumpery stuff; rubbish.

> WAUGH. 1867. — It's my own brewin', and there's no mak o' *preawt* in it. *Tattlin' Matty,* p. 14.

> B. BRIERLEY. 1868. — Factories an' railroads, an' o' sich ne'er-do-good *prowt.* *Irkdale,* c. i., p. 7.

PULLEN, *sb. pl.* poultry.

> WAUGH. 1855. — This wur his buttery, wheer he kept *pullen,* an' gam, an' sich like. *Lanc. Sketches: Cottage of Tim Bobbin,* p. 54.

PUMMER, *sb.* anything very large.

> WAUGH. 1865. — "Well," said Ben, "aw'll just taste wi' tho. Hello! there's no quart here, Ehoch!" "Well; aw nobbut had one poo [pull] at it,—but it wur a *pummer,* owd lad; for aw wur as dry as soot." *Besom Ben,* c. iii., p. 31.

> IBID. 1868. — "Lumps!" said Ben; "Ay, an' *pummers* too, some on 'em." *Sneck-Bant,* c. ii., p. 30.

PUNCE, *v.* to kick. The same as M.E. *bunsen.* See BOUNCE in Skeat's Etym. Dict.

BAMFORD.
1840.

Iv th' dur wurno oppent when he coom, he'd ha *punst* it oppen. *Life of a Radical*, vol. i., p. 134.

WAUGH.
1855.

Nawe! lev th' dur oppen, or else he'll *punce* it in. *Lanc. Sketches: Heywood and Neighbourhood*, p. 183.

IBID.
1867.

Iv awd been at th' back o' that chap, aw could ha' *punce't* him, see yo! *Home Life of Factory Folk*, c. xi., p. 106.

B. BRIERLEY.
1868.

Aw've a good mind to gie thi shins a *punce*, an' see if that'll rooze thee. *Fratchingtons*, p. 55.

PURR, *v.* to kick. Gaelic *purr*, to push, thrust, drive. See PORE (2) in Skeat's Etym. Dict.

COLL. USE.
1881.

Howd! (hold) tha munnot *purr* him when he's deawn.

PUSH, *sb.* energy, determination.

COLL. USE.
1881.

He'll never make nowt on it—he's no *push* in him.

PUTTIN'-ON, *sb.* a makeshift.

WAUGH.
1879.

I thought it would be a bit of a *puttin-on*, till to-morn. *Chimney Corner*, p. 99.

PUT-TO, *v.* tried, perplexed.

COLL. USE.
1881.

He wur hard *put-to*, poor lad, to make ony sort of a livin'.

PYANET (N. Lanc.),
PYNART (S. Lanc.),
PYNOT (general),
PYOT (Cartmel),

} *sb.* a magpie.

COLLIER.
1750.

Tim. I saigh [saw] two rott'n *pynots.*
Mary. That wur a sign o' bad fortin, for I yerd meh gronny say hoo'd as lief ha' seen two Owd Harrys as two *pynots.* *Works*, p. 50.

WAUGH.
1867.

He walks by me i'th street as peart as a *pynot.* *Home Life of Factory Folk*, c. xi., p. 106.

EDWARD KIRK.
1876.

The magpie, locally called a "*pynet*," still crosses your path, when you correct its forebodings by making a cross with your foot on the ground, and repeat

One for anger, two for mirth,
Three for a wedding, and four for death.

Papers of Manchester Literary Club, vol. i. Art.: *A Nook of North Lancashire*, p. 109.

PYANOT, *sb.* the peony.

PYTCH, *sb.* a hive for bees. Probably cognate with "pitch" of a roof, or "pitch" a covering of anything as a defence against weather. A breakwater is said to be "pitched" with stones on the surface.

Q.

QUALITY,
QUALITY-FOLK, } *sb.* the gentry.

COLL. USE.
1881.

They wanten us t' think ut they're *quality-folk ;* but they're nowt o'th soart, mon,—not they.

QUARLES (Worsley), }
QUARRELS, } *sb. pl.* square, or rather diamond-shaped, panes of glass in a latticed window.

QUELT, *sb.* a blow.

COLL. USE.
1881.

He gan him a *quelt* at th' side of his yed ut nearly knock'd him o'er.

QUERK, *sb.* a moulding in joinery.

QUERK (N. Lanc.), *v.* to cheat, to over-reach.

QUERN (N. Lanc.), *sb.* a hand-mill for grinding corn. A.S. *cweorn ;* Icel. *kvern.*

SHAKSPERE.
1599.

Skim milk, and sometimes labour in the *quern.*
Mids. N. Dream, ii. i. 36.

QUEST, *sb.* an inquest.

SHAKSPERE.
1602.

What lawful *quest* have given their verdict up
Unto the frowning judge ?
Richard Third, i. iv. 1899.

IBID.
1603.

"But is this law ?" Ay, marry is't ; crowner's *quest* law.   *Hamlet,* v. i. 23.

COLL. USE.
1881.

Th' crunner's (coroner's) *quest* is sittin' o'er him to-day.

QUICK-STICKS, *sb.* a short space of time.

COLL. USE.
1881.

Aw'll shift thee in *quick-sticks,* see if aw dunnot.

QUIFT, *v.* to quaff, to tipple.

QUIFTIN', *part.* quaffing.

QUIFTIN'-POT, *sb.* a half-gill.

COLLIER.
1750.

Beside, there's two tumblers, three *quiftin'-pots,* an' four pipes masht.   *Works,* p. 53.

WAUGH.
1879.

Here, Betty, bring us a quart an' a *quiftin'-pot.*
Chimney Corner, p. 150.

QUIT-OF,
QUIT-ON, } *compound prep.* without, delivered from.

    COLL. USE.   " Han yo' getten *quit-on* him ?"   " Aye, he's gone at
    1881.   last ; but he were a hard un to shift."

QUOCK (Fylde), *v.* to vomit.

QUOCK,
QUOKE, } *v.* to go a-shearing or harvesting from home.

QUOCKER, *sb.* one who goes harvesting to a distance.

R.

RABBLEMENT, *sb.* a crowd of disorderly folk ; a mob.

SPENSER.
1590.

And after all the raskall many ran,
Heaped together in rude *rablement*.
F. Queene, canto xii., st. 9.

SHAKSPERE.
1600.

Still as he refused it the *rabblement* hooted.
J. Cæsar, i. ii. 245.

COLLIER.
1750.

Donned mo like a meawntybank's foo, to mey [make]
th' *rabblement* fun.   *Works*, p. xxxvi.

WAUGH.

Aw don't want to be a show for ony mak o' *rabblement*
'at happens to be i' th' tap-reawm.—*Sneck-Bant*, p. 88.

RABBLETY, *sb.* a small rabble or crowd.

RACKAN-HOOK, } *sb.* a hook placed in the chimney so that it
RECKIN-HOOK, } can be swung over the fire, and intended to
hold a pot or kettle.   Applied figuratively to an idle, lazy fellow,
who prefers sitting in the chimney corner to working.   [See
Reek-airn in Atkinson's Cleveland Glossary.   The suggestion
there made, that *reckin* or *rackan* stands for *reek-airn*, *i.e.* reek-
iron or smoke-iron, is a very plausible solution of a difficult
word.—W. W. S.]

WAUGH.
1875.

An' then we sang glees,
Till th' *rack-an'-hook* rung.   *Old Cronies*, p. 54.

IBID.
1879.

Thou'rt too idle to make ony brass for thisel'—thou
loungin' *rack-an'-hook*—an' if onybody else con make
ony, thou'll make it away for 'em.
Chimney Corner, p. 152.

RACKETTY, *adj.* careless, thoughtless.

WAUGH.
1879.

That's another *racketty* slotch !
Chimney Corner, p. 155.

RACKLE, *adj.* reckless; also hasty, rash.   M.E. *rakel*, rash.   See
Chaucer's Maunciple's Tale, lines 174 and 235.   This *rakel* is
the word which was afterwards corrupted into *rake-hell*.

WAUGH.
1867.

Owd Tip's th' better chap i' th' bottom, iv he be a bit
rackle.   *Owd Blanket*, c. iv., p. 89.

IBID.
1876.

" Is there ony news o' that *rackle* brother o' thine?"
" Ay."   " What's he doin'?"   " He's wrostlin' th' cham-
pion."   " What champion ?"   " Drink."
Hermit Cobbler, p. 29.

RACKLESOME, *adj.* reckless.

> WAUGH.
> 1875.
> Hoo're as hondsome a filly as mortal e'er see'd,
> But hoo coom of a *racklesome*, natterin' breed.
> *Owd Cronies*, p. 50.

RACK-O'-MUTTON, *sb.* a saddle of mutton.

RAD (Fylde), *adj.* loosely knit.

RADDLE, *v.* to thrash, to beat—*i.e.* to thrash with a rod ; from *rad* = *rod*.

> WAUGH.
> 1879.
> They *raddle't* my bwons to some tune, I can tell tho';
> an' that's how I geet these lumps upo' my yed.
> *Chimney Corner*, p. 173.

RADDLE-AN'-DAUB, *sb.* a material anciently used for building, and consisting of stones and wood, mixed with mud or plaster ; or of twigs and plaster only. *Raddle* = little rod ; dimin. of *rad*.

RADDLIN, *sb.* wicker work on which plaster is laid.

RADLINS, *sb. pl.* hazel or other twigs used for laying plaster upon.

RAG, *sb.* hoar frost.

RAGAMUFFIN, *sb.* a disreputable and ill-clothed person. See note to *P. Plowman*, Text C, xxi. 283, where *Ragamoffin* occurs as the name of a demon.

> SHAKSPERE.
> 1597.
> I have led my *ragamuffins* where they are peppered.
> *1 Henry IV.*, v. iv. 36.

RAGGED-ROBIN, *sb.* the meadow-lychnis. *Lychnis flos-cuculi.*

> TENNYSON.
> 1859.
> The Prince
> Hath pick'd a *ragged-robin* from the hedge.
> *Enid*, l. 724.

RAGGOT, *sb.* a rough, disorderly person; a ragged vagabond.

RAGGOTIN', *part.* rambling about ; living in a disorderly way.

RAGGY, *adj.* broken and stormy.

> WAUGH.
> 1879.
> There's bin so mich *raggy* weather upo' th' moors that there's bin a great lot o' sheep lost.
> *Chimney Corner*, p. 376.

RAITHER-OF-OATHER, *adv.* almost ; equivalent to the phrase " on the whole."

> WAUGH.
> 1879.
> Owd Mary 'll be turn't three-score; an' I think her husban' would be *raither-of-oather* th' owder o' th' two.
> *Chimney Corner*, p. 146.

RAKE, *v.* to cover or heap up a fire with coals or cinders in order to keep it alive.

> COLL. USE.
> 1881.
> We mun ha' this foire *raked* afore we goo to bed—there 'll be no toime to leet it i' th' morn.

RAM, }
RAMMY, } *adj.* strong-scented, offensive to taste or smell. Icel. *ramr.*

RAM-BAZZ, *adv.* suddenly and with great force.   Cf. RAM-JAM.

> WAUGH.
> 1879.
> As owd Ben wur waddlin' whoam fuddle't, one winter neet, he coom *ram-bazz* again th' gate post, an' down he went.   *Chimney Corner*, p. 276.

RAMBLIN', *adj.* loose, talkative, untrustworthy.

> COLL. USE.
> 1881.
> Never heed him; he's a *ramblin'* soart of a chap.

RAM-JAM, *adv.* tightly packed, superlatively full.

> WAUGH.
> 1879.
> Aw geet *ram-jam* into th' middle.
> *Chimney Corner*, p. 40.

> IBID.
> If I wur *ramjam* full o' sixpences, I shouldn't feel comfortable.   *Ibid.*, p. 46.

RAMPAGE, *sb.* a loose, disorderly, or riotous condition.

> COLL. USE.
> 1881.
> Owd Ned's on the *rampage* again—drunk from mornin' till neet.

RAMPS (N. Lanc.), *sb.* wild onions, *Allium ursinum*.   Short for *ramsons.*

RAMSHACKLE, *adj.* disjointed, dilapidated.   Icel. *ramskakkr.*

> COLL. USE.
> 1881.
> Aw'st trust none o' my bones i' that *ramshackle* consarn—its haaf i' pieces a'ready.   [Alluding to an old and broken-down carriage.]

RAN-TAN, *sb.* a loud noise or knocking.

> COLL. USE.
> 1881.
> What's yon' *ran-tan* at th' dur [door]?

RAPSCALLION, *sb.* a wild and reckless person.

> COLL. USE.
> 1881.
> What a *rapscallion* thou art !   When wilt'a sattle deawn an' be quiet?

RASCOT, *sb.* a rascal.

> COLLIER.
> 1750.
> This mays [makes] me neaw, to cross these *rascot's* ends,
> To send agen to my owd trusty friends.
> *Works*, p. xxxiii.

RASPS, *sb. pl.* raspberries.

> LORD BACON.
> 1597.
> In May and June come *Rasps*.
> *Essay 46 : Of Gardens.*

> JOHN PHILIPS.
> 1708.
> Now with the Corinths, now the *Rasps* supply
> Delicious Draughts.   *Cyder : A Poem.*

> COLL. USE.
> 1881.
> Goo into th' garden an' get a twothree *rasps*—there's plenty on 'em ripe.

RATCH, *v.* to stretch, to extend; figuratively to exaggerate.   Lowland Scotch *rax.*

> WAUGH.
> 1876.
> I think thoose that chatter'n so mich mun *ratch* a bit.
> *Hermit Cobbler*, p. 66.

RATCH, *sb.* the space in a loom betwixt the yarn-beam and the healds.

RATEY (Rossendale), *adj.* rough ; applied to the weather.

RATTON,) *sb.* a rat. Icel. *rotta*, which is, however, a borrowed
ROTTON,) word from F. or Low Latin. M.E. *ratoun*, O. Fr.
ratoun, from Low L. *ratonem*, acc. of *rato*, a rat.

> WAUGH.   A sharper, seawnder set o' dog-teeth never snapt at a
> ratton !   *Lanc. Sketches*, p. 80.

RAW-HEAD, *sb.* a term of horror, used to frighten children. Probably the monumental skull in connection with the cross-bones.

> COLL. USE.   Husht ! go to sleep—*raw-head* an' bloody-bones 'll
> 1881.   fetch thee.

RAWKY (N. Lanc.), *adj.* damp, foggy. *Roky* in Norfolk ; the same
as *reeky.*

RAYLEE, *adv.* pronun. of really.

> WAUGH.   *Raylee* o' me, Matty, I dunnot like takkin' it.
> 1879.   *Chimney Corner*, p. 144.

READ, *v.* to perceive, to make out, to understand. A common
Lancashire saying among old folks is "Aw con *read* that as ne'er
wur printed."

> WAUGH.   " Are they for gettin' their baggin' up yon, thinksto?
> 1867.   They're seechin' summat, bith look on 'em." "Nay,"
> replied the other, "aw connot *read* yon."
> *Dulesgate*, p. 29.

REAR AN' FERRIN (Fylde), *sb.* the ridge and furrow in a field.

REAWK, *v.* to get together ; to associate ; to spend time in idle
gossip in neighbours' houses. See ROOK, *sb.*

REAWLY, *adj.* sleepy, unwashed.

RECKLIN,) *sb.* the last of a litter, which is generally the smallest ;
RICKLIN,) the youngest of a family or brood. Icel. *reklingr.*

REDDY, *v.* to prepare, to set right ; also to comb or straighten,
applied to the hair. A corruption of Lowland Scotch *red*, which
is allied to Icel. *ryðja*, to clear, and to E. *rid*. Turned into *ready*
or *reddy* by a popular etymology.

> WAUGH.   Come in, an' sit tho deawn while eawr lasses getten
> yon kitchen *readied* a bit.—*Owd Blanket*, c. iii., p. 53.

> IBID.   Here; tak howd o' this horn, an' *ready* thi yure a bit.
> 1879.   *Chimney Corner*, p. 168.

REDDYIN'-COMB, *sb.* a comb for the hair.

RED-RADDLE, *sb.* soft fibrous iron ore, used for marking sheep.
Raddle = ruddle, *i.e.* red stuff. *Red-raddle* is tautological.

RED-ROBIN, *sb.* the redbreast.

RED-SHANK, *sb.* a bird, *Scolopax calidris ;* applied figuratively and
contemptuously to any bare or red-legged person. It has been

commonly used in Lancashire ever since the retreat of the bare-legged Scotch rebels in 1745.

> WAUGH.
> 1859.
>
> Dody felt at his axe, an' he said, "Thou young foo';
> Thou'lt get a rare twiltin' for stoppin' fro' schoo';
> Hie tho' off like a *red-shank*, or th' dur may be teen'd,"
> An' he gan him a bit of a lifter beheend.
> *Lanc. Songs : Grindlestone.*

REEAM, *sb.* cream.   Icel. *rjómi.*

> COLLIER.
> 1750.
>
> Estid o' hittin' me, it hit th' *reeam*-mug ot stood o' th'
> hob, an keyvt aw th' *reeam* into th' foyar.—*Works*, p. 66.

REEAMIN', *part.* foaming.

REECH, *sb.* smoke.   A.S. *réc.*   Cf. Scotch *reek.*

> WAUGH.
> 1855.
>
> Neaw, win yo have a *reech* o' bacco ?
> *Lanc. Sketches*, p. 53.

> IBID.
> 1879.
>
> This is th' reet mak of a country for takkin' th' white
> out o' yo'r shirts.   There's bin nought nobbut *reech* an'
> rain sin' I coom.   *Chimney Corner*, p. 251.

REECH, *v.* to emit smoke or steam.

> WAUGH.
> 1879.
>
> Afore lung my clooas began o' *reechin'* like a lime kil'.
> *Chimney Corner*, p. 170.

REELER, *sb.* a mill operative who winds yarn on to a large reel or barrel.

REE-SUPPER, *sb.* a second supper.

REESTY, *adj.* rusted or discoloured ; also applied to bacon which has become strong and rancid.

RENDER, *v.* to melt.

RICKIN', *part.* making a noise ; also scolding.

> WAUGH.
> 1867.
>
> " Awve plenty o' brass, mon," said Tip, *rickin'* abeawt
> four-pen'oth o' copper in his pocket.
> *Owd Blanket*, c. iv., p. 86.

RICKLE, *v.* to make a noise, to chatter.

> B. BRIERLEY.
> 1867.
>
> Aw con tell him by th' *rickle* of his clog buckles.
> *Marlocks of Merriton*, p. 26.

RICKLIN, *sb.* gambling.   *Ricklin'-i'-th'-hat,* shaking pence in a hat.

RID, *v.* to separate.   Icel. *ryðja,* to clear, to *rid ;* all one with Mod. E. *rid.*

RIF-RAF, *sb.* worthless odds and ends ; the *residuum ;* low company.

> COLL. USE.
> 1881.
>
> What a lot o' *rif-raf* we'n getten at this end now.   It
> used to be a quiet, daycent place.

RIFT, *v.* to belch.   Icel. *repta,* pronounced *refta.*

RIGGIN, *sb.* the ridge of the roof.

> WAUGH.
> 1879.
>
> Away he went on to th' *riggin* o' th' house, an' started
> o' sweepin' like mad.   *Chimney Corner*, p. 296.

RIGGOT, *sb.* a narrow channel, a gutter.

RINDLE, *sb.* a small stream or brook. A.S. *rynel*, a stream or runnel.

> WAUGH. 1859.
>
> Yon dainty *rindles*, dancin' deawn
> Fro' meawntains into th' plain.
> *Lanc. Songs: Au've worn my bits o' Shoon.*

RIPPER, *sb.* a thoughtless dare-devil.

> COLL. USE. 1881.
>
> He's a reg'lar *ripper*—ready for owt i' th' way o' mischief.

RIPSTITCH, *sb.* a reckless person ; literally, one who tears his clothes.

> COLL. USE. 1881.
>
> What a *ripstitch* that lad is ! If aw send him out i' th' mornin' wi' his things o' reet an' tidy, he'll come back at neet like a scarecrow.

RIVEN, RIVVEN, } *part.* torn ; also figuratively, vexed, out of temper, angry.

> WAUGH. 1867.
>
> A pratty seet he looked ; his clooas wur *rivven*, and daubed wi' slutch. *Owd Blanket*, c. iii., p. 64.

> IBID. 1879.
>
> What's th' matter that thou'rt so *rivven* to-neet ?
> *Chimney Corner*, p. 255.

ROADY, *adj.* mixed ; applied to bacon which has alternate layers of fat and lean.

> COLL. USE. 1881.
>
> Gi' me an egg an' a collop o' *roady* bacon—that's the sort of a breakfast for me.

ROBIN-RUN-I'-TH'-HEDGE, *sb.* the plant bedstraw. *Gallium.*

ROB-MAWKIN, *sb.* a scarecrow. See MAWKIN.

ROG, *v.* to shake with a rattling din.

> WAUGH. 1867.
>
> Well ; what does he do, but starts a-*roggin'* at th' dur, as iv th' heawse wur a-fire.
> *Tattlin' Matty*, c. ii., p. 21.

> IBID. 1867.
>
> Then he *rogged* at the door, and shouted "Hello !"
> *Owd Blanket*, c. i., p. 7.

ROM, *v.* to force with violence ; to ram.

> COLL. USE. 1881.
>
> Tha'll not *rom* that deawn my throat, aw con tell thi— *i.e.*, you will not get me to accept or believe what you say, however much persuasion you may use.

RONDLE, *v.* to pull the ears as a punishment.

ROOK, *sb.* a heap, a number together, a lot.

> B. BRIERLEY. 1868.
>
> He'd be makkin' o' sorts o' marlocks wi' th' bed-clooas an' cheears an' drawers—tumblin' 'em o' of a *rook* like an' owd goods shop. *Irkdale*, p. 47.

> WAUGH. 1879.
>
> I've made fourpence, to-day, wi' gettin' a *rook* o' coals in. *Chimney Corner*, p. 251.

ROOT, *v.* to search for anything by feeling with the fingers, or with a stick. Icel. róta, to turn up ground, as a swine ; to *rout* about.

WAUGH.
1879.
"Wheer's mi purse ?" said Jack, *rootin'* amung th' slutch i' th' pig-pen. " Nay, thou doesn't need to *root* theer !"
Chimney Corner, p. 271.

ROOTIN', *part. adj.* meddlesome, inquisitive.

COLL. USE.
1881.
He's a *rootin'* tootin' sort of a chap.

ROPS, *sb.* the bowels, intestines. A.S. *roppas*, the bowels, entrails.

ROTTON, *sb.* a rat. See RATTON.

ROUGH-SPUN, *adj.* coarse but honest.

COLL. USE.
1881.
He's a bit *rough-spun ;* but he's o' reet.

RUBBIN'-STONE, *sb.* a small stone used for scouring and whitening the flagged floors of cottages. "White sand an' *rubbin'-stones* for rags and bones" was the cry formerly used by men who went about the country with small carts or panniered asses, selling the sand and stones to the cottagers, or exchanging them for rags and bones.

RUBBIN'-STOOP, *sb.* an upright pillar of stone or wood, set up in the pastures for the cattle to rub themselves against.

WAUGH.
1876.
Billy stons bi hissel' i' th' world, like th' *rubbin'-stoop* i' th' middle o' th' ten-acre feelt yon.
Hermit Cobbler, p. 18.

IBID.
1879.
It's like shoutin' to a lot o' *rubbin'-stoops* in a moor-end pastur !
Chimney Corner, p. 361.

RUCK, *sb.* a heap, a lot. Another form of *rook*.

RUD, *adj.* red.

RUN-A-BER, }
RUNBER, } *sb.* a run to get a force, an impetus. *Ber* = Lowland Scotch *beir*, force, impetus.

B. BRIERLEY.
1869.
On we went, as if th' train wur takkin a *run-a-ber*, an' wur gooin' to jump o'er Lunnon, an' land somewheer in France.
Ab-o'-th'-Yate in London, p. 10.

RUNAGATE, *sb.* an unattached person ; one ready to run at any one's bidding. In the Old English authors, Tyndale, Latimer, Raleigh, Shakspere, and Thomas Fuller, the word means a fugitive, a runaway. A singular corruption, due to popular etymology, of *renegate*, which occurs in Chaucer. See RENEGATE in Skeat's Etym. Dict.

TYNDALE.
1578.
A vagabond and a *runagate* shalt thou be in the earth.
Genesis, iv. 12.

SHAKSPERE.
1602.
Stanley :   Richmond is on the seas.
K. Rich. : White-liver'd *runagate*, what doth he there ?
Richard Third, iv. iv. 464.

PRAYER BOOK.
But the *runagates* continue in scarceness.
Psalms lxviii. 6.

RUNT, *sb.* a dwarf; a stunted animal or tree.

RUSH-BEARIN', *sb.* a Lancashire rustic festival.

> BAMFORD.
> 1859.
>
> The *rush-bearing* was the great feast of the year, and was held on the anniversary of the dedication of the church. *Early Days,* p. 147.

> HARLAND AND WILKINSON.
> 1873.
>
> The festival of *rush-bearing* does not always, however, coincide with the feast of the dedication. At Altcar the church is dedicated to St. Michael, September 29, yet the *rush-bearing* is celebrated in July. Mr. Roby speaks of it as an unmeaning pageant still practised in the northern and eastern parts of Lancashire, for the purpose of levying contributions.
> *Legends and Trad. of Lancashire,* p. 110.

RUSH-BOWTS, *sb. pl.* sheaves of rushes used in making a rush-cart. See RUSH-CART.

> BAMFORD.
> 1859.
>
> Others, again, are culling the finest of the rushes, and making them into *bowts*. *Early Days,* p. 152.

RUSH-CART, *sb.* a cart trimmed with newly-cut rushes, and used at the festival called Rush-bearing.

RUSHLEET, *sb.* a candle made of rush pith dipped in tallow; used also for any small candle, and metaphorically for a feeble attempt or display.

> COLL. USE.
> 1881.
>
> Come on wi' thi farthin'-*rushleet,* an' let's see what tha con do.

RUTE, *sb.* a hasty, violent determination; a fit of passion, a paroxysm of anger.

> BAMFORD.
> 1854.
>
> He went away in a great *rhute.*
> *Dial. S. Lanc.* p. 216.

RYEN, *sb.* a narrow channel or footpath. See RINDLE.

RYZEN, *adj.* twisted. Not the original sense. A.S. *hris,* brush-wood, small twigs; M.E. *rys, ris;* prov. E. *rice.* A *ryzen* hedge is a hedge twisted with hedge growth and stakes—called *stake and ether* hedge in Wilts Glossary (E. D. S.).

S.

SACK, *v.* to dismiss from work ; also *sb.* dismissal.

COLL. USE.   1. He *sack'd* me straight off, bout (without) a word.
1881.   2. "Is yon lad eawt o' wark again ?"   "Aye, they
gan him t' *sack* a week sin'."

SAD, *adj.* heavy, solid ; mostly applied to bread which has not been successfully leavened.

REV. W. GASKELL.   When a pudding or paste, or any mixture of a similar
1854.   kind, is made too thick, not sufficiently fluid, it is spoken
of as being too "*sad*."   Such a meaning may perhaps be
obtained from the Anglo-Saxon *sadian*, to saturate ; but
I am disposed to think we get it more directly from the
Welsh word *sad*, which signifies "firm ;" *sadiaw*, to
make firm ; just as the Lancashire people say of a mixture
for a pudding—"*sadden* it a bit."—*Lect. Lanc. Dialect*,
p. 9.
[The A.S. *sadian*, verb, is a mere derivative of *sæd*,
adj., sated, satisfied, firm ; and the W. *sad* is merely
borrowed from the same A.S. adjective.—W. W. S.]

SAFE, *adj.* sure, certain.

REV. W. GASKELL.   In Welsh *sef* signifies certain, and in Lancashire the
1854.   ordinary expression instead of "he is sure to do it," is,
"he is *safe* to do it," which is not quite the meaning of the
word in common English.—*Lect. Lanc. Dialect*, p. 11.

SAID, *p. p.* silenced, commanded.

COLL. USE.   Be *said*, wilto, or aw'll knock thi deawn, tha young
1881.   whelp !

SAIN (N. Lanc.), *sb.* lard, fat.   M.E. *saim* (Stratmann); but also
F. *sain.*

SAL (N. Lanc.), *v.* shall.

SAND-KNOCKER, *sb.* a sand-grinder.   This occupation was formerly much more common in Lancashire than now, sand being more frequently used, not only for the purpose of cleaning, but as a kind of ornament, and to preserve cleanliness.   After a floor had been washed, to "sand" it was almost the universal custom.

WAUGH.   There is a race of hereditary sand-sellers or "*sond-*
1855.   *knockers*," in Smallbridge ; a rough, mountain breed,
who live by crushing sandstone rock, for sale in the town
of Rochdale and the villages about it.   This sand is
used for strewing upon the flagged house-floor, when the
floor has been clean washed.—*Lanc. Sketches*, p. 130.

SAP, *sb.* an apple.

SAP-HEAD,
SAP-SKULL, } (N. Lanc.), *sb.* a blockhead ; a soft, silly person.

DR. BARBER.
1870.

T' *sapheead* rooart owt for help.—*Forness Folk*, p. 6.

SAPLESS, *adj.* foolish, witless.

SARK, *sb.* a shirt.   Icel. *serkr.*

BURNS.
1786.

There's some *sark*-necks I wad draw tight.
The Cry and Prayer.

BAMFORD.
1859.

An' if hat an' *sark* be drest.—*Early Days*, p. 153.

SARKLESS, *adj.* shirtless.

SARRA (N. Lanc.), *v.* to serve.

DR. BARBER.
1870.

I've a lile pig, an' I went out yā day to *sarra* it.
Forness Folk, p. 60.

SATTLE, *v.* to settle, to sit down.

WAUGH.
1859.

Come, Jamie, an' *sattle* thisel in a cheer.
Lanc. Songs : Jamie's Frolic.

SAUCE, *v.* to scold ; also *sb.* blame, recrimination, impertinence.

COLL. USE.
1881.

1. Hoo'll *sauce* thi weel for that, owd lad.
2. If tha 'd hit mo, an' gi' me less o' thi *sauce*, aw should be better pleäz'd (pleased).

SAUP,
SOPE, } *sb.* a sup, a drink.

WAUGH.
1867.

What 'll tho ha' to sup?   A *saup* o' summat warm would be th' best, aw think.   *Owd Blanket*, p. 57.

IBID.

Sup up, woman ; an' have a *saup* moor.—*Ibid.*, p. 61.

SAUT-PYE, *sb.* a salt-box.

SAUT-PYE-BIGGIN', *sb.* a building slated only upon one side—(of the same shape as a salt-box).

SAWGH, *sb.* a willow.   A.S. *sealh*, cognate with (not derived from) Lat. *salix.*

SCALE,
SKAIL, } *v.* to stir, to root out, as, "Skail that fire" = root out the ashes.

WAUGH.
1866.

Ben took up the poker to *scale* the ashes out of the firegrate.   *Ben an' th' Bantam*, c. i., p. 14.

SCALLION, *sb.* a young onion, a shallot.   [O.F. *escalogne ;* Lat. *ascalonia*, so named from Ascalon in Philistia.—W. W. S.]

B. BRIERLEY.
1869.

I'd as lief have a buttercake an' a *scallion* as owt.   If yo'n no *scallions*, a two-thri o' thoose tother yarbs ud do as weel.   *Ab in London*, p. 94.

SCAPLINS, *sb. pl.* stone chips, broken stones.

WAUGH.
1865.

Robin favvurs a chap at's bin brought up o' yirth-bobs an' *scaplins*.   *Barrel Organ*, p. 18.

SCAW (Ormskirk), *sb.* the scalp.

SCOANCE, ⎫ *sb.* a lantern. [From O.F. *escons*, hidden, due to Lat.
SCONCE, ⎭ *absconsus*, used for *absconditus*, hidden. It hence
meant any kind of protection. The Du. *schans*, a fort, and Icel.
skons, are merely borrowed from O. French. The O. F. *esconse*,
fem. of *escons*, occurs in the sense of a dark lantern.—W. W. S.]

> COLLIER.   It begun t' be dark, an' I'r beawt *scoance* in a strange
> 1750.   country.   *Works*, p. 50.

SCOG, *v.* to argue, to dispute ; also (Ormskirk) to tell ironical jokes.

SCOG, *sb.* a quarrel or dispute.   Allied to *shock*.

> WAUGH.   Tummus wur too mony for her.   Never a day passed
> 1879.   but they'd a bit of a *scog* o' some mak.
>   *Chimney Corner*, p. 129.

SCOPPEREL, *sb.* a round flat piece of bone with a hole in the
middle, frequently made into a spinner or teetotum ; also applied
metaphorically to a young rascal.   Icel. *skoppa*, to spin like a
top ; *skoppara-kringla*, a top (the toy).

> WAUGH.   Give o'er wuzzin up an' deawn th' floor.   Thae turns
> 1866.   me mazy.   Thae'rt war [worse] nor a *scopperil*.
>   *Ben an' th' Bantam*, p. 211.

> DR. BARBER.   T' wind fair-ly tuk me an' skirled me round like a
> 1870.   *scopperel*.   *Forness Folk*, p. 60.

SCORRICK, *sb.* a fragment, a crumb.

> COLL. USE.   He ett (ate) it o' up in hauve o' minnit—they 'r not a
> 1881.   *scorrick* laft.

SCOWBANK, *v.* to loiter in idleness ; to hang about a place without
an object.

> COLL. USE.   Come, tha mun shift thi shop ; aw 'll not ha' thi *scow-*
> 1881.   *bankin'* abeawt here ony lunger.

SCRAN, *sb.* food, bread ; sometimes refuse food.

> WAUGH.   Nat's bin out o' wark a good while ; an' he's bin ill
> 1879.   put to't for a bit o' *scran* now an' then.
>   *Chimney Corner*, p. 116.

SCRANNEL, ⎫ *sb.* a lean person.
SCRAMMIL, ⎭

> MILTON.   Their lean and flashy songs
> 1637.   Grate on their *scrannel* pipes of wretched straw.
>   *Lycidas*, 123.

> COLL. USE.   He's a poor *scrammil* as ever crope on two legs.
> 1881.

SCRANNY, *adj.* poor, meagre, generally applied to food.

> WAUGH.   Hard wark, an' pitiful pay, an' poor *scranny* livin'.
> 1867.   *Owd Blanket*, c. iii., p. 71.

SCRAT, *v.* to scratch.   Cf. Swed. *kratta*, to scrape.

> B. BRIERLEY. Th' owd sweeper wur *scrattin'* away wi' his stump of
> 1869.   a besom.   *Ab in London*, p. 23.

SCRAT, *sb.* the devil; generally used with the adjective "owd"— *i.e. Owd Scrat.*

SCRAUM, *v.* to scramble awkwardly.

> B. BRIERLEY.
> 1869.
> As I seed I'd no chance o' gettin' nowt beaut I helped mysel', I *scraumt* howd of a hontful o' buttercakes.
> *Ab in London,* p. 94.

SCRAUMIN, *adj.* large and straggling.

SCRAWL, *sb.* a mean or despicable person.

> SHAKSPERE.
> 1595.
> By heaven, these *scroyles* of Angiers flout you.
> *K. John,* ii. ii. 373.

> ———

> COLL. USE.
> 1881.
> As mean a *scrawl* as yo 'll meet in a day's walk.

SCREED, *sb.* a shred, a fragment. A.S. *scredde,* a shred.

SCREEVE, *v.* to froth at the mouth, as in a fit.

SCRIMPED, } *adj.* small, pinched. Mr. Blackmore in *Christowell,*
SCRIMPY, } c. 45, says, "Dartmoor is not often *scrimped* with drought." Cf. Lowl. Sc. *scrimpit,* dwarfish; allied to *shrimp* and *shrink.*

> COLL. USE.
> 1881.
> He 'r a little *scrimpy* chap—moor loike a choilt than a mon.

SCROG, *sb.* a fragment.

SCROWE, *sb.* a disturbance, an uproar; a bewildering state of affairs.

> WAUGH.
> 1874.
> Dunnot stop a minute upon 't road, or thou 'll be to lat, an' there 'll be sic a *scrowe* as nivver.
> *Jannock,* p. 63.

SCRUNCH, *v.* to crush, to crush with a grating sound.

SCRUNT, *adj.* over-worn or worn out.

> COLLIER.
> 1750.
> A felly weh o little reawnd hat on' o *scrunt* wig.
> *Works,* p. 63.

SCRUNT, *sb.* brushwood, stunted undergrowth.

SCUFF, } *sb.* the nape of the neck. "Frisian, *skuft,* the withers of
SCUFT, } a horse, properly the tuft of hair which a person mounting lays hold of to help himself up. Goth. *skuft,* hair of the head."—Wedgwood. Mr. R. D. Blackmore in his Devonshire story, *Christowell,* chap. 39, has "*scruff* of the neck."

> WAUGH.
> 1868.
> They very near poo'd me in bith *scuft* o'th neck, or else aw'd ne'er a stopt theer, thae may depend.
> *Sneck-Bant,* p. 8.

> IBID.
> 1874.
> Turn him out, I tell ye, or I'll rive him out bi' t' *scuft* o' t' neck.
> *Jannock,* p. 90.

SCUFT, *v.* to strike, to beat.

> COLL. USE.
> 1881.
> Aw 'll *scuft* him warmly if aw catch him—see if aw dunnot.

SCUFTER (N. Lanc.), } *sb.* hurry.
SCUTTER (S. Lanc.),

SCUT, *sb.* a short coat or other garment.

SCUTCH, *v.* to beat; to clean by beating or tearing open. Scutching is a process in the preparation of cotton, which is now performed by a machine usually called the "devil;" formerly this was done by women who beat the cotton with what were termed "batting-sticks." Allied to Norweg. *skoka*, a "scutch" or swingle for beating flax.

SCUTTER, *v.* to run. The same as Prov. E. *scuttle*, to run.

WAUGH. 1855. Witches *scutterin'* through th' slifters o' th' wole by theawsans. *Lanc. Sketches*, p. 199.

B. BRIERLEY. 1870. If childer meeten him anywhere, they *scuttern* away like a lot o' chickens when there's a dog abeawt. *Ab on Times and Things*, p. 41.

SEA-NEE, *sb.* a small fresh-water eel.

SEAWL, } *sb.* a relish taken with bread; water mixed with sugar,
SEWL, } treacle, fat, or other condiment, to take along with bread. In Rossendale the word is or was applied to anything eaten with bread and potatoes. Cf. Icel. *sufl*, whatever is eaten with bread; A.S. *sufol;* Dan. *suul*. See *Havelok*, lines 767, 1143, 2905.

COLLIER. 1750. What wofo times are these! Pot-baws are scant, an' dear is *seawl* an' cheese. *Works*, p. 33.

SEAWTERSKULL, *sb.* a blockhead.

SEECH, *v.* to seek.

RAMSBOTTOM. 1864. To help mi mother, ut's so kind, Aw'm here an' *seechin'* wark so late. *Lanc. Rhymes*, p. 7.

SEED, *v.* saw.

SEELY, *adj.* silly, foolish, simple. This word in its older sense— simple, happy—is spelled by Chaucer as it is pronounced in Lancashire—*sely*, and sometimes by Shakspere as *seely*. A.S. *sœlig*, orig. happy, lucky, seasonable; from *sœl*, a fit season, time.

WAUGH. 1879. Sich *seely* wark!—*Chimney Corner*, p. 153.

SEEMIN'-GLASS, *sb.* a looking-glass, a mirror.

WAUGH. 1867. She handed him the looking-glass, or "*seemin'-glass*," as country folk call it. *Owd Blanket*, c. i., p. 18.

IBID. 1879. "I wish thou could see thisel!" "Well; fot (fetch) a *seemin'-glass*, an' let's have a look." *Chimney Corner*, p. 151.

SEET, *sb.* sight, a spectacle.

WAUGH. 1881. An' eh, hoo wur sich a *seet* when hoo londed! Hoo're as thin as a lat (lath). *Owd Blanket*, p. 73.

SEETH (Ormskirk), *v.* to sift.

SEG, *sb.* a small hard place on the skin of the hand or foot, caused by much work, or by friction.

B. BRIERLEY.
1868.
They startn o' feightin' theere as soon as they con walk, an' never gi'en o'er till they'n *segs* ole o'er 'em.
Irkdale, p. 64.

SEN, *v. pres. pl.* say—*i.e.* "they *sen.*"

RAMSBOTTOM.
1864.
My prattiest things they co'n em feaw,
Or quietly *sen* they're wantin' nowt.
Lanc. Rhymes, p. 55.

B. BRIERLEY.
1870.
Well, they *sen* it's better for t' be born lucky than rich.
Ab on Times and Things, p. 52.

SEN (N. Lanc.), since. Short for Mid. Eng. *sithen.*

J. P. MORRIS.
1867.
When I was a varra lile lad—that's a conny lang time *sen* now. *Siege o' Brou'ton*, p. 3.

SENNIGROON, *adj.* having stiffened sinews.

COLL. USE.
1881.
1. He's as stiff and *sennigroon* as an owd tit (horse).
2. Stir abeawt mon ; tha 'll be *sennigroon* if ta sits i' that cheer much lunger.

SETS, *sb. pl.* large paving stones.

SETTLE, *sb.* a long wooden couch, with arms and wooden back. A.S. *setl*, a seat. See LONG-SETTLE, *ante* p. 185.

WEST MIDLAND DIALECT.
1320.
And he sete in that *settel* semlych ryche.
Sir Gawayne, l. 882.

REV. W. GASKELL.
1854.
A kind of rude sofa or long wooden seat, with a back and arms to it, goes by the name of a *settle ;* and under A.D. 796, in the Saxon Chronicle, we meet with "dom-*setl*," the judgment seat. In the Saxon version, Christ's overturning the seats of them that sold doves is rendered, "Hyra-*setlu*, he to brœc ;" and in the translation of Psalm i., even in Edward the Third's reign, we have, "Ne sat in *setel* of storme ungode."
Lect. Lanc. Dialect, p. 17.

SET-TO, *sb.* a fight, a contest, a dispute.

COLL. USE.
1881.
They'd a rare *set-to* deawn i't' kloof ; but t' constables dropt on 'em an' stopt ther gam (game).

SET-TO, *v.* to begin.

COLL. USE.
1881.
Come, may (make) no moor bawks, but *set-to.*

SHAD,
SHED, } *v.* to surpass, to excel.

COLLIER.
1750.
This had lik't to *shad* aw th' tother.—*Works*, p. 49.

B. BRIERLEY.
1869.
I're in as good romancin' fettle as ever Fause Juddie wur, an' he *shad* Gulliver. *Ab in London*, p. 98.

WAUGH.
1879.
"Well if ever !" cried Betty ; "that *sheds* o'."
Chimney Corner, p. 276.

SHAFFLE, *v.* to excuse, to delay.

SHAFFLE-HORN, *sb.* one who shirks work; a shiftless person.

SHAMMOCK, *v.* to hesitate, to trifle deceptively, to act awkwardly or in a shame-faced way.

> WAUGH. 1865.
> Wheerever hasto bin *shammockin'* an' doin' till this time o' th' neet? *Besom Ben,* c. ix., p. 104.

> B. BRIERLEY. 1869.
> Men wi' blank faces are *shammockin'* wearily in an' eaut. *Ab in London,* p. 74.

SHAMMOCK, *sb.* an awkward, confused, shame-faced person.

SHAMMOCKIN', *adj.* shy, abashed, bungling, confused.

> B. BRIERLEY. 1870.
> Hoo wonders heaw soon some *shammockin'* lad 'll be lookin' soft at her. *Ab on Times and Things,* p. 80.

SHAN, *v. pl.* of shall—*i.e.* "they *shan.*"

SHANDRAY, *sb.* a one-horse carriage.

SHANDRYDAN (N. Lanc.), *sb.* a cart fitted with springs; an ancient and dilapidated carriage. Also, a shandray with a hood or cover set up behind.

SHANK, *v.* to walk.

> B. BRIERLEY. 1869.
> Well, I set eaut, *shankin'* it o th' road, an' a weary treaunce I find it. *Ab in London,* p. 67.

SHANKLE, *v.* to shuffle and idle about.

SHANKS'S-PONY, *sb.* a person's legs. One who walks is said to "ride on *shanks's-pony.*"

SHAP, SHAPE, } *v.* to go, to finish, to manage, or contrive, or attempt.

> WAUGH. 1855.
> Roddle said, "*Shap* off whoam as fast as tho con." *Lanc. Sketches,* p. 130.

> IBID. 1865.
> Come, lads; aw want to be *shappin'* off—Lobden gate on. *Besom Ben,* c. iv., p. 41.

> IBID. 1867.
> "Theer, thae's *shap't* that at last, as how!" said one of these to his friend, who had just finished [his basin of soup], and stood wiping his mouth complacently. "*Shap't* that," replied the other, "ay, lad, aw can do a ticket and a hafe (three pints of soup) every mornin'." *Cotton Famine,* p. 61.

> COLL. USE. 1881.
> He *shaps* weel at any rate—*i.e.* he manages or attempts well.

SHARP-SET, *adj.* hungry.

> WAUGH. 1855.
> Beef's noan sich bad takkin, if yor ony ways *sharp-set.* *Lanc. Sketches,* p. 103.

SHEED, *v.* to spill. A.S. *sceádan*, to divide; *part.* shed.

WAUGH.
1866.

His jackass knocked my gronmother o'er, an' broke her pitcher an' *sheeded* th' milk, an' hoo'll ha to be paid. . . . . Are yo noan beawn to pay for th' milk 'at wur *shed*, then ?—*Ben an th' Bantam*, c. iv., pp. 79, 80.

SHEEDER, *sb.* one who spills liquor.

WAUGH.
1879.

"Hello, Sam, I've knocked my ale o'er !" "That's reet, my lad," said Sam (the landlord); "one good *sheeder's* worth two fuddlers."—*Chimney Corner*, p. 178.

SHEPSTER, *sb.* the starling. So named from settling on *sheeps'* backs.

SHIFT, *v. imperative*, equivalent to "move out of the way."

SHIFT, *sb.* energy, power of motion.

COLL. USE.
1881.

He's no moor *shift* in him than a kittlin (a kitten).

SHILTHER,
SHOOTHER, } *sb.* shoulder.

B. BRIERLEY.
1869.

Th' little waiter kept on grinnin' at me, an' hutchin' his *shoothers* up. *Ab in London*, p. 61.

SHINDY, *sb.* a game played with a stick and a round piece of wood or cork. Sometimes called "nurr and spell"—a form of golf.

SHIPPON, *sb.* a place for housing cattle. A.S. *scypen*, the same. See Chaucer, *C. T.*, l. 2000 [*or* 2002].

COLLIER.
1750.

I gan a glent into th' *shipp'n*, an seed a mon stonnin' i' th' groop. *Works*, p. 56.

SHIRL, *adj.* shrill. The following appears on a tomb-stone in the grave-yard of Rochdale Parish Church :—

Here must he stay till Judgment day,
While Trumpets *shirl* do Sound,
Then must he Rise in Glorious wise,
And Gloriously be Crown'd.

SHIVE,
SHOIVE, } *sb.* a slice, generally a slice of bread; sometimes used for bread itself. Icel. *skifa*. Hence Mod. E. *shivers*, splinters, bits.

SHAKSPERE.
1594.

Easy it is
Of a cut loaf to steal a *shive*.
Titus Andron., ii. i. 87.

MISS LAHEE.
1865.

Mi mother fotched her a gradely *shive* o' curran' loaf an' cheese. *Betty o' Yep*, p. 4.

COLL. USE.
1881.

Tha foo ! wear thi brass (money) o' *shoive*, an' not o' drink.

SHOE-LEATHER, *sb.* used figuratively for a shoe.

WAUGH.
1879.

A honsomer, sweeter-lookin' owd couple never stept *shoe-leather*. *Chimney Corner*, p. 146.

SHOG, *v.* to jog or jolt ; to go uneasily.

> DRYDEN.   Which with a *shog* casts all the hair before.
> 1676.   *Epilogue to The Man of Mode.*

SHOO, *v.* to drive anything before you, at the same time making a sound like that of "shoo."

> COLL. USE.   Here, Nanny, *shoo* these geese eawt o' th' fielt.
> 1881.

SHOOF, *sb.* a shoe.

SHOOL, *sb.* a shovel.   A.S. *scofl.*   See "Who Killed Cock Robin ?"—

> "I," said the owl,
> "With my spade and *showl,*
>   I'll dig his grave."

> WAUGH.   Come, shap off, afore aw fling a *shool*-full o' red cinders
> 1867.   at yo !   *Owd Blanket*, p. 11.

SHOON, *sb. pl.* shoes.

> CHAUCER.   His *shoon* of cordewane.   *Sir Thopas*, l. 21.
> 1390.
>
> SHAKSPERE.   *Jack Cade.* Spare none but such as go in clouted
> 1592.   *shoon.*   *Second Henry Sixth*, iv. ii. 192.
>
> MILTON.   The dull swain
> 1637.   Treads on it daily with his clouted *shoon.*
>   *Comus*, 635.
>
> KEATS.   When the soundless earth is muffled,
> 1817.   And the caked snow is shuffled
>   From the ploughboy's heavy *shoon.*   *Fancy.*
>
> COLLIER.   I thowt meh heart wou'd ha' sunk int' meh *shoon.*
> 1750.   *Works*, p. 59.
>
> WAUGH.   Aw've just mended th' fire wi' a cob;
> 1859.   Owd Swaddle has brought thi new *shoon.*
>   *Lanc. Songs: Come Whoam.*

SHOOTHER, *v.* to push, to hustle.   See **SHILTHER.**

> B. BRIERLEY.   Sam *shoothered* me into th' cab.   *Ibid.*, p. 88.
> 1869.

SHORE, *sb.* a sewer.

> SHAKSPERE.   Empty
> 1607.   Old receptacles, or common *shores*, of filth.
>   *Pericles*, iv. vi. 185.
>
> COLL. USE.   They're breakin' into th' main-*shore* again.
> 1881.

SHOT, *sb.* an account owing, a reckoning.   Icel. *skot.*   See **ALE**-**SHOT,** *ante*, p. 8.

> COLLIER.   I thowt I'll know heaw meh *shot* stons.—*Works*, p. 55.
> 1750.
>
> ALEX. WILSON.   When th' *shot* wur paid, an' th' drink wur done.
> 1842.   *Songs: Johnny Green's Wedding*, p. 58.

SHUDE, *sb.* the husk of grain, chaff.

COLL. USE.
1881.

"What's to do wi' thi porritch?" "What's to do wi' it? It could na be mich worse. It's sour, sauty (salty), *shudy*, and scaudin' (scalding) hot."

SHULL, *sb.* the husk or integument. See also HULL. Shakspere gives the word as "shale:" "Leaving them but the *shales* and husks of men."—*Hen. V.*, iv. ii. 18.

SHUT, *v.* to be rid of, quit of.

WAUGH.
1866.

Howd te din, an' lie still a bit, till aw get *shut* on him. *Owd Blanket*, p. 13.

MISS LAHEE.
1875.

Tha con howd it up when tha's getten *shut* o' thi load. *Charity Coat*, p. 14.

SHUTS, *sb. pl.* shutters.

WAUGH.
1879.

I wur puttin' *shuts* to, wi th' long brush i' my hands, an' th' brush hit th' window.—*Chimney Corner*, p. 301.

SHUTTANCE, *sb.* riddance.

WAUGH.
1879.

Good neet to tho, my lad, an' a good *shuttance*. *Chimney Corner*, p. 317.

COLL. USE.
1881.

"Is he gone?" "Aye; an' a good *shuttance* it is."

(Used also as an ironical "God-speed," *i.e.*, "Good *shuttance* to thi." "Good *shuttance* to bad rubbish" is a common expression.)

SHUTTER, *v.* to slide off, out, or down, as snow from a roof. A variant of *scutter*.

WAUGH.
1855.

Bodle lost his howd, an' he coom *shutterin'* deawn again, an' o' th' soot i' th' chimbley wi' him. *Lanc. Sketches*, p. 30.

B. BRIERLEY.
1868.

Aw could *shutter* eawt o' th' world as yessily as gooin' to sleep. *Irkdale*, p. 102.

SHUZ or CHUZ, } *adv.* so.

COLL. USE.
1881.

1. Aw'st goo to-morn *shuz* what comes.
2. *Shuz* heaw tha talks, it'll mak no difference.

SIB, *adj.* related, akin. A.S. *sib*, peace, relationship; Icel. *sifjaðr*, *adj.* related; Mœso-Goth. *sibja*, relationship. Langland has *sibbe* and *syb*, *P. Plow.*, B-text, Passus V., ll. 634 and 636.

SPENSER.
1579.

If that my grandsire me sayd be true,
Sicker [sure] I am very *sibbe* to you.
Shepheardes Calender: May, l. 267.

COLLIER.
1750.

Yoar *sib* to thoose Gotum tykes otteh [that you] complen'n so, on ar ne'er satisfy'd. *Works*, p. 33.

REV. W. GASKELL.
1854.

Another old word which has clung to this part of the country is *sib*, signifying related to. In the Mœso-Gothic, one term for disciples is *siponia*. In Anglo-Saxon *sibbe* or *sib* meant alliance or relationship. In the *Harrowing of Hell*, the earliest of the miracle-plays in English which has been preserved, we meet with a later form of the noun :—

> For thi godnesse art thou myn,
> More for thi godnesse
> Than for eny *sibnesse*.

The adjective frequently occurs in the old English stage of the language. We have it in Robert of Gloucester, and in Chaucer. It is one of the words, too, which Spenser employs both in the *Faerie Queene* and the *Shepheardes Calender*. *Lect. Lanc. Dialect*, p. 21.

WAUGH.
1879.

O' th' childer i' th' country met (might) ha' belunged to 'em, for everything 'at they let on seemed to tak to 'em, as if they were'n ever so *sib* (akin).
Chimney Corner, p. 146.

SICH-LIKE (*i.e.* such-like), *adj.* of the same kind.

WAUGH.
1867.

Sich-like sleeveless wark as that.—*Tattlin' Matty*, p. 18.

SIDE, *adj.* deep, long. A.S. *sīd;* Icel. *sīδr*, long, hanging.

BAMFORD.
1850.

A curtain or garment is said to be *side* when it hangs low : "A *side* shirt ;" "it hangs very *side ;*" "it's made too *side.*" *MS. Glossary.*

SIDE, *v.* to clear, to make tidy.

WAUGH.
1875.

Get this place *sided* up ; th' coach 'll be here directly.
Old Cronies, p. 20.

IBID.
1879.

Here, Sally, help me to *side* this table.
Chimney Corner, p. 36.

SIDLE *v.* to go aside or sideways ; to get away unnoticed.

COLL. USE.
1881.

He *sidled* up to his mother an' axed her t' forgive him for this once.

SIDTH, *sb.* depth, length. See SIDE, *adj.*

SIKE, *v.* to sigh, to sob. A.S. *sīcan.*

CHAUCER.
1380.

For fere of which he quook and *syked* sore.
Monkes Tale, l. 3394.

RAMSBOTTOM.
1864.

An' his mother, eh, Lord ! heaw hoo *soikt.*
Lanc. Rhymes, p. 17.

SIKE, *sb.* a drain, a gutter. M.E. *sike* (Stratmann) ; Icel. *sīk.*

SILE (Lytham), *v.* to strain milk. Icel. *sīa*, to filter. See Halliwell.

SIMNEL, *sb.* a cake, made of flour, spice, and currants, eaten in Lancashire on Mid-Lent Sunday, usually with the accompaniment of braggat or spiced ale.

REV. W. GASKELL.
1854.

There is a kind of cake for which the town of Bury is famous, and which gives its name in these parts to Mid-Lent Sunday—I mean *symnel*. Many curious and fanciful derivations have been found for this ; but I feel no doubt that we must look for its true origin to the Anglo-Saxon *simble* or *simle*, which means a feast, or, *symblian*, to banquet. *Simnel* was evidently some kind of the finest bread. From the Chronicle of Battle Abbey we learn that, in proof of his regard for the monks, the Conqueror granted for their daily use 36 oz. of "bread fit for the table of a king, which is commonly called *simenel;*" and Roger de Hoveden mentions among the provisions allowed to the Scotch king at the court of England "twelve *simenels*." "Banquet bread," therefore, would seem to come very near the meaning of this word. I may just observe, in passing, that the baker's boy who in the reign of Henry VII. personated the Earl of Warwick, was most likely called "Lambert Simnel" as a sort of nickname derived from his trade.

Lect. Lanc. Dialect, p. 18.

[But it is now well known that the word is French· It is spelt *simenel* in *Havelok* and in Old French; *siminellus* in Low Latin (Ducange). It is a corruption o *similellus* (the double *l* being differentiated), a derivative of Lat. *simila*, wheat flour of the finest quality. It was so called because made of the best flour. Cf. G. *semmel*, wheat-bread, borrowed from Latin. The A.S. word has nothing whatever to do with it.—W. W. S.]

SIMNEL-SUNDAY, *sb.* the festival of Mid-Lent.

SIMPLE, *adj.* poor, lowly.

COLL. USE.
1881.
Gentle an' *simple*, o' together, an' o' alike.

SIN', *adv.* since.

SINGLET, *sb.* a waistcoat; also a woollen under-shirt.

COLLIER.
1750.
I donned meh Sunday jump o' top o' meh *singlet*.
Works, p. 41.

WAUGH.
1865.
The most remarkable part of his dress was a slack, short jacket, or *singlet*, with sleeves. The front of it was of undressed calf-skin, with the hair outside.
Besom Ben, c. i., p. 6.

SINK, *sb.* a drain, the eye of a sewer.

SINK-STONE, *sb.* a stone slab or shallow trough connected with the drain, and used for washing dishes, &c. See SLOPSTONE.

WAUGH.
1879.
Hoo lays howd of a greight tin can 'at stood upo' th' *sink-stone*. *Chimney Corner*, p. 129.

SIPE, *v.* to drink. Allied to *sip* and *sup*.

SIPEIN, *part. adj.* dripping.

WAUGH.
1879.
One day, when th' rain wur peltin' down, Tummy coom runnin' into th' kitchen, out o' th' garden, *sipein'* weet. *Chimney Corner*, p. 129.

SITTER, *sb.* a festered burn.

SKARN, *sb.* dung. Icel. *skarn.*

SKEDLOCK, *sb.* charlock, a weed which grows among corn and in waste places. *Sinapis arvensis.* See KEDDLE-DOCK (*ante*, p. 172), which, however, is not the same plant.

> WAUGH. 1867.　　Eawr Billy 'd ha' to wear a *skedlock* in his hat.
> *Ben an' th' Bantam*, p. 52.

SKEER (N. Lanc.), *sb.* a stone patch or bed on the sea-shore or on sand-banks.

SKELBOOSE, *sb.* a passage by the side of a cattle stall, made so that a man can get to the fodder-rack in front of the cattle. See BOOSE.

SKELP, *v.* to hit or strike violently. See Jamieson's Scottish Dict.

SKELP, *sb.* a blow.

> COLL. USE. 1881.　　He gan him a *skelp* o't' side of his yed 'at sent him spinning into t' ditch.

SKEN, *v.* to squint.

> WAUGH. 1855.　　He *skens* ill enough to crack a looking-glass, welly.
> *Lancashire Sketches : Bury to Rochdale*, p. 27.

> B. BRIERLEY. 1868.　　Aw connot help thinkin' abeawt booath on 'em at onct ; a sort o' *skennin* thowt, yo' seen, same as lookin' at two pint pots till they booath go'n int' one.
> *Irkdale*, p. 196.

SKEP, *sb.* a hive. See SKIP.

-SKEW (Ormskirk), *v.* to fly sideways. A hawk *skews* about.

SKEW-WHIFT, *adj.* awry, askew, on one side ; used also metaphorically to express an awkward temper.

> COLL. USE. 1881.　　He's a bit *skew-whift* in his mind, tha knows.

SKIFT, *v.* to remove, shift.

> WAUGH. 1865.　　The instant Dimple felt his touch he shot out his hind-feet like lightning, catching Twitchel a little below his dinner-trap. "O—oh !" cried Twitchel, laying his hands upon his belly, "that's *skifted* my baggin above a bit !"
> *Besom Ben*, p. 26.

SKILP (N. Lanc.), *sb.* a shelf.

SKINFLINT, *sb.* a stingy person, a miser.

SKIP, *sb.* a large and coarse wicker basket. Such baskets, square in shape, are much used in the Lancashire mills for packing cotton weft. Icel. *skeppa, skjappa.* See SKEP.

> REV. RICH. MORRIS. 1876.　　*Skep*, a basket, in the *Cursor*, is widely known. In the North it is a deep, round, coarse basket. In Sussex it means a flat bushel, a vessel for yeast, a bee-hackle, a bee-hive (as in Norfolk), and even a hat.
> *Survival of Early Eng. Words.*

SKIP, *sb.* an infant's gown.

SKIRL (N. Lanc.), *v.* to cry, to call loudly. Cf. E. *shrill.*

SKRIKE, *v.* to shriek ; *sb.* a shout, an outcry, a shriek.

DR. JOHN DEE. 1581.	Somewhat like the *shrich* of an owle, but more longly drawn, and more softly, as it were in my chamber. *Private Diary*, p. 11.
WAUGH. 1879.	I thought I'd go too, an' give a bit of a *skrike* for summat or another, among th' lot. *Chimney Corner*, p. 40.
B. BRIERLEY. 1868.	Th' wimmen seet up a *skrike* as loud as if Owd Sooty had popt his horns in at th' dur. *Irkdale*.

SKRIKE-O'-DAY, *sb.* daybreak.   Literally, the first voice or call of the day.

| COLLIER. 1750. | I geet up be *skrike-o-'day* on seet eawt.
Works, p. 41. |
| WAUGH. 1875. | They crope off one mornin' just afore *skrike o' day*.
Old Cronies, p. 13. |

SKUG (Oldham), *sb.* dirt.

SKYME, *v.* to refrain, to decline a thing, to be indifferent or disinclined, to draw up the nose scornfully.   As : " What arto *skymin'* at ? "   " Eat, an' dunno *skyme*."

SKYMOUS, *adj.* squeamish, fastidious in eating, indifferent.   *Skoymose* in Halliwell.

SLACK, *sb.* the loose or baggy part of the trousers.

| WAUGH. 1879. | I took it bi th' *slack* o' th' breeches, an' chuckt it into th' pond.   *Chimney Corner*, p. 229. |

SLACK, *sb.* a hollow place ; a hollow between sand-hills on the coast.   Also a depression between hills, corresponding with that which in Welsh is called a " Bwlch."   Icel. *slakki.*

| ANON. 1880. | The great interest of the sandhills is the " *slacks*," as the country people call the low-lying hollows between. Every here and there the hills have receded and formed a little flat valley, where there is something like soil, and where the rain lodges and the mosses grow. This is a " *slack ;*" and in the Lancashire *slacks* may be found some of the most beautiful, and certainly one of the rarest—perhaps the very rarest—of English flowers. .   .   .   Arenaria, or the sand pyrola, is to be found nowhere except among the *slacks* of the Lancashire sand-hills.   *Pall Mall Gazette*, Sept. 11, 1880. |
| LEO H. GRINDON. 1882. | At Birkdale, in the moist hollows among the sand-hills, called the " *slacks*," the marsh epipactis and the Orchis latifolia grow in profusion.
Illustrations of Lancashire, p. 78. |

SLACK,
SLACK-JAW, } *sb.* derisive talk.

| WAUGH. 1867. | I never seed a lot o' chaps so altered sin' th' last February. At that time no mortal mon hardly could walk through 'em beawt havin' a bit o' *slack-jaw*, or a lump o' clay flung at him. But it isn't so neaw.
Factory Folk, p. 122. |

SLACK, *sb.* small coals.

> COLL. USE.
> 1881.
>
> Come, wi mun ha' some cobs ; this coal 's aw *slack*.

SLACK, *v.* to cover the fire with small coals so as to make consumption slow.

SLACK, *adj.* not busy ; short of work.

> COLL. USE.
> 1881.
>
> "Is yore factory stopp'd ?" "Aye, we've bin *slack* now for mony a month."

SLAMP,
SLANK, } *adj.* slack, thin, soft.

> WAUGH.
> 1879.
>
> I'm as *slamp* as a sack-full o' swillin's.
> *Chimney Corner*, p. 113.

SLANCE, *v.* to steal, to pick up furtively, to take pickings from meat.

SLAPE, *adj.* smooth, bare, slippery. Icel. *sleipr.*

SLAT, *v.* to dash water or other liquid on anything ; to spill. Icel. *sletta.*

> WAUGH.
> 1865.
>
> How would to like me to *slat* tho o' th' face wi' a stockin'-full o' slutch, some Sunday, when thae 'rt swaggerin' at front o' th' parson ?
> *Barrel Organ.* (Altered to "*slap*" in last edition.)

SLATTER, *v.* to spill (as water) or scatter (as sand). Frequentative of *slat.* Hence E. *slattern.*

> B. BRIERLEY.
> 1868.
>
> Some on 'em took to an' *slattert* ther tears same as if they'd lost th' corks o' ther e'en. *Irkdale*, p. 49.

> WAUGH.
> 1868.
>
> Do be quiet, an' let me set these things. Thae'll make me *slatter* 'em *Sneck-Bant*, p. 14.

SLAY, *sb.* the hand-board of a loom. See *Sley* in Halliwell.

SLECK, *sb.* small fine coal. See SLACK.

> WAUGH.
> 1868.
>
> Th' fire 'll tak care ov itsel'. Aw put some *sleck* on.
> *Sneck-Bant*, p. 55.

SLECK, *v.* to slake.

SLECKIN', *sb.* the slaking of thirst.

> WAUGH.
> 1879.
>
> Seven pints ! What's seven pints to a mon o' my size ? I need more *sleckin'* than these under-size't kitlins.
> *Chimney Corner*, p. 362.

SLED, *sb.* a sledge. M.E. *slede.* Prompt. Parv. Icel. *sleði.*

> WAUGH.
> 1875.
>
> The lad darted into the house with his wooden "*sled*" upon his back. His mother said, "Put that *sled* o' thine out o' th' gate." *Old Cronies*, p. 28.

SLEDS (Lancaster), *sb.* shoes.

SLEEVELESS, *adj.* useless, unprofitable, shiftless.   See Shak.,
Troilus and C., v. iv. 9.

> COLLIER.   Meh mind misgives meh ot yoar'n gooin' a *sleeveless*
> 1750.   arnt [arrant, errand].   *Works,* p. 42.

> WAUGH.   He thinks o' nought i' th' world but race-runnin' an'
> 1867.   wrostlin', an' pigeon-flyin', an' single-step doancin', an'
>   sich like *sleeveless* wark as that.—*Tatlin' Matty,* p. 18.

SLIFT, *v.* to slide.

SLIFTER, *sb.* a crevice.

> WAUGH.   He could see witches scutterin' through th' *slifters* o' th'
> 1855.   wole [wall] by theawsans.   *Lanc. Sketches,* p. 199.

> IBID.   There is'nt a *slifter,* nor a ginnel, nor a gorse-bush 'at
> 1879.   'ud house aught bigger than a mowdiwarp.
>   *Chimney Corner,* p. 170.

SLIM, *v.* to do worthless work.   Cf. Icel. *slæmr,* vile.

SLIPPY, quick.

> B. BRIERLEY.   Goo whoam an' be *slippy.*   *Irkdale,* p. 34.
> 1868.

SLIVVIN, *sb.* a number of hanks of yarn put together.

SLOPSTONE, *sb.* a place for washing.   See SINK-STONE.

SLOTCH, *sb.* a drunkard, a disgusting fellow.

> WAUGH.   Owd Trinal ! That's another racketty *slotch !*
> 1879.   *Chimney Corner,* p. 155.

SLOVEN, *part. adj.* split, cloven, *p. p.* of *slive;* M.E. *sliven,* from
A.S. *slifan,* to cleave.

SLOYTHER, } *v.* to loiter ; to go about carelessly ; to draw the
SLUTHER, } feet listlessly along the ground.

SLUBBINGS, *sb. pl.* slightly twisted cops of woollen or cotton yarn.

SLUR, *sb.* a slide on the ice.

SLUR, *v.* to slide.

> WAUGH.   Betty cried out, "Stop it ! Do stop it ! Aw'm *slurrin'*
> 1868.   off !"   *Sneck-Bant,* p. 83.

SLUTCH, *sb.* mud.   Also, *sludge* in Southern Eng.

> WAUGH.   A drunken slotch, as thou art,—keawerin' i' th' chimbley
> 1879.   barkle't wi' *slutch !*   *Chimney Corner,* p. 152.

SMIDDY, *sb.* a smithy.   Icel. *smiðja.*

SMIDDY-SMUDGE or **SMITHY-SMUDGE,** *sb.*   The fine coal-
dust of a blacksmith's shop and forge.

> WAUGH.   Of his caligraphy he seemed particularly proud, for he
> 1855.   declared that "Tim [Bobbin] could write a clear print
>   hond, as smo' [small] as *smithy-smudge.*"
>   *Lanc. Sketches,* p. 55.

> IBID.   Aw'm as dry [thirsty] as *smithy-smudge.*
> 1865.   *Besom Ben,* p. 9.

SMITE, *sb.* a bit ; a small portion of anything. Lit. "a smear ;" the E. verb *smite* meant originally to smear or rub, as well as to hit. Hence *smut.*

> WAUGH.
> 1865.
> If thae gets thi back turn't, thae doesn't care a *smite* for noather me nor th' childer. *Besom Ben,* p. 104.

> IBID.
> 1867.
> "Nonsense !" said the landlady. "It 'll not do tho a *smite* o' harm, lass." *Owd Blanket,* p. 61.

SMITTLE (N. Lanc.), *adj.* infectious. A.S. *besmítan,* to pollute.

SMOOR, *v.* to smother. A.S. *smorian.*

> WAUGH.
> 1867.
> He seized her round the neck, and kissed her so heartily that she cried out, "Oh, Ben ; thae'll *smoor* mo ! Give o'er ; do !" *Owd Blanket,* p. 22.

> IBID.
> 1867.
> Another woman took her clog off, and held it up, saying, "Look at that. We're o' walkin' o' th' floor ; an' *smoort* wi' cowds" [colds]. *Home Life of Factory Folk,* 18.

SMOOT, *adj.* smooth.

> COLLIER.
> 1750.
> Hoo's os *smoot* os o mowdiwarp. *Works,* p. 57.

SMOUCH, *sb.* a kiss.

> COLLIER.
> 1750.
> Ney, Meary, le meh ha' one *smeawtch* ot partin'. *Works,* p. 71.

SMUDGE-HOLE, *sb.* the chimney.

> WAUGH.
> 1855.
> He set tone foot onto th' top bar, an' up he went into th' *smudge-hole.* *Lanc. Sketches,* p. 28.

SMUSH, *adj.* smart, finely dressed.

> COLL. USE.
> 1881.
> What's up this mornin'—thae'rt as *smush* as if it wur Sunday.

SNAFFLE, *v.* to speak through the nose. Cf. Du. *snavel,* a horse's muzzle ; whence E. *snaffle-bit.*

SNAPE, *v.* to pinch or starve ; to check or restrain ; to snub. Icel. *sneypa,* to disgrace ; Tudor E. *sneap,* to chide.

> SHAKSPERE.
> 1593.
> Like little frosts that sometime threat the spring, To add a more rejoicing to the prime, And give the *sneaped* birds more cause to sing. *Lucrece,* 331.

> WAUGH.
> 1875.
> When they *snapen* your heart, an' they stinten your fare, It's time to be joggin' away. *Old Cronies,* p. 24.

> COLL. USE.
> 1881.
> Tha's *snap'd* him neaw ; he 'll not speyk (speak) again to-neet.

SNARL, *v.* to twist, to entangle. From E. *snare.*

SNARL, *sb.* a knot or tangle in a thread of yarn.

SNECK, *sb.* a small catch or latch upon a door. Cf. Icel. *snikka*, to cut, in allusion to the notch of the catch.

SNECK-BANT, *sb.* a string coming through a hole in a door just below the "sneck," by means of which the latch is lifted from the outside.

> WAUGH.   In some of these old settlements [about Smallbridge
> 1855.   and Wardle] there are houses where the door is still
>   opened from without by a "*sneck-bant*," or "finger-
>   hole."   *Lanc. Sketches*, p. 124.

SNERP, ⎱ (N. Lanc.), *v.* to shrivel up.
SNERPLE, ⎰

SNICKET, *sb.* a naughty or forward girl.

> WAUGH.   Nay, sure; is it that impident *snicket?*
> 1879.   *Chimney Corner*, p. 26.

SNICK-SNARLES, *sb. pl.* entanglements in thread, the result of being too much twisted. See SNARL.

SNIE, ⎱ *v.* to rain or snow thickly. Halliwell gives *snee*, to abound,
SNEE, ⎰ swarm.

SNIFT, *v.* to whimper. Allied to *snivel* and *sniff.*

SNIFT, *sb.* a moment, a short space of time, as: "Aw con do it in a *snift.*"

> COLLIER.   I clum th' steigh [ladder] in o *snift.—Works*, p. 44.
> 1750.
> WAUGH.   Stop a minute; aw'll be deawn in a *snift.*
> 1867.   *Owd Blanket*, p. 14.

SNIG, *sb.* an eel. *Snig*-pie was formerly a common dainty in Lancashire. Cf. Icel. *snigill*, a snail.

> WAUGH.   By th' mon, Ben, thae'rt as lennock as a *snig.*
> 1868.   *Sneck-Bant*, p. 29.

SNIG, *v.* to snatch.

SNIGGED (Failsworth), *part.* twisted suddenly and roughly.

SNIGGER, *v.* to laugh derisively or in a hidden manner.

> WAUGH.   Ay; thou may weel *snigger* and laugh!
> 1879.   *Chimney Corner*, p. 151.

SNIGH, *v.* to draw the nose together; to sniff.

> COLL. USE.   "Ate (eat) thi dinner: wot arto *snighin'* at? Wot
> 1881.   dosto *snigh* up thi nose at? Is it no good enough?"

SNIPPET (Ormskirk), *sb.* a dish of baked meat and potatoes.

SNOD, *adj.* smooth, easy, snug, comfortable. Icel. *snauðr*. Cf. *Snodgrass.*

> WAUGH.   Rough and free as so many *snod*-backed mowdiwarps
> 1855.   [*i.e.* smooth-backed moles].   *Lanc. Sketches*, p. 189.

SNOOZE, *v.* to sleep.

SNOOZE, *sb.* sleep, a short sleep.

SNOUT-BAND, *sb.* the iron on the toes of a clog sole.

SNUDDLE, *v.* to lie close together. Cf. *snod.*

SNUFT, *sb.* the burnt wick of a candle.

> WAUGH.   Then he deed. He went out as quiet as th' *snuft* o' a
> 1879.   candle.   *Chimney Corner*, p. 146.

SNURCH, *v.* to snort or snigger in a smothered kind of way.

> WAUGH.   Nae then, come. Aw yer yo' *snurchin'* an' laughin'
> 1865.   theere.   *Besom Ben*, p. 43.

> B. BRIERLEY.   "Dick, dunno sit *snurchin'* theere." "It's yo uts
> 1868.   *snurchin'*, noa me," Dick retorted.   *Irkdale*, p. 237.

SODDEN, *adj.* heavy with water; applied also to bread which has
been imperfectly leavened. See THODDEN.

SOLCH,) *sb.* the noise made by treading or falling on a morass or
SOLSH,) damp place; *adv.* in a mass, heavily.

> WAUGH.   My shoon made a weet *solch* every time aw planted a
> 1868.   hoof.   *Sneck-Bant*, p. 7.

> IBID.   I let [alighted] *solsh* up to th' middle i' some slutch.
> 1879.   *Chimney Corner*, p. 174.

SOLOMON'S-SALE, *sb.* Solomon's-seal.   *Polygonatum multiflorum.*

> WAUGH.   It 'll cost thrippence or fourpence for *Solomon's-sale* to
> 1879.   get thi een reet !   *Chimney Corner*, p. 154.

SOMEBRY, *sb.* somebody. [In Norfolk, I have heard *noburu*—
pronounced nearly as E. no-borough—for *nobody.* W. W. S.]

> WAUGH.   If I had ony company I'd pike *somebry* 'at wur some
> 1879.   bit like daycent.   *Chimney Corner*, p. 155.

SOOF,   )
SOUGH, } *sb.* a drain or sewer.   *Sough* in Halliwell.
SUFF,   )

> B. BRIERLEY.   Like rottens [rats] in a *soof.*—*Ab in London*, p. 119.
> 1869.

SOSS, *sb.* the sound caused by a soft body falling.

SOSS, *v.* to sit down heavily or clumsily.

SOUR-DOCK, *sb.* meadow sorrel.   *Rumex acetosa.*   Called also in
Lancashire—*green-sauce.*

> 1440.   *Sowre dokke* (herbe)   *Prompt. Parv.*

SOWE, *sb.* the mixture of flour and water used by the hand-loom
weaver for sizing the warp. Now called *size.*

> B. BRIERLEY.   I've known th' owd lad sit at his loom wi' a stick at th'
> 1870.   side on him fort' keep th' childer fro' atin his *sowe,*
>   they'rn so clemmed.—*Ab on Times and Things*, p. 15.

SPACK, *v.* to entice, to prevail upon, to reconcile. Perhaps merely a form of *speak*.

> WAUGH.
> 1876.
> Hoo took a deeol o' *spackin* (enticing, reconciling) to th' shop when we first geet wed.
> *Hermit Cobbler*, p. 59.

SPANK, *v.* to provoke, to irritate; also, to beat.

SPANKIN', *part. adj.* dashing, bold. A certain Roger Aytoun, formerly a well-known commander of volunteers in Manchester, was always called "Spanking Roger."

SPAN-NEW, *adj.* quite new.

> COLL. USE.
> 1881.
> Ther's bin a wind-fo' somewheer; everythin' 'at he's getten on 's *span-new*.

SPARK-OUT, *adv.* entirely extinguished.

> COLL. USE.
> 1881.
> He'll goo *spark-out*—*i.e.* be entirely lost or forgotten.

SPARRABLES, *sb. pl.* sparrow-bills, small nails used by shoemakers.

SPEAN (N. Lanc.), *v.* to wean. See *spane, speans*, in Halliwell.

SPEAR, ⎱ *sb.* a wooden partition beside the door of a cottage, which
SPEER, ⎰ opens directly into the living room of a house. Lit. a *spar*.

> B. BRIERLEY.
> 1868.
> "Mally, this *spear* wants painting." "Aye," aw said, "but ther's a ale-shot wants payin' an' rubbin' off afore we can paint it." *Irkdale*, p. 266.

SPEEL (Preston), *sb.* a splinter. M.E. *speld*, a splinter.

SPELK, *sb.* a chip of wood; a splinter to bind a broken limb. Cf. E. *spelicans*, a word of Dutch origin.

> WAUGH.
> 1879.
> We mun ha' tho *spelk't* up a bit, owd craiter, or else thou'll be tumblin' i' lumps.—*Chimney Corner*, p. 113.

SPER, *v.* to enquire, to ask. A.S. *spyrian*, to track, from *spor*, a track; Icel. *spyrja;* Sc. *speer*.

> WEST MID. DIALECT.
> 1320.
> Not fer fro that note place That ye han spied and *spuryed* so specially after.
> *Sir Gawayne*, l. 2092.

> COLLIER.
> 1750.
> I went t' Rachdaw [Rochdale], on *sperr'd* this mon eawt. *Works*, p. 58.

> REV. W. GASKELL.
> 1854.
> Instead of to ask, or inquire, a word frequently used by a Lancashire man is *spir*, equivalent to the Scotch *speer*. This, again, is genuine Anglo-Saxon. In his translation of Boethius, King Alfred uses it when he says "he wile *spyrian*," meaning he will inquire.
> *Lect. Lanc. Dialect*, p. 16.

> WAUGH.
> 1879.
> "Mistress, can yo tell me wheer Jenny Pepper lives?" "I know nought about her. *Sper* fur [=ask further on], an' shut th' dur." *Chimney Corner*, p. 31.

SPICK-AN'-SPAN, *adj.* neat and new ; bright and fresh.

> COLL. USE.
> 1881.
> He's as *spick-an'-span* as a new hauf-creawn. (The meaning is the same as in the more modern phrase, "He looks as if he came out of a band-box.")

SPINK, *sb.* the chaffinch. *Fringilla cœlebs.*

SPOON-MEAT, *sb.* soft or liquid food, in opposition to meat which has to be masticated.

> WAUGH.
> 1879.
> "Thou'rt welcome, if thou'll have a bit." "Nay; aw'm livin' o' *spoon-meight* at present."
> *Chimney Corner*, p. 39.

SPREE, *sb.* a frolic ; a bout of drinking. Introduced from Ireland ; Irish *spre*, animation.

> WAUGH.
> 1859.
> A frolic 'll just be the physic for me !
> Aw'll see some fresh places,
> An' look at fresh faces—
> An' go have a bit of a *spree.*
> *Lancashire Songs : Jamie's Frolic.*

SPRIG, *sb.* a small sharp nail having no head.

SPRINT, *sb.* a short quick race. See *sprunt* in Halliwell ; allied to E. *spurt* = a violent exertion.

> WAUGH.
> 1867.
> Kempy was a famous "*sprint*-runner," well known all over the country side. *Owd Blanket*, p. 82.

SPROD, *v.* to swagger, to pretend.

SPROD, *sb.* salmon-trout.

SPROTE, *v.* to brag, to amplify, to exaggerate, to display.

SPROZE, *v.* to talk big, to swagger. Bamford gives *Sprozin'*, self-exalting ; *Sprozt*, self-exalted.

STADLES, *sb. pl.* marks of the smallpox.

STAGGED-UP, *participial phrase*, exhausted. Cf. Scotch *steek*, E. *stick*, verb, *stuck*, *i.e.* stuck fast.

> WAUGH.
> 1866.
> "Is that one of thy childer at sits atop o' th' jackass?" "Nawe," replied Ben in a whisper, "it belungs this woman here. Aw let on her o' tother side Ye..ley Ho'; quite *stagged-up*." *Ben an' th' Bantam*, p. 71.

> IBID.
> 1879.
> Th' owd lad wur as clemmed as a whisket, an' he wur fair *stagged-up* o' gates [all ways].
> *Chimney Corner*, p. 116.

STALE, *sb.* a long handle for a brush or mop. M.E. *stale, stele*, handle ; A.S. *stel*, a stalk. Allied to *stalk*. Mr. R. Jeffries (*Wild Life in a Southern County*, p. 70) says : "The peculiar broad-headed nail which fastens the mop to the stout ashen '*steale*' or handle, is also made in the village. I spell '*steale*' by conjecture, and according to pronunciation. It is used also of a rake : instead of a rake-handle they say rake-*steale*."

SPENSER.
1590.

And in his hand an huge pole-axe did beare, Whose *steale* was yron-studded.

F. Queene, Bk. V., c. 14.

STALLED,
STAWED, } *part.* full to repletion.

COLL. USE.
1881.

" Wilto have another plate o' beef before aw put mi tools away ?" " Nay, aw'm *stalled* at last ; aw couldn't find another corner shuz what aw did."

STALL-OFF, *sb.* a pretence, an equivocation.

COLL. USE.
1881.

Tae no notice on him—it's nobbut a *stall-off.*

STANG, *sb.* a pole. A.S. *steng ;* Icel. *stöng* (gen. sing. *stangar,* whence the prov. E. word).

WAUGH.
1879.

Dan o' Swapper's said, "Now, then, Caleb,—we'n made it for thee to carry th' pow." An' he ga' me howd of a greight *stang,* about twelve feet long.

Chimney Corner, p. 172.

STANG-RIDIN', *sb.* a mode of punishment, consisting of the riding of a man on a pole.

REV. W. GASKELL.
1854.

In Anglo-Saxon a pole was *steng,* and in Danish it is *stang,* which is the word used in Lancashire, especially in connection with a curious custom which formerly prevailed, and may still in some parts of the county, called " riding *stang.*" The only time I can recollect witnessing it, it was intended for the punishment of a wife who had beaten her liege lord. A boy was mounted on a pole, the *stang,* and carried through the street in which she lived, reciting some doggrel rhymes, in which the offender's name was brought in and held up to scorn, and accompanied by a drumming of pans and kettles. Mr. Bamford gives a somewhat different account of *stang-ridin'.* He says, " The unfortunate wife is carried through the village on a *stang,* while some witty neighbour proclaims, often in rude rhyme, the poor fellow's sufferings and humiliations at home, in some such words as these :—

' Ting, tang, to the sign of the pan !
Our good neighbour's wife
She has beat her good man.
It was neither for boiled nor for roast.
But hoo up with her fist, an'
Knocked down Mesther, post.' "

Lect. Lanc. Dialect, p. 30.

HARLAND AND WILKINSON.
1873.

The practice of what is locally called *stang-ridin'* was practised in Lancashire some forty years ago. When a man or woman is detected in an act of unfaithfulness, a framework of two long poles is procured, across which is placed a flat board, to serve as a seat. The person who has offended is caught by the crowd, and tied fast to the seat with cords. A procession is formed, and the

R

culprit is carried aloft on the shoulders of four men,
attended by a crowd, who make all the discordant noises
they can, on pots, pans, and tea-trays, as they pass along
the road.   Arrived at the front of any house, the procession halts, and the leader proclaims the names of the
parties, with the time and place when the fault has been
committed.   When the real parties cannot be captured a
substitute is found, and the procession takes place as if
the offenders were really present.   The writer accompanied one of these processions, in the neighbourhood of
Blackburn, when quite a youth ; and the feud thus created
was not allayed for many years.

Leg. and Trad. of Lanc., p. 174.

STANNER (Lytham), *sb.* a ridge of stones formed by the sea.

STARK, *adj.* superlative or duplication of stiff, as " Aw'm *stark* wi'
walkin'," and " He's stiff an' *stark* by this time," *i.e.*—" He is
dead." A.S. *stearc.*

SHAKSPERE.   Shall, stiff and *stark* and cold, appear like death.
1591-3.   *Romeo,* iv. i. 103.

STARK-NAK'T, *adj.* entirely naked; an emphatic form of "naked."

SHAKSPERE.   Stood *stark-naked* on the brook's green brim.
1599.   *Passionate Pilgrim,* p. 80.

COLL. USE.   " Had he nowt on ?"   " Not he—he was as *stark-*
1881.   *nak't* as when he wur born."

STAW (Ormskirk), *v.* to stop : a horse if pulled up when drawing a
cart is *stawed.   Staw = stall;* see *Stall* (5) in Halliwell.

STAWMP, *v.* to stagger clumsily.

STEAWND, *v.* astound, *i.e.* confound.

WAUGH.   The dule *steawnd* thee and thi Uncle Joe too !
1866.   *Ben an' th' Bantam,* p. 96.

STEAWNGE, *v.* to cause a sharp, intense, and poignant pain.   Allied
to E. *sting.*   Cf. Lowl. Scotch *stang,* a sting.   Burns begins his
Address to the Toothache, " My curse upon thy venom'd *stang.*"

WAUGH.   Every time I set my foot down there's a *steawngin'*
1879.   pain strikes straight up from my toe to th' top o' mi yed.
                                  Chimney Corner, p. 18.

IBID.   It *steawnges* an' lutches to that degree that I sometimes
          wish my yed would fly straight off.   *Ibid.,* p. 143.

STEE (N. Lanc.),   ⎱ a ladder, a stile.   A.S. *stígan,* to climb, to
STEIGH (S. Lanc.), ⎰ rise, to ascend ; Icel. *stegi, stigi.*

COLLIER.   I clum th' *steigh* in o snift.   *Works,* p. 44.
1750.

STEGG (N. Lanc.), *sb.* a gander.   Same as E. *stag ;* see Icel. *steggr,
steggi.*

STEP-MOTHER'S-BLESSING, *sb.* a little break or soreness in the skin below the nail.

STICK-FAST, *v.* to take firm hold. *Stuck-fast*, to be in a dilemma or position of difficulty.

> COLL. USE.
> 1881.
>
> 1. Neaw lads, *stick-fast;* if that rope slips we're dun for.
> 2. He's *stuck-fast* neaw, if ever he wur in his loife.

STIDDY,
STITHY, } *sb.* an anvil. Icel, *stedi.*

> CHAUCER.
> 1380.
>
> The smyth
> That forgeth scharpe swerdes on his *stith.*
> *Knightes Tale,* l. 1167.

STINGO, *sb.* strong ale; metaphorically, anything powerful.

STIR, *v.* to depend, to rely; literally to move upon.

> WAUGH.
> 1879.
>
> Well, he's nought mich to *stir* on, for sure; but he helps me as weel as he con.—*Chimney Corner,* p. 144.

STIR, *sb.* a merry-making, a party, a tumult.

> COLL. USE.
> 1881.
>
> "Yo'n had a rare *stir* last week." "Aye; it wur eawr Mall's first christenin'."

STON, *v.* to stand.

> BAMFORD.
> 1859.
>
> Yon's eawer Daniel wife spirit, as sure as I *ston* heer.
> *Early Days,* p. 167.

STOOP, *sb.* a stump.

> COLLIER.
> 1750.
>
> A mon restin' 'im on a *stoop* ith' lone.—*Works,* p. 52.

> WAUGH.
> 1867.
>
> Whatever's th' lad stonnin' i' th rain for—like a *stoop!* Come in witho! *Owd Blanket,* p. 52.

STOUP-AN'-ROUP, *sb.* a complete clearance; "He's eatin' o', *stoup-an'-roup.*"

STRACKLIN', *sb.* a giddy foolish person.

STRACKT, *part.* distracted, distraught, demented.

STREY, *sb.* straw.

STRIKE, *sb.* a measure of capacity. Bamford defines it as containing two pecks.

> MISS LAHEE.
> 1865.
>
> Tha mun start an' brew another *strike* at once.
> *Carter's Struggles,* p. 26.

STRINES, *sb.* handles of a barrow; the sides of a ladder.

STROLLOP, *sb.* an untidy woman, commonly used without the "s"—*trollop.*

STROPPIN', *part.* (Ormskirk), giving milk slowly. Allied to *strip.* See *Strippings* in Halliwell.

STUBBY, *adj.* short and stiff. Applied to the stature or "build" of a man, and also to the hair of the beard.

STUT, *v.* to stutter, stammer. M.E. *stoten;* Icel. *stauta.*

> WAUGH.
> 1876.
> Thou's had plenty to sup, I doubt, for thou *stuts* a bit.
> *Hermit Cobbler,* p. 16.

SUAGE, } *v.* to soften; to remove a swelling by fomentation.
SWAGE, } Short for *assuage.*

> COLL. USE.
> 1881.
> He'll *suage* it away wi' camomile an' poppy-heads.

SUMMAT, *sb.* something; *adv.* somewhat.

> B. BRIERLEY.
> 1868.
> Dost think theaw could make *summat* [something] o' that sort. *Irkdale,* p. 27.

> WAUGH.
> 1868.
> It's no use lettin' it lie theer. It 'll come in for *summat* [something] better nor mendin' th' hee-road wi.
> *Sneck-Bant,* p. 10.

> COLL. USE.
> 1881.
> I want a thing *summat* [somewhat] like this.

SUMPH, *sb.* a soft fellow, a simpleton.

SUMS, *sb. pl.* exercises in arithmetic; used also for arithmetic itself.

> COLL. USE.
> 1881.
> He's larnin' readin' an' writin', but he's not getten into *sums* yet.

SWAD, *sb.* a husk or shell. See SHULL. Cf. E. *swathe.*

> WAUGH.
> 1865.
> Like peighs i' one *swad.* *Besom Ben,* p. 24.

SWADDLINS, } *sb.* wrappers for children. See SWAD.
SWATHELINS, }

SWAILER, *sb.* a wholesale dealer in corn and provisions.

SWAMMEL (N. Lanc.), } *v.* to climb a pole or tree.
SWARM (General), }

SWANKIN' (N. Lanc.), *adj.* very large.

SWAP, } *v.* to exchange or barter; to change or alter, and, figura-
SWOP, } tively, to be disappointed or mistaken.

> GEO. ELIOT.
> 1876.
> But how could a fellow push his way properly, when he objected to *swop* for his own advantage?
> *Daniel Deronda,* Book II., p. 324.

> WAUGH.
> 1865.
> Th' owd lad wur i' sich a fluster, that istid o' stoppin' it, he *swapped* the barrel to another tune.
> *Barrel Organ.*

> IBID.
> 1866.
> He's a pluck't-un is that lad, or else aw'm *swapt.*
> *Ben an' th' Bantam,* p. 86.

WAUGH.
1867.

Iv ever thae *swaps*, thae'll ha' to mend, for thae'rt as ill as tho con be neaw. *Owd Blanket*, p. 18.

IBID.
1868.

He made me ston o' one leg two hours, an' every five minutes aw had to *swap* legs. *Sneck-Bant*, p. 28.

SWEEL, *v.* to burn, to blaze, to burn and melt. A.S. *swélan*, to burn; Icel. *svæla*. A candle is said to *sweel* when the wick burns down upon the tallow and causes it to melt or run. A fire or anything else is also said to *sweel* when it burns fiercely.

SWEEL, *sb.* a great blaze.

SWEEL (Ormskirk), *v.* to singe. Icel. *svæla*.

SWEELIN', *v.* firing the heather on the moors in winter.

SWELTED, *part.* well boiled; hot and perspiring. Allied to E. *sweltry*, now spelt *sultry ;* and to *sweel* (above).

SPENSER.

Which like a fever fit through all his body *swelt*.
F. Q., Bk. I., c. vii., st. 6.

REV. W. GASKELL.
1854.

When a Lancashire man is overheated, he says he is "welly *swelted*." *Lect. Lanc. Dialect*, p. 17.

SWING, *adj.* sloping. A *swing-road* has a ditch at one side only, and slopes uniformly towards the ditch, so that the top side is dry for foot passengers.

SWINGIN' (g soft), *part. adj.* big, bulky, large.

SWINGIN'-STICK, *sb.* a hazel stick for beating wool. In the cotton manufacture the same thing was called a *battin'-stick*. See SCUTCH.

SWIPPER, *adj.* active, lithe. Cf. Icel. *svipall*, *svipull*, shifty, changeable.

B. BRIERLEY.
1868.

Hoo's as *swipper* as a new tipt shuttle, hoo is.
Irkdale, p. 176.

WAUGH.
1875.

They were a lot o' th' *swipper'st* lads i' Christendom wur th' Lancashire Volunteers. *Old Cronies*, p. 95.

IBID.
1879.

He 're as *swipper* as a kitlin', an' as strung as a lion.
Chimney Corner, p. 199.

SWITHEN (Ormskirk), *adj.* crooked.

SWITHER, *sb.* a great heat; a swoon. Allied to *sweat*. Cf. Sanscrit *svid*, to sweat; Icel. *sviði*, a burn.

B. BRIERLEY.
1869.

Lorjus, heaw I swat ! I felt as if I're gooin' off in a *swither*. *Ab in London*, p. 93.

SWITHER, *v.* to dry up, to scorch. Icel. *sviðar*, to burn, singe.

SWOL, *v.* to fasten by the neck; as "To *swol* a beast in a shippon."

SWOP, *sb.* pronun. of soap.

<small>WAUGH.
1865.</small>

Two peawnd o' breawn [brown] *swop*. Ay! Aw'll put th' *swop* into these clogs; or else eawr Betty 'll happen be slappin' it into th' pon wi' th' beef.

Besom Ben, p. 7.

SWORD, *sb.* the outside skin or rind in a rasher of bacon.

<small>1440.</small>

Swarde, or *sworde* of flesche (swad or swarde), *Coriana*. A.S. *sweard*, cutis porcina. *Prompt. Parv.*

<small>COLL. USE.
1881.</small>

It 'll ate owt mon—potato-pillin's, bacon-*swords*, an' cabbage-stalks.

SYKE, *sb.* a ditch, a hollow place. Icel. *sík*, a gutter. In Yorkshire it is also a channel for water; also the current of water along a channel, which sometimes runs with great impetuosity down the side of a moor.

T.

TACK, *sb.* a flavour, a disagreeable taste.

> TUSSER.
> 1580.
>> Martilmas beefe doth beare good *tack*
>> When countrie folke doe dainties lack.
>>> *Husbandrie*, c. 12.
>>
>> What *tacke* in a pudding, saith greedy gut wringer.
>>> *Ibid.*, c. 76.

> COLL. USE.
> 1881.
>> There's some soart of a nasty *tack* abeawt this broth; tha's had it in a dirty pon (pan).

TACKLE, *v.* to attempt, to take in hand.

> REV. W. GASKELL.
> 1854.
>> A Lancashire man talks of *tacklin'* a horse, for harnessing it; and he says, "I'll *tackle* the felly," meaning "I'll set him right," generally by what he calls "giving him a dressing." *Lect. Lanc. Dialect*, p. 11.

> COLL. USE.
> 1881.
>> It's too big for him, mon; he'll noan *tackle* a job like that.

TACKLER, *sb.* a name given to an overlooker in a weaving mill.

TAISTRIL (Fylde and N. Lanc.), } *sb.* a vicious, ill-conditioned
TEASTRIL (S. Lanc.), } person.

> COLLIER.
> 1750.
>> This *teastril* proffert bring meh clear off for hoave o ginny [half a guinea]. *Works*, p. 65.

> J. P. MORRIS.
> 1867.
>> Thow drukken *taistril*, thow.—*Lebby Beck Dobby*, 8.

TAK-ON, *v.* to exhibit grief or anger in a violent manner.

> COLL. USE.
> 1881.
>> Tha munnot *tak-on* o' thattens—tha'll only mak thisell ill.

TALLY-BOARD, *sb.* a tally, a piece of wood on which an account is notched or chalked; a board on which a record of a weaver's work is kept.

TAN, *v.* to beat. A figurative expression used only in connection with the word "hide" or skin.

> WAUGH.
> 1859.
>> Iv ony mon says wrang to me,
>> Aw'll *tan* his hide to-day! *Lanc. Songs: Chirrup.*

TANG (Lytham), *sb.* a long tongue-like seaweed. Danish *tang;* Icel. þang.

TANGLE, *sb.* seaweed. Icel. þöngull.

TANGLES, *sb.* locks of hair; also entanglements.

TANKLIN', *sb.* a dangling thing; a pendant.

> WAUGH. 1879.
>
> "Hello, Dick, what's that bit o' th' *tanklin'* thou's getten thrut o'er thi shoolder?" "It's a cock-chicken, owd lad. I'm beawn t' ha' this brid to mi tay."
>
> *Chimney Corner*, p. 216.

TANTRUM, *sb.* a fit of rage or passion; a silly exhibition of impatience.

> COLL. USE. 1882.
>
> Aw'll ha' none o' thi *tantrums* here; dunnot thee think tha'll get owt wi' sich wark as that.

TASTRIL, *sb.* a small keg or barrel.

TATCHIN'-END, *sb.* a thread with a bristle attached to it; used in shoemaking.

'TATOE-HASH, *sb.* flesh-meat and potatoes boiled together, a dish very common in Lancashire.

> COLL. USE. 1881.
>
> What, han we *'tatoe-hash* again to-day? Let's have a bit of a change to-morrow!

TATTER-CLOUT, *sb.* a beggar, a poorly-dressed man or woman.

> WAUGH. 1879.
>
> A mon owd enough to be thi faither—a poor *tatter-clout* 'at's nought noather in him nor on him—a clemmed craiter 'at doesn't get a gradely belly-full o' meight in a week's time. *Chimney Corner*, p. 153.

TAX-WAX,
TAXY-WAXY (Preston), } *sb.* gristle; the tendon in a leg of mutton. In other parts of the country, *pax-wax*
and *fix-fax*.

TAY,
TAK, } *v.* to take. Scotch *ta'*.

> WAUGH. 1855.
>
> *Tay* thy wynt a bit, Bodle; thir't safe londed, iv it be hard leetin'. *Lanc. Sketches*, p. 30.

TEAGLE, *sb.* a wooden crane projecting from the upper part of a building, and used for raising or lowering goods.

TEA-THINGS,
TAY-THINGS, } *sb.* the earthenware or other vessels used at tea.

TEDDISOME (N. Lanc.), *adj.* tedious, fretful.

> DR. BARBER. 1870.
>
> He duddent set mich be the'r *teddisum* bis'ness.
>
> *Forness Folk*, p. 25.

TEEM,
TEAM, } *v.* to pour. Icel. *tœma*, to empty out, from *tômr*, empty.

> B. BRIERLEY. 1869.
>
> Hoo *temmed* me a cup o' tae eaut.
>
> *Ab in London*, p. 92.

> COLL. USE. 1881.
>
> Come, *teem* eawt, an' let's be suppin'; aw'm dry.

TEEN, *v.* to shut or close. See TINE.

WAUGH.
1855.
The folks in the house used to say, " Hello! so-an-
so's comin'; *teen* th' dur !" whereupon the landlord
would reply, " Nawe, nawe, lev it oppen, or else he'll
punce it in !"   *Lanc. Sketches*, p. 183.

IBID.
1859.
Hie tho' off, like a red-shank, or th' dur may be *teen'd.*
                                Lanc. Songs: Grindlestone.

TEEND, *v.* to light, to kindle. A.S. *tendan, tyndan,* to set fire to.
Icel. *tendra,* to make a fire, to light.

SPENSER.
1596.
In their stubborne mind.
Coles of contention and whot vengeance *tind.*
                                            F. Queene, ii. viii. xi.

REV. W. GASKELL.
1854.
Another common phrase is " *teend* th' fire," that is,
light it. This is only a slight change from the Anglo-
Saxon verb *tendan,* to set on fire, from which " tinder"
is, no doubt, derived. We are told that in the Fylde
district, " the last evening in October is called the
' *Teanlay* night ;' at the close of the day, till within late
years, the hills which enclose that district shone brightly
with many a bonfire, the mosses rivalling them with their
fires, kindled for the object of succouring their friends in
purgatory."   *Lect. Lanc. Dialect,* p. 15.

[Strictly speaking, *tinder* is not " derived" from A.S.
tendan, but both words are from the same root.—W. W. S.]

TELL-TALE-TIT, *sb.* a tale-bearer ; one who discloses a secret.

TEMS (Fylde and S. Lanc.), *sb.* a sieve. See *Temse* in Halliwell.

TENNIL, *sb.* a large basket.

TENT, *v.* to watch, to mind.

WILLIAM MORRIS.
1869.
And sheep, and swine, fed on the herbage sweet,
Seeming all wild as though they knew not man,
For quite *untented* here and there they ran.
                                            Jason, p. 179.

WAUGH.
1859.
Eawr Matty helps my mother, an'
Hoo sews, an' *tents* eawr Joe.
                                Lanc. Songs: Eawr Folk.

WAUGH.
1875.
I wish thou'd manage to do thi wark beawt so mich
tentin'.   *Old Cronies,* p. 20.

TENTER, *sb.* a watcher ; one who has charge of certain machines
in a mill.

TEWIN', *part.* toiling. Same as E. *taw,* to curry leather. A.S.
tawian, to prepare, get ready, also to scourge ; always with the
sense of violent exertion.

WAUGH.
1867.
Aw sometimes think it's very weel that four ov eawrs
are i' heaven—we'n sich hard *tewin'* to poo through wi'
tother, just neaw.   *Factory Folk,* p. 35.

IBID.
1867.
Owd wed folk finden one another's bits o' ways eawt,
wi' livin', an' *tewin',* an' pooin', an' feightin' th' world
together.   *Tattlin' Matty,* p. 12.

TEWIN', *part.* teasing, persuading, urging.

> REV. W. GASKELL.
> 1854.
>
> When a Lancashire man would express strongly the way in which another plagues or teases him, he says, "Yo're awlus *tewin'* on me, that yo are!" This seems to be the same as the Anglo-Saxon *teogan*, to pull, whence our word "tug." We have it in the Lancashire form in Drayton's *Polyolbion*, where he says—
>
> The toiling fisher here is *tewing* of his net.
>
> *Lect. Lanc. Dialect*, p. 16.

TEWIT, *sb.* the lapwing or green plover. *Vanellus cristatus.*

TEWITISH (Fylde), *adj.* wild, foolish.

THARCAKE, *sb.* a cake made from meal, treacle, and butter, and eaten on the night of the fifth of November. Short for *Tharf-cake*, M.E. *therf-cake* in P. Plowman. A.S. *theorf*, *thærf*, unleavened.

> COLLIER.
> 1750.
>
> Os thodd'n os a *tharcake*. *Works*, p. 57.

> WAUGH.
> 1867.
>
> [He thought] of the carols and festivities at Christmas, the *Thar-cake* or *Thor-cake*, and the nightly fun of Hallow-mass Eve. *Owd Blanket*, p. 34.

THAR-CAKE MONDAY, *sb.* the first Monday after Halloween, which is the vigil of All Saints' Day, which is on the first of November. The second of November is All Souls' Day. In the *Festa Anglo-Romano* we read, "The custom of *Soul Mass Cakes*, which are a kind of oat cakes, that some of the richer sorts of persons in Lancashire (among the Papists) use still to give the poor on this day." The name, however—*Thar-cake*, or *Thor-cake*, suggests a still older origin.

> WAUGH.
> 1879.
>
> "How owd arto?" "Five-an'-twenty, come *Thar-cake Monday.*" *Chimney Corner*, p. 366.

THAT, *adv.* used for the adverb "so."

> COLL. USE.
> 1881.
>
> He's *that* nowt (naughty) he doesn't know what to do wi' his-sel.

THEAWM-ROPE, *sb.* a hay band.

THEFNICUTE or **FEFNICUTE**, } *sb.* a sneaking person, a hypocrite.

THEIRSELS, *pro.* themselves.

> WAUGH.
> 1879.
>
> Folk 'at never did a hond's-turn for *theirsels* sin they wur born into th' world. *Chimney Corner*, p. 141.

THIBBS, *sb.* the shafts of a cart.

THIBLE, *sb.* a porridge stick; a piece of flat wood used to stir meat in cooking.

> COLLIER.
> 1750.
>
> I went for t' borrow their *thible*, to stir th' furmetry weh. *Works*, p. 40.

> WAUGH.
> 1859.
>
> Sin th' day hoo broke my nose i th' fowd
> Wi' th' edge o' th' porridge *thible*.
> *Lanc. Songs: Margit's Comin'.*

THICK, *adj.* friendly, intimate.

B. BRIERLEY.
1868.
The children were already "as *thick* as inkle-weavers," notwithstanding their short acquaintance.
Irkdale, p. 60.

COLL. USE.
1881.
Thoose two are a deol too *thick*, aw con tell thi; tha' mun watch 'em; they're brewin summat o' no good between 'em.

THICK-AN'-THIN, *sb.* all sorts of things, difficulties, obstacles.

COLL. USE.
1881.
He's the mon to do it : he'll feight thro' *thick-an'-thin*, but he'll have his own road at last.

THICK-AN'-THREEFOLD, *adv.* in great numbers.

COLL. USE.
1881.
They'd nobbut been married abeawt three months when trouble begun o' comin' on 'em *thick-an'-threefold.*

THICK-NECK (Heysham), *sb.* a false growth in corn; the growing of several stalks together.

THICKYED, *sb.* (thickhead) an obtuse or stupid person.

COLL. USE.
1881.
He's a born *thickyed :* he knows nowt, an' he'll larn nowt.

THI'DD'N, *pro. and v. pl.* they had.

WAUGH.
1855.
After Owd Neddy an' Bodle had been fuddlin' o' th' o'erneet, *thi'dd'n* just getten a yure o' th' owd dog into 'em. *Lanc. Sketches*, p. 28.

THILL, *sb.* the shaft of a cart or waggon. See *thylle* in Prompt. Parv.

THILLER, *sb.* the horse between the shafts. See *thylle-horse* in Prompt. Parv.

THILLIN', *part.* working in the shafts.

THINGS, *sb. pl.* clothes, personal apparel.

SPENSER.
1595.
Set all your *things* in seemely good aray.
_____ *Epithalamion.*

COLL. USE.
1881.
" Arto' gooin' to th' owd lad's buryin'?" "Nawe ; aw've no *things* good enoof to goo in."

THINK-ON, *v.* to remember.

COLL. USE.
1881.
1. Be sure an' *think-on* what aw tell thee.

2. Mi head's noan worth a rap ; aw connot *think-on* beawt (unless) aw put it deawn.

3. Tha mun *think-me-on* to-morn ; if tha doesn't, aw'st be sure to forget it.

THISEL, *pro.* thyself.

WAUGH.
1879.
Now, rap *thisel'* weel up !—*Chimney Corner*, p. 145.

THISSEN, } *adv.* in this way.
THISSENS, }

> COLLIER. 1750.
> Theyd'n better t' be o *thiss'n.*   *Works,* xxxv.

> WAUGH. 1866.
> Thae 'll be gettin' wrang again. Aw never like to see tho o' *thissens.*   *Ben an' th' Bantam,* p. 18.

THO', *pro.* thee.

> WAUGH. 1879.
> Wi' a lot o' little childer yammerin' round *tho'.* ·
> *Chimney Corner,* p. 144.

THODDEN, *adj.* applied to bread or dough which has not risen in consequence of failure in the yeast; and, figuratively, to anything which is close-grained or heavy.

> COLLIER. 1750.
> Os *thodd'n* os a tharcake.   *Works,* p. 57.

> B. BRIERLEY. 1869.
> Childer, drinkin' nowt strunger than churn-milk, till their bones are gradely set an' their flesh as *thodden* as leather.   *Ab-o'-th'-Yate in London,* p. 64.

THOLE, *v.* to suffer, to endure. A.S. *tholian;* M.E. *tholen;* formerly very common.

> BURNS. 1786.
> Poor tenant bodies, scant o' cash,
> How they maun *thole* a factor's snash.   *Twa Dogs.*

THREEP, } *v.* to argue, to contend for a special point, to dispute.
THREAP, }   A.S. *threápian;* cf. Icel. þrefa, to wrangle.

> COLL USE. 1881.
> He'd *threap* o' neet if yo'd hearken him.

THRIMBLE, *v.* to crumble bread; also to tremble, to trifle, to hesitate.

> BAMFORD. 1854.
> Whot dusto ston *thrimblin'* theer for?
> *Dial. S. Lanc.,* p. 247.

THRINTER, *sb.* a three-year-old sheep.

THRODDY, *adj.* short, dumpy. Cf. Icel. þrutinn, swollen; þrútna, to swell.

> COLLIER. 1750.
> A fattish, *throddy* gentleman coom in a trice.
> *Works,* p. 56.

> EDWARD KIRK. 1876.
> *Throddy* means stiff, or low and stout; dumpy, if you will. "A little *throddy* fellow" is applied to a fine fat child or a short stout-set man.
> *Manch. Guardian,* Jan. 3, 1876.

THRODKIN, *sb.* a cake made of oatmeal and bacon.

> EDWARD KIRK. 1876.
> *Throdkin* is the name of a cake peculiar, I believe, to the Fylde district, where it was reckoned a staple dish a quarter of a century ago. It is made of meal and water kneaded well together, and afterwards placed upon a large deep plate, often made of tin, and in depth not unlike a soup plate. The cake was about an inch and a half in thickness, and was well pressed with the thumb upon the plate. The surface was covered with slices or scraps of fat bacon. When baked the *throdkin* was cut tart fashion, and served with the slices of bacon. Eaten fresh and warm it was not an unwelcome dish, and a little of it went a long way with the keenest appetite of a thresher.   *Manch. Guardian,* Jan. 3, 1876.

THROE, *sb.* a forked stick, laid across a mug to support a sieve whilst milk or other liquid is strained through.

THRONG, } *adj.* busy, full of work. Icel. *þröngr.* Cf. A.S.
THRUNG, } *thringan,* to press, urge.

BURNS.
1786.

Twa dogs, that were na *thrang* at hame.—*The Twa Dogs.*

ALEX. WILSON.
1842.

'Twur *thrung* as Eccles wakes, mon.—*Songs of Wilsons.*

WAUGH.
1868.

They wur as *thrung* as Throp wife together.
Sneck-Bant, p. 25.

COLL. USE.
1881.

1. We connot do with you to-day, mestur—we're too *thrung.*

2. It's a *thrung* shop is this, an' no mistake.

THRUMS, *sb. pl.* the ends of a warp. Icel. *þrömr,* an edge.

THRUT, *v.* threw; also thrown.

WAUGH.
1855.

Hoo wur welly *thrut* eawt o' bed.
Lanc. Sketches, p. 208.

IBID.
1875.

Owd Jud *thrut* him o'er th' hedge—just like cob'in a catch-bo'.
Old Cronies, p. 40.

IBID.

One said it was a jackdaw, an' another he said "Nay; It's nobbut an' owd blackin'-brush 'at somebry's *thrut* away."
Old Cronies, p. 59.

THRUTCH, *v.* to push, to press, to crowd; and, figuratively, *thrutched* is to be troubled or distressed. A narrow ravine on the river Spodden, near Rochdale, is called the "Thrutch." A.S. *thryccan,* to press.

COLLIER.
1750.

Yet I'm war [worse] *thrutcht* between two arran rogues.
Works, xxxiii.

WAUGH.
1867.

"Aw think thae'rt a bit *thrutch't* i' thi mind this mornin' abeawt summat, artn'to?" "*Thrutch't* or no *thrutch't,* aw'll thank yo to be *thrutchin'* off this dur-stone!"
Owd Blanket, p. 10.

IBID.
1875.

There wur three folk i' that hole that wur as ill *thrutched* i' their minds as ony poor craiters i' Christen-dom could be.
Old Cronies, p. 45.

IBID.
1879.

They olez say'n there's th' most *thrutchin'* wheer there's th' least reawm.
Chimney Corner, p. 40.

THRUTCHINS, *sb.* the whey which is last pressed in the making of cheese.

COLLIER.
1750.

A lyte weter-podditch an' some *thrutchins.*
Works, p. 68.

THATTEN, } *adv.* in that way.
THATTENS, }

COLL. USE.
1881.

If tha' gwos on o' *thattens* ony lunger tha'll be ruin't (ruin'd).

THUNGE, *v.* to knock in a violent fashion.

MISS LAHRE.
1865.
One o' th' women fot me a *thungin'* rap between th sheaulders.   *Betty o' Yeps*, p. 9.

WAUGH.
1879.
They *thunged* at owd Fullocker's dur [door].
Chimney Corner, p. 173.

THWANG, *sb.* a thump, a blow.

THWITE,
THWITTLE, } *v.* to cut. A.S. *thwítan*, to cut.

WAUGH.
1875.
I've seen tho *thwite* very hondsomely at a goose afore now.   *Old Cronies*, p. 32.

THWITTLE, *sb.* a knife. Cf. Icel. þveita, þvita, a kind of axe or chopper. See above.

CHAUCER.
A Scheffield *thwitel* bar he in his hose.
——   *Reeves Tale*, l. 13.

COLLIER.
1750.
Os good veeol [veal] os ever deed on a *thwittle*.
Works, p. 42.

B. BRIERLEY.
1869.
A bit of as nice mutton as ever greased a *thwittle*.
Ab-o'-th-Yate in London, p. 55.

WAUGH.
1879.
I see'd him with a pluck-an-liver i' one hond, an' a *thwittle* i' th' tother.   *Chimney Corner*, p. 376.

TICKLE, *adj.* nice, dainty ; also precarious. M.E. *tikel*, unstable. Chaucer, Miller's Tale, l. 242.

WAUGH.
1868.
Hoo's nobbut in a *tickle* state of health.
Sneck-Bant, p. 79.

IBID.
1879.
"What are yo for havin'?" said the landlady. "Well," said Bockin, "we'n just have aught 'at yo'n a mind to give us, Mally. I'm noan *tickle*; an' I'm sure Billy isn't."   *Chimney Corner*, p. 73.

TICKLE-BUT, *adv.* headlong, impetuous.

WAUGH.
1876.
An ill-willed keaw (cow) coom *tickle-but* bang through th' fair, wi' th' yed down, an' th' tail up.
Hermit Cobbler, p. 16.

IBID.
1879.
At it he went, *tickle-but*, like a bull at a gate.
Chimney Corner, p. 115.

TICK-TACK-TOE, *sb.* a child's game.

S. ROWLANDS.
1600.
At *Tick-tacke*, Irish, Noddie, Maw, and Ruffe; At hot-cockles, leape-frogge, or blindman-buffe.
Notes to Stubbes's Anatomy of Abuses.

TIE-IN (Oldham), *v.* to set in ; especially used of a sickness which follows in addition to one already there.

TIG, *v.* to touch. M.E. *tek*, a slight touch ; Prompt. Parv.

TIMMERSOME, *adj.* timid, afraid.

COLLIER.
1750.
Boh yoar'n bowd; I'st o bin *timmersome*.
Works, p. 48.

WAUGH.
1855.
Ever sin it happened hoo gets quite *timmersome* as soon as it draws toawrd edge o' dark.
Lanc. Sketches, p. 208.

TINE, *v.* to shut or close. See TEEN. A.S. *týnan,* to enclose, to shut in, formed (by regular change of *ú* to *ý*) from *tún,* an enclosure = E. town.

> COLLIER. 1750.
> It wur one o'clock afore I could *toyn* me een.
> *Works,* p. 54.

> REV. W. GASKELL. 1854.
> In Anglo-Saxon, *tynan* meant to shut; as "*tynde* he his bec," he shut his books. In Lancashire it is still common to say, "*tin* th' dur," that is, shut the door. In Tim Bobbin we read, "Owey they seete to' th' leath on *toyn* t' dur." *Lect. Lanc. Dialect,* p. 15.

TINGE, *sb.* a small red bug.

TIPPLE, *sb.* any kind of intoxicating drink.

> COLL. USE. 1881.
> Sup up; it's a good *tipple*—it 'll warm thi.

TIT, *sb.* a nag, a small horse.

> TUSSER. 1580.
> By *tits* and such
> Few gaineth much.
> *Husbandrie,* c. 15.

> COLLIER. 1750.
> Sum cryed'n eawt a Doctor, a Doctor, while others mead'n th' londlort go saddle th' *tit* to fotch one.
> *Works,* p. 52.

> B. BRIERLEY. 1868.
> Dost think theaw could mak' summat o' that sort for yon *tit* o' mine? *Irkdale,* p. 27.

> WAUGH. 1875.
> "Jack, that's noan an ill mak of a *tit.*" "Nawe, bi th' mass," replied Jack, "it's as bonny a bit o' horseflesh as ever I clapt een on." *Old Cronies,* p. 22.

TITHERUP, *sb.* a hand-gallop. From the sound. Also called *tit-up.*

TITTER, *sb.* a ringworm.

TITTER-OR-LATTER, *adv. phrase,* sooner or later. Icel. *tiðr,* frequent; Mid. Eng. *titter,* more quickly. See Hampole's *Pricke of Conscience,* l. 2,354.

> WAUGH. 1879.
> It brings 'em down, *titter or latter,* as how strong they are. *Chimney Corner,* p. 8.

TITTIVATE, *v.* to dress up, to adorn.

> COLL. USE. 1881.
> Hoo'll stond *tittivating* hersel afore th' glass for an hour.

TITTY, *sb.* the breast, also the milk from the breast.

TIZIKY, *adj.* asthmatical, short of breath, having a troublesome cough. From *tisic,* corruption of *phthisic,* adj. from *phthisis.*

> SHAKSPERE. 1594.
> A whoreson rascally *tisick* so troubles me.
> *Troilus and C.,* v. iii. 101.

> COLL. USE. 1881.
> He's like a *tiziky* owd mon, tho' he's noan forty yet.

TO, *pro.* thou ; as *wilto, hasto, conto.*

TOAD-RUD, *sb.* the spawn of toads.

TO-BE-SURE, *adv. phrase,* equivalent to certainly, without question.

> COLL. USE.   " Do'st think he'll come ?"   " *To-be-sure* he will."
> 1881.

TOD (N. Lanc.), *sb.* the fox.   Cf. Icel. *taδ*, dung ; prob. from the smell.

TO-DO, *sb.* a row, a bustle, an uncommon occurrence or occasion.

> WILLIAM BLACK.   Dear, dear, what a *to-do* there was when he ran away.
> *Three Feathers,* c. xl.

> COLL. USE.   1. What's *to-do ?* (What is the matter ?)
> 1881.   2. There wur a rare *to-do* (famous doings).

TOIT (N. Lanc.), *v.* to turn over, to upset.

TO-MORN, *sb.* to-morrow.

> WAUGH.   It's Kesmass *to-morn* thou knows.
> 1875.   *Old Cronies,* p. 29.

TONE, *adj.* one.   Due to the old phrase *the tone,* corruption of *thet one = that one, i.e.,* the one.   The initial *t* is due to the final *t* of *that.*   So also in *the tother = that other.*

> ALEX. WILSON.   We donned eawr bits o' ribbins too,
> 1840.   One red, one green, an' *tone* wur blue.
> *Songs of Wilsons.*

> WAUGH.   Tay thy cheer to th' *tone* side a bit, an' may reawm for
> 1855.   him.   *Lanc. Sketches,* p. 25.

> MISS LAHEE.   Yo hannot yerd *tone* hauve [half] on it yet.
> 1865.   *Betty o' Yeps,* p. 13.

> B. BRIERLEY.   He're like a mon ut had lost *tone* hawve of hissel afore
> 1868.   he'd been wed three months.   *Irkdale,* p. 26.

TONE-AN'-TOTHER, *adj. phrase,* the one and the other.

> TUSSER.   Of two sorts of men, the *tone* good, and *tother* bad,
> 1580.   out of S. Augustine.
> Since first the world began, there was and shall be still,
> Of humane kind, *thon* good and *thother* ill.
> *Husbandrie,* c. 110.

> WAUGH.   There'd be about six o' *tone* an' hauve-a-dozen o' *tother.*
> *Chimney Corner,* p. 349.

TOOT, *v.* to search, pry, meddle.   M.E. *toten,* to peep out.

> SPENSER.   With bowe and bolts in either hand,
> 1579.   For birds in bushes *tooting.*
> *Shepheardes Calender:* March.

TUSSER.
1580.

Ill huswiferie *looteth*,
  To make hir selfe brave,
Good huswiferie looketh
  What houshold must have.   *Husbandrie*, c. 94.

WAUGH.
1859.

Through th' woodlan' green aw *tooted* keen,
For th' little window winkin'.
        Lanc. Songs: Goblin Parson.

IBID.

An' he *tooted* about o'er th' neighbourin' ground;
Still, never a soul to turn th' stone could he find.
        Ibid.: Grindlestone.

COLL. USE.
1881.

He's allus rootin' an' *tootin'* abeawt.

TOOTH-AN-NAIL, *adv.* with determination, with all one's strength.

COLL. USE.
1881.

He's at it mon *tooth-an'-nail* from mornin' till neet.

TOOTHSOME, *adj.* dainty, palatable.

WAUGH.
1855.

We'n a bit o' nice cowd beef, an I'll bring it eawt.
But it's bhoylt (boiled), mind yo ! Dun yo like it bhoylt ?
Yo'n find it middlin' *toothsome.*—*Lanc. Sketches*, p. 24.

TOOTH-WARCHE, *sb.* toothache.

WAUGH.
1879.

It isn't to tell how a bit of a thing like th' *tooth-warche*
can potter a body.   *Chimney Corner*, p. 143.

TOOTLE, *v.* to flute, to whistle.

B. BRIERLEY.
1869.

"Handel !" I said, "has Handel o' Jone's getten to
that height wi' his *tootlin'* ?" He said he wur no Handel
o' Jone's, but th' great Handel of o.
        Ab-o'-th'-Yate in London, p. 39.

WAUGH.
1875.

"An odd tot a-piece bring,"
  Said Rondle, "an' then,—
Like layrocks o' th' wing,
  We'n *tootle* again."
We *tootle't* an' sang
Till midneet coom on.   *Old Cronies*, p. 55.

TOPPER, *sb.* something surpassingly great or better than common.

WAUGH.
1859.

Eawr Tummy's taen to preitchin'—
He's a *topper* at it, too !
        Lanc. Songs: Eawr Folk.

TOPPIN, *sb.* the hair of the head.

WAUGH.
1867.

Let him alone, wilto ?—or else aw'll poo that *toppin* o'
thine, smartly, aw will !   *Factory Folk*, p. 166.

TOPPIN-FAT, *sb.* hair oil.

WAUGH.
1879.

(Referring to an over-dressed woman) Yon's worn
[spent] some brass o' ribbins an' *toppin-fat*, I'll awarnd
yo !   *Chimney Corner*, p. 26.

TORE, *v.* to try hard, to endeavour strenuously ; *torin'*, labouring assiduously and faring hardly ; *torin'-on,* to contrive to exist by the hardest labour and on the barest means. Perhaps a corruption of *taw,* the same as *tew.* See TEWIN'.

| BAMFORD. 1854. | Poor things, they hanno a gradely livin', theyn nobbut a *torin on.* *Dial. S. Lanc.,* p. 249. |
| WAUGH. 1875. | So they *toart't* on, o' this ill fashion, year after year, till·at last Nan wur ta'en ill. *Old Cronies,* p. 52. |

TO-RIGHTS, ⎫ *adj.* right, straight, in proper order or condi-
TO-REETS, ⎭ tion.

| COLL. USE. 1881. | He'll put 'em *to-reets* if ony body con. |

TOT, *sb.* a small drinking vessel ; also a small quantity of drink.

| WAUGH. 1865. | Their ale-*tots* stood, some on the hob, and some on the round table, at the landlord's elbow. *Sexton's Story,* p. 6. |
| IBID. 1876. | Theer they sit ; an' nought would do but I mut have a *tot* wi' 'em. *Hermit Cobbler,* p. 18. |

TOTHER, *adj.* the other. See TONE.

WAUGH. 1868.	Him an' this *tother* wur as thick as inkle-weighvers. *Sneck-Bant,* p. 25.
B. BRIERLEY. 1868.	Clinker ! stick to her *tother* hont. *Irkdale,* p. 6.
COLL. USE. 1831.	I'll tak tone hawve if tha'll tak *tother.*

TOUCHER, *sb.* a shave, *i.e.,* a close shave.

| B. BRIERLEY. 1869. | Hoo're as nee as a *toucher* makkin a mistake. *Ab-o'-th'-Yate in London,* p. 5. |

TOWEL, *v.* to beat.

TOWELLIN', *sb.* a beating.

| WAUGH. 1879. | He started o' givin' him a gradely good *towellin'.* *Chimney Corner,* p. 161. |

TRAPES, *v.* to walk to no purpose ; to go about foolishly or on an useless errand. Mr. Thomas Hardy (*Far from Madding Crowd,* c. viii.) has "they all had a *traypse* up to the vestry."

TRASH, *v.* to go slipshod.

TRASHES, *sb.* worn-out shoes ; also slippers.

| COLL. USE. 1881. | He'd nowt on his feet but a pair o' *trashes* that let o' his toes through. |

TRAWNCE, *sb.* a tedious walk, a roundabout journey.

| COLLIER. 1750. | I've had sich o' *trawnce* this mornin' as eh neer had e' meh life. *Works,* p. 40. |
| WAUGH. 1879. | "Arto tire't, my lad ?" "Ay—a bit." "Ay—an' thou may weel. It's a lung *trawnce,* an' thou's walked it like a drum-major." *Chimney Corner,* p. 86. |

TRAWNCE, *v.* to tramp.

> WAUGH.
> 1867.
>
> Thae'rt th' owdest o' th' two, an' thae'rt noan fit to *trawnce* up an' deawn o' this shap.
>
> *Factory Folk*, p. 195.

TRAYCLE, *sb.* treacle, molasses.

> WAUGH.
> 1879.
>
> I've bin havin' baum-tay, sweeten't wi' *traycle*, for a while.
>
> *Chimney Corner*, p. 142.

TREST, *sb.* a strong bench; a butcher's block. Cf. E. *trestle.*

TRIG, *v.* to evade by moving quickly round corners or obstacles.

TRINDLE, } *sb.* a hoop; the wheel of a barrow; the neck ruffle
TRUNDLE, } of a shirt. A.S. *tryndel*, a circle, hoop.

> B. BRIERLEY.
> 1869.
>
> We seed a hippopotamus—a thing wi' a meauth ut ud howd a wheelbarrow, *trindle* an' o.
>
> *Ab-o'-th'-Yate in London*, p. 47.

TRIPPIT, *sb.* a quarter of a pound.

TROD, *sb.* road, highway. M.E. *trod*, Ancren Riwle, p. 380, note *g.*

> WAUGH.
> 1855.
>
> The district is far out of the common *trod*, as Lancashire people say. *Lanc. Sketches*, p. 72.

TROLLOPS, *sb.* a slattern, a slovenly woman.

> WAUGH.
> 1866.
>
> He's taen up wi' some mak ov a durty *trollops* 'at he's let on upo' th' road, an' he's carryin' her chylt upo' th' jackass. *Ben an' th' Bantam*, c. iv., p. 74.

> IBID.
> 1868.
>
> Aw should as soon think o' gettin' wed to a co'n-boggart as sich a *trollops*. *Sneck-Bant*, p. 91.

> IBID.
> 1879.
>
> "It's th' new sarvant at th' Buck. What a *trollops* to be sure!" "Aye—hoo's a gradely daggle-tail."
>
> *Chimney Corner*, p. 28.

TROT, *v.* to joke, to chaff, to make sport of. A "Bolton *Trotter*" is one who practices upon another the kind of chaff common in Bolton.

TRUCK, *sb.* trade, business, communication. M.E. *trukken*, to barter; Ancren Riwle, p. 380; from F. *troquer*, to barter.

> WAUGH.
> 1866.
>
> "Well, bring it [a cat] in," said the landlord. "Nay," replied Ben, "aw'll ha' no moor *truck* wi't. Tak it for yoursel." *Ben an' th' Bantam*, c. ii., p. 47.

> IBID.
> 1867.
>
> "Ben, here, would do it for a trifle; wouldn't tho, Ben?" "Nay," replied Ben, "aw'd rayther ha' no *truck*." *Owd Blanket*, p. 102.

> IBID.
> 1876.
>
> As soon as I'd stable't Brown Jenny, I set off into th' market to look after mi *truck* [trade].
>
> *Hermit Cobbler*, p. 16.

> COLL. USE.
> 1881.
>
> Aw'll ha' no *truck* wi' thee, aw con tell thee; so tha con pike off.

TULLET (Fylde), *sb.* a small gull.

TUN, *v.* to pour.

COLL. USE.
1881.

(Said of a man drinking) " Eh, he did *tun* it into him."

TURMIT, *sb.* a turnip.

WAUGH.
1866.

Sam, get some potitos, an' a two-three carrits an' *turmits.*   *Ben an' th' Bantam,* c. ii., p. 31.

TUSH, *sb.* a tooth ; *tushie,* a baby's tooth. See Shakspere, *Venus,* l. 617. A.S. *tusc.*

COLLIER.
1762.

Ho, 'onist mon whot munneh gi' yo t' drea
A *tush* ot pleagues me awmust neet un dea.
     Works, p. 448 : *Hob and the Quack Doctor.*

TWELL, *sb.* a turn or twirl, as of a wheel. E. *twirl.*

WAUGH.
1859.

I connot howd th' axe an' turn th' hondle mysel' ;
Thou'st a nice lad o' somebry's—come, give us a *twell !*
     Lanc. Songs: Grindlestone.

TWILTIN', *sb.* a beating. Also a *quilting* in some parts.

WAUGH.
1859.

Thou young foo',
Thou'll get a rare *twiltin'* for stoppin' fro' schoo'.
     Lanc. Songs: Grindlestone.

TWINDLES, *sb.* twins.

TWINTER, *sb.* a two-year-old sheep. Lit. *two-winter.*

TWITCH-CLOCK, *sb.* the common black beetle.

WAUGH.
1879.

Nay ; it's nobbut a *twitch-clock,* or cricket, or summat.
     Chimney Corner, p. 325.

TWITCHEL, *sb.* a short wooden lever with a loop of rope fastened to one end ; the rope is put round the lower jaw of an unruly horse, and the stick is twisted round so as to get a tight hold of the jaw and subdue the horse.

TWITCHEL, *v.* to pinch, to nip ; more correctly, to get into a noose. See TWITCHEL, *sb.*

B. BRIERLEY.

If ever I catch 'em among dacent folk, I'll *twitchel* 'em, if ther's a pair o' owd cans or tin kettles to be fund i' Lunnon.   *Ab-o'-th'-Yate in London,* p. 44.

TWITCHELT, *adj.* in a noose.

WAUGH.
1855.

He wacker't an stare't like a *twichelt* dog.
     Lanc. Sketches, p. 130.

B. BRIERLEY.
1868.

He made her squeal as leawd as a *twichelt* gonner.
     Irkdale, p. 193.

WAUGH.
1879.

Theer he stoode, swillin' it round, an' starin' like a *twichelt* earwig.   *Chimney Corner,* p. 9.

TWO-DOUBLE, *adj.* bowed with age or infirmity.

COLL. USE.
1881.

Tha'll never have a mon loike that, wilto ? Why, he's nearly *two-double.*

TWO-THRE, *adj.* two or three ; a few.

B. BRIERLEY. 1868.	He's a *two-thri* letters want 'liverin'. *Irkdale,* p. 252.
WAUGH. 1875.	Clock's just upo' th' stroke o' twelve. It'll be Christmas Day in a *two-thre* minutes.—*Old Cronies,* p. 100.
IBID. 1879.	I flang a *two-thre* oddments mysel'. *Chimney Corner,* p. 41.

TYKE, *sb.* an overgrown man or beast ; a queer or awkward fellow. Icel. *tík,* a bitch, dog.

TYPE, *v.* to overturn. Cf. mod. E. *tip over*.

TYPE-O'ER, *v.* to fall ; figuratively, to die.

| WAUGH. 1868. | " How's Owd Grime gettin' on ?" " Oh, he's gone ! Th' owd lad *type't o'er* abeawt a fortnight sin." *Sneck-Bant,* p. 27. |
| IBID. 1879. | In a bit he *type't o'er*, an' o' wur still. *Chimney Corner,* p. 377. |

U.

ULLERT,
ULLET, } *sb.* a young owl, owlet.   A.S. *úle,* an owl.

UM, *pr.* them ; also, when pronounced with closed lips and accompanied by an inclination of the head, equivalent to "yes." *Um* in the former sense answers to M.E. *hem,* them, common in Chaucer.

UMBRELL, *sb.* an umbrella.

WAUGH.   It's a good job yo brought yo'r *umbrell.*
1879.   *Chimney Corner,* p. 361.

UN, *con.* and.

UN, *adj.* one.

COLL. USE.   There's another *un* comin' up th' loan (lane).
1882.

UNBEKNOWN,
UNBEKNOWNST, } *adv.* not known, secretly.

JOHN SCHOLES.   Aw've slipt thoose things in *unbeknown* to her.
1857.   *Jaunt to see th' Queen,* p. 25.

MISS LAHEE.   He bought it for me *unbeknown* to Jim.
1870.   *Esther's Divvy,* p. 30.

UNBETHINK, *v.* to remember, to reflect.   Lit. "to think about." The prefix *un-* is for *um-;* A.S. *ymb-,* about.   "Þatt te birrth *ummbethennkenn* agg," *i.e.* that it behoves thee always to consider. *Ormulum,* 1240.

COLLIER.   On then I *unbethowt* me o' me sawt.—*Works,* p. 49.
1750.

WAUGH.   Aw'll have a wift o' 'bacco whol aw *unbethink* mo a
1866.   bit.   *Ben an' th' Bantam,* c. iii., p. 51.

IBID.   That's hur 'at I wur beawn to get wed to at first ; but
1879.   I've *unbethought* mysel' sin then.
                             Chimney Corner, p. 20.

IBID.   He forgeet Jone, as clean as a whistle, an' he drove
             through Middleton, an' straight on to Rachda', afore he
             unbethought his-sel'.   *Ibid.,* p. 353.

UNCUTH, *adj.* strange.   A.S. *un-cúð,* unknown.

LANGLAND.   *Unkouth* knightes shul come thi kyngdom to cleve.
1377.   *P. Plowman,* B-text, Pass. vii., l. 155.

SPENSER.
1590.

They three together traveiled
Through many a wood and many an *uncouth* way.
F. Queene, Bk. III., canto x., st. 34.

T. L. O. DAVIES.
1875.

Uncouth once meant "unknown." Bishop Hall speaks of an apparition of a good angel as being in modern days "wonderful and *uncouth*" (*Invis. World*, i. 8); but the prejudice which is often felt against that which is strange led to its present sense of "rough" or "awkward."
Bible English, p. 183.

WAUGH.
1877.

"How are things shappin' down i' th' cloof, yon?" "About th' owd bat. There's nought *uncuth* agate 'at I know on." *Chimney Corner*, p. 114.

UNCUTH,
UNCUTHS, } *sb. pl.* something new, strange, or uncommon.

COLLIER.
1750.

Then (as I thowt he talkt so awkertly) I'd ash him for th' wonst whot *uncuths* he'd yerd sturrin'.
Works, p. 51.

B. BRIERLEY.
1867.

"What is it theau has to tell me; an *uncouth* or a tale?" "An *uncouth*, Mary; the feyver's abeaut."
Marlocks of Meriton, p. 73.

WAUGH.
1868.

They were telling one another the "*uncuths*" (bits of strange news) of their separate neighbourhoods.
Sneck-Bant, p. 24.

UNDERBREE (N. Lanc.), *sb.* a bright light appearing under clouds.

UNDERNEIGH, *adv.* underneath.

UNFORBIDDAN (N. Lanc.), *adj.* disobedient. A.S. *un*, not, and *forbebdan*, to forbid.

J. P. MORRIS.
1869.

Thou's a varra *forbiddan* barne.
Words of Furness, p. 104.

UNGAIN, *adj.* awkward, inconvenient.

———

The lady seyde, We ryde ylle,
Thes gates [roads] they are *ungayne*.
Le Bone Florence, l. 1420; in Ritson's Metrical Romances, vol. iii., p. 60.

COLL. USE.
1882.

He's taen th' *ungainst* road he could find.

UNHOMED (Fylde), *part. adj.* unpolished.

UNKERT, *adj.* strange. See UNCUTH. Also *unkid, unked*, in other dialects; all corruptions of *uncouth*. "Into an *uncod* place," *i.e.* into a strange place; Political Poems and Songs, .ed. T. Wright, p. 364 (Record Series).

UNNISH (Fylde), *v.* to starve. [Put for *hunish*. In my notes to P. Plowman, p. 237, I give examples of the rare M.E. word *honesschen*, to chase away, do away with, kill, &c. I there connect it with *hunch*, to push; but I now think it was originally due to the O.F. *honir*, to disgrace (as in *honi soit qui mal y pense*); *hun-ish* being formed from the stem of the pres. part. *honiss-ant*. It may have been confused with E. *hunch*, to push, as it is used in a considerable variety of senses.—W. W. S.]

UN-SNECK, *v.* to unlatch or unfasten a door.

UP-END, *v.* to set on end, to raise up.

> WAUGH.
> 1876.
> I left him about two minutes sin' *up-ended* i' bed yon, croodlin' a bit of a tune.—*Manchr. Critic*, January 14.

UPHOD,
UPHOWD, } *v.* to guarantee, to vouch for. Lit. "to uphold."

> WAUGH.
> 1855.
> Beside, he's somebory's chylt, an' somebory likes him too, aw'll *uphowd* him.
> *Lanc. Sketches: Bury to Rochdale*, p. 27.

> J. P. MORRIS.
> 1867.
> Gert letherin' yung chaps, fell-bred, I'se *uphod* 'em.
> *Siege o' Brouton*, p. 3.

> WAUGH.
> 1879.
> There wur a bonny racket i' that hole for a bit, I'll *uphowd* to!
> *Chimney Corner*, p. 90.

UPPISH, *adj.* proud, conceited.

UPS-AN'-DOWNS, *sb. pl.* changes, good and ill fortune.

> COLL. USE.
> 1882.
> Th' owd lad's had his *ups-an'-downs* aw con tell yo, tho' he's getten into a quiet shop at last.

UPSET, *sb.* a round loaf of bread, baked like a cake on the oven-bottom.

UPSIDES, *adj.* equal.

> COLL. USE.
> 1882.
> Aw'll be *upsides* with him yet—see iv aw dunnot!

UPSTROKE, *sb.* end, finish.

> WAUGH.
> 1879.
> Thou'd better look out, or thou'll find thisel' i'th' wrung shop when th' *upstroke* comes.
> *Chimney Corner*, p. 53.

URCHIN, *sb.* an hedgehog. See *irchon* in *Specimens of English*, ed. Morris and Skeat, p. 32; and *urchin* in *Tempest*, i. ii. 326.

> COLLIER.
> 1750.
> A tealier fund an *urchon* i'th' hadloont-reean.
> *Works*, p. 37.

URLED (N. Lanc.), *adj.* stunted.

URSELS, *pr. pl.* ourselves.

> WAUGH.
> 1855.
> At th' most o' times, we'n to kill *ursels* to keep *ursels*, welly.
> *Lanc. Sketches*, p. 32.

US, *pro.* our. In a Friesic version of the *Merchant of Venice*, printed at Gröningen in 1829, Shakspere's line—"Like as God's sun sweetly *our* world o'ershines"—is translated "Lyk az God's sinne swiet *uus* wrâd oerschijnt." A.S. *úser*, our; more commonly *úre.*

> COLL. USE.   It's a wild soart of a neet, lads; we's be best off at *us*
> 1882.   own fireside.

USHEAW, *adv.* so how; equivalent to "no matter how."

> COLL. USE.   Yo need'nt fear; he'll come *usheaw* it is.
> 1882.

UT, *pro.* that. M.E. *at,* that. "Thai slew the veddir *at* thai bar" = they slew the weather which they bore; Barbour's *Bruce,* vii. 152.

> RAMSBOTTOM.   We're mixt wi' stondin paupers, too,
> 1864.   *Ut* winno wortch when wark's t' be had.
>   *Lanc. Rhymes,* p. 24.

UZZIT, *sb.* the letter Z. Also called in other dialects *izzard, izzet* (Halliwell).

> B. BRIERLEY.   When aw're th' age o' yon lass, aw're as straight as a
> 1868.   pickin'-peg. But neaw, aw'm as croot as a *uzzit.*
>   *Red Windows Hall,* c. ii., p. 12.

V.

VARRA (N. Lanc.), *adj.* and *adv.* pron. of very. The same pronunciation is given by Shakspere—"No, sir; but it is *vara* fine." *Love's L. Lost,* v. ii. 487.

> DR. BARBER.   I sud ha' thowte ivvery body kent aad Bat *varra* near.
> 1870.   He was *varra* notable, wos Bat.—*Forness Folk,* p. 133.

VIEWLY,
VIEWSOME, } (N. Lanc.), *adj.* handsome, striking to the eye.

W.

WACKER, *v.* to shake, tremble, quiver.　Cf. E. *wag, waggle.*

COLLIER.
1750.

As soon as I could speyk for *whackerin'*, I asht him
wher ther wur on aleheawse.　　　　*Works*, p. 52.

ELIJAH RIDINGS.
1845.

My yure stood up, my pluck wur deawn,
　　Aw *wackert* cowd an' pale.　　*Lanc. Muse*, p. 30.

WAUGH.
1879.

Thou *wackers* about like a tripe doll.
　　　　　　　　Chimney Corner, p. 113.

WAENY, *adj.* tending to wane or grow less.

WAFT, *sb.* a draught.

COLL. USE.
1881.

He took it deawn at a *waft.*

WAKIN'-TIME, *sb.* the time or period of the wakes.

WAUGH.
1859.

Aw wish that Candlemas day were past,
　When *wakin'-time* comes on.
　　　　　　Lanc. Songs: Sweetheart Gate.

IBID.
1866.

Aw'st ha' sarve't thoose folk wi' besoms neaw aboon
seven year, come *wakin'-time.*
　　　　　　　Ben an' th' Bantam, p. 53.

WALK-MILL, *sb.* a fulling mill.　M.E. *walker*, a fuller.　See
Walker in Ray, p. 71.　In the early Manchester directories all
the fullers and cloth-dressers were called *walkers.*

WAUGH.
1866.

He wur a *walk-miller* when he're young.
　　　　　　　Ben an' th' Bantam, p. 64.

WALLOW, *adj.* (Fylde and E. Lanc.), insipid.　See *Walsh* in Ray.

WAMBLE, *v.* to shake, to stagger, to move unsteadily from side to
side.　The word is often applied to food in the stomach.

WAUGH.
1879.

I lost about nine on 'em o' together; an' thoose 'at's
left are *wamblin'* about like chips in a ponful o' warp-
sizin'.　It'll be a good while afore my teeth getten sattle't
again.　　　　　　　*Chimney Corner*, p. 39.

WAMBLY, *adj.* weak, faint, shaky, sickly.　See above.

WAUGH.
1855.

He used to be as limber as a treawt (trout) when he're
young; but neaw he's as *wambly* an' slamp as a barrow
full o' warp-sizin'.　　　　*Lanc. Sketches*, p. 130.

B. BRIERLEY.
1869.

I went as *wambly* as a lad after smokin' his first pipe.
　　　　　　　　Ab in London, p. 43.

WAUGH.
1879.

I feel very *wambly*, for sure.　I'm as slamp as a seck-
full o' swillin's.　　　　*Chimney Corner*, p. 113.

WANG-TOOTH (N. Lanc.), *sb.* a molar tooth. A.S. *wang*, cheek, jaw. See *wanges* in Chaucer's *Reeves Tale*, l. 110.

WANKLE, *adj.* weak, unstable. A.S. *wancol*, unstable, fluctuating.

> J. P. MORRIS. "That barne's terble *wankle* on its legs," is a very
> 1869. common expression in Furness.
> *Words and Phrases of Furness*, p. 107.

WAP, *sb.* a glance, a glimpse.

> WAUGH. It wur th' cat; I just geet a *wap* o' its tail as it wur
> 1879. gooin' out o' seet. *Chimney Corner*, p. 176.

WAP, } *v.* to move or turn quickly; to go by swiftly; as "He
WHAP, } *wapt* eawt o' th' dur;" "He *wapt* past me like leetnin' (lightning)." Cf. M.E. *wippen*, to move quickly.

WAR, *adj.* worse. A.S. *wœrra*, worse.

> SPENSER. They sayne the world is much *war* than it wont.
> 1579. *Shepheardes Calender:* September.

> WAUGH. Hoo co'de [called] me *war* than a pow-cat.
> 1879. *Chimney Corner*, p. 91.

> COLL. USE. Aye, lad; things are gettin' *war* and *war* (worse and
> 1882. worse); we's come to 't fur-eend soon.

WARCH, *v.* to ache. A.S. *wœrc*, pain; Icel. *verkr*, pain; M.E. *werk*, pain, *werchen*, to ache.

> SIR T. MALLORY. But I may not stonde, myn hede *werches* soo.
> 1469. *Le Morte Darthur*, Lib. xxi., cap. v., l. 1.

> COLLIER. I gran, an' I thrutcht, till meh arms *wartcht* agen.
> 1750. *Works*, p. 44.

> B. BRIERLEY. I shaked his hond till my arm *wartcht*, then he shaked
> 1869. mine till his arm *wartcht*. *Ab in London*, p. 78.

> WAUGH. Dick o' Belltinker's is for havin' one of his front teeth
> 1879. poo'd out, if it doesn't give o'er *warchin'*.
> *Chimney Corner*, p. 114.

WARM, *v.* to beat.

> WAUGH. Shaking the lad by the shoulder, she whispered in his
> 1879. ear, "I'll *warm* thee, gentleman, when we getten
> whoam!" *Chimney Corner*, p. 15.

WARTY, *sb. pl.* working-days. Short for *wark-day*.

> B. BRIERLEY. Ther's very little difference neaw between ther Sunday
> 1867. an' ther *warty* clooas.—*Marlocks of Merriton*, p. 61.

> COLL. USE. He ne'er stops, mon; he's at it Sunday and *warty* o'
> 1881. alike.

WASTREL, *sb.* a good-for-nothing fellow, a spendthrift. Also applied as an *adj.* to articles spoilt in the making through some flaw in the material, as a *wastrel* casting in iron, a *wastrel* bobbin, which splits in the turning. From the verb to *waste*. M.E. *wastour*. Piers Plowman, B-text, vi., l. 176.

> B. BRIERLEY. Look at his feyther, a gamblin', thievin', chettin', black-
> 1868. leggin', God-forswearin' *wastrel*. *Irkdale*, p. 75.

WAUGH.
1879.

It's Dick o' Fiddler's.   A bigger *wastrel* never kommed
(combed) a toppin' !   He's bin sold up three or four times,
an' he owes brass o' up an' down this town.
Chimney Corner, p. 30.

WATER-GAIT, *sb.* a gully or reft in the rock, which in summer is
the bed of a streamlet, but in winter is filled by a torrent.

GRINDON.
1881.

The desolate complexion of these winter-torrent gullies
(in Lancashire phrase, "*water-gaits*") in its way is complete, though often charmingly redeemed by innumerable
green fern-plumes on the borders.
Illustrations of Lancashire, p. 49.

WATER-PORRIDGE, *sb.* oatmeal porridge.   Oftener called
"Thick-porridge."

WAUGHISH, *adj.* weary, faint.   Cf. *wallow.*   *Waugh-ish* =
wallow-ish.

COLLIER.
1750.

I'r wofo weak an' *waughish.*   *Works*, p. 60

WAUT, *v.* to upset; to turn completely over; to fall on one side.
M.E. *walten.*   See Allit. Poems and Sir Gawayne ; also *Walt* in
Ray, p. 72.

B. BRIERLEY.
1868.

If aw *waut* my cart i' theere, Nan, awse want a
strunger tit nor thee for t' poo me eawt.
Irkdale, p. 161.

WAUGH.
1879.

At th' end of o', th' Smo'bridge chaps *wauted* th'
Marlan' cart into th' river.—*Chimney Corner*, p. 196.

WEAN, *sb.* a child.

BURNS.
1786.

Himsel, a wife, he thus sustains,
A smytrie o' wee duddie *weans.*   *Twa Dogs*.

COLLIER.
1750.

Theaw'rt none sitch a feaw *whean* nother.
Works, p. 71.

WEAR,
WARE, } *v.* to spend.   See *Ware* in Ray, p. 72.

SPENSER.
1590.

That wicked wight his dayes doth *weare.*
F. Queene, i. i. 31.

COLLIER.
1750.

I thowt I'll know heaw meh shot stons afore I'll *wear*
moor o meh brass o' meh brekfast.   *Works*, p. 55.

WAUGH.
1879.

There may be here an' there a collier 'at's no moor wit
nor *wearin'* his hard-won brass o' sich like prout as
champagne.   *Chimney Corner*, p. 56.

COLL. USE.
1881.

He'll *ware* his brass wheer he loikes.

WEARY, *adj.* sad, disreputable, regrettable.

COLL. USE.
1881.

It's a *weary* job, this ; aw wish we'd ne'er begun on it.

WEBSTER, *sb.* a weaver. M.E. *webstere.*

> LANGLAND.
> 1377.
>
> Wolle *websteres* and weveres of lynnen.
> *P. Plowman,* B-text, Prol., 219.

> BURNS.
> 1785.
>
> *Wabster* lads
> Blackguarding frae Kilmarnock. *The Holy Fair.*

WEEK, *sb.* pron. of wick—the wick of a candle or lamp. M.E. *weke.*

> LANGLAND.
> 1377.
>
> As wex and a *weke* were twyned togideres.
> *P. Plowman,* B-text, xvii. 204.

> SPENSER.
> 1590.
>
> True it is that, when the oyle is spent,
> The light goes out, and *weeke* is throwne away.
> *F. Queene,* ii. x. 30.

WEEMLESS (N. Lanc.), *adj.* spotless; without a fault. A.S. *wem,* spot, blemish; Icel. *vammlauss,* spotless.

WE'N, } *pro.* and *v.* we have; also, we will have. (1) *We'n = we*
WE'EN, } *han,* we have. (2) *We'n = we willen,* we will. See WIN.

> B. BRIERLEY.
> 1868.
>
> *We'n* [we have] made it up for t' have a buryin'.
> *Irkdale,* p. 29.

WEET, *prep.* and *pro.* with it.

WEIGHS, *sb. pl.* a pair of scales.

WELLY, *adv.* well-nigh, nearly. Put for *wel-ny.* M.E. *ny,* nigh.

> WAUGH.
> 1859.
>
> Er Joseph's *welly* blint, poor lad.
> *Lanc. Songs: Eawr Folk.*

> B. BRIERLEY.
> 1868.
>
> Aw *welly* geet eawt o' conceit wi' folk.
> *Irkdale,* p. 42.

WELLY-NEAR, *adv.* very near.

> COLL. USE.
> 1881.
>
> He wur *welly-near* drownt when they geet him eawt;
> another minute 'ud 'a' done th' job for him.

WENCH, *sb.* a girl, a young woman; usually but not exclusively used to describe an unmarried woman.

> B. BRIERLEY.
> 1868.
>
> Gone deawn to th' Grange wi' some moore schoo'
> *wenches* ut wanted to see that lad. *Irkdale,* p. 191.

WESH, *v.* pro. of wash.

> TYNDALE.
> 1526.
>
> Goo *wesshe* the in the pole of Siloe.
> *Trans.: Gospel of St. John,* chap. ix.

WE'ST, *pr.* and *v.* we shall.

> WAUGH.
> 1855.
>
> A sawp o' deawnfo' 'ud do a seet o' good just neaw;
> an' *we'st* ha' some afore long, or aw'm chetted.
> *Lanc. Sketches,* p. 203.

> B. BRIERLEY.
> 1867.
>
> This comes o' thi workin' ov a Sunday. *We'st* ha'
> some sort o' bad luck beside, aw reckon, through it.
> *Marlocks of Merriton,* p. 70.

WHA (N. Lanc.), *pro.* who. A.S. *hwá,* who.

WHANG (N. Lanc.), *sb.* a shoe-tie ; a thong.

WHANG (N. Lanc.), *sb.* a blow.

WHAU, *adv.* why.

WHEANTLY, *adv.* hearty, pretty well.

> COLLIER.   Aw could ha' gone on *wheantly*.   *Works*, xxxvi.
> 1750.

> BAMFORD.   " Heaw arto this mornin' ? "   " Well, awm *weantly*,
> 1854.   thank yo."   *Dial. S. Lanc.*, p. 255.

WHEEM, *adj.* handy, convenient.   See *Wheam* in Ray, p. 73.

WHEEM (N. Lanc.), *adj.* innocent-looking, quiet.

WHEMMEL (N. Lanc.), *v.* to knock down, to upset.   E. *whelm.*

WHEWT, *v.* to whistle.

> COLLIER.   *Whewt* on Tummus an' Mary.   *Works*, p. 39.
> 1750.

> WAUGH.   Hoo'd hauve-a-dozen colliers *whewtin'* an tootin' after
> 1879.   her every neet.   *Chimney Corner*, p. 29.

WHICK, *adj.* alive, sprightly.   A.S. *cwic*, living, quick, active.

> COLLIER.   It's moor in bargain o't I'm oather *whick* or hearty.
> 1750.   *Works*, p. 40.

> WAUGH.   The trippers looked the brighter for their out, and, to
> 1855.   use their own phrase, felt "fain at they'rn *wick.*"
> *Lanc. Sketches*, p. 44.

> B. BRIERLEY.   We persuaded Donny for t' bury th' wife while hoo're
> 1868.   *wick*.   *Irkdale*, p. 28.

WHICKS, *sb. pl.* quicks, thorns.

WHIRLBONE, *sb.* the round of the knee ; " but," says Bamford,
" all large bones of the thigh and leg are included in the term."
Properly the round end of a bone, which *whirls* or turns round
in the joint.

> COLLIER.   I'd th' skin bruzzed off th' *whirlbooan* o' meh knee.
> 1750.   *Works*, p. 45.

WHIRLERS, *sb. pl.* extra stockings, or hay-bands, worn around the
ankles.

WHISHT, *adj.* quiet, noiseless.

> WAUGH.   Nea then ; yo mun be as *whisht* as mice !
> *Besom Ben*, p. 52.

WHISKET, *sb.* a wicker basket.   See *Whisket* in Ray, p. 73.

> B. BRIERLEY.   Theau gets as writhen as an owd *wisket.*
> 1868.   *Fratchingtons*, p. 68.

> WAUGH.   Th' owd lad wur as clemmed as a *whisket.*
> 1879.   *Chimney Corner*, p. 116.

WHITSTER, *sb.* a bleacher.   This word is now almost obsolete,
but " *Whitster's* Arms " is still a common alehouse sign.

WHOAM,
WHOM, } *sb.* pron. of home.

WHOR, *pro.* what.

WAUGH.
1867.
"What's your son getting, Mary?" said the chairman. "*Whor?*" replied she. "Aw'm rayther deaf. What say'n yo?" *Factory Folk*, p. 18.

WHOT, *adj.* hot.

DR. JOHN DEE.
1581.
Wheruppon rose *whott* words between us. *Private Diary*, p. 12.

SPENSER.
1590.
Nether to melt in pleasures *whott* desyre, Nor frye in hartlesse grief. *F. Queene*, ii. ii. 58.

WAUGH.
1855.
A *wot* churn-milk posset, weel sweet'nt. *Lanc. Sketches*, p. 22.

WHUT-CAKE,
WUD-CAKE, } *sb.* oatcake.

WI', *prep.* abbreviation of *with*.

WICHURT,
WITCHOD, } *adj.* wet-shod.

LANGLAND.
1377.
Wolleward and *wete-shoed* went I forth after. *P. Plowman*, B-text, xviii. 1.

WAUGH.
1867.
One woman pleaded hard for two pair of clogs, saying, "Yon chylt's bar-fuut; an' he's *witchod*, an' as ill as he con be." "Who's *witchod?*" asked the chairman. "My husban' is, an' he connot ston it just neaw." *Factory Folk*, p. 18.

WICKEN, *sb.* the mountain ash, the rowan tree of Scotland. At Seal Bank, near Greenfield, Saddleworth, there is a place called the *Wicken*-hole, from the abundance of trees of this kind growing there.

WICKEN-WHISTLE, *sb.* a whistle made out of a piece of the mountain ash, the tender bark of which is easily manipulated.

WAUGH.
1879.
She saw him cutting a twig with his knife. "William!" cried she, "whatever arto doin'?" "I'm makin' a *wicken-whistle*. *Chimney Corner*, p. 5.

WICKEYIN', *part.* reversing a suit at cards.

WICKSTART, *sb.* an upstart. Cf. M.E. *wippen*. See WAP, p. 278.

WAUGH.
1879.
A lot o' camplin', concayted *wickstarts*, 'at hannot had time to reckon their limbs up gradely. *Chimney Corner*, p. 141.

WI'DD'N, *pr.* and *v. pl.* we had. Wi'dd'n = *we hadden*, we had.

WAUGH.
1855.
Sam an' me's gettin owd, an' *wi'dd'n* raythur be quiet for th' bit o' time at wi' ha'n to do on. *Lanc. Sketches*, p. 26.

WIMBLE (Lancaster), } *v.* to tilt, to raise one end, to incline.
WIMLE, }   Variant of WHEMMEL, *q.v.*

WIN, *pr. pl.* will = *willen.*

> B. BRIERLEY.
> 1868.
>   Well, but heaw *win* th' two wimmen do when they find it eawt ut they booath belung to one husbandt?
>   *Irkdale,* p. 197.

WINBERRY, } *sb.* the whortleberry. *Vaccinium myrtillus.* A.S.
WIMBERRY, } *win-berige;* lit. wine-berry, from the resemblance
to a diminutive grape.

WINDLES, *sb. pl.* blades of grass, or corn, or anything blown astray
by the wind.

WINDLESTRAW, *sb.* coarse wiry grass.

WINROW, *sb.* a row of hay in the meadow = *wind-row.* See
Windrow in Ray, p. 95.

WISEMAN, } *sb.* a fortune-teller.
WISEWOMAN, }

> POTTS.
> 1613.
>   The said Peter was now satisfied that the said Isabel Ratey was no Witch, by sending to one Halesworths, which they call a *Wiseman.*
>   *Discovery of Witches,* p. 46.

WITHIN, *prep.* against, opposed to.

> COLL. USE.
> 1881.
>   Aw'm not *within* gooin', if aw'm wanted.

WITHOUT, *conj.* unless.

> COLL. USE.
> 1881.
>   Aw'st not put a hond to it *without* tha'll help at same time.

WOBBLE, *v.* to move from side to side.

WOISTY, } *adj.* large and empty.
WYESTY, }

> COLLIER.
> 1750.
>   So Margit shew'd meh a *wistey* reawm (room).
>   *Works,* p. 54.

> JOHN SCHOLES.
> 1857.
>   Awm gooin' ov o' lung *wysty* journey.
>   *Jaunt to see th' Queen,* p. 20.

WOLE, *sb.* pron. of wall.

> WAUGH.
> 1855.
>   He's hardly wit enough to keep fro' runnin' again *woles* i' th' dayleet!   *Lanc. Sketches,* p. 28.

WON, *v.* to reside, live at. A.S. *wunian,* to dwell; M.E. *wonen,*
to dwell.

> CHAUCER.
> 1380.
>   A Schipman was ther, *wonyng* fer by weste.
>   *Prol. Cant. Tales,* 388.

> SPENSER.
> 1590.
>   In those same woods ye well remember may How that a noble Hunteresse did *woune.*
>   *F. Queene,* iii. v. 27.

> COLLIER.
> 1750.
>   An owd cratchenly gentleman *wooans* ot yon heawse.
>   *Works,* p. 56.

WOODE, WUD } *adj.* mad, insane. A.S. *wód*, mad.

SPENSER.
1590.
Through unadvized rashness woxen *wood.*
F. Queene, i. iv. 34.

COLLIER.
1750.
" Neaw, Meary, whot cou'd onny mon do?" " Do !
I'st o' gone stark *woode*." *Works*, p. 42.

WOPPER, *sb.* anything very large of its kind.

COLL. USE.
1881.
"Is it a wench ?" "Nawe, it's a lad, an' a *wopper*,
too."

WORCH, *v.* to work. A.S. *weorcan ;* M.E. *werchen.*

WAUGH.
1855.
There isn't a wick thing i' this world can *wortch* as it
should do, if it doesn't heyt (eat) as it should do.
Lanc. Sketches, p. 31.

IBID.
1879.
Colliers *worchen* for their livin'—that's one thing i'
their favour for a start. *Chimney Corner*, p. 56.

WORKY-DAY, *sb.* working-day as opposed to Sunday.

GEO. HERBERT.
1633.
The *worky-daies* are the back-part ;
The burden of the week lies there.
The Temple : "Sunday."

COLL. USE.
1881.
Which clooas (clothes) mun aw put on—my *worky-day*
or my Sunday uns ?

WORRIT, *v.* to harass, to perplex, to annoy by trifling irritations.

COLL. USE.
1882.
Hoo means nowt wrung ; but hoo *worrits* me till aw'm
fit to knock her deawn.

WOTZEL, *sb.* a spindle used for making holes by burning.

WOUGH, *sb.* a wall. M.E. *wowe.* See *Wogh* in Ray, p. 74.

WEST MID. DIALECT.
1360.
In the palays pryncipale upon the playn *wowe.*
E. Allit. Poems, B. 1531.

1440.
Wowe or wal, murus. *Prompt. Parv.*

1553.
The jury order that James Oldom shall on penalty
uphold a *wough* or wall betwixt the houses.
Manchr. Court Leet Records.

WRYTHE, *v.* to twist; allied to *wreathe.* A.S. *wriðan*, to twist;
whence *wræ'ð*, a wreath.

B. BRIERLEY.
1868.
Aw'll *wrythe* thy neck reawnd till it's as twisted as a
cleawkin' bant. *Irkdale*, p. 71.

WRYTHEN, *part. adj.* twisted, gnarled. A.S. *wriðen*, p. p. of the
strong verb *wriðan*, to writhe.

WUTHER, *adj.* swift, forcible.

WUTHERIN', *part. adj.* rushing, overpowering.   A "*wutherin'*" felley" is a powerful, overbearing man.

WAUGH.   He'll be a greight, stark, strung-backed, *wutherin'*
1879.   Englishman, o' th' owd breed, if he's luck.
                                        Chimney Corner, p. 157.

WYE-CAUVE, *sb.* a she-calf.   See *Whye* in Ray, p. 74.

B. BRIERLEY.   Aw've bin browt up as marred as a *wye-cauve* ut's bin
1868.   licked with its mother till it con do nowt for itsel'.
                                        Irkdale, p. 263.

WYNT (*y* long), *sb.* breath.

B. BRIERLEY.   He're an owd Jacobin, wur my feyther, an' cusst church
                an' king as lung as he'd *wynt*.   *Irkdale*, p. 47.

WAUGH.   He oppen't his gills, for he lippen't o' lettin' th' ale
1879.   down o' at a *wynt*.   *Chimney Corner*, p. 9.

WYTHINS (*y* long), *sb. pl.* osiers, withies.

WYZEL (*y* long), *sb.* the haulm or stalk of the potato.

Y.

YĀ,
YAN, } (N. Lanc.), *adj.* one.

J. P. MORRIS.
1867.   Sooa *yā* day, bless ye, ther' wos sich a noration as nivver wos seen.   *Invasion o' U'ston*, p. 4.

IBID.   Anudder fella oppen'd t' secks *yan* by *yan*.
     Ibid., p. 5.

YAD or
YAUD, } (N. Lanc.), *sb.* a horse.   Cf. E. *jade*.

YALLOW-YORIN' (N. Lanc.), *sb.* the Yellow-Bunting or Yellow-Hammer. *Emberiza citrinella.*

YAM (N. Lanc.), *sb.* pron. of home.

J. P. MORRIS.
1867.   It wos varra leeàt at neet when o' t' Coniston fellows gat *yam.*   *Invasion o' U'ston*, p. 7.

DR. BARBER.
1870.   What a deal o' things a body may larn if he nobbut gangs frae *yam* a lile bit !   *Forness Folk*, p. 35.

YAMMER, *v.* to long for, to yearn after ; also to cry or whimper. M.E. *yeomerian*, to lament ; A.S. *geómrian*, to lament. Cf. Icel. *jarma*, to bleat.

COLLIER.
1750.   Boh aw *yammer* t' hear heaw things turn'd eawt at th' eend of aw.   *Works*, p. 62.

BAMFORD.
1840.   His feyther, dead an' gwon as he is, wud no ha' ston sighen' an' *yammerin'* as this does.
     Life of Radical, i. 134.

WAUGH.
1855.   Eh, dear o' me ! To see poor folk's little bits o' childer *yammerin'* for a bite o' mheyt, when there's noan for 'em.   *Lanc. Sketches : Bury to Rochdale*, p. 32.

IBID.
1859.   We wandern abeawt to find rest on't,
An' th' worm *yammers* for us i' th' greawnd.
     Lanc. Songs : God Bless these Poor Folk.

IBID.
1875.   The lads of the village lingered about the doorway of the Boar's Head, *yammering* and sniffing at the odours of the kitchen.   *Old Cronies*, c. iii., p. 28.

YANCE (N. Lanc.), *adv.* once.

J. P. MORRIS.
1867.   O' at *yance* ther' strack up a meeàst ter'ble rumpus.
     Invasion o' U'ston, p. 5.

YARB, *sb.* herb ; also occasionally used for hay-grass.

WAUGH.
1855.   I bethought me of an old herbalist, or "*yarb* doctor," who lived somewhere thereabouts—a genuine dealer in simples.   *Lanc. Sketches*, p. 21.

IBID.   We'n the finest *yarb* (grass) i' yon top meadow at ever I clapt een on.   *Ibid.*, p. 228.

YARBER, *sb.* a gatherer of herbs.

YARBIN', *part.* gathering herbs.

YARK, *v.* to strike hard, to hit earnestly.   Cf. E. *jerk.*

YARKIN', *sb.* a beating, a thrashing.

YARRISH, *adj.* of a harsh taste.

YARY, *adj.* acrid, strong-flavoured.

YATE, *sb.* a gate, a fence.   A.S. *geat,* a gate.

WEST MID. DIALECT.
1360.

Vch pane of that place had thre *yates.*
E. E. Allit. Poems, A. 1033.

B. BRIERLEY.
1870.

Hoo says th' owd *yate's* nowt like what it wur th' day
I took her through it.—*Ab on Times and Things,* p. 28.

YEARNSTFUL, *adj.* earnest, with great yearning ; lit. *earnest-ful.*

COLLIER.
1750.

Bless me Meary ! theaw'rt so *yearnstful,* 'at teaw'll
naw let me tell me tale.   *Works,* p. 69.

JOHN SCHOLES.
1857.

Oytch body lookt wi' sich *yearnstfo* een as iv thi lipp'nt
o' summut leetin' eawt o' th' cleawds.
Jaunt to see th' Queen, p. 42.

YEARNSTFULLY, *adv.* earnestly.

WAUGH.
1855.

Bodle begun o' lookin' very *yearnstfully* at th' fire-hole.
Lanc. Sketches : Bury to Rochdale, p. 28.

YEARTH, *sb.* pron. of earth.   The use of *y* before the vowel, as
in this word, is very common in Lancashire.   It also frequently
takes the place of H, as in *head,* pronounced *yed.*   The same
thing will be found in Tusser—

Thresh cleane ye must bid them, though lesser they
yarn (earn).   *Five Hundred Pointes :* November.

And in Spenser—

My due reward, the which right well I deeme
I *yearned* have.   *F. Queene,* vi. vii. 15.

So also in Shropshire, *yep = heap.*

YEBB, *sb.* Edmund.

YED, *sb.* pron. of head.

BAMFORD.
1859.

"Sithe," said the latter, "if ta dusna say 'Deawn
wi' th' Rump,' theawst goa *yed* fost inta that dam."
Early Days, p. 17.

YED-BEETLER, *sb.* the head beetler, the head man of a company
of beetlers ; also applied figuratively to any foreman or man in
charge.

WAUGH.
1879.

He wur a mak of a *yed-beetler* amung th' porters, up
at th' railway-station.   *Chimney Corner,* p. 146.

YEDDERS (N. Lanc.), *sb. pl.* wattling bands for hedges. *Yeather* in Ray, p. 75.

YED-WARCH, *sb.* headache. See WARCH.

YEL, *sb.* an awl.

YELLS, *sb. pl.* healds of a weaver's loom.

YEM, *sb.* Edmund.

YEPSINTLE, *sb.* two handfuls. See *Yaspen* in Ray, p. 95.

COLLIER.
1750.
Of aw th' spots i' th' ward [world], there wou'd not I ha comn for a *yepsintle* o' ginneys [guineas].
Works, p. 67.

YERR, *v.* to hear.

WAUGH.
1869.
"Aw con tell tho heaw to cure th' worms," said Ben. "Let's be *yerrin'* then," replied Skudler.
Yeth-Bobs, c. iii., p. 45.

IBID.
1879.
If hoo *yerd* a foot passin' th' house, hoo geet up, an looked through th' window. *Chimney Corner*, 147.

YERST, *sb.* a hearse.

WAUGH.
1866.
"But it's a berrin-coach." "A what?" "A *yerst*." "What's that?" "One o' thoose coaches 'at they carry'n coffins in at funerals." *Ben an' th' Bantam*, p. 226.

YETTER, *sb.* = heater, *i.e.* a piece of iron which is made red-hot in the fire and then used for heating a kind of smoothing-iron called a "box-iron." Also, in another shape, for heating what is called a "tally-iron."

WAUGH.
1855.
Others, like Nut Nan, prowling about shady recesses of the woods, "wi' a poke-full o' red-whot *yetters*, to brun nut-steylers their een eawt."
Lanc. Sketches: Heywood and its Neighbourhood, p. 190.

IBID.
1867.
Her face wur as red as a *yetter*.—*Tattlin' Matty*, p. 24.

YEZZINS, *sb. pl.* the eaves. See EASINS, *ante*, p. 114.

YEZZY, *adj.* pron. of easy.

WAUGH.
1867.
Go thi ways whoam, Ann; neaw do; or else aw shan't be *yezzy* abeawt tho. *Factory Folk*, p. 194.

IBID.
1876.
It 'll be a good deal *yezzier* when it comes to a yed. *Chimney Corner: Manchr. Critic*, March 17.

YIGH,
YOI, } *adv.* yes.

WAUGH.
1876.
"This is th' house, isn't it, Matty?" "*Yigh*. We're just i' time."
Chimney Corner: Manchr. Critic, March 17.

YIRTH-BOBS,
YETH-BOBS, } *sb. pl.* tufts of heath.

WAUGH.
1855.

If yo 'rn up at th' Smobridge, yo'dd'n be fit to heyt *yirth-bobs* an' scaplins, welly.
Lanc. Sketches: Rochdale to Blackstone Edge, p. 131.

IBID.
1869.

Hello, Ben! Is that thee? Heaw arto gettin' on among yon *yirthbobs* upo' Lobden Moor?
Yeth-Bobs an' Scaplins, c. i.; p. 16.

YO, *pron.* you.

WAUGH.
1879.

"What dun *yo* want?" "Mistress, can *yo* tell me wheer Jenny Pepper lives?" "Who, sayn *yo*?"
Chimney Corner, p. 31.

YOANDURTH, *sb.* the forenoon. See *Aandorn* in Ray, p. 29.

COLLIER.
1750.

Sed I, aw'r theer th' last oandurth, an hee'd leet o' one th' *yoandurth* afore. *Works*, p. 56.

YO'DD'N,
YOAD'N, } you had; also you would. For (1) *yo hadden*, (2) *yo wolden*.

WAUGH.
1855.

Whau, mon, *yo'dd'n* sink into a deeod sleep, an' fair dee i' th' shell, iv one didn't wakken yo up a bit, neaw an' then. *Lanc. Sketches, Bury to Rochdale*, p. 26.

YO'N, *pron.* and *v.* you will, you have. (1) *Yo willen;* (2) *yo han* (= *haven*).

WAUGH.
1865.

"Cant or not cant, aw'll shap this job for yo, *yo'n* see," replied Roddle. *Besom Ben*, c. vi., p. 82.

IBID.
1866.

"Aw'll not have sich gooin's on!" cried she. "Look what lumber *yo'n* made."
Ben an' th' Bantam, c. ii., p. 41.

YONDERLY, *adj.* anxious, absent-minded, vacant.

WAUGH.
1859.

Come, Jamie, an' sattle thisel in a cheer;
Thae's looked very *yonderly* mony a day;
It's grievin' to see heaw theawr't wearin' away.
Lanc. Songs: Jamie's Frolic.

B. BRIERLEY.
1868.

What's do wi' thee; theaw's lookt o mornin as *yonderly* as if theaw'd lost th' guiders o' thy een?
Irkdale, c. ii., p. 74.

YO-NEET (Fylde), *sb.* a merry night. Short for *yule-neet*.

YORNEY, *sb.* a fool.

B. BRIERLEY.
1867.

Did t' think he'd bin such a *yorney* as he is?
Marlocks of Merriton, p. 29.

YORT, *sb.* a yard, a fold.

YO'ST, *pron.* and *v.* you shall. See *Aw'st*, *ante*, p. 18.

WAUGH.
1867.

"Iv yo two connot agree," said the mother, "aw'll tak that dish away; an' *yo'st* not have another bite this day." *Factory Folk*, c. xix., p. 166.

YOWER (N. Lanc.), *sb.* the udder of a cow. Icel. *júgr*.

YOWL, *v.* to howl. M.E. *yollen;* allied to E. *yell.*

WAUGH.
1865.

"Jem," cried the landlady again, "heaw lung are yo beawn to sit *yeawlin'* theer?"—*Sexton's Story*, p. 11.

IBID.

The organ *yowlt* on. *Barrel Organ*, p. 29.

YURE, *sb.* hair.

WAUGH.
1859.

One neet aw crope whoam when my weighvin' were o'er,
To brush mo, an' wesh mo, an' fettle my *yure.*
Lanc. Songs: Jamie's Frolic.

IBID.
1879.

He wur like a grey-*yure't* [grey-haired] chylt, in his ways. *Chimney Corner*, p. 146.

YUREY, *adj.* hairy, furry.

WAUGH.
1874.

There coom in a rough-lookin' chap wi' a *yurey* cap on.
Chimney Corner: Manchr. Critic, August 14.